Drug Diplomacy in the Twentieth Century

Drug Diplomacy is the first comprehensive historical account of the evolution of the global drug control regime. The book analyzes how the rules and regulations that encompass the drug question came to be framed. By examining the international historical aspects of the issue, the author addresses the many questions surrounding this global problem. Including coverage of substances from heroin and cocaine to morphine, stimulants, hallucinogens and alcohol, *Drug Diplomacy* discusses:

- The historical development of drug laws, drug-control institutions, and attitudes about drugs
- International control negotiations and the relationship between the drug question and issues such as trade policy, national security concerns, the Cold War, and medical considerations
- The reasons why the goal to eliminate drug abuse has been so difficult to accomplish

William B. McAllister is Lecturer in History and Faculty Consultant at the Teaching Resource Center at the University of Virginia.

Drug Diplomacy in the Twentieth Century

An international history

William B. McAllister

London and New York

First published 2000
by Routledge
11 New Fetter Lane, London EC4P 4EE

Simultaneously published in the USA and Canada
by Routledge
29 West 35th Street, New York, NY 10001

Routledge is an imprint of the Taylor & Francis Group

© 2000 William B. McAllister

Typeset in Baskerville by
BC Typesetting, Bristol
Printed and bound in Great Britain by
TJ International Ltd, Padstow

British Library Cataloguing in Publication Data
A catalogue record for this book is available from the British Library

Library of Congress Cataloging in Publication Data
McAllister, William B., 1958–
    Drug diplomacy in the twentieth century: an international history
/ William B. McAllister.
          p.   cm.
    Includes bibliographical references and index.
    1. Narcotics, Control of – Government policy – History – 20th
century.   2. Narcotics, Control of – International cooperation –
– History – 20th century.   3. Drug abuse – Prevention – History – 20th
century.   I. Title.
HV5801.M335   1999
363.45′0904–dc21
                                                          99-18225
                                                          CIP

ISBN 0–415–17989–0 (hbk)
ISBN 0–415–17990–4 (pbk)

To Toastie

Contents

Preface

During the mid-1980s I worked for a juvenile crime and delinquency prevention program. I taught American fifth and sixth graders about positive problem-solving strategies, communication skills, and the dangers of engaging in self-defeating behaviors. Drugs and drug abuse figured as a key topic in the curriculum, always stimulating considerable interest among students, parents, school administrators, and funders. I often heard the sort of black-and-white questions that eleven- or twelve year-old students are wont to ask: What is a drug? Are drugs really all that bad? What is the difference (if any) between "drugs" and "medicine?" Why do people use substances that are so obviously harmful? Why is alcohol legal (at least for adults), considering its many negative effects? Why don't other countries quit making drugs – don't they see it's bad? Why can't the police keep it out? Who determines which drugs are bad and which are good? How do they decide?

I offered prerehearsed responses to the students' queries, but over time I found them increasingly unsatisfactory. I wondered how the rules and definitions that encompass the drug question came to be framed. Everyone seemed to agree that "eliminating drug abuse" was a desirable goal. Why, then, was this laudable objective so hard to accomplish? Aware that the drug question was a global problem, I especially wanted to know how the issue played out in the international arena.

I concluded the key to my questions lay in understanding the international historical aspects of the issue. How did drug laws, drug-control institutions, and attitudes about drugs develop over time? The drug question touches on many different fields – which factors and agents were most important in influencing the course of drug diplomacy? How did the history of drug control fit into the larger story of human-environmental interaction? The books I consulted for explanations deepened my understanding, but left me with even more questions. I decided to embark on my own research journey in hopes of satisfying my curiosity.

This book represents the result of many years of investigation. I discovered that, for more than a century, people all over the world have wrestled with the same haunting questions my students asked me. I still have no simple answers; this book does not propose magic-bullet policy solutions to eliminate the evils associated with drug abuse. Indeed, *Drug Diplomacy* suggests that the "drug problem" cannot be solved but only managed. If, however, this work provides greater understanding and stimulates further inquiry, I shall consider my attempt to honor those whose questions set me along this path successful.

Acknowledgements

Although a single author's name appears on the title page, an undertaking of this magnitude is truly a corporate exercise. I can recognize here only the principal contributors to the production that follows.

This work has benefitted from the incisive comments of colleagues at the University of Virginia, including Stephen Schuker, Melvyn Leffler, Robert Beck, Hans Schmitt, Enno Kraehe, John Duffy, Herbert Braun, Marva Barnett, and Brian Owensby. William O. Walker III has taken a special interest in my project since its early stages. Discussions with Erwin Schmidl, Jessica Gienow-Hecht, David Courtwright, John McWilliams, David Musto, Caroline Acker, Jill Jonnes, and Paul Gootenberg proved valuable as well. Responsibility for remaining faults are rightfully laid at my doorstep alone.

Many others rendered aid in conducting my research. The University of Virginia, the Institute for the Study of World Politics, the Canadian Studies Program, the American Institute of the History of Pharmacy, the Albert Gallatin Foundation for the Study of International Affairs, and the Virginia Foundation for the Humanities all provided support for this project. I am indebted to the many archivists and librarians who helped me locate material. I learned much from fruitful conversations with numerous individuals, both active and retired, who played some role in the history of international drug control.

I also amassed considerable personal debts in completing this work. Erwin Schmidl and Bill and Brenda Jones shared their homes as well as their insights. My immediate and extended family made innumerable contributions that enabled me to complete the task. My mother and father extended the sort of support only one's parents can provide. My long-suffering wife, Terri, was most intimately involved from beginning to end. Her willingness to make personal sacrifices, provide me with a listening ear, and offer unstinting encouragement enabled me to see the task through. By their very presence, our children have furnished much-needed perspective to my work. In return for such bounteous charity I can only offer my thanks and present, most humbly, the fruits of this labor.

Abbreviations

ACC	accession number
AOIB	Anti-Opium Information Bureau
AP	Harry J. Anslinger Papers, the Pennsylvania State University
BLI	British Library of Information (New York)
BNDD	Bureau of Narcotics and Dangerous Drugs, United States (1968–72)
BP	Raymond L. Buell Papers, Library of Congress
CAB	Cabinet Records, Great Britain
CND	Commission on Narcotic Drugs, United Nations (1946–present)
CP	Papers of Neil Chayet, in possession of author
DEA	Drug Enforcement Administration, United States (1972–present)
DND	Division of Narcotic Drugs, United Nations (1946–present)
DNHW	Department of National Health and Welfare, Canada
DSB	Drug Supervisory Body (1933–67)
ECOSOC	Economic and Social Council, United Nations (1946–present)
FBN	Federal Bureau of Narcotics, United States (1930–68)
FBNA	FBN archival records (RG 170), WNRC
FPA	Foreign Policy Association
FPAA	FPA Archives, Madison, Wisconsin
FO	Foreign Office, Great Britain
INCB	International Narcotics Control Board (1968–present)
HO	Home Office, Great Britain
IO	India Office, Great Britain
IOA	India Office Library and Records, Great Britain

IOpC	Interdepartmental Opium Committee, Great Britain (1927–46)
IOC	International Organisations Committee, Great Britain (1946–present)
IP	John Ingersoll Papers, in his possession, Asheville, North Carolina
KMT	Kuomintang (Chinese Nationalist Party)
LF	Lot File
LN	League of Nations
LNA	League of Nations Archives, Geneva
LNd	League of Nations document(s)
LSP	Lyndon F. Small Papers, Library of Congress
NA	National Archives, United States
OAC	Opium Advisory Committee (Advisory Committee on the Traffic in Opium and other Dangerous Drugs), League of Nations (1920–46)
OHRO	Oral History Research Office, Columbia University
PAC	Public Archives of Canada, Ottawa
PCOB	Permanent Central Opium Board (1928–67)
PRC	People's Republic of China (1949–present)
PRO	Public Record Office, Great Britain
PS	FDC Reports – "The Pink Sheet," archived at FDC Reports, Chevy Chase, Maryland
RG	record group
SD	State Department, United States
SP	Arthur Sweetser Papers, Library of Congress
UN	United Nations Organization (1946–present)
UNA	United Nations Archives, New York
UNDCP	United Nations Drug Control Program, Vienna
UNDCPA	United Nations Drug Control Program Archives, Vienna
UNd	United Nations Document(s)
UNFDAC	United Nations Fund for Drug Abuse Control
WHO	World Health Organization
WHOA	World Health Organization Archives, Geneva
WNRC	Washington National Records Center, Suitland, Maryland

Terms and definitions

CONSUMING STATES In its pure form refers to states that neither produce nor manufacture drugs but require them for medicinal purposes (i.e the majority of the world's nations). The term sometimes connotes a "victim state" because such are at the mercy of both producers and manufacturers for the supply of essential medicines (at whatever price the traffic will bear). Any state, however, may consider itself a consumer since all require medicaments. Most states have considered themselves consuming nations when advantageous.

CONTROL Observers frequently use *prohibition* when *control* more accurately reflects the design of legislation and other measures. Control denotes regulation, restriction, and/or limitation, but not proscription. At both the national and international levels, substances are rarely banned altogether.

DERIVATIVES Salts, isomers, ethers, esters, and other preparations derived from basic drugs. Employed commonly in medical practice. Important to the control regime because if not restricted, illicit drug peddlers could create slightly altered chemical configurations that escaped regulatory strictures.

DRUG One enduring difficulty of the drug issue is that the word itself is rarely defined. The international treaties, for example, only do so in a functional way by enumerating which substances fall under control provisions. Zimring and Hawkins offer a useful definition: "a psychoactive substance capable of being used recreationally."[1] Such a description encompasses not only the traditional focus on opiates, coca products, and cannabis, but also alcohol, sedatives, stimulants, and hallucinogens. Caffeine and tobacco/nicotine stand on the margins of this definition, which suits their unregulated status in the international control system. One purpose of this book is to point out how the definition of certain substances as outside the purview of control (alcohol and tobacco since the beginning, psychotropics until the 1960s) privileged some actors and their preferences over others.

DRUG ADDICTION AND DEPENDENCE Participants and chroniclers have usually avoided defining this concept in any specific way, despite its centrality to the drug question. Zimring and Hawkins again offer a functional definition, focusing on measurable behavior rather than speculations about physical or psychological effects: "Drug use that is habitual and assumes a functional importance for the individual concerned, such that it renders his or her other social roles and preferences increasingly unimportant."[2]

MANUFACTURING STATES The states that house the majority of advanced pharmaceutical companies' factories. This group includes the United States, Great Britain, France, Germany, Switzerland, the Netherlands, and Japan. Secondary manufacturing states include Belgium and Italy.[3] *MANUFACTURE/MANUFACTURING* refers to the process of rendering agricultural raw materials and synthetic products into more pharmacologically sophisticated concoctions. The principal manufactured drugs early in the twentieth century included heroin, morphine, codeine, and cocaine. As synthetic opiates and psychotropics were developed, the term applied to those substances as well.

NARCOTICS Drugs prized primarily for their analgesic qualities, although also utilized for a variety of other purposes. Usually derived from opiates or their synthetic substitutes.

OPIATES Drugs derived in whole or in part from opium or its derivatives.

PRODUCING STATES Agrarian countries that grow agricultural raw materials such as opium, coca, marijuana/hashish, and qat. The major countries in this group include Bolivia, China, French Indo-China and its successor states, India, Iran, Peru, Thailand, Turkey, and Yugoslavia. Secondary states in this group include Afghanistan, Bulgaria, Greece, the Dutch East Indies/Indonesia, and Mexico.[4] *PRODUCTION/PRODUCING* refers to the process of growing such agricultural raw materials.

PSYCHOTROPICS Umbrella term used in international control nomenclature that refers to several categories of manufactured substances including: stimulants (such as [meth]amphetamines), depressants (tranquilizers and sedatives such as barbiturates and benzo-diazaepines), and hallucinogens (such as LSD, mescaline, PCP, MDMA, etc.).

REGIME Defined most simply as a ruling or prevailing system. No consensus exists among international relations specialists about the existence, definition, or impact of regimes. I follow Skran in utilizing a generalized definition of regimes as "governing arrangements created by a group of countries to deal with a particular issue in world politics," although I would add that non-state actors contribute to creating and modifying those arrangements.[5] As noted in the text, the drug control apparatus is nested within overarching international structures that privilege national sovereignty and liberal market systems, and that reflect the preferences of dominant actors.

SYNTHETICS   Refers to drugs, most often narcotics, manufactured without recourse to agricultural raw materials by utilizing chemical substitutes and/or equivalents.

Introduction

In a cramped Geneva hotel meeting room and the lobbies nearby, a
tense atmosphere suffused the 1931 Conference on the Limitation of
Manufactured Drugs. Under the auspices of the League of Nations,
delegates had gathered in hopes of forging an agreement that would
limit the supply of morphine, heroin, codeine, and similar substances
to legitimate medicinal needs. Most people assumed that restricting
supplies would curb the excess manufacture and unregulated distribution that, they believed, caused drug abuse. Yet the conference rejected
the draft narcotics control treaty laboriously crafted by Sir Malcolm
Delevingne, head of the British delegation and the world's senior drug
diplomat. Delevingne proposed instituting a quota arrangement that
would divide the licit market among the world's principal pharmaceutical companies, but his plan foundered amid numerous objections.
Manufacturers could not agree on how to "slice the pie." Delegates
argued about whether widely used medicines like codeine should fall
under the same restrictions applied to more powerful substances such
as heroin. Opinions differed on what constituted "legitimate" medicinal requirements, especially in areas lacking medical systems defined
as "advanced" by westerners. Governments proved unwilling to restrict
commerce during a time of worsening economic depression. States also
declined to reveal the magnitude of their military stockpiles.

Stung by the rejection, Delevingne refused to assist as the conference
struggled to create an alternative accord. Instructing his deputies not
to participate, he indignantly read a newspaper amidst the proceedings.
When his colleagues appealed to Delevingne for help on a problematic
issue, he replied with a curt, "Certainly not!" Colonel Clem Sharman,
the chief Canadian delegate and a rising star among drug diplomats,
retorted, "Sir Malcolm, your attitude would be much more convincing
if you did not read your London *Times* upside down."[1]

Sharman's rejoinder relieved the immediate tension, and Delevingne eventually re-entered the negotiations after overcoming his disappointment. The Conference successfully fashioned a landmark regulatory treaty that clarified the distinction between the licit drug trade and illicit traffic. The underlying tensions that animated drug diplomacy, however, remained unresolved. Much like Sir Malcolm, who eventually put aside his newspaper, the issues surrounding international drug control proved irritating yet irresistible to all concerned.

The drug diplomats of 1931, like their predecessors and successors, pursued multiple, often contradictory goals in a complex environment. The "drug question" has always intertwined with issues of national security and economic growth, competing policy objectives, maneuvering for bureaucratic position, defense of cultural prerogatives, and the vicissitudes of personality. This work situates the historical development of international drug control efforts within those political, economic, defense, social, intellectual, cultural, and interpersonal contexts. In so doing *Drug Diplomacy* elucidates the intractability of the "drug problem." Studying the history of drug regulation in the global arena provides a frame through which one catches an illuminating glimpse of the modern world.

The scene in Geneva encapsulates the principal elements at work throughout the history of international drug control. The major categories of actors active throughout the era of drug diplomacy participated in the 1931 negotiations. States, both the "great" and those considered less powerful by the conventional calculus, played significant roles.[2] Imperial governments, such as Delevingne's, had to consider colonial interests in fashioning policy. Pharmaceutical company lobbyists, representatives of drug-suppression societies, spokesmen for the medical profession, emissaries from government ministries, agents of enforcement organizations, and other sub-national and transnational actors populated the hallways in Geneva, attempting to influence the proceedings.[3] Representatives of international organizations such as the League of Nations and the Permanent Central Opium Board (created by an earlier drug control treaty) acted as intermediaries, but also strove to advance their own interests.[4] International civil servants forged alliances across national and other boundaries as coalitions vied for administrative dominance.[5] As the exchange between Delevingne and Sharman illustrates, interpersonal relations, often between individuals sporting idiosyncratic personalities, also influenced the outcome. At various junctures small groups and even single individuals played critically important roles in shaping the trajectory of the control system.[6]

The 1931 negotiations addressed the perennial dilemmas of drug diplomacy, which center around the dynamic that arises when regulatory efforts intersect with factors relating to demand and supply. Control advocates aimed to limit the deleterious effects of drug misuse, but they did not want to restrict access for legitimate purposes or quash the incentives that produce valuable new substances. Forging consensus on the definition of fundamental concepts such as "drug" and "drug abuse" proved impossible. Disputes about which drugs warranted regulation, and on what grounds those determinations should be made, reflected fundamental conflicts of interest. Negotiators also debated how best to implement controls – whether governmental agencies, medical professionals, or some other entity should regulate access to powerful medicines.

The Geneva discussions highlighted the abiding ideas that underpinned international control efforts. The logic of supply control suffused all drug negotiations. Restricting quantities to "legitimate" purposes appeared the best approach to those who designed the rules. Supply-side calculations centered on "bottleneck thinking" – control advocates assumed that regulating this or that supposed choke point in the producer-to-user drug flow would curb drug abuse. Those who resisted control efforts often did not object to regulation altogether, but wished rather to structure restrictions that operated to their advantage. Only rarely did opponents arise who challenged the supply-control thesis directly. Beliefs about addiction also informed drug negotiations. In the western countries that most strongly influenced the drug-diplomatic agenda, a distinction between medical (i.e. "legitimate") use and recreational (i.e. "illegitimate") abuse developed among professionals and public. Addicts increasingly came to be perceived as threats. Majority opinion held that society had a responsibility to intervene. Additionally, attitudes about the superiority of western scientific methods, bureaucratic procedures, and pharmaco-industrial prowess undergirded participants' views about which drugs merited attention and how control measures should be constructed.

Structural factors shaped the contours of the drug regime as well. The drug control system emerging over the half-century that preceded the 1931 negotiations developed within an international liberal free trade regime that ostensibly favored western governments and (often multinational) corporations, but also bestowed certain advantages upon producers and even non-state actors such as traffickers. Control advocates worked in an atmosphere that stressed the primacy of national sovereignty over international authority. Technology, in its largest sense, played key roles in drug creation, dissemination, use, abuse, and regulation. Improvements in transportation, enhanced communications, agricultural innovation, the increasing pace of pharmaceutical research, development and industrial manufacture, more sophisticated marketing techniques, the evolution of bureaucratic practice, the development of professional expertise, and the expansion of governmental capacities all contributed to forming the international drug regime's parameters.

This book is divided into four sections that trace the evolution of international drug control efforts from the later nineteenth century to the beginning of the twenty-first. Part I, which covers developments prior to 1920, outlines why governments and other actors came to treat psychoactive substances as an issue of diplomatic importance. Since at least the early modern era, societal appraisals of drugs' efficacy generally followed a cycle characterized by euphoria (often based on purported medicinal applications), then disillusionment, and finally a more sober assessment. When the negative aspects of use became apparent (or became associated with a substance for other reasons), the inclination to limit access, either informally or formally, followed. Around the turn of the twentieth century, control advocates emerged who favored international regulation of addicting drugs. Other constituencies resisted, or attempted to modify, the control impetus. Fundamental conflicts of vision and interest, first articulated during this period, animated subsequent drug diplomacy. By 1920, the movement to regulate the drug trade gained sufficient momentum to become a permanent feature of international discourse.

Part II, focusing on the years 1920–31, discusses the negotiations that created the basic rules and structures of the international drug control regime. Control advocates and opponents forged an uneasy compromise between competing aims: the desire to minimize drug abuse, the need to maximize medicinal assets, the necessity of avoiding injury to commerce, and the demands of states, international organizations, pharmaceutical companies, and other corporate actors to protect their institutional prerogatives. These key players emphasized supply control at the expense of alternative conceptions about the nature of the drug problem and how to deal with it. Limitations embedded in the resultant regulatory arrangements created opportunities for both cooperation and conflict in the international arena.

Part III details how the principals attempted to implement, modify, and/or contest the global regulatory scheme in the fluctuating circumstances of mid-century. During the 1930s control advocates struggled to apply the rules amidst the breakdown of international comity. Owing to the remarkable efforts of a few key officials, the regulatory apparatus not only survived the disruptions of World War II but appeared well positioned to make progress in the postwar years. After 1945, however, efforts to enforce control measures on a worldwide basis foundered. Strife within the drug-control community, resistance from without, and global geopolitical complications led to an undulating, fluidic stalemate. By the later 1950s, even some supporters of the regime's goals questioned how and whether they might be achieved. This phase culminated in the 1961 Single Convention, which consolidated but did not advance the agenda of control advocates.

Part IV examines the course of drug diplomacy during 1961–2000, an era of unprecedented trial and opportunity. An explosion of demand beginning in the 1960s forced a reconsideration of the tenets underlying the control regime. Illicit trafficking took on alarming proportions that threatened states, societies, and economies worldwide. Alternative strategies for dealing with the drug question received renewed attention, yet the supply-control approach remained remarkably robust. Attempts to fashion bureaucratic and policy responses to these altered circumstances ran afoul of the dilemmas inherent in the control/ demand/supply equation that have bedeviled drug diplomats from the outset.

Before proceeding, one caveat is in order: although sensitivity to demand-side dynamics permeates this work, readers will find little mention of individual drug users. The problems of addicts and addiction often did not feature prominently in international deliberations. Until the late twentieth century, owing to the dominant supply-control mentality and the ostracizing of substance abusers, decision makers considered it unnecessary to examine why or how people used drugs. Moreover, statistical evidence about the extent of drug addiction, until at least the 1970s, is not necessarily reliable.[7] In the United States, the chief purveyor of addiction statistics through the latter 1960s, the Federal Bureau of Narcotics, adjusted the number of addicts reported, sometimes abruptly, to suit its purposes. Few other states attempted systematic assessment before the 1960s. Impressionistic anecdotes and historical epidemiological investigations can give, at best, a rough outline of trends in drug use. Government reports to international agencies indicate more about the political nature of the issue than any objectively evaluated reality. Additionally, as the later chapters indicate, a large number of individuals who became addicted to psychotropics escaped notice for years; a major drug epidemic developed right under the noses of control advocates. It is, therefore, unwise to assume any direct connection between the (purported) number of drug users, which translated into a "drug problem", and which consequently affected the configuration of regulatory regimes. Drug diplomacy routinely focused on other concerns.

And now the beginning. The story of international drug control traces a serpentine path from obscure origins to its current global extent. After a brief historical overview, the first chapter picks up the trail in Asia, following a route laced with opium.

Part I

Setting the stage

1 Drugs through the ages to 1920

[German officials] don't understand action based on humanitarian motives and . . . the Reichstag would understand it still less when called on to enact legislation to restrict German traders in the legitimate business of poisoning Hindoos and Chinese.[1]

Drugs in historical perspective

Humans have always used psychoactive substances for medicinal, social, religious, and nutritional purposes. Consumption of beer, wine, opium, marijuana, tobacco, coffee, betel, coca, kava, qat, hallucinogens, and many other drugs originated in prehistory. Communities around the globe took advantage of climatic conditions and local resources to develop substances for altering consciousness, alleviating pain, and providing stamina for the hard work of day-to-day living. Drugs also served as social signifiers; certain substances might be reserved for the elite, utilized to delineate between class or caste, or dedicated to religious ceremony. Cultures generally developed taboos against misuse and imposed sanctions upon those transgressing behavioral norms. Drugs comprised an important trade item since the beginning of commercial interaction. Merchants, migrants, and conquerors introduced their culture's substances to others, thereby stimulating the traffic. Commenting upon historical, anthropological, and archeological evidence indicating that *Homo sapiens* have always sought psychoactive experience, Andrew Sherratt notes that drugs "have been central to the formation of civilizations, the definition of cultural identities, and the growth of the world economy."[2]

At the dawn of the modern era the cross-cultural exchange of goods, including psychoactive substances, accelerated as Europeans ventured across the oceans. Asians exported tea; Europeans marketed strong alcoholic beverages. Demand increased for coffee from the Near East and Africa, tobacco from the Western Hemisphere, and chocolate from South America.

In a pattern that recurs down to the present, perceptions concerning novel substances usually progressed through three stages: euphoria, disillusionment, and equilibrium. When first introduced drugs engendered enthusiasm, featuring much ado about supposed beneficial (often medicinal) properties. After some period, disenchantment set in as a substance's inefficacies and undesirable aspects became apparent. Finally, increased familiarity with a drug resulted in a more even-handed view of its qualities. New drugs also often acquired symbolic importance as indicators of social status, cultural identity, political inclination, or religious creed.[3]

During the seventeenth and eighteenth centuries, reliable supplies, reduced transportation costs, more sophisticated distribution and marketing arrangements, and an enhanced financial establishment facilitated an expansion of world trade. Drugs comprised an important commodity in this global marketplace. Europeans became accustomed to their coffee and tea. Alcohol lubricated the slave trade as tobacco sustained it. Governments, especially those with overseas empires, derived important revenue from taxing or monopolizing the traffic. Most importantly for the subsequent history of international drug control, opium became a key item in Asian societies and economies.[4]

Opium in Asia[5]

China had long exercised the upper hand in its economic relations with the Occident. Silks, teas, fine pottery, and other items flowed west. Yet the Middle Kingdom desired little from outside. Europeans emptied their coffers to buy the goods they craved. Attempts to redress this imbalance provided a principal impetus for western expansion. The eastern emperors limited westerners' physical and material encroachment; although Europeans established limited trading enclaves at Macao, Canton, and other peripheral entrepôts, those concessions only highlighted the Celestial Kingdom's predominance.

The growing popularity of opium smoking provided a partial solution to trade imbalances with China. The Dutch, Portuguese, and English had all trafficked in opium for some time, primarily to Southeast Asia and the East Indies in exchange for spices and other goods. The seventeenth-century introduction of tobacco altered traditional use patterns of other drugs. Individuals experimented, mixing opium with smoking tobacco. Over the course of the seventeenth and eighteenth centuries, smoking opium without tobacco became increasingly popular throughout Asia and the East Indies. The Chinese developed a particular affinity for opium smoking. Western traders and governments seized upon the opportunity. Macao alone imported 160,000 pounds of opium in 1767, and by the early nineteenth century imports from India totalled over 720,000 pounds per annum.[6]

Circumstances in colonial Asia contributed to this increase in the China opium trade. Throughout the eighteenth century British East India Company officials attempted to foster stability in the volatile opium sector of the agricultural economy. They settled on a company-run monopoly, which provided farmers advance payments and bought the opium produced. The Honourable Company then sold the opium to independent wholesalers at a profit, thereby earning much-needed revenue. Portuguese officials implemented a similar scheme, buying opium produced in the independent Malwa states and reselling to exporters debarking from the west coast of India. At the same time, opium smoking increased in Southeast Asia and Indonesia. Most colonial governments established farm systems for opium distribution, auctioning exclusive rights to retail sales in a designated territory. Responding to this dependable demand base, opium acreage in India increased steadily. Excess supplies in some years produced a glut in search of a market.[7]

Encouraging the China opium trade, therefore, solved several related problems for colonial governments. Opium production provided a living for numerous peasants, merchants, bankers, and government officials. Exports to China earned hard currency, thereby reducing specie outflows. Monopolizing opium buying in India and farming out sales in other colonies provided revenue for hard-pressed colonial administrations. Three global wars between 1757 and 1815 featured significant military operations in the Indian Ocean basin, further straining colonial budgets. Increasing opium sales appeared an attractive method to help redress the imbalance.

Yet promoting the opium trade presented international political problems. Official China considered opium smoking a moral vice and, increasingly, an economic threat.[8] In 1729, Peking issued an Imperial edict against the practice. The Emperor's injunction, however, had little effect in the face of opium's addictive qualities. As the Chinese appetite for opium expanded, Western traders imported increasing quantities, usually with the connivance of local officials. The situation drifted until the end of the eighteenth century, by which time officials in Peking perceived that opium imports presented a serious threat. The social costs of addiction had become apparent, and silver exited the country in noticeable quantities to pay for the drug. In 1785 the Emperor prohibited the export of specie for opium purchases. Imperial edicts promulgated in 1796 and 1799 banned opium imports altogether.

The responses to Chinese governmental action illustrate an enduring pattern of regulatory history: the control impetus is inextricably intertwined with supply and demand. A thriving illicit traffic soon supplanted the previously semi-legitimate trade; smugglers developed networks for supply, delivery, investment, and enforcement of contracts that circumvented state authority.[9] In the early nineteenth century western commercial firms imported increasing amounts of opium to well-armed receiving ships offshore. Compradors then smuggled the goods onto the mainland. Price competition broke out between suppliers. Both the British and the Portuguese stimulated Indian production, attempting to corner the market. Other players, sensing profit opportunities, entered the fray. American shippers pioneered new supply routes, buying Persian and Turkish opium for export to the Far East. Favored indigenous groups, such as the Parsi in British India, participated in the traffic as well. The oversupply of opium encouraged the opening of new smuggling channels, and Chinese imports increased steadily. By the 1830s exports to the Middle Kingdom exceeded four million pounds annually.[10]

China *in extremis*[11]

After the Napoleonic wars, European and American companies acted more aggressively to penetrate the China market. They flaunted Imperial trade restrictions in conjunction with local officials who shared the profit. The Peking government, slowly losing its grip on the provinces, appeared impotent to redress the situation. By the late 1830s tension came to a head over the issue of trade.

Opium sparked a conflagration. In 1838, a new Imperial commissioner arrived in Canton determined to rein in the foreigners. He moved against fellow countrymen engaged in trafficking and challenged the Europeans by confiscating their opium. Chinese actions precipitated the Opium War with Britain. The English utilized their technologically superior navy to inflict an embarrassing defeat on the Middle Kingdom. The settlement of hostilities provided increased access to Chinese markets, although opium remained contraband.[12]

In subsequent decades the Imperial government could not enforce dictates against the drug. The relaxed trade restrictions only enhanced the opium traffic. Chinese imports increased steadily, averaging over 6.5 million pounds during the 1840s and exceeding 9.5 million pounds in the 1850s. Contemporaries estimated the traffic as "probably the largest commerce of the time in any single commodity."[13] The potential for profit engendered stiff competition. Clipper ships, for example, carried opium and the mail from India to the East, returning with loads of Chinese specie.[14] Trade wars between 1856 and 1860, in conjunction with the Taiping and other internal rebellions, brought the Imperial government to its knees. Westerners exacted extensive trade privileges and China lost its tariff autonomy. Peking rescinded the opium ban, deciding instead to enhance its treasury by imposing taxes on the drug.[15]

Changes in regulatory climates again altered the relationship between control, supply, and demand. With governmental restrictions removed, Chinese opium consumption skyrocketed. The colonial Indian government promoted opium production in support of policies designed to encourage development, self-sufficiency, and capital accumulation. During the 1880s India alone exported an astounding 13 million pounds annually to the Middle Kingdom. In Persia, local industry withered, unable to compete with cheap European manufactured goods. Many Persian farmers turned to opium as a cash crop. Exports, primarily to the Far East, increased steadily after 1850. The Imperial Malayan government colluded with Chinese tin mine operators to control coolie labor by supplying cheap opium via the farm system. Most importantly, Chinese cultivators began producing for the home market. Domestic production eventually exceeded imports, and per-capita consumption reached unprecedented levels.[16]

By the turn of the century, China's existence as a cohesive entity seemed threatened, yet opium permeated all aspects of society and economy. Widespread addiction existed at all levels, from the lowliest pauper to the Imperial household. The Chinese government and economy became addicted as well. With the imposition of import and internal transit taxes on opium during the 1870s, officials at all levels increasingly relied on those revenues. In addition to its value as a cash crop, opium served as a medium of exchange and contributed to the development of a market economy, especially in cash-starved interior provinces. Consequently, intermittent Imperial attempts to institute pogroms against opium met resistance. Jonathan Spence describes opium use during this period as a "phenomenon that radically affected all levels of Chinese society."[17]

Drugs in the west

The dire straits of China, however, cannot alone explain why drug control, aimed at certain substances and not others, emerged as an issue of international concern around the turn of the twentieth century. Prohibition movements directed at tobacco or alcohol, for example, existed alongside anti-opium agitation in the later nineteenth century, yet neither engendered any appreciable international response.[18] A constellation of additional factors, centered on the industrializing west, brought the opium question to governmental attention. Occidental developments in medical practice and organization, technological advances, commercial interests, social reform movements, cultural anxieties, the advent of international organizations, religious sentiment, and the world's geopolitical configuration all shaped the manner in which drug control became an issue of diplomatic import. In both east and west, the drug question intertwined with numerous other concerns and interests; drug control served not only as an end in itself but also as a means to achieve other aspirations.

The technological fix[19]

Major currents of nineteenth-century science, research, technology, industry, business organization, and marketing converged in the realm of drugs. These factors combined to produce new substances at an increasing rate, to make them widely available at decreasing prices, and to tout their purported benefits to wide audiences. The development and spread of coca/cocaine illustrate these phenomena.

Long recognized as possessing analgesic, stimulant, and other desirable qualities, coca use remained limited until a variety of factors converged during the mid-1880s. The time required to transport the leaves out of their native Andean region and across the ocean depleted their potency. In the nineteenth century, more efficient sea transport enabled coca leaves to arrive in Europe relatively fresh. After mid-century, patent medicine manufacturers incorporated coca extract in medicinals, instituted aggressive advertising campaigns, and increased sales. In an early example of agro-industrial espionage for profit, Imperial botanical organizations smuggled coca plants out of the Andes, perfected cultivation techniques at central stations such as Kew Gardens, and transplanted samples to colonies under their control. Researchers attempted to establish the efficacy of the crystallized extract of the coca leaf, utilizing the experimental-scientific method then coming into prominence. Yet a lack of available cocaine of consistent quality hindered their efforts.

During the mid-1880s demand for cocaine skyrocketed. In the early 1880s, pharmaceutical companies for the first time reliably manufactured small amounts of cocaine containing a sufficient quantity of active ingredient. Medical publications, becoming established as reliable sources of information based on scientific method and peer review, featured articles about the drug's clinical applications. Cocaine appealed to physicians not only because it promised better treatment for a variety of maladies, but also because it represented "progress" and modern scientific techniques that reinforced their specialist expertise. Modern methods of administration, such as the hypodermic needle, appeared to offer an exactitude of treatment heretofore unavailable. In the absence of regulation, pharmaceutical companies stimulated demand by touting cocaine not only to physicians, but to patent medicine manufacturers and the general public as well.

The mid-1880s euphoric reception of cocaine set off a chain reaction. Pharmaceutical companies rushed to fill orders, but fresh coca leaf was unavailable in sufficient quantity. Consequently, the price skyrocketed. To meet demand and share in the profit, several imperial powers stepped up efforts to develop commercially salable coca. The Dutch proved most successful, producing a variety with double the alkaloid content of Peruvian leaf. Chemists developed various methods to produce crude cocaine, which entailed semi-processing coca leaves to capture the active ingredient in non-perishable form. Peruvians hoped to utilize local crude cocaine manufacture as a springboard for industrialization, economic integration, and modernization. Meanwhile, German chemists led the way in recovering the greatest amount of alkaloid from coca leaves and crude cocaine. Within a few years, coca production increased dramatically, coca paste processing became commonplace, coca leaves became a commodity traded on the international market, and pharmaceutical manufacturers competed for business on the basis of price, availability, and quality of product.

Hardly available in 1885, cocaine quickly became emblematic of the modern, technological, international, political economy. Attempts to monopolize the trade vertically or horizontally failed; production, refining, manufacturing, distribution, and financing alliances crisscrossed national borders. States erected tariff barriers to protect domestic industries. Prices dropped dramatically as supply caught up with, and stimulated, demand. By the early twentieth century, cocaine ranked third in terms of dollar value among drugs. The popularity of the two drugs superseding cocaine, morphine and quinine, resulted from the same constellation of factors – a burgeoning pharmaco-industrial complex. The profits from such early successes ensured that the pace of research and development quickened, which in time resulted in the creation of an increasing variety of substances possessing both therapeutic and addiction potential. Although less dramatic than cocaine, many drugs produced by the science-pharmaceutical juggernaut enjoyed a similar initial enthusiastic reception. Experience soon indicated, however, that unrestricted access to drugs entailed unacceptable costs.

The home front [20]

By the early twentieth century, western societies generally viewed unrestricted drug availability and use with concern. The older notion that psychoactive substances, the individual, and social setting contributed roughly equally to drug-related problems gave way to an emphasis on the drug as the key agent engendering negative consequences. A longstanding *laissez-faire* attitude toward drug use, which privileged consumer choice and self-treatment over medical expertise, appeared inappropriate to the new era's changed circumstances. A variety of material and mental factors contributed to quickening the control impetus. By the early twentieth century the question was not *whether* access to drugs ought to be regulated, but *what* level and type of regulation was appropriate.

Growing medical expertise and professional considerations contributed to a redefinition of the drug question. As physicians gained experience with newer, more potent drugs and methods of administration, they witnessed the negative side effects of those substances. Indiscriminate opiate use, for example, caused widespread iatrogenic addiction, which in turn injured the emerging medical-professional ethos. As part of their campaign toward professionalization, physicians wished to gain control over the right to prescribe such powerful substances. Gradual medico-technological advances, such as the creation of aspirin, made it possible to restrict, at least somewhat, wide-spectrum use of more potent analgesics. Control of addicting substances, therefore, appeared more feasible to the medical community. Pharmacists were willing to acquiesce in this encroachment on their traditional prerogatives as long as they received exclusive rights to retail distribution. This emerging medical establishment attacked the patent medicine trade, marginal practitioners, and self-medication as threats to public health as well as to their professional aspirations.

Availability and misuse caused increasing concern among the general public as well. Aggressive marketing of patent medicines highlighted the dangers of an unrestricted market. Scandals, such as the doping of babies by working-class mothers, were the subject of government investigations. Journalists revealed adulteration, lack of quality control, and fraud, especially among over-the-counter medicines. Medical organizations highlighted the threat posed by unscrupulous or uninformed doctors. Revelations about drug hazards fit the late-nineteenth century desire to protect the public interest from the excesses of an overweening industrial society. Many called for measures to ensure the safety of food and medicines.

Changes in user groups also caused concern and shifted responsibility for drug abuse from society toward individuals increasingly defined as deviant. As the century drew to a close, a heterogeneous collection of addicts, including wounded veterans from the wars of mid-century, those dependent on unregulated habit-forming analgesics, iatrogenic cases, and eclectics, declined. Mainstream social status and the nature of their addiction – private pain relief – epitomized that cohort. A more frightening group of users replaced them, primarily younger, urban addicts, often minorities, who took drugs openly rather than in isolation, and for pleasure rather than to relieve pain. These marginal members of society were associated with an emerging underground scene that rejected bourgeois convention. Drug use of that type symbolized for many the social deviancy and moral deficiency inherent in increasingly public displays of vice. In the minds of contemporaries, a perceived decline in traditional morality, especially among the underclass, merited a more punitive response.

As the principal user cohort changed, conceptions about addiction focused increasingly on individual pathology and perceived deviation from social norms. Physicians, armed with a somewhat wider range of drug therapies, bolstered by experience, and supported by an increasingly sophisticated medical press, began to distinguish between medical and recreational use. Moral judgements about intention figured as much as observations about physical symptoms in determining drug-abuse treatment strategies. Non-medicinal use of drugs appeared pathological in nature. Some attributed such addiction to physiological defect. Others maintained that addiction reflected a psychological condition. Still others detected a pathology of the soul, a moral deficiency, at the root of addictive behavior. Treatment consisted of some combination of: curtailing or terminating use, therapy for discernible physical afflictions associated with drug use, and bolstering the addict's will to

resist the craving for drugs. Those who considered addiction a con-
tagious disease were likely to view drug abusers as societal pathogens;
social quarantine – incarceration in hopes of inculcating moral
sensibilities – seemed the proper response.

Whether one preferred medicalization or criminalization, regulating
access to, and use of, drugs seemed the logical response. Medical/
professional and government controls promised to help not only those
currently addicted, but also to prevent others from falling into the
same affliction. Vigilance against foreign substances (whether micro-
bial, inanimate, or human) and resort to quarantine appealed to
contemporary sensibilities. At the same time, instituting controls
reinforced the authority of the medical profession, government
agencies, and moral entrepreneurs.[21]

Social reform groups that focused on public health, child welfare,
social work, and especially temperance, saw drug regulation as both an
end in itself and a means to their central goals. Reformers hoped drug
controls would remove an important impediment to enhancing the
social milieu. To bolster their arguments in a self-consciously modern
era, they utilized social scientific methods to define, describe, and offer
solutions to problematic voluntary behaviors such as drug and alcohol
abuse. In their fight against inebriety, many temperance workers
perceived little practical difference between "dangerous drugs" and
alcohol. Others viewed drug regulation, more pragmatically, as an
expedient precedent. They hoped to take advantage of anti-drug sentiment in their battle against the ultimate enemy – demon rum.

The drug question appealed especially to women activists, who
exerted considerable influence in bringing such issues into the policy
arena. Women sometimes occupied positions of leadership and
comprised the majority of the rank-and-file support. Women usually
adopted the maternalist mantle, claiming a special feminine interest in
issues relating to hearth and home. In advocating drug restrictions,
most female activists hoped simultaneously to civilize national
behavior, gain a hearing for their concerns, and carve out space for
women in the public arena.

Anxieties brought on by increased cultural interaction animated
sentiments against drugs perceived as foreign. The Chinese diaspora,
caused in part by western-instigated, opium-related turmoil at home,
brought the opium habit in its wake. Many westerners believed over-
wrought reports concerning the habit's spread. Although grossly exaggerated, fears about the opium dens' effect upon young white men and
women fed nativist resentment against foreigners. Coca, in part because
of its mixture into popular unregulated libations such as Vin Mariani

and Coca Cola, acquired a negative image as well. In the United States, cocaine's popular association with blacks fueled regulatory passions based on racial discrimination.

A gendered view of drug use also contributed to the control impetus. Recreational drug use implied irrationality, sensuality, and a loss of control suggestive of femininity. To counteract the perceived weakness of such behavior and attitudes, many viewed a firm hand – substantive regulation – as the proper antidote.

The trajectory of control followed a pattern that moved from informal to formal restriction. During the nineteenth century, few advocated an active governmental role in regulating what was seen as personal behavior. Variable, context-dependent social limitations acted as the principal brake on drug availability and use. Polite society frowned upon public inebriety, regardless of drug type. As the negative effects of drugs such as cocaine became apparent, many physicians restricted therapeutic employment and many pharmacists ended indiscriminate sales. Cocaine, although legal, could often only be obtained from shady purveyors, frequently at a higher price that reflected the social opprobrium attached to non-medicinal use.

Around the turn of the twentieth century, western attitudes about formal control measures shifted. Allowing individuals the freedom to exercise self-administration had proved problematic; access filtered through professional expertise and public agencies appeared to offer the protections that most people desired. Localities, states, and national legislatures mandated food-and-drug-purity laws, restricted retail sales of addicting substances, and empowered medical and pharmacists' professional organizations to enforce standards. "Ethical" pharmaceutical companies (the term appeared around this time to distinguish them from patent medicine makers) acquiesced in regulations that provided legitimacy for their product lines. Patent medicine makers either changed their formulas or exited the business.

By 1914, most western societies had arrived at a control synthesis, opting to privilege expert knowledge and bureaucratic regulation at the expense of a democratic, every-man-his-own-doctor approach. Once in place, the control paradigm carried a logic of its own. If some substance appeared to present a danger, demands upon public authorities for regulation were sure to follow. When some user group engendered sympathy or enmity, calls arose for enforcement measures designed to protect innocents and punish perpetrators. Moreover, given the nature of the relationship between demand, supply, and regulation, governmental restrictions inevitably propelled the control impetus into the international arena.

Internationalism[22]

A new type of international cooperation also contributed to creating a multilateral drug control regime in the early twentieth century. Pioneered during the mid-1800s, numerous organizations emerged to confront issues that required trans-national attention in an increasingly interconnected world. Calls for an international meeting to discuss the East Asian opium traffic arose out of this tradition. Those interested in the drug issue drew upon a half-century's experience in international cooperation. A generally accepted protocol for multilateral negotiations existed; states and non-state actors gradually refined methods to promote their interests in that setting.

The missionary crusade[23]

In the same way that a variety of domestic actors played key roles in instituting local and national controls, the cumulative influence of missionary societies, civil servants, businessmen, and politicians resulted in attention to the international aspects of the drug question. The Dutch addressed an "internal" concern by focusing on their colony in the East Indies. Anglo-American efforts were directed primarily at the international traffic into China.

Dutch reformers, primarily missionaries along with some civil servants and soldiers who had served overseas, objected to the farm system long employed in the East Indies. They argued that selling concessions to the highest bidder encouraged corruption, smuggling, and addiction. Moreover, many feared the influence of ethnic Chinese who grew wealthy by dominating the traffic. Although some advocated prohibition, most recognized that a ban would foster smuggling. In a compromise typical of late-nineteenth-century western reform efforts, in 1893 the government appropriated the right of opium distribution by instituting a state monopoly. The Dutch *opium regie* placed salaried civil servants in charge, a move intended to break the power of the opium farmers, eliminate the profit temptations associated with a commission system, and end violence linked to opium trafficking. The monopoly aimed to reduce health risks by ensuring drug purity and to discourage smuggling by manipulating price. In response to the moral sensibilities of the new age, the *regie* ultimately hoped to eliminate drug abuse by registering addicts, who could only obtain opium legally through government sources. Once all the current users in a locale had registered, no new smokers could be added to the list. In theory, addiction would die out with the demise of registered users. Other nations' imperial administrations followed the Dutch example in succeeding years.[24] Thus, in response to calls for reform, colonial governments became directly involved in, and derived revenue from, selling opium. The moral and practical implications of this involvement became a central point of contention in succeeding decades.

British and American missionaries, who occupied the leading positions among those proselytizing in China, became stalwart opponents of the international opium trade. Despite valiant effort and substantial funding, decades of labor produced few converts in China. While on home leave, missionaries regularly addressed congregations about their work, noting the need for further contributions. By the late 1800s, however, lack of "success" led many to question whether the effort should continue. Missionaries cited opium as a key impediment. Addiction ruined lives and deadened morals; Westerners' association with the drug damaged churches' reputations among the people. Many missionaries had travelled to their stations in ships carrying opium, and the irony was not lost upon them.[25]

In the second half of the nineteenth century, British clergy founded several anti-opium societies dedicated to ending India's role in debauching China. Likening their cause to the great anti-slavery crusade a generation earlier, anti-opiumists publicized the immorality of the trade. Generating numerous petitions to lay before the government, they secured Parliamentary allies who vigorously interrogated the Queen's ministers. Women provided crucial support in the anti-opium campaigns, exercising their maternalist prerogatives for a cause they believed morally just. Agitation crested in the 1890s, culminating in an official investigation.

The anti-control defense[26]

In the course of the investigation, many opposed curbing the India-to-China trade and the very notion of regulating the international movement of drugs. Foes of regulation voiced a combination of sophistry and irrefutable logic in defense of their prerogatives. Subsequent players objecting to the control synthesis repeatedly employed similar arguments, whether applied within or beyond national borders.

One tactic involved challenging a drug's negative image. Defenders of India's opium exports claimed that critics exaggerated opium's deleterious effects. Many users carried on with little apparent dysfunction, and some even claimed that opium enhanced their quality of life. In succeeding debates, pro-control advocates generally assumed drugs engendered universal effects, regardless of circumstances. Opponents of control often argued in favor of specificity; drug use engendered different outcomes depending on culture, society, living conditions, or other circumstances. Throughout the twentieth century, anti-control advocates maintained that a drug's effects could not necessarily be condemned as universally negative.

Economic factors figured strongly in anti-control arguments as well. The Indian government required opium revenues; control advocates did not support raising British taxes to make up the difference. Moreover, many individuals derived a living from the trade. Depriving them of their livelihood punished the innocent. When confronting moral dilemmas about government complicity in fostering drug trading, those opposed to control often highlighted the costs of regulation rather than its benefits.

Differing political philosophies also played an important role. Both sides utilized classical liberal thought, which decried government interference in commerce. Pro-control advocates noted that the Indian monopoly system featured substantial government involvement. Anti-control forces condemned the government involvement inherent in restrictive legislation. The monopoly merely collected opium and sold it to independent wholesalers; the Indian government, they claimed, could hardly take responsibility for the final destination of commodities leaving its ports. In subsequent contests, control opponents frequently contested assumptions about the polity that prejudiced their case, often emphasizing liberty for individuals at the expense of socially-determined norms of responsibility.

Global competition, often combined with blaming countries that housed drug users, comprised another element of the anti-control thesis. Even many conceding a distaste for the trade appreciated the dilemmas presented by a substantive control effort. The government of India, in fact, disliked the negative publicity attached to the opium traffic, and would have been willing to forgo the revenue. Yet, if India suspended opium shipments, other suppliers would simply increase their market share. The Portuguese continued to ship Malwa opium to their outpost at Macao, and Persian and Turkish exports increased steadily as the new century dawned. Even in the unlikely event that all imports could be eliminated, the Chinese themselves produced thousands of tons of opium each year. Until China got its own house in order, many otherwise ill-disposed toward the traffic saw little merit in denying India a legitimate share of the trade. In ensuing years, defenders of the status quo habitually attempted to transfer responsibility for the drug problem beyond regulatory reach.

Both sides recognized the links between opium trading and larger issues of commerce. On the one hand, suspending opium imports might set an undesirable precedent. Although opium still generated tremendous profits for the governments, banks, and shippers involved, several other commodities exported to China had surpassed it by the late nineteenth century. If Great Britain renounced its right to sell opium, the Chinese might attempt to prohibit imports of other items. Conversely, British officials understood that continued opium shipments strained London's relations with China. Increasing criticism at home and a rising tide of resentment in China against foreign encroachment symbolized by opium caused concern among British officials.

The British debate highlighted a key dilemma that surfaced in all subsequent deliberations: the drug issue could not be separated from its larger political, economic, social, and cultural contexts. In this instance, British India's policy remained unchanged until a solution to the global problems of competing imports and Chinese overproduction materialized. From the beginning, control advocates had to negotiate a tangle of issues that infinitely complicated their task.

The great game[27]

In considering the fate of the opium trade, British policymakers had to consider the East Asian geopolitical situation. Toward the end of the nineteenth century, western powers employed increasingly aggressive measures to pry China open. They imposed an Imperial Maritime Customs Service that collected tariffs and ensured protection of foreigners' trade rights. Peking tried to play the barbarians off against one another, but the Powers took advantage of Most Favored Nation status to claim privileges granted to their rivals. Extraterritoriality agreements enabled foreigners to break Chinese laws with relative impunity, further weakening Imperial authority. Japan precipitated a war in 1894, easily besting the moribund (and opium-besotted) Chinese. Peking ceded Taiwan in the peace settlement, renewing the race for territorial concessions. Britain, France, Japan, Russia, and Germany soon carved out spheres of influence, and it appeared that the entire country might be partitioned in a fashion reminiscent of the "scramble for Africa." The Boxer rebellion only reinforced perceptions about the impending disintegration of the Middle Kingdom. In its aftermath the industrialized states imposed an indemnity and other punitive concessions on China, further crippling the central government's ability to control the country.

In conjunction with domestic pressure and anti-opium-trade arguments, concerns about Chinese viability finally tipped the balance against continued Indian exports. Officials in London generally agreed that Great Britain's interests were best served by maintaining Chinese territorial integrity. British sales and investments were more widespread throughout the Middle Kingdom than were those of any of her rivals. The opium habit clearly contributed to China's weakened position. With the Liberal electoral victory of 1906, the English anti-opium coalition gained supporters. The new government soon intimated its willingness to curtail the India-to-China trade.

The Chinese government reached a similar conclusion at approximately the same time. After the Boxer rebellion, Imperial officials belatedly implemented a program to restore China's fortunes. Opium figured prominently in their plans. In September 1906, Imperial edicts announced a gradual suppression of domestic opium cultivation and use. Acreage for poppy production would be reduced by one-tenth annually, bringing opium production to an end after ten years. Opium smokers would gradually reduce their consumption as well. Peking announced its desire to curtail opium imports in support of those domestic measures.[28]

The Ten Year Agreement of 1907[29]

British officials viewed China's latest pronouncement with skepticism, but popular opinion, larger trade considerations, and concerns about the Middle Kingdom's territorial integrity spurred them to treat with Peking. After protracted negotiations, Britain agreed to reduce Indian opium exports by 10 percent annually,[30] provided China eliminated domestic production at the same rate. To allay fears that unreported domestic production might upset the scheme, British officials insisted upon independent verification of Peking's progress in eradicating poppy cultivation. Three years after implementing the agreement, London would designate an inspector who would be allowed unlimited access to the interior. If the inspector pronounced initial Chinese efforts a success, both parties would continue reductions over the ensuing seven years. The Emperor assented, and the agreement went into effect on 1 January 1908.

In its initial phase, the "Ten Year Agreement" between India and China succeeded better than expected. To general surprise, the Imperial government kept its part of the bargain. Between 1908 and 1910, poppy acreage declined precipitously. The British inspector, travelling extensively during 1910–11, expressed satisfaction with

Chinese efforts. Although some provinces had not kept to the schedule, others had eliminated poppy cultivation completely. Reflecting a nascent nationalism, anti-opium sentiment became a *cause célèbre* among leading elements in China. The Chinese National Assembly, meeting for the first time in 1910, advocated an accelerated program to eliminate opium use. In response, Indian officials stepped up their own timetable for ending the trade, despite concerns that early prohibition jeopardized the principle of free access to Chinese markets. British India shipped its last licit chest of opium to China in 1913.

Just as China appeared capable of kicking the habit, however, the country's central authority disintegrated. In November 1911 the Manchu dynasty succumbed to revolution. A weak republic established in 1912 proved unable to hold the country together, and fighting developed between warlords for control over the provinces. After the Great War broke out in 1914, the European powers turned their attentions homeward. Japan exploited the situation, exacting concessions that engendered further disintegration. China descended into civil turmoil.

Under such conditions, the anti-opium crusade evaporated. Profit-hungry warlords encouraged, even compelled, poppy cultivation. Opium again became a medium of exchange, facilitating its recrudescence. Whether demand had ever receded significantly is doubtful, but in any case widespread addiction plagued the country. As early as 1912–13, opium cultivation reappeared in some areas where it had been suppressed. After 1915 the anti-opium campaign lost all momentum. By the mid-1920s extensive poppy-growing existed in fourteen of China's eighteen provinces, and total domestic production approximated the levels of a generation earlier.[31] Even as Chiang Kai-Shek extended the Nationalist banner over much of China during the late 1920s and the 1930s, opium continued to afflict the country. His Kuomintang government depended upon opium revenues to fill its coffers; many provincial authorities and semi-independent officials became similarly addicted to the profits reaped from the opium trade and the benefits of consorting with traffickers who could provide information, arms, muscle, and connections.[32]

Legacy

The Ten Year Agreement served as an influential model for the next six decades. Succeeding generations of drug control advocates harkened back to the 1907 pact as the prime example of a successful opium treaty. They believed the Indian/Chinese agreement demonstrated that drug control was primarily a matter of national will. States that really *wanted* to impose effective drug restrictions could do so in relatively short order; had the Chinese government maintained control, the opium scourge would surely have been defeated.

The "success" of the Ten Year Agreement also set the tone for later negotiations by focusing attention on the control of supply. The most direct method for ending the drug problem appeared to be elimination of excess quantities available for abuse. Consequently, questions about what caused addiction, the relationship between supply and demand, and whether formal controls fostered illegal activity received little attention.

Control advocates stubbornly refused to acknowledge important faults in their analysis. Although India eliminated shipments to China, Indian exports to Asian colonial opium monopolies continued. Indian domestic consumption remained unaffected as well. The Indian/Chinese agreement also did nothing to curtail shipments from Persia or Turkey. Additionally, the 1907 pact fomented increased domestic and international smuggling. Moreover, the success of Chinese efforts to eliminate cultivation was probably exaggerated. Even if domestic production had decreased substantially in the early years, there is no reason to assume that subsequent efforts would have proceeded smoothly. Provincial officials no doubt started with the easiest areas first, both in hopes of providing an example and to show good progress. The Chinese government would have encountered increasing resistance and more smuggling in the later stages of the anti-opium campaign. A related ominous development appeared at this time as well. As opium availability declined, heroin and morphine imports rose. China provided the first evidence that control efforts would have to account for addicts' adaptive propensities; rather than eliminating abuse, regulatory changes often modified patterns of use.[33]

Most importantly, domestic and international factors in Britain, India, and China came to a rare point of intersection between 1906 and 1911. Before and after that period such a commonality did not exist. The pact hinged on Peking's agreement to surrender a portion of its sovereignty. The inspection clause of the Ten Year Agreement represented an exceptional concession, granted under duress by the government of a quasi-occupied country. Although control advocates repeatedly attempted to impose independent inspection clauses in later agreements, the targets of such provisions refused to surrender their sovereignty.

Nevertheless, the Ten Year Agreement haunted international drug control negotiations for sixty years. Control advocates repeatedly exhibited great faith in treaties featuring reduction of excess supplies, even when such documents merely papered over fundamental conflicts. This belief in the efficacy of the supply control model provided a clear goal and unifying rationale for control advocates, but it also presented the largest stumbling block to their aspirations.

Enter America[34]

The advent of the United States as a Western Pacific power provided the final catalyst leading to international drug control. American traders and manufacturers disliked opium because they believed it reduced Chinese demand for other goods. With no effective ability to project power on the Asian mainland, the United States attempted instead to gain access to Chinese markets by currying favor with Imperial authorities. In 1887 Washington barred American ships from carrying opium to China. In ensuing decades, the US government generally supported Chinese efforts to end opium imports.

Upon acquiring the Philippines at the conclusion of the Spanish–American War, Washington inherited an opium problem. Madrid, like other Asian colonial powers, employed a government-sanctioned scheme for distribution of smoking opium. The policy offended American moral sensibilities, particularly among temperance advocates and supporters of missionary activities. Washington imposed a policy of suppression, excepting medical needs, upon the Philippines.

After 1898 America's East Asian interests, like Great Britain's, were best served by maintaining Chinese territorial integrity. Through the Open Door notes and subsequent initiatives, Washington sought to protect American trading, investment, and development opportunities throughout the Celestial Kingdom. An anti-opium policy complemented this general approach. No significant US interests were involved in the opium trade, and curbing addiction would certainly bolster a tottering China. Moreover, such a policy garnered domestic support among temperance groups, missionary societies, merchant organizations, and those concerned about the spread of alien drug-using subcultures. American policymakers, therefore, were predisposed to view favorably proposals for restricting the Asian opium traffic.

During 1906–7, the same period that witnessed the British–Indian–Chinese rapprochement, the United States government first entertained the notion of calling an international meeting to consider the opium question. The initiative emanated from Bishop Charles Henry Brent, a Canadian-born Anglican minister who had served as Episcopal Bishop of the Philippines since 1901. Brent took an extreme

Charles Henry BRENT (1862–1929). United States. Born in Ontario, Episcopal Bishop of the Philippines and later western New York State. Longtime laborer in the field of opium reform. Possessed the strengths and weaknesses of the moral crusader.

prohibitionist position on the opium question. He viewed any non-medical use as immoral, and opposed state-sponsored opium distribution monopolies because he believed they corrupted both government and populace. Brent feared that continued East Asian opium trafficking would undermine the new Philippine prohibition policy. Moreover, he sided with the missionary societies then agitating against the China trade. Brent utilized personal contacts with Philippine Governor William Howard Taft, President Roosevelt, and other high-ranking officials to lobby for an international meeting to discuss ending the traffic. The Bishop originally envisioned limiting participation to the principal Far Eastern powers and restricting discussions to the Chinese situation. Brent was the first of many to discover the difficulty of maintaining control over the agenda and the invitation list.

Predisposed to view such a meeting favorably, the State Department circularized a number of governments after mid-1906. Several expressed interest, but registered reservations as well. Some claimed that the issue could not properly be discussed unless all the major producing, manufacturing, and consuming nations attended. To placate the wary, Washington expanded the invitation list and agreed that the delegates would act in an advisory capacity only. Under these conditions, all the colonial powers[35] agreed to attend, as did China and Siam. Persia consented only after the application of considerable diplomatic pressure. Italy and Austria-Hungary, not wishing to abdicate their positions among the Great Powers despite a paucity of interest in the issue, asked to be invited as well. In an ominous sign of future developments, Turkey declined to attend. Conferees met in Shanghai in February 1909.

The Shanghai Opium Commission[36]

As the first gathering convened to consider drugs as an international concern, the 1909 Shanghai Opium Commission acted as a prototype for later meetings. Despite the fact that delegates possessed no plenipotentiary powers, the representatives clashed on several issues.

Hamilton WRIGHT (1867–1917). United States. Physician claiming expertise in tropical diseases. Became addicted to the cause of opium suppression upon first exposure in 1909. Abrasively enthusiastic, his outspoken dedication caused irritation even among allies.

Bishop Brent assumed the presidency of the meeting, leaving physician Hamilton Wright to lead the American offensive. Dr. Wright's reputation as an expert in tropical medicine and experience in the Far East earned him a place on the US delegation. He devoted himself to the cause until his untimely death in 1917. In Shanghai, Wright attacked the prerogatives of the colonial powers, engendering an adversarial atmosphere that carried over into subsequent negotiations.

Wright worked in conjunction with the Chinese delegation to pressure the colonial powers. He attempted to discuss the recently completed Ten Year Agreement, primarily in hopes of accelerating the cessation of Indian imports. Insisting on treaty rights and cognizant of the larger trade issues involved, the British representatives refused to discuss the issue. The Americans also posited a restrictive definition of legitimate use, claiming that any consumption not related to medical and scientific purposes (as defined in terms of western medicine and science) should be considered illicit. The colonial powers objected strenuously to any contention that eating, smoking, and other applications of opium in traditional preparations produced deleterious results. They advocated recognizing "quasi-medical" opium use as legitimate, stressing the practical difficulties governments would encounter by suppressing such use without an alternative. Considering opium's long medicinal history and the general state of colonial medical services, the likelihood of providing a culturally acceptable substitute at reasonable cost seemed remote.

Governments accused of abetting the opium scourge attempted to deflect attention from themselves. Several raised the issue of increasing heroin and morphine abuse in the ostensibly reformed China. Producing nations pointed out the sins of pharmaceutical firms located in manufacturing states, which placed no constraints on exports, thereby highlighting the complicated nature of the drug abuse phenomenon. The colonial powers also objected when the US delegation floated a resolution proposing a follow-up plenipotentiary conference. Those states with vested interests in the extant *laissez-faire* arrangements disapproved of any attempt to draft a drug control treaty that would impose binding obligations upon signatories.

The delegates agreed upon a series of diluted recommendations to lay before their governments. The fundamental differences aired at the 1909 Shanghai Opium Commission, however, remained central points of contention for decades.

Path to The Hague[37]

The governments represented at the 1909 meeting followed their own inclinations rather than the Commission's recommendations. Most colonial powers, and the Persians as well, took no action. The British had already declared their intentions concerning the India–China trade, but they indicated no desire to alter their policies regarding other colonies. Under pressure from Brent and, by extension, the US government, India agreed to end opium exports to jurisdictions that prohibited its import. This concession removed one contentious issue by ending the licit trade to Philippine ports. China pursued its suppression campaign until political breakdown precluded further progress.

The United States, however, continued to champion the cause. Brent and Wright, now the State Department's official adviser on international narcotics matters, agitated for further action. Regardless of the Ten Year Agreement, they noted that opium still entered China from territories controlled by other states, particularly the Portuguese. Smuggling also appeared to be on the rise. Increased trafficking in morphine, heroin, cocaine, and marijuana caused concern as well. The global nature of the drug trade spurred Wright and Brent to call for an international plenipotentiary convention to address the full range of issues.

The State Department and executive branch, with Brent's friend Taft now in the White House, viewed the proposal sympathetically. The moral and practical merits of the anti-opium cause contained considerable appeal. A survey conducted by Wright in preparation for the Shanghai meeting reported widespread addiction in America. Wright probably overstated the problem's severity, but his findings heightened concerns about opiate abuse among Chinese and its spread to the general populace. Wright utilized reports about rising cocaine and marijuana use among blacks to bolster his case. Trade considerations also proved influential. Washington hoped its efforts on behalf of China would redound to the benefit of American business interests in the Far East. Brent and Wright, in fact, had proposed revision of certain tariff agreements as part of their overall campaign to eliminate the drug scourge, shore up China's revenues, and benefit US commerce.

American officials endorsed the effort. In September 1909 the State Department circularized governments that attended the Shanghai meeting, expressing interest in convening a plenipotentiary conference to consider an international drug control treaty. Among a lengthy list of items the United States proposed for discussion, the most controversial included control of the production, manufacture, and distribution of opium; limiting opium cultivation so that reduced Indian plantings would not result in increases elsewhere; uniform national control and penal regulations; reciprocal notifications concerning opium imports and exports; governmental regulation of opium exporters; and granting reciprocal rights to search vessels suspected of carrying contraband opium.[38] Wright and Brent refrained from proposing controls over cocaine, marijuana, and manufactured drugs. They assumed that other states would do so, and wished to avoid the appearance of unduly influencing the proceedings. Nevertheless, the general thrust of US drug control proposals changed little for decades. In 1909 the United States had already articulated a supply-oriented vision of international drug regulation to which other actors had to respond.

The American proposal generated a lukewarm reception. During 1910–11, Brent and Wright pestered reluctant governments until all agreed to attend. Brent generated support from British and American anti-opium lobbies. He highlighted the plight of imperial subjects in Far Eastern territories, arguing they had the right to be free of opium practically forced upon them by colonial administrations that profited from the business. In a maneuver that would be repeated many times by subsequent American officials, Wright threatened to convoke a plenipotentiary meeting under the auspices of the United States government. Wright calculated, correctly, that such a move would animate the sluggish European powers. The prospect of meeting in the midst of the moralistic American populace held little appeal for the Great Powers. After much foot dragging, the principal states agreed to meet at the Hague on 1 December 1911.[39]

Several governments, however, insisted on amendments to the agenda. Italy, experiencing difficulty curbing a long-established trade in marijuana and hashish through its African possessions, called for international controls over those drugs. Portugal proclaimed that it would not take any steps to injure the Macao opium trade unless all other governments, whether represented at the conference or not, agreed to do the same. Russia would not countenance the restriction of poppy cultivation, because in that country the plant was grown primarily for its oil and seeds. France refused to consider provisions requiring amendment of its domestic legislation. Both Paris and London objected to proposals concerning the reciprocal right of search on the high seas. Hoping to deflect attention from India's continuing role as an opium producer and exporter, Great Britain also insisted that the conference take up the issue of manufactured drugs such as morphine, heroin, and cocaine. Germany, the principal exporter of those drugs, objected to the British proposal. Turkey refused to attend under any circumstances. To ensure the participation of other governments, the United States offered assurances that the agenda remained open to revision. Although that maneuver enabled the meeting to proceed, the representatives arrived with widely divergent expectations about the scope of the Conference.

Although not generally recognized at the time, the events of 1909–11 proved a more accurate harbinger of the future than the negotiations surrounding the Ten Year Agreement. The attitude of the principal players did not augur well for those advocating stringent international control standards. Governments demonstrated their inclination to protect interests at the expense of pursuing moral objectives. Even in the United States, which acted as leader of the drug control crusade, governmental officials allowed Brent and Wright free rein only because their program dovetailed with other policy goals. When competing domestic or international considerations changed the political calculus, Washington would subordinate international cooperation to other objectives. Non-governmental actors, such as the anti-opium societies, missionary groups, and temperance advocates, could cajole officials and counteract economic and cultural influences only to a point. The pressure of public opinion might bring nations to the bargaining table, but considerations of morality proved unable decisively to influence the negotiations.

Moreover, states opposed to the imposition of international controls proved adept at obfuscation. By insisting that all nations must adhere to any treaty negotiated at the Hague, the Portuguese guaranteed themselves a loophole. Theoretically, of course, Lisbon raised a valid point. In fact, subsequent developments showed that anything short of complete international cooperation could indeed jeopardize global control efforts. Nevertheless, the Portuguese government cared little for such larger considerations; Lisbon simply wanted to protect a profitable trade for its Macao colony. Similarly, the British expanded the agenda to include manufactured drugs because they hoped the Germans and Dutch would balk. The German pharmaceutical industry led the trade in morphine and cocaine, and defended its prerogatives vigorously despite government attempts to cooperate in forging the new regime. If the Hague talks failed to produce a satisfactory control instrument, London would not have to shoulder the opprobrium. A viable treaty, on the other hand, would enable British pharmaceuticals to compete with German products on a level playing field as well as placate British colonials urging restrictions on manufactured drugs. Other key states, such as Switzerland and Turkey, refused to participate at all.

In an oft-repeated pattern, the first plenipotentiary drug control conference engendered widely differing views about what sort of program should be pursued. The Americans espoused radical measures, not least because the principal enforcement burdens fell on other governments. Germany, Switzerland, the Netherlands and other states possessing significant pharmaceutical industries might support controls over raw materials, but they objected to limitations on manufactured drugs. Producing states such as Persia, Turkey, and India considered domestic drug use an internal matter, not subject to interference from other states. They also insisted on the right to export opium to those states that did not prohibit the trade. Territories that consumed large quantities of (smoking) opium, primarily the colonies of Southeast Asia and Indonesia, worried that reducing licit supplies would simply foment increased smuggling. They viewed attempts to enforce prohibition as irresponsible and unrealistic. Unable to agree in advance on the agenda, representatives compromised on the spot. Needless to say, such conditions were not conducive to reaching agreement smoothly.

The Hague Opium Conference[40]

At the Hague Opium Conference, delegations adopted positions similar to those espoused in the pre-negotiations of 1909–11. Bishop Brent once again took the president's chair, leaving Wright to lead American efforts. With the Chinese delegation as his main support, Wright attempted to implement a stringent program of controls. Other delegations rebuffed the American initiatives by weakening the treaty's provisions.

Chapters I and II called upon signatories to restrict the trade in raw and prepared (smoking) opium. This section included a clause preventing the export of such drugs to states that prohibited their import. Those provisions represented one of the Conference's most important achievements. On the other hand, Chapters I and II did little to curb excess imports into treaty ports such as Macao, Hong Kong, and other centers of worldwide opium smuggling. The principal producing territories, represented by Great Britain and Persia, defeated provisions requiring signatories to reduce opium cultivation. Moreover, although states agreed gradually to suppress opium smoking, the treaty set no timetable. Those wishing to avoid enacting substantive changes could do so by employing sundry excuses.

Chapter IV dealt specifically with measures to reduce the drug traffic in China. Peking utilized the opportunity to gain cooperation in its anti-opium campaign. Several articles in Chapter IV also implied a reduction of extraterritorial rights exercised by foreign nationals in the Middle Kingdom. This section constituted another important Chinese accomplishment, although the country's subsequent disintegration largely nullified the effect.

Chapter III, which covered manufactured drugs such as morphine, heroin, codeine, and cocaine, proved the most problematic. As the British anticipated, Germany objected to curtailing manufacture or export. Berlin's representatives refused to sacrifice their predominance in the international marketplace unless all conceivable rivals followed suit. The German delegation succeeded in removing codeine from consideration altogether. The pertinent articles called for a variety of licensing, manufacturing, and distribution controls, but the Germans ensured that the provisions remained vague. They further weakened Chapter III by insisting on language that allowed governments to "use their best efforts" to enact the relevant provisions. Once again, governments not inclined to impose substantive controls could choose from among several escape clauses.

Despite the loopholes included in Chapter III, Berlin's representatives demanded additional protections. The German delegation, supported by France, insisted that even minor producing, manufacturing, and consuming states, totalling thirty-four governments in all, ratify the treaty before it entered into force. They argued that, until states not represented at the conference (the most important of which included Bolivia, Peru, Turkey, Serbia, and Switzerland) adhered to the treaty's provisions, the drug business would simply migrate to the country featuring the least restrictive regulatory environment. Despite the extraordinary nature of the proposal, the other delegations acquiesced when it became clear that Germany and perhaps France would not sign without it.

The Conference completed its work on 23 January 1912. In a typical manifestation of pre-1914 internationalism, the Netherlands government took responsibility for administering the Hague Opium Convention. Nations deposited ratifications with the Hague, and the Dutch government acted as the communication point for matters concerning the treaty.

Post-Hague developments

The Hague Convention reinforced the position of Americans who favored strong domestic enforcement measures. The Senate ratified the treaty in 1913. An initiative launched by control advocates, including Hamilton Wright, to enact national legislation bore fruit the following year. The Harrison Narcotics Act of 1914 inaugurated federal involvement in drug control, and provided the country's basic law for decades. To circumvent prevailing constitutional strictures, which did not allow for a direct federal role in criminalizing drug use, Wright fashioned the Harrison Act as a revenue measure. The burden of enforcing the law therefore fell to the Treasury Department. Wholesalers, retailers, and physicians applied for a tax stamp, at a nominal fee, in order to dispense drugs. The real intent of the law, however, was to limit use by restricting access. Physicians and pharmacists who dispensed large quantities of controlled substances could be prosecuted for maintaining addicts, a practice disapproved of by the Harrison Act's supporters. In the ensuing decade, the Harrison Act underwent numerous court challenges. Federal officials often cited the international obligations incurred under the 1912 Hague Opium Convention as a key justification in defending the statute. The peculiar character of American arrangements for drug control, which criminalized illicit use by way of the tax code, survived. Nevertheless, the shaky legal ground underpinning American statutes compelled federal officials to seek further buttressing by way of international agreement.[41]

After the Hague Conference adjourned, the issue of universality presented a roadblock. Persuading thirty-four nations to ratify the International Opium Convention proved a daunting task. Over the next thirty months efforts by Wright, Brent, the State Department, the British Foreign Office, and the Dutch government produced eight ratifications and twenty-four promises to adhere. Serbia and Turkey, however, rejected all overtures. Once the Great War broke out in August 1914, more pressing matters took precedence. During 1915 the United States, China, the Netherlands, Norway, and Honduras put the International Opium Convention into force among themselves, but beyond that the issue remained in abeyance until the cessation of hostilities. Once again, control advocates thought they had come tantalizingly close to success. If only Serbia and Turkey had ratified, they believed, the 1912 treaty could have been implemented. The effect of the war, however, had been more profound than anyone supposed.[42]

The Great War and its aftermath

Drug scares emanating from wartime conditions engendered increased support for both domestic and international controls. Reports of abuse among Allied troops in France surfaced during 1915. London tabloids also featured accounts of prostitutes doping and robbing soldiers on leave in England. Smuggling increased in Europe and the Far East as shortages encouraged illicit entrepreneurial activity. Wartime regulations highlighted how control measures could impact the phenomenon of poly-drug use; limitations on alcohol consumption and pub operations made relatively uncontrolled substances like cocaine and opiates attractive alternatives. Curfews drove night life underground, exacerbating related illicit activities. Inadequate legislation emerged as the principal culprit; unscrupulous physicians and pharmacists could dispense addicting substances with impunity, while shippers were under no import or export restrictions. Exaggerated stories about an increased drug threat caused concern; drug use forced contemporaries to confront phenomena wrought by wartime exigencies such as malleable gender roles, anxieties about modernity, and a frayed social fabric. Great Britain utilized the Defense of the Realm Act to tighten domestic controls, focusing on punitive measures for trafficking in or possession of cocaine and opium. Germany, Canada, and other states instituted similar programs designed to restrict access to drugs, conserve vital medicinal resources, and deter smuggling. These ad-hoc wartime administrative arrangements generally solidified after 1918, leaving enforcement in the hands of agencies not necessarily suited to the task.

Wartime smuggling and shortages demonstrated that laxity in one jurisdiction imperiled the efficacy of legislation elsewhere. The dilemma highlighted the international dimensions of the drug control equation. In response, the Home Office introduced a system of import/export authorizations designed to ensure that all drug shipments into and out of Britain had a legitimate destination. Those regulations subsequently provided a de-facto standard for control agencies in other countries.[43]

The peace process directly benefitted the Hague Opium Convention. Through a complicated series of overtures, both the British and American delegations to the Paris conference concluded that a clause requiring ratification of the Hague Opium Convention should be included in the peace treaties. The Chinese insisted on German and Austrian adherence as a condition for concluding peace. The proposal presented an unexpected boon to control advocates. With the stroke of a pen, the requirement of the 1912 treaty for near-universal adherence was satisfied. Two of the principal recalcitrants, Turkey and Germany, were forced to comply in order to conclude peace. Consequently, the Hague Opium convention came into general application between 1919 and 1921.[44]

Most significantly, through the League of Nations the drug question gained a permanent place on the international agenda. Article 23c of the Covenant conferred upon the League responsibility for supervising execution of the 1912 Hague treaty. By virtue of its leading position in the promotion of social, medical, and humanitarian affairs, the League became the center of international efforts to resolve the drug dilemma. For better and worse, all paths to drug control passed through Geneva.[45]

At the same time, the war exacerbated the supply dimension of the drug problem. Germany had acted as the world's premier supplier of morphine, heroin, and cocaine in the prewar years. The sudden cessation of that trade in 1914 left allied nations and neutrals in dire straits. In response, Great Britain, France, and Japan significantly increased their pharmaceutical manufacturing capabilities. Dutch firms expanded cocaine manufacture, and sold to all comers. European hostilities also caused US officials to recognize that their country possessed neither adequate manufacturing facilities nor satisfactory research and development capabilities. Washington introduced programs to redress those gaps.

Thus, several key industrial states emerged from the Great War with significantly augmented manufacturing capabilities and enhanced research facilities. In reacting to wartime exigencies, crash drug development programs spawned new constituencies with a direct interest in international control negotiations. With the cessation of hostilities, pharmaceutical companies sought markets for their expanded productive capacities, and generally took a dim view of efforts to limit their prerogatives. Research and development consortia also sought to advance their objectives in relation to the emerging international regime. Their efforts ensured protection for scientific endeavors, but they also reinforced the tendency to treat the drug question as a problem of excess supply.[46]

Conclusion

By 1920, the principal elements and relationships contributing to drug diplomacy had materialized. Addicting substances moved in the mainstream of the international flow of capital and goods. The cultural preferences and manifest power of the western industrialized nations determined which drugs escaped limitation and which suffered censure. Abundant supplies and insatiable demand, however, ensured that the traffic would assume a subterranean nature wherever serious enforcement efforts took hold; supply, demand, and regulation were inextricably intertwined in networks of collaboration that crossed legal, political, economic, social, and cultural boundaries. All over the world, farmers, pharmaceutical manufacturers, retailers, medical professionals, and traders, both scrupulous and unscrupulous, derived some portion of their livelihood from drugs. Insurgents and participants in civil wars utilized the many benefits derived from drug trafficking to support their activities.[47] Technological advances introduced new substances and new methods of administration, while increasingly sophisticated business and marketing organizations facilitated dissemination of those products. The evolution of technology and scientific research promised to accelerate the pace of drug development. Both advocates and opponents of control measures had identified their principal arguments and forged alliances with like-minded groups at home and abroad. National control agencies arose to oversee enforcement and deal with their counterpart organizations in other countries. Buffeted by domestic interest groups, international factors beyond their control, and competing governmental priorities, state drug-control administrators pursued their own bureaucratic interests as a primary goal. Governments, whether they wished to or not, had to confront the drug question's impact on trade, security, and other international issues. The League provided a venue for multileveled interactions between numerous state and non-state actors. The League also introduced a further layer of administrative abstraction into the equation. An international secretariat, dedicated to promoting the control regime but beset by numerous impediments, sometimes hindered as much as it advanced the cause. Under this superstructure lay a multitude of addicted individuals, whose propensity to procure habituating substances proved the most incalculable factor of all.

Developments since the late nineteenth century indicated both the likely evolution of the regime and alternate conceptions about the drug question. Both the 1907 Ten Year Agreement and the Hague Opium Convention emphasized supply control. Many questioned, however, the utility of attempts to impose substantive regulations on a worldwide basis. Smuggling presented a perennial problem. Moreover, many addicts had already demonstrated a discouraging tendency to circumvent control efforts by switching between alcohol, opium, cocaine, heroin and other drugs in accordance with the local regulatory climate.[48] Moreover, some medical professionals and social reform advocates stressed the primacy of etiological factors. They hoped to curb drug addiction, or at least its most deleterious effects, by reducing demand. Although a minority of the rising expert class, it remained to be seen how these dissenters might influence the main currents of drug control.

The landmark Hague Opium Convention exemplified the emerging regime's possibilities and limitations. The treaty urged much but required little. States inclined to enhance controls found ample justification in the convention's stipulations. Indeed, the United States cited treaty obligation as a principal reason for reforming domestic legislation. The treaty's equivocal provisions, however, allowed recalcitrants to avoid enacting substantive measures. Through the Paris peace treaties control advocates overcame the obstacle created by the Hague Convention's near-universal ratification clause, but whether states would take their obligations seriously remained unclear.

Despite such uncertainties, control advocates remained optimistic. The 1912 Convention and subsequent adoption of the cause by the League of Nations represented a diplomatic achievement of significance. States came together to deal with a complicated diplomatic, social, economic, political, and legal issue. Even if the regime lacked a full set of teeth, a fault not yet fully apparent, control advocates considered it a good beginning. Building on the foundation provided by the Hague agreement and the League's prestige, opponents of the "drug scourge" envisioned a bright future.

Part II
Establishing the system

2 Laying the foundation –
1919–25

On its face it would seem a proposition simple enough: Opium, morphine, heroin, cocaine, hasheesh, or whatnot other habit-forming drug is dangerous stuff. Its production, distribution and use should be limited and controlled so as to confine it to purposes strictly medical and scientific. . . .
But it is not so simple as that.[1]

With the resumption of peacetime conditions, drug diplomacy received renewed attention. Economic considerations, socio-medical concerns, political interests, cultural presuppositions, and religious–moral motivations continued to figure prominently in the calculations of control advocates, their opponents, and those interested in utilizing the drug issue to advance other causes. Domestic sentiment favoring increased international restrictions, widespread in the West, spurred governments to the negotiating table. At the same time, officials in manufacturing states had to take account of constituencies desiring to protect capacity expanded during the late unpleasantness. Colonial governments viewed attempts by outsiders to impose controls over domestic production and consumption as an unwarranted invasion of sovereign rights. Producer countries objected to the export of western standards at the expense of indigenous ambitions. Consumer states, lacking both raw materials and manufacturing facilities, desired access to vital medicaments at reasonable cost. The anemic state of world trade caused nervousness in many quarters; proposals to limit the commerce in drugs might encourage other barriers to trade. The conflicts likely to erupt between such disparate interests portended a bumpy ride along the road to drug control.

Larger political concerns also impinged upon and were influenced by the global traffic in addicting substances. The establishment of the

League of Nations and its secretariat introduced a new factor into international equations. After 1919, a supra-national organization with its own employees and interests would shape, and be shaped by, the drug issue. The United States wished to play a leading role in drug negotiations, but could only do so by confronting its spurned progeny, the League. Great Britain could not play a constructive role without reconciling the disparate interests of metropole and empire. Political instability in China continued to bedevil all concerned with the East Asian drug question.

By 1925, this constellation of factors produced a fledgling control regime that reflected both the limited program upon which parties could agree and the aspirations of control advocates. A foundational treaty called upon governments to oversee imports and exports of dangerous drugs, but did not impinge significantly on the production, manufacture or consumption of those substances. Governments also agreed to the creation of a semi-independent control body, the Permanent Central Opium Board, but crippled its ability to overcome the prerogatives of states. The negotiations of the early 1920s resulted in a statutory emphasis on supply control that overshadowed alternative approaches to the problem, while at the same time highlighting the difficulty of reproducing a breakthrough like that achieved in the 1907 Ten Year Agreement.

New kid: the League of Nations

The League created several entities to deal with drug matters. The "Advisory Committee on the Traffic in Opium and Other Dangerous Drugs," usually referred to as the Opium Advisory Committee (OAC), served as the focal responsible organization.[2] Composed of governmental representatives, the OAC met quarterly during its early years, annually later on. The League designated an "Opium and Social Questions Section" (hereafter referred to as the Opium Section) within the secretariat for administrative and executive support. Dame Rachel Crowdy was named head of the Opium Section.[3] The League Health Committee (forerunner of the World Health Organization) took responsibility for advising on medical matters.[4]

The League showed great interest in the drug issue; success in multilateral drug negotiations strengthened the organization while failure weakened it. For example, after the US Senate rejected the Versailles treaty, League officials maneuvered carefully to influence American public opinion in hopes of building support for a reversal. They launched a publicity campaign that downplayed the League's political

Dame Rachel Eleanor CROWDY (Dame Rachel Thornhill) (1884–1964). Great Britain. Chief of Opium Traffic and Social Questions Section, 1919–31. The highest ranking woman ever to serve in the League Secretariat. Trained as a nurse, she earned an Apothecary's certificate, served with the Territorial Army's Voluntary Aid Detachments, and as lecturer at the National Health Society. During the Great War she took charge of British Voluntary Aid Detachments on the Continent. After Crowdy left the League she continued in a variety of voluntary positions focusing on disarmament and the peaceful resolution of conflicts. Enigmatic, witty, outspoken, and inquisitive, contemporaries considered her a formidable, idiosyncratic activist.

work, stressed its practical, welfare, and humanitarian efforts, and appealed to American interests rather than to moral sensibilities. Carefully leaked revelations, including reports about how Washington's intransigence hindered the fight against drugs, embarrassed Washington. American Arthur Sweetser, a League official and well-connected proponent of US participation, hoped the United States might join the OAC and other League Committees in piecemeal fashion until a "fairly complete infiltration will have taken place in the majority of League activities."[5] Secretary-General Sir Eric Drummond and other League officials harbored similar hopes that reaching an accord with the United States on the drug question would redound to the League's benefit, although Drummond advocated quiet diplomacy in contrast to Sweetser's more public approach. Most observers took a less sanguine view. British officials, for example, considered the prospect of American association with the League unlikely. Even if Washington were completely satisfied – a doubtful prospect – they believed the drug question did not possess sufficient gravity to draw the United States into the League's orbit.[6] Many Americans, though favorably disposed toward internationalism and peace activism, did not support the League. Nevertheless, the secretariat apprehended the essential point. The post-war atmosphere featured a deep desire for international cooperation. The League represented the most tangible expression of that yearning. Yet exercising leadership on drugs and other international issues would require the League to confront problematic governments such as the United States. A good public image was vital to League interests.[7]

The secretariat paid particular attention to the League's status because that issue presented both opportunities and obstacles. On the one hand, the personal and bureaucratic interest of the secretariat necessitated operating a functional, strong, expansive drug control apparatus. Such a regime would display administrative prowess and afford opportunity for advancement. Members of the Opium Section had every incentive to make the drug regime work.

Conversely, political factors hampered the Secretariat's pursuit of bureaucratic interest and communal obligations. Although Geneva assumed responsibility for administering the Hague treaty, many signatories, most notably the United States and several Latin American countries, were not League members. Instigating effective international controls involved evaluating whether governments complied with treaty obligations. If not, the situation could be rectified only by publicizing infractions. The political representatives of the OAC shouldered the primary responsibility for that task. Nevertheless, since information passed through the secretariat, its position enabled assessments independent of governmental representatives. In the course of performing their duties, secretariat members offered suggestions, acted as intermediaries, and negotiated compromises. Yet the ethos instigated by Secretary-General Drummond required that secretariat members act as neutral administrators. Difficulties most often arose when national representatives perceived the secretariat as criticizing their government or favoring another. Political considerations affected appointments, even to relatively low-level secretariat positions, which further exacerbated the situation. Secretariat members might jeopardize their careers by offending any government. Given such complexities, officials of the Opium Section had two choices: either lead strongly or keep a low profile. The latter usually prevailed.[8]

The League goes to work

The League provided a key venue for grappling with international socio-medical concerns. Phenomena such as child welfare, women's rights, health care, labor legislation, malnutrition, and drug abuse could be viewed through many prisms. Defining the scope of such problems required striking a balance between economic, social, health, and police aspects. Determining the "root cause" of maladies associated with each issue involved questions about the individual, social, environmental, and structural factors at play. The League provided opportunities for redefining parameters: an issue like prostitution, traditionally considered a domestic matter, became, when constituted to include "white slavery," a transnational problem touching on human rights, economic opportunity, women's status, and legal reform. Governments tended to tolerate information requests and statistics gathering about such phenomena, but were wary about endorsing international legislation that might restrict their prerogatives. Treaties created standards of behavior, even if honored only in the breach. International organizations devoted to humanitarian causes might pose a threat to national aspirations by providing funding, direction, and a platform for domestic and foreign critics. Some issues, drugs included, could expose the divergence between metropole and colonies that damaged the imperial image. Transnational expert communities, philanthropic entities, women's groups, promoters of particular causes, and internationalists all tried to take advantage of the League structure to achieve their aspirations. Drug diplomacy took place within these currents.[9]

Like other League organizations wrestling with similar questions, the drug control organs focused considerable initial effort on gauging the extent of the problem. The OAC requested information about imports, exports, re-exports, consumption, and reserve stocks. The staggering proportions of the drug problem soon became apparent. Conservative estimates suggested that world production of opium and coca exceeded "legitimate" need (for medical and scientific purposes as defined by western standards) by a factor of ten. Pessimistic observers calculated that raw material production surpassed licit requirements a hundredfold. A substantial percentage of manufactured drugs were also sold for non-medicinal purposes. Imposing substantive control would affect the livelihood of millions; the licit slice of the opium pie was minuscule by comparison.[10] As a first measure, the OAC urged states to adopt an import/export certification scheme modeled after the British system introduced during the war.[11]

League organs also attempted to define the parameters of "legitimate" demand. That task proved impossible because the process touched upon fundamental questions of definition, causation, and responsibility. Rival League bodies proposed different standards, but both incorporated the same basic assumption: if the limits of legitimate need were determined, the OAC could then restrict the trade to that quantity.

The League created a Mixed Sub-Committee charged with the task of finding answers to the following broadly drawn questions:

1   What is the aim of the work undertaken by the League?
2   What constitutes an abuse?
3   How do abuses occur?

4   How can these abuses be ascertained?
5   How can abuses be prevented?

Despite this mandate to pursue basic definitional and etiological issues, mundane material considerations quickly preoccupied the Mixed Sub-Committee. Three medical experts from the League Health Committee, two non-physician OAC members (including John Campbell), and an OAC member who was also a physician comprised the Mixed Sub-Committee's membership. Although the Mixed Sub-Committee's instructions focused on the medical aspects of the question, all three OAC representatives wished to protect their domestic production or manufacturing capabilities. Additionally, John Campbell insisted on the legitimacy of quasi-medical opium use. Consequently, the three OAC representatives argued for a liberal estimate of the world's legitimate needs. The physicians from the League Health Committee, on the other hand, were concerned with the medical effects of drugs, including iatrogenic addiction and the attendant damage to professional status. They advocated a lower ceiling for licit consumption. The political representatives of the OAC eventually imposed their views.

   Its concentration on supply-related issues brought the Mixed Sub-Committee into conflict with efforts the League Health Committee. The Health Committee had independently created a commission to determine an appropriate per-capita figure for opium and cocaine consumption. Once it became clear that the position of the non-physicians would prevail in the Mixed Sub-Committee, the two bodies prepared competing reports. The Mixed Sub-Committee arrived at a figure for opium consumption 33 percent higher than that recommended by the physician-dominated League Health Committee. The Mixed Sub-Committee made no pronouncement on an appropriate figure for

---

Sir John CAMPBELL (1874–1944). Born in Scotland, civil servant in the government of India. Chairman of the International Tin Committee and Vice-Chair of the Greek Refugee Settlement Commission. Representative for India on the OAC 1921–34. Gruff, aggressive, and intolerant with opponents. Saw the opium question in absolute terms, staunchly defending his government's position. A sore loser.

cocaine, claiming paucity of information. The League Health Committee suggested a maximum for cocaine, but admitted that inadequate information precluded a definitive determination. In a victory for producing and manufacturing interests, both committees acknowledged their estimates applied only to countries with "advanced" medical systems. Their calculations could not apply to most of South America, Africa, and Asia. Both committees publicized their findings in hopes of influencing the OAC at its January 1923 session.[12] As a result, questions about why individuals used drugs, what measures might be taken to prevent abuse, how social factors affected drug taking, and other etiological issues received short shrift.

No countervailing forces operating in the international arena intervened to redirect this internecine quantitative dispute. Conceptions about drug users became increasingly pessimistic; dependence in general and drug addiction in particular came to be viewed as dysfunctional. Cognizant of their paying constituencies, the League health and welfare organizations shied away from studying the problems of "non-productive" members of society. The League concentrated on helping "normal" and "deserving" people, not least because doing so enabled all parties to avoid troublesome questions about societal factors contributing to deviant behavior. Philanthropic organizations interested in health and welfare issues generally preferred to fund narrowly defined projects that appeared solvable rather than complicated social-medical problems. Predominant eradication concepts borrowed from epidemiology, which focused on eliminating specific disease vectors, appeared applicable within a supply-oriented approach to the drug question: eliminating excess quantities seemed analogous to killing mosquitos. Such thinking also enabled professional communities to pursue an attractive research agenda. The search for a "magic bullet" – a non-addicting yet potent analgesic – appealed to scientists, pharmaceutical companies, and independent funding agencies. Women at the League spoke often about the drug question, but their pronouncements focused primarily on redefining women's positions within the international system and the value of creating international norms. They generally supported the emerging control paradigm that emphasized regulation of substances, marginalization of users, and exploration in search of better drugs. As a result of such factors, the international drug control regime came to be defined primarily as outside the social and medical spheres. While social and medical questions never disappeared entirely, the system focused on economic calculations, regulatory statutes, and enforcement measures. Medical expertise played an important role in defining which drugs possessed addiction potential, but those determinations focused on narrow physiological manifestations and eschewed the larger social implications of addiction. Supply control emerged as the regime's *raison d'être*.[13]

Consequently, the League's efforts to investigate fundamental etiological questions quickly stalled. Rather than exploring alternative approaches, League organs degenerated into debates over relatively narrow aspects of the supply-control paradigm. The plight of the individual user received scant attention; the system stumbled in its first effort to understand the addict. The dispute between the Mixed Sub-committee and the League Health Committee delayed OAC discussions about etiology, and in the interim the United States reentered the arena. Subsequent American interventions derailed internationally-oriented investigations into the factors contributing to drug abuse.

The American conundrum

In light of OAC revelations of the early 1920s about the magnitude of the drug traffic, control advocates recognized that the international effort required American participation. The United States counted among the greatest of both manufacturing and consuming nations. Yet the American aversion to the League threatened to stifle cooperation. Washington avoided direct communications with Geneva and pursued independent initiatives that jeopardized League undertakings. American behavior in the realm of drug diplomacy reflected this unhelpful policy. For example, the United States recognized the Netherlands government as responsible for administering the Hague Opium Convention while all other adherents dealt directly with the League. The Dutch acted as go-between, passing information and communications between Geneva and Washington. Rather than alleviating this awkward situation by communicating with the League, in 1922 the House of Representatives called for a conference to be held in Washington to draft a new international treaty.[14]

Other key players could not countenance an anti-opium agreement concluded outside League auspices. League and British officials took the initiative, redoubling efforts to coopt the United States. Drummond and Crowdy feared an American-sponsored convention would hinder League efforts. The Secretary-General formally invited Washington to join the OAC. Senior British officials implored the State Department to accept; London perceived in the League program the kind of control system that accommodated its wider interests.[15] To show good

Sir Malcolm DELEVINGNE (1868–1950). Great Britain. Deputy Undersecretary of State, Home Office, 1922–31. Charged with responsibility for domestic and international aspects of drug control. UK representative to OAC, 1921–34. After retirement, elected to PCOB 1935–48. Longtime proponent of welfare, health, and safety measures for industrial workers. Largely responsible for improved Factory Acts and mining safety. A lifelong bachelor, Delevingne lived with his two spinster sisters. Small and thin, with a high, reedy voice, Delevingne did not suffer fools gladly. Although wise enough to use diplomatic language on paper, Delevingne's sharpness of tongue often caused difficulties in face-to-face negotiations. Respected by his colleagues and a little feared by the Foreign Office. A loveable curmudgeon.

faith, the chief British drug-control official, Sir Malcolm Delevingne, vigorously reported drug trafficking cases to the League, cracked down on domestic offenders, and prodded the French, Germans, and Swiss to follow suit.[16]

Those entreaties encountered an unexpectedly positive response because American policy had shifted by early 1923. Domestic and international developments inclined the Harding administration toward accommodation with the League. Some even believed the drug question presented a pivotal opportunity to foster US-League ties. Anti-League constituencies and irreconcilable control advocates, however, decisively influenced American drug policy. Ironically, American participation in international drug control negotiations produced discord rather than harmony.

Geopolitical concerns, sometimes linked to drugs, contributed to the shift in American policy. Independent US foreign policy initiatives of the early 1920s, especially arms control negotiations, yielded disappointing results, highlighting the need for global cooperation. Mounting difficulties between France and Germany endangered reparations negotiations, disarmament talks, and economic stabilization efforts. Widespread narcotics abuse threatened further to weaken China. Even staunch League foes, fearing instability abroad, sought a more cooperative international approach. International businesses and chambers of commerce also preferred an orderly world in which to employ their capital.[17]

Helen Howell MOORHEAD (1883–1950). United States. Driving force behind the FPA's Opium Research Committee and hostess with the mostest. A woman of strong but closely held opinions. Master of private negotiations. Less well known than her contemporary, E. W. Wright, but more effective in international negotiations. Her behind-the-scenes style matched both the sensibilities of drug diplomats and the gender expectations of the age. She enjoyed the confidence of her fellow-travellers in narcotics circles more than the company of her own family.

American Pro-League organizations followed a parallel course. The Carnegie Foundation, the World Peace Foundation, and the League of Nations Association promoted closer ties that might eventually produce American membership in the League. The Foreign Policy Association (FPA), the premier organization dedicated to educating ordinary Americans about international issues, took a special interest in international drug control. They recognized the symbolic value of the drug question. The FPA hoped a high-profile effort to publicize the issues surrounding drug control would increase membership and revenues, thereby supporting its other activities. In 1922 the FPA created an Opium Research Committee, naming Helen Howell Moorhead secretary. She immediately set to work. After discovering little policy coordination in Washington, Moorhead urged federal officials to cooperate with the League, even if that meant pruning American drug control objectives to accommodate other powers.[18]

Such efforts heightened attention to international issues among key American constituencies. Those groups that forged the original control impetus held various opinions about the League, but generally favored some sort of international cooperation in the fight against drugs. Law-enforcement officials, charged with implementing the Harrison Narcotics Act, concurred. In the 1922 elections Republicans suffered significant losses. Most observers interpreted the result as a rebuke of Harding's equivocal approach to international affairs. By late 1922 the administration concluded it must engage with Geneva, but, typically, only on (ostensibly) non-political technical issues such as health and welfare. Noting "immense public interest" in an acute national problem that could be solved only through international collaboration, the State Department announced that it would send an observer to the January 1923 OAC meeting. Drug diplomacy necessitated the first high-profile contact between Washington and the League.[19]

An uncompromising approach, however, accompanied American involvement. Pro-League organizations proved unable to influence the content of US policy. Pro-control constituencies, such as missionary groups, religious organizations, temperance workers, and supporters of China tended to favor prohibition. They wished the United States to retain its self-proclaimed moral leadership on the drug question. These groups advocated a radical supply-control agenda, arguing for the elimination of all opium and coca production except that required for medical and scientific needs. American activists also contended that opium smoking and opium eating, which colonial governments considered quasi-medical use (and therefore legitimate), should be outlawed. That such an agenda afforded little opportunity for cooperation with other states did not factor in American control advocates' calculations.

Over there

The Harding Administration sent former Surgeon-General Rupert Blue[20] to the January 1923 OAC meeting, though only as an "unofficial observer" in order to placate isolationist sentiment. His instructions embodied strong pro-control positions: elimination of excess production; opposition to a proposed government-controlled opium monopoly in China; and protest against continuing quasi-medical opium use in India. The State Department's directive abjured compromise.[21]

Blue indelibly influenced the proceedings. At his insistence, the Mixed Sub-Committee altered its report, redefining drug abuse to include all non-medical use and declaring quasi-medical opium use "not legitimate."[22] Blue advocated restriction of poppy cultivation, sending a clear message to producing nations: the United States proposed radical alteration of their economies and cultures. The OAC postponed voting on the Mixed Sub-Committee's report until its next session, allowing states time to respond.[23]

Blue's interventions caused an important shift in the international debate. He further politicized a thorny question by focusing on agricultural production and non-medical use in Asian territories. Colonial governments considered both issues purely domestic concerns. Blue's demeanor indicated that the United States intended to promote its position vigorously. Other governments could scarcely ignore American views.

Preparations for the fifth OAC session

This initial encounter spurred American interest in the drug issue. Blue recommended sending a larger delegation, with wider expertise, to the next meeting. The Foreign Policy Association concurred, hoping a more considered policy might result. With quiet urging from the League secretariat, the FPA also planned to send Helen Moorhead as an observer.[24] Anti-opium and prohibitionist groups also supported sending a larger delegation, assuming it would follow the policy expounded by Blue. Most importantly, Representative Stephen Porter of Pennsylvania, the anti-League chairman of the House Foreign Affairs Committee, expressed interest in the issue.

With widespread support, albeit in pursuit of differing ends, the State Department decided to send a delegation headed by Porter to the spring 1923 OAC meeting. Porter would be accompanied by Blue, Bishop Brent, and Edwin L. Neville, a consular official with long experience in the Far East. The delegation included the most prestigious combination of political leadership, moral authority, medical prowess, and technical expertise yet sent by the United States to Geneva.[25]

The appointment of a notable American delegation, combined with anti-opium broadsides launched by Porter,[26] indicated the upcoming OAC meeting might produce a showdown. If members of the League did not cooperate, the US might act independently. The other principal actors prepared accordingly.

Secretary-General Drummond's position predisposed him to favor appeasement. He approached officials in London, suggesting that the Indian and British delegations should include parliamentary members responsible for opium matters; the distinguished nature of the American delegation required the presence of equally notable representatives from India and Britain. Moreover, Drummond feared the explosive potential inherent in placing the prickly Delevingne and combative Campbell in the same room with the bombastic Porter. Drummond

---

Stephen G. PORTER (1869–1930). United States. Studied medicine, but opted for law. In a twenty-year congressional career (D-Pittsburgh), rose to chair of House Foreign Affairs Committee in 1919. He served longer in that capacity than any of his predecessors, and travelled extensively. Acquired the status of *Czar* over American drug policy during the 1920s, and behaved in a manner appropriate to the appellation.

also urged the Foreign Office to impress upon the India Office the need for compromise language concerning the issue of "legitimate" opium consumption.[27] The Foreign Office rejected Drummond's suggestions. British sources indicated that the American delegation was more interested in grand-standing than substantive results; Porter hoped to acquire domestic political capital by assuming an intransigent position. Delevingne and Campbell possessed an unrivalled comprehension of the issues and were best-equipped to counter American charges. Officials in White-hall, aware of the precarious balance between Delevingne's cantankerous nature and his preeminent expertise, also feared strained relations with the Home Office if they displaced him. The Foreign and India Offices instructed their delegates to present their cases firmly, with the aim of converting rather than antagonizing the Americans.[28]

The Foreign and Home Offices, in fact, hoped to turn the situation to advantage by playing the more extreme forces off against one another. On the one hand, the upcoming meeting afforded them the opportunity to educate an ignorant Porter about the realities of the drug question without alienating him. At the same time they would attempt to use American pressure to pry concessions out of the India Office, the French, and other recalcitrant governments. The Foreign and Home Offices hoped this strategy would result in a compromise along moderate lines, precisely what would most benefit British interests.

The fifth OAC session[29]

The international climate, however, did not lend itself to sweeping new initiatives. As the OAC met during May and June 1923, the spiraling Ruhr crisis occupied center stage. OAC deliberations received scant attention from civil service superiors or from legislators responsible for political oversight. In addition to the standard reasons for opposing additional controls, representatives to the OAC preferred a go-slow approach during a time of turmoil. The American delegation, however, evinced little concern about the larger issues of that summer, despite Washington's involvement in their resolution.

At OAC meetings, Porter's demeanor and proposals engendered an equally intransigent response. The colonial powers defended established forms of opium use in Asia and rejected substantive restrictions on poppy cultivation. When Porter threatened withdrawal, Delevingne forged compromise resolutions that placated both sides but did nothing to resolve fundamental differences. In hopes of appealing over the head of Porter to American public opinion, Moorhead and Drummond concocted a statement outlining the extensive measures already taken by the OAC that fulfilled US principles.

Most importantly, to accommodate the Americans, one ambiguously worded OAC resolution recommended new plenipotentiary negotiations. The Ruhr occupation crisis made it imperative to avoid the open breach that might have occurred had the US delegation not been placated. When the international climate cooled later in 1923, however, it became evident that governments interpreted the recommendation differently. The OAC resolution did not make clear whether one or two meetings should be convened, how many governments would be invited, or what subject matter should be addressed.[30]

Mr Smith goes to Geneva

Early US encounters with the League altered the trajectory of international drug control efforts. American inflexibility elicited more, rather than less, rigidity from other states. Deliberations about the nature and etiology of drug abuse abruptly ended. When the League revisited questions of causation during the later 1930s, the international legal and institutional structure already incorporated the prevailing inexact notions about drug abuse and etiology. Research concerning causation and cure continued, but at the national level, where authorities with overriding governmental, professional, and political interests controlled its direction.[31] States abjured the opportunity to create a more rigorous definition of drug abuse, one that might apply universally or that might distinguish between the phenomena experienced in the industrialized west and the rest of the globe. Instead, governments plunged headlong into the process of protecting interests within a paradigm that emphasized supply control and excluded other possibilities. Questions about the efficacy of control measures also received short shrift. American actions deflected attention from concerns about what effect regulatory legislation might have on illicit manufacture, smuggling, and poly-drug addicts.[32]

American intervention also lessened the chances of producing a document US negotiators might find acceptable. To placate Washington, the other powers accelerated the timetable for negotiating a new international treaty. Many governments had insufficient time to gather the information necessary for intelligent decision-making. The pre-negotiations intended to produce a workable draft were conducted in a hurried atmosphere.[33] Finally, US expectations remained both high and brittle. The all-or-nothing American approach portended trouble ahead.

Toward the Geneva drug conferences

Early efforts to fashion a League-sponsored international drug control system climaxed between mid-1924 and early 1925. In addition to fundamental policy disagreements, external circumstances decisively affected the outcome. Great Britain underwent two changes of government in 1924. Difficulties within and without also precipitated cabinet changes in France. In the United States, politicians indulged in election-year posturing. The Franco-German crisis and its attendant financial conundrum overshadowed negotiations. Sun Yat-Sen's growing debility and eventual death fostered instability in China. Such geopolitical factors complicated the task of drug negotiators struggling to overcome profound differences between producing and manufacturing states. Nevertheless, Geneva hosted signing ceremonies for two drug control treaties in early 1925. Both documents reflected the environment in which they were negotiated – they contained limited provisions and met with limited approval.

Setting the stage[34]

Delevingne viewed the increased American presence as a mixed blessing. On the one hand, he recognized the importance to Great Britain of US participation in the international arena. Yet the American position created headaches.

The prospect of negotiating new treaties presented Delevingne with domestic difficulties. Once he opened the drug question for debate within the government, several ministries would put forward conflicting views. Forging a consensus would be an unpalatable and lengthy process.

The main responsibility for creating an international consensus also rested upon Delevingne. The Americans had already demonstrated an uncompromising position. Nor was Delevingne encouraged by the attitudes of other governments. Paris and The Hague demurred at the prospect of serious restrictions on opium trading or consumption, while Tokyo and Lisbon exhibited open hostility. Nanking insisted that the colonial powers were responsible for the situation in the Far East, but lack of civil control inside Chinese borders clearly exacerbated the problem. The Turks and Swiss had yet to ratify the Hague treaty – Delevingne could hardly expect them to contribute toward a more exacting agreement. The Persians appeared likely to seize any export business relinquished by India. South American coca states, defending material interests, a progressive ideology, and cultural prerogatives, declared baldly that, at most, they would agree not to *increase* production.[35]

No matter what policy His Majesty's Government decided upon, or what consensus he could forge among other states, Delevingne suspected his efforts would not silence US criticism. Federal policy seemed hostage to moralists and publicity-seekers who advocated an absolutist and unrealistic agenda. As Delevingne saw it, the Americans posed as much of a problem as the opium.[36]

To negotiate the labyrinth, Delevingne designed a double-pronged approach. He proposed two international plenipotentiary meetings, the first opened only to producers, the second only to manufacturers. He hoped in this way to keep the meetings small, with perhaps a dozen governments attending each. Limiting the size and scope of each meeting would, he calculated, enhance the chances of success.

Delevingne pinned his hopes on agreement among manufacturing states. He aimed to control the manufacturing bottleneck. A relatively small number of factories in a few industrialized states manufactured the world's morphine, heroin, cocaine, and similar substances. Delevingne reasoned that, if those governments limited output, excess supplies would dry up. This proposal met the primary American concern – the flow of illicit manufactured drugs to the United States would be curtailed. Delevingne hoped to enlist American aid in negotiating the agreement, thereby doing his part to enhance US relations with Britain and the League.

Simultaneously, Delevingne recognized that the Asian problem remained insoluble, even if a successful agreement among manufacturers were forthcoming. While marginal improvements in the opium production/opium smoking situation might be possible, the kind of fundamental change that the Americans demanded could only be instituted over a long period. Consequently, he wanted to limit discussion of the Far Eastern situation to those states directly involved. Delevingne sought to exclude the United States from this group. He believed the Americans would only make trouble by proposing unworkable solutions and inciting discord.

After much intricate maneuvering, Delevingne secured League endorsement for two conferences. The first would focus exclusively on the Far Eastern opium situation. The League encouraged the colonial powers to end the trade in and use of raw and prepared opium, as called for by the Hague Convention. Additionally, the meeting would discuss measures to deal with the illegal production and use of opium in China. The League scheduled this meeting for the first two weeks of November 1924.[37]

The League charged the second conference with concluding an agreement (1) to control the production of manufactured drugs such as morphine, heroin, and cocaine, and; (2) to limit the amounts of raw opium and coca imported for manufacturing and other medical and scientific purposes. The second conference was scheduled to follow directly after the first. Over Delevingne's objections, the League invited all governments to participate.

Delevingne got most of what he wanted. By separating the issues of production and manufacture, he could focus his energies on shrinking the manufacturing bottleneck. Since the United States did not receive an invitation to the first conference, the Americans had no platform from which to pursue their quixotic desire to limit agricultural production in remote parts of the globe.[38]

Yet the relationship between the two conferences remained unclear. Was the first conference a self-contained entity? Was it to act as a sub-committee of the second conference? Could the second conference consider matters discussed by the first conference? What if the first conference did not finish its deliberations in the allotted two weeks? Could the second conference proceed without the final report of the first?[39]

Preparatory negotiations [40]

All sides left such questions in abeyance, however, as they began preparations for the November conferences. The League convened a series of meetings intended to create a draft treaty. Participants included the United States, now fully immersed in the proceedings, Great Britain, France, the Netherlands, and several technical experts. These discussions demonstrated considerable divergence between key players.

Consul Neville, the most technically adept of the American participants, presented proposals that combined the maximum level of control commensurate with minimum imposition on the US interests.[41] Harkening back to the 1907 Ten Year Agreement, American stipulations called for a cut-off date, perhaps 10 or 15 years in the future, for the production, trade in, and use of non-medicinal drugs. Not wishing to prejudice US exports, Neville proposed to bar states from increasing customs taxes as a substitute for lost drug revenue. Neville advocated extending controls to derivatives. Notably, he did not rule out a cartel or monopoly, as long as US manufacturers received a fair slice of the pie. Ironically, Neville also proposed language that would require states to submit statistics on production, imports, exports, stocks, and consumption – information that the US itself was notably tardy in supplying to the OAC.

Finally, Neville proposed creating an entity to oversee fulfillment of the treaty's provisions. The essence of this concept eventually emerged as the Permanent Central Opium Board, one of the enduring facets of the international drug control system. The idea of a central supervisory organ reflected the inclinations of the period's internationalists and American progressives, who favored expert committees, independent evaluators, and disinterested quasi-judicial bodies. The Board outlasted many such organizations and continues to operate today. Its successes and failures, discussed in subsequent chapters, illustrate the strengths and shortcomings of the international drug regime's governing arrangements.

Delevingne proposed a less ambitious agenda. He thought it possible to control coca production in Latin American states, but not opium growing in British colonies. Concerning manufacture Delevingne proposed his favorite solution: a quota scheme. Governments would estimate their needs and manufacturing states would then divide up the orders according to a predetermined formula. An import/export certification system would support the quota arrangement. Delevingne echoed the proposal for a central board to superintend the system.

The other participants adopted openly mercenary positions. The Dutch plan would have given the Netherlands a monopoly on coca production and manufacture. The French delegate made no proposals at all. Given their recent financial crisis and the drubbing they took in the negotiations that produced the Dawes Plan, Paris would not entertain any scheme that might injure exports or colonial finances.[42]

The preparatory meetings only highlighted the barriers to agreement. Since no consensus existed on the parameters of world legitimate requirements, it proved impossible to determine target figures for production or manufacture. The monopoly and quota schemes foundered because each state desired a too-large percentage of the trade. Moreover, all wanted the freedom to purchase raw materials and/or manufactured drugs at the lowest price. Finally, opponents pointed out that monopolies and quotas would likely encourage price increases, more smuggling, and new production and manufacture in states not party to the agreement. This failure to forge consensus augured ill for the success of the two conferences, scheduled to begin less than four months hence.

At its August 1924 meeting, the OAC inherited the task of finding some basis for negotiation.[43] States with export-oriented pharmaceutical industries, most notably the French, Germans, and Swiss, rejected direct controls over manufacture. Similarly, the Far Eastern colonial powers avoided any commitment to limit production. Delevingne and Neville, apprehending the limits of the possible, conceded those issues in return for a strengthened commitment to "indirect control" in the guise of the central board.

As other substantive proposals disappeared, the relative importance of the estimates system and of the central board increased. The OAC hammered out a draft treaty in which those two factors figured prominently. Governments would submit to the board estimates specifying quantities of raw material and manufactured drugs they planned to import. Governments would also submit estimates of exports, re-exports, stocks, and consumption. Notably, the draft empowered the board to determine estimates for states that failed to submit them. The board could also question estimates that appeared excessive. To ensure proper monitoring of raw materials and manufactured drugs, the draft proposed a system of import certificates and export licenses. The plan also provided for an expansion of controls to substances not covered in the Hague Convention.[44]

Nevertheless, the draft avoided the most problematic aspects concerning the board and the estimates system. The board, through the estimates, might exercise considerable power over the drug trade. The OAC considered carefully what statistics governments would be required to submit, when and how those estimates would be submitted, and what powers the board would exercise. Representatives could reach no agreement on those issues and held them over for the upcoming plenipotentiary meeting. Another key issue involved the selection procedure for board members. After much debate, the OAC recommended that the League Council appoint board members, *on the advice of the OAC*. Recalcitrant states acquiesced in an ostensibly independent board because the latter provision enabled them to influence the selection process. OAC delegates also riddled the draft with reservations.

After six months of intense negotiations, the principal players had uncovered little common ground. They produced a draft only by papering over the fundamental issues that remained unresolved. Domestic considerations, however, prevented key states from reconsidering their positions.

Britannia founders

In addition to his international maneuvering, Delevingne simultaneously attempted to forge a British/Imperial consensus on drug policy. He required collaboration from abroad in order to enforce domestic drug regulations. Yet Delevingne could not secure cooperation from other states as long as Britain's image remained tarnished by the policies of the Indian government and other colonial administrations. Ultimately, his efforts proved as unsuccessful at home as abroad. In mid-1924, Delevingne requested a complete review of British drug control policy. The Colonial Office prepared a series of reports on the opium situation in the Far Eastern colonies. The Foreign Office solicited information from overseas posts concerning the posture of other governments and conditions in China. Delevingne did not request input from the India Office because he had already concluded that His Majesty's Government should commit itself both to the eventual suppression of the opium trade and the elimination of quasi-medical use of opiates. Knowing the reception such notions would receive from Campbell, Delevingne wanted to have the other principal departments in line before broaching the subject.

Delevingne's plan never got past the first hurdle. Although the reports from colonial governments indicated a wide variance in conditions, all believed suppression of opium smoking to be impracticable. They cited the impact on governmental revenues, the impossibility of enforcing a ban on an unwilling populace, and the smuggling, hoarding, speculation, and corruption likely to result. Some even questioned the cultural assumptions underpinning control, including Hong Kong officials who pointed out that alcohol and marijuana use caused more deleterious effects than opium, yet the Empire permitted consumption of those substances.[45]

The Foreign Office preferred Delevingne's position because of its public relations advantages, but they did not wish to overrule colonial governments. B. C. Newton of the Far Eastern department believed it was time to admit that the government could do no more to eliminate opium use. Repudiating the objectives of the international drug control system, however, meant rejecting the assumptions underpinning it. Such a departure from official policy would stir up a hornet's nest of opposition at home and abroad. At the same time, the Home government could hardly impose restrictions on recalcitrant colonial governments supported by the Colonial Secretary. A decision on this matter could only be made by the Cabinet.[46]

The Home Office, Colonial Office, and India Office, which had got wind of Delevingne's plans, presented their cases to the Cabinet. Unable to reconcile the differences, the Cabinet postponed the issue several times. By early October time was running short; all sides appealed for a decision as soon as possible.[47]

At precisely that juncture, with little warning and lightning speed, the Labour Government fell. Prime Minister Ramsay MacDonald lost a vote of confidence on 8 October 1924 and Parliament was dissolved the next day. Elections were scheduled for 29 October, only five days before the opening of the first conference in Geneva. Preoccupied with the campaign, cabinet members had no time to meet in regular session.

The ill-considered timing of the conferences, an unintended result of attempts to placate the United States, now loomed large. British officials privately contacted Drummond, requesting a delay until the new Cabinet could consider the issue. The Secretary-General refused, noting that any postponement of the first conference would upset the timetable for the second. Moreover, domestic and international public opinion could not be ignored. Whitehall concluded that a British-instigated delay would simply provide ammunition for those who believed Great Britain wanted to shirk its drug-control obligations.[48]

As an emergency measure, the Foreign, Home, and Colonial offices worked out skeletal recommendations for Delevingne. He could agree to marginal improvements in control measures, but should demur on suppression of opium smoking and import controls. Delevingne received no directions concerning the second conference. He would have to tele-graph for instructions as matters developed.[49]

After several years of determined effort, Delevingne's attempts to negotiate the domestic and international minefields attendant to the drug issue came to naught. Less than three weeks before the opening gavel, Great Britain had no policy on the question of opium smoking, the central issue of the first conference. The protracted interdepart-mental negotiations left Delevingne with no instructions concerning the second. That Delevingne himself was the individual primarily responsible for defining the scope of the meetings added to the irony. Mired in intragovernmental conflict, mindful of domestic constitu-encies, harried by US pressure, plagued by the unwillingness of other states to compromise, and hobbled by the propensity of drug users to circumvent control measures, the British delegation resigned itself to conducting a public relations exercise designed to indicate its sincerity.

US preparations[50]

On the other side of the Atlantic, preparations for the Geneva drug conferences proceeded without tumult. Control advocates, following a logic similar to that which informed America's alcohol prohibition policy, focused on reducing supply. Anti-opium crusaders, the medical establishment, and astute politicians determined the international drug policy of the United States government.

By the second decade of the twentieth century, government, medical, and reform-oriented officials in America conceived of the drug problem as a two-sided issue. On the one hand, most agreed that physicians caused numerous drug abuse cases. Inappropriate or excessive prescribing of narcotics produced what contemporaries referred to as "medical addiction." As doctors altered their therapeutic practices, iatrogenic addiction declined. Physicians and police also identified a newer category of drug users often referred to as "criminal addicts." Predominantly lower class and disproportionately non-white, this cohort acquired drugs from illicit channels and committed crimes to support their habits.[51]

Between 1914 and the mid-1920s the United States Government took steps to address medical addiction. The 1914 Harrison Narcotics Act empowered the federal government to regulate, albeit in the guise of a revenue measure, narcotic transactions between physicians, pharmacists, and individuals. The Treasury Department, with the aim of eliminating non-medical use, restricted access to and dispensation of narcotics. Tested in the courts, the Treasury Department position, with some revisions, prevailed by 1920. The Federal government then closed maintenance clinics and pressured physicians and pharmacists to acquiesce in a thoroughgoing encroachment on their prescribing and dispensing prerogatives.

Federal officials and advocates of stringent control measures, believing they had made a good start within the country, maintained the scourge could only be eliminated through international cooperation. Enforcement officials worried especially about the growing ranks of criminal addicts. Assuming that elimination of the illicit supply would cause addiction to cease, officials advocated eradicating excess production. Publicists including Hamilton Wright's widow, Elizabeth Washburn Wright, missionary societies, and international anti-opium organizations also viewed the solution to both America's problem and the world's problem as lying overseas. They highlighted the injustices perpetrated on Asians by moneygrubbing colonial masters. Britain, possessing the world's largest empire, suffered the lion's share of the criticism. The conclusion was inescapable: the United States required international concurrence to meet its domestic and global responsibilities. Utilizing the League machinery seemed the best alternative at the moment. Control advocates would not compromise, however, on basic US principles.[52]

Elizabeth Washburn WRIGHT (1876–1952). United States. Took up the opium standard upon the death of her husband, Hamilton Wright. Master of the unaimed broadside. As a member of the American delegation to the International Opium Conference of 1924–25, Wright was the first American woman granted plenipotentiary powers by the US government. Ambitious scion of a family of politicians (her father was a senator and several brothers served in Congress), she was not capable of operating in private. Intelligent enough to consider others' ideas, yet too dangerous to share one's opinions with. Insistent to a fault, she bombarded contacts with a steady stream of information, proposals, and offers of aid. A stranger to subtlety, even her handwriting assaulted correspondents.

Congressman Porter installed himself as the pilot of American international anti-opium efforts. After his initial foray to Geneva in 1923, he saw the publicity potential inherent in the drug question.[53] Porter spearheaded an appropriation funding the American delegation to the second conference. Debate on the issue was surprisingly muted considering Porter's resolution proposed, for the first time, formal United States representation at a League-sponsored plenipotentiary gathering. Some pro-League Democrats expressed the hope that attendance would create a precedent for increased formal ties with Geneva. Porter, however, insisted that allotting funds for US representation did not indicate a more general endorsement of the League.

When the Porter resolution passed to the Senate, that body attached an amendment barring the American delegation from signing any agreement that did not (1) recognize the principle of limitation to medical and scientific uses and (2) control the production of raw materials. This stipulation, allowing the American delegation no room for maneuver, complicated even further the already problematic negotiations in Geneva. Why Congress tied the hands of the delegation in this manner is unclear. Most likely members simply indulged in election-year grandstanding. With vocal support from the anti-opium and anti-British lobbies, taking an extreme position appeared to offer little risk.

In a vain attempt to moderate the US position, FPA representatives met with Porter before he left for Geneva. Porter indicated that "he was in charge of the opium work [in the US] and wished no gratuitous advice or assistance." After this exchange Helen Howell Moorhead doubted prospects for an agreement. The FPA Executive Committee persuaded her to go to Geneva in the hope of averting calamity.[54]

In May 1924 the United States set in stone the uncompromising attitude that animated its international drug control strategy for the remainder of the decade. Indeed, for the rest of the century, the elusive quest – control of agricultural production in the field – remained a central tenet of US drug policy. Such a strategy required little sacrifice from Americans while demanding fundamental social and institutional change from others. The State Department was not sanguine about the policy's prospects for success; diplomatic soundings indicated that producer states would not acquiesce to American demands. Yet staking out an extreme position at the outset of international negotiations is not unusual. Combined, however, with the Congressional no-compromise injunction and Porter's demonstrated propensity to abjure concessions, American policy was, by its own standard, doomed to failure.

Other states' positions

Germany and Switzerland, although not members of the League, received invitations to the second conference. Representatives of those important manufacturing states, desiring to protect material interests in the international drug trade, scrutinized any treaty language that required substantive regulation.

The Netherlands also viewed the proceedings with caution. Financial considerations predominated; the Dutch pharmaceutical industry, leaders in cocaine manufacture, and the East Indian *Opium Regie* involved considerable private investment and generated substantial public revenues. A differing social calculus also separated The Hague from Washington. Unlike the Americans, the Dutch had concluded that addicts should be considered a medical rather than a police problem. The elaborate control mechanisms applied in the United States did not appear to help addicts. Dutch officials considered the US position hypocritical; Americans could not enforce their moral-behavioral standards at home, but wished to impose them abroad. Moreover, experience with the *Regie* paralleled that of British colonies; overenthusiastic attempts to suppress opium use increased clandestine trafficking and corruption. Appreciating the phenomenon of polydrug usage, some also feared opium restrictions would lead to a rise in consumption of alcohol, heroin, or other drugs.[55]

Producer states attending included Bolivia, Bulgaria, Greece, Hungary, Persia, Siam, Turkey, Venezuela, and Yugoslavia. Heavily dependent on agricultural exports, those governments objected to controls on raw materials. The international coca market, for example, was highly competitive; through agro-technological investment Dutch East Indian planters had largely supplanted Andean producers. Japanese coca cultivators on Taiwan made increasing inroads as well. South American states feared controls would inhibit their attempts to recover market share. Social, cultural, and political motivations animated producer states as well: Peru did not attend the conference in part because coca represented a path to self-sufficiency, modernization, and national prowess. Coca's supporters defended its utility, at least among indigenous users, rejecting the disparagements of western medical science. The condemnation implicit in an international control regime's configuration would damage liberal hopes that Peru might engage the world on its own terms. Owing to their relatively weak positions, however, representatives of producer states rarely took the lead at the Geneva negotiations; they merely exercised the veto when proposals appeared too onerous.[56]

Canada emerged on the international scene as the most visible representative of a third class of states, usually referred to as "consuming countries." Canada neither produced raw material nor manufactured drugs, yet required the finished product for medicinal purposes. Canadian policy opposed any monopoly scheme that might unduly increase the price of drugs. Additionally, Canada typified many states in that it suffered from illicit trafficking. Clandestine shipments of drugs often passed through Canadian territory. The Canadian conception of their domestic drug abuse problem approximated that in the United States; addicts fell into categories based on their propensity toward criminality.[57] Canadian authorities supported inviting all states to the second Geneva conference. Ottawa wished to have its own, non-British voice in the proceedings.[58]

The 1924–25 Geneva conventions[59]

The first Geneva conference[60]

The first conference, scheduled for 3–17 November 1924, considered measures for suppressing opium use in the Far East. Additionally, China agreed to entertain suggestions about improving opium controls within its borders.

The first conference soon stalled over a dispute between Great Britain and Japan that reflected larger geopolitical concerns. British consular reports and other states' communications to the OAC repeatedly implicated Japanese nationals in Far Eastern trafficking cases. In particular, it appeared that Britain played an unwilling indirect role; shippers using import certifications issued by Japanese opium monopoly officials were diverting opium (including some purchased in India) transshipped through British colonial territories. Such drug trafficking symbolized Japan's increasing penetration of China, which London viewed as a threat. In 1924 Britain began denying export certificates if the Japanese import authorization appeared suspicious. Still smarting from the British denunciation of their longstanding alliance, the League's failure to adopt a racial equality clause, and recent American legislation barring Japanese immigration to the US, Tokyo took this latest measure as a further affront to the country's dignity. The Japanese insisted that all import certifications should be honored, and they threatened to withdraw if the conference did not meet their demands.[61]

Delevingne suggested direct negotiations with Tokyo to avoid derailing the Geneva proceedings. Whitehall concurred and requested Washington's support. Surely the State Department, considering the fire-eating position just unveiled by the US delegation at the second conference (see below), would back London on an issue central to the maintenance of effective control. Yet the State Department demurred, indicating it could not control Porter and wished to disassociate itself from his mission. The response dismayed the Foreign Office. Not only could Delevingne expect no help from the United States, but Porter's own government considered him a loose cannon. Porter stated as much when he told Drummond that he acted "independent of [Secretary of State] Hughes and the State Department."[62]

After intense negotiations, the British and Japanese reached a compromise when London agreed to scrutinize all import and export certificates equally. Japan ensured that the same standards would be applied to all governments while Britain held firm in its opposition to weakening the import/export certification system.[63]

Beyond resolving that controversy, the first conference achieved little. The colonial powers would not commit to a date for elimination of opium smoking. All insisted that the situation would not improve until China controlled its internal production. The Chinese exploited the conference to publicize grievances about extraterritoriality, claiming that they could not alleviate the problem as long as foreigners escaped Chinese justice. At the same time, the Chinese refused to admit the magnitude of the problem within their own borders. The final document provided for only minor refinements in the domestic control systems of Far Eastern colonial administrations.

Owing in large part to the British–Japanese controversy, the first conference ran twice as long as planned. The delay compelled the second conference to begin without the results of the first conference at hand. In early December the treaty produced by the first conference was ready for signature, yet only India did so at that time. The other seven delegations withheld their signatures because the lack of substantive accomplishment at the first conference had become the center of controversy in the second. By failing to achieve a breakthrough, the first conference disappointed the hopes of the American delegation. Porter's dissatisfaction wrought havoc on the proceedings.

The second Geneva conference[64]

The second Geneva drug conference began its deliberations on 17 November 1924. Unlike the clubby first conference, forty-one governments attended the second meeting. Many delegates served as resident representatives in Geneva – consuls, *chargés d'affaires*, and the like. They knew little of the subject, and over time the majority attended less frequently. A core of producing, manufacturing, and consuming states performed the heavy lifting.

The American delegation took the initiative immediately. Porter announced a set of "suggestions" based on the assumption that the general American principles previously endorsed by the OAC constituted the agenda. All parties expected Porter to make certain proposals, especially the establishment of a central board and the creation of a standardized import/export certification system. Two further propositions generated immediate controversy. Porter proposed (1) to emulate the 1907 Indian–Chinese agreement by eliminating opium smoking within ten years, and (2) restricting opium and coca production to medical and scientific needs.

Porter's pronouncement threw the proceedings into an uproar. The Chinese welcomed it, claiming their nation was the chief victim of international drug trafficking and the extraterritoriality that supported it. Most other delegations involved in the preliminary negotiations contended that the draft treaty recommended by the OAC, worked out with the active participation of US observers, comprised the only legitimate agenda. Indian delegate Campbell emphasized that his instructions allowed him to consider only those topics outlined in the OAC's agenda. The French and Japanese, initially favorable, distanced themselves once they understood the implications of the American proposals.[65]

Delevingne also reacted with consternation. He believed that the Americans had agreed to the agenda as constituted at the August OAC meeting. He acknowledged that the American principles should serve as an ultimate goal. To attempt, however, to bring them about immediately was foolhardy. The proposition that governments should control excess (i.e. non-medical) production of raw opium and coca leaves clearly lay outside the competence of the conference and was in any case a practical impossibility. Delevingne also objected to the suggestion that governments should reduce opium smoking by 10 percent per year. The first conference had dealt with this matter and failed to reach agreement. Discussing it again would not produce a better result.[66]

Within a few days, the issue required the Secretary-General's attention. Drummond attended the negotiations and even participated in some subcommittee discussions. The acrimonious exchanges between Campbell and Porter shocked Drummond. He urged London to compromise, fearing the conference might break up, with disastrous consequences for the League and Great Britain. British officials, faced with an intra-governmental impasse, could make no concessions. The Foreign Office and Delevingne found themselves supporting the Indian position in spite of their reservations about its morality, utility, and long-term defensibility.[67]

The debate about the competence of the second conference soon overshadowed its proceedings. During the second week of December, matters came to a head. The US delegation won a vote that referred the question of raw opium production to the appropriate subcommittee. Porter then attempted to bring the question of prepared (smoking) opium before the conference. The governments represented at the first conference, save the Chinese, opposed that move. The British and Indian delegations considered withdrawing. Herluf Zahle, president of the second conference, threatened to resign. Facing the imminent demise of the second conference, several delegations suggested adjournment. On 16 December the conference suspended proceedings until mid-January, allowing delegations a chance to consult with their governments.[68]

Defeated in detail

While the controversy about competence grabbed the headlines, the substantive work proceeded largely unnoticed. Porter and Brent, preoccupied with the heights, neglected the trenches. Six subcommittees dealt with various sections of the draft treaty. The key sections concerned the interconnected issues of statistical reporting, the estimates system, and the powers of the central board.

Proponents of a workable control regime, led by Delevingne and Neville, believed that stringent reporting requirements figured as an integral component of the system. They wanted governments to report regularly (preferably quarterly) their actual consumption, imports, exports, manufacture, production, and stocks on hand. They envisioned a system in which governments also submitted binding (probably annual) estimates of future requirements. If governments predicted their requirements and reported their actual consumption, it would be possible to identify non-compliant states quickly because their estimates and/or statistics would not match comparable countries. Provision also had to be made for special circumstances. In case of medical emergency, governments might require more raw material or manufactured drugs than originally anticipated. The scheme therefore allowed the submission of revised estimates. As representatives of states with substantial manufacturing interests, Delevingne and Neville wanted to maintain a free market. The provision for revised estimates also enabled manufacturers to take advantage of agricultural surplus. In years of abundant crop production pharmaceutical companies could increase inventory at the lowest price possible. The draft recommended by the OAC included the basic elements of this scheme.[69]

Over the objections of some manufacturing states (led by the French and Swiss) Delevingne and Neville retained a large portion of the original estimates scheme.[70] The final version of the treaty required signatories to submit annual statistics concerning the production of raw opium and coca leaves, manufacture of morphine, heroin, cocaine and some (but not all) of their derivatives, stocks on hand (except those held by governments), and consumption (other than for government purposes).[71] The treaty required signatories to submit quarterly statistics of imports and exports of raw materials and manufactured drugs. The agreement also called upon states in which opium smoking was "temporarily permitted" by the provisions of the Hague treaty to submit statistics concerning their manufacture and consumption of prepared opium. All states would submit by December 31 non-binding estimates of their requirements for the following year. The provision for revised estimates remained intact. Although advocates of strong reporting measures could not secure language providing for binding estimates, in the main they prevailed.

Delevingne and Neville, however, knew that victory on the estimates question was not as great as it appeared. Governments reported statistics and estimates to the central board. To gain concessions on the estimates they accepted provisions weakening that body's powers.

The original proposals of mid-1924 envisioned a board with wide powers. The board would have the authority, after receiving estimates from governments, to determine the amount of drugs manufactured each year. Imports and exports would be limited to the quantities specified in the estimates. The board could fix estimates for countries that failed to submit their own and question estimates that seemed excessive. The board could also impose sanctions on states that exceeded their allotment by prohibiting other governments from exporting raw material or manufactured drugs to the offending country.

France, supported by Switzerland and the Netherlands, led the opposition to a strong board. During preliminary deliberations they insisted upon circumscribing board powers. At the second conference they further reduced its prerogatives. The final document provided for a board with no compulsory powers and only limited authority to scrutinize trade. The board had no right to question statistics submitted by governments unless sufficient evidence indicated that a certain country acted as a center of the illicit traffic. In that case the board could request an explanation, but only through the Secretary-General. If the central board declared a state to be a center of the illicit traffic, it could only recommend an embargo.

Opponents of a strong central board further weakened it by enfeebling the language concerning its composition. The French, Dutch, and others interested in a weak board wished to subject it to League authority. They wanted board members appointed for short three-year terms. To ensure the protection of their interests, several delegations called for a board designed to represent producing, manufacturing, and consuming states. Delevingne insisted that the board should consist of independent experts rather than representatives of interests. The final version called for a mixed board, combining "in equitable proportion, persons possessing a knowledge of the drug situation, both in the producing and manufacturing countries on the one hand, and in the consuming countries on the other hand, and connected with such countries."[72] To be eligible for election to the board, individuals could not hold any office that made them dependent on their governments.

The relationship between the central board and the League complicated matters further. Those favoring a weak organ wished to make the board's secretariat an integral part of the League. It being generally understood that the next Secretary-General would be a Frenchman, the French delegation contended that the Secretary-General should have control over personnel matters.[73] The British, on the other hand, wanted to create a board independent of the League. They feared that if the Board were too closely associated with Geneva, the United States might not cooperate with it. Delevingne also believed that a board independent of the encumbrances associated with the League secretariat would be more likely to act judiciously.[74]

British officials also wished to avoid turning over control of the board secretariat to Opium Section head Crowdy.[75] They feared that Crowdy, an outspoken, idiosyncratic individual, might propel the board toward extreme pronouncements. Worried that an overly aggressive board could drive nations with a lukewarm commitment out of the drug control system, British officials inserted a provision that empowered the board to nominate its own candidate for Secretary. The Secretary-General, unwilling to surrender completely his administrative prerogatives, retained the right to appoint the Secretary, subject to approval by the League. Since all parties implicitly understood that Great Britain would be accorded a seat on the new board, Delevingne and Foreign Office officials could indicate to that person their concerns about Crowdy.

Article 20 of the treaty, which attempted to reconcile the contending positions about the relationship between the board and the League, created instead an inherently disharmonious structure.[76] The demarcation line between the League and the board remained unclear. Uncertainties persisted about how much leeway the board possessed in the hiring of staff other than its Secretary, who defined the limits of the board's "technical independence," and whether the League had to shoulder the board's expenses. Was the board an entity of the League, or was it independent – a creature of the 1925 International Opium Convention? Such questions, buried under the press of events, surfaced repeatedly afterward. In ensuing years the equivocal nature of the board's relationship to the League hindered its work and engendered conflict within the secretariat. Ironically, that same ambiguity saved the board from extinction during World War II.

Despite the efforts of Delevingne and Neville, opponents of a strong board succeeded. On the rare occasions when the high-profile US representatives, Porter and Brent, intervened at this more mundane level of debate, they did so to good effect. The confrontational approach that gained them so little in the public arena could yield notable successes at the drafting level. Had the leading American representatives applied themselves to the details of the agreement, they would have found the final treaty more acceptable.[77]

Christmas break

Although the December recess averted immediate disaster, League officials grew increasingly fretful. Conference president Zahle saw no purpose in reconvening if the impasse could not be broken. Arthur Sweetser recommended that the key European powers name high-ranking diplomats or politicians to head their delegations. Sweetser urged compromise: if the Colonial powers did not attempt to meet American demands the US delegation would probably withdraw, perhaps with other delegations in tow. Upon reading Sweetser's memorandum, an alarmed Assistant Secretary-General Joseph Avenol took up the matter with the French government. The secretariat made quiet but strong representations at The Hague. Drummond contacted London, acknowledging that, short of a major capitulation from the colonial powers, all hinged on whether Porter would compromise. Drummond underscored the importance of conciliating Porter. If a treaty could be successfully negotiated, Porter would have to defend it (and the League) before Congress. Porter's advocacy of League drug control efforts would be a boon when related issues that involved control mechanisms, such as the Traffic in Arms Conference, came up for discussion in the United States.[78]

Drummond's arguments did not impress the Foreign Office. Whitehall doubted whether the United States could be brought into the League at all, and certainly did not believe that Porter could serve as the agent of such a change. The League secretariat did little for its own prestige by recommending unreasonable concessions. Drummond had to shift for himself – British policy would be determined by its own interests.[79]

In London, the India and Colonial Offices besieged the newly installed Conservative government with their grievances, prompting a series of inter-ministerial meetings. B. C. Newton of the Foreign Office reiterated his belief that the time had come to admit openly that the government could not fulfill certain obligations under the Hague treaty. The civil disturbances in China precluded doing so. The government should seek a revised interpretation of the Hague agreement relieving signatories of unattainable obligations. Although many officials concurred, they also recognized the political impossibility of taking such a stance publicly. Moreover, Cabinet members wished to demonstrate that the Conservative Party was as keen on drug control as Labour and the Liberals.[80]

Given internal governmental disagreement and external pressure to do something, the Cabinet attempted to steer between the shoals. Great Britain would sign the treaty produced by the first conference, even though it represented only a minor improvement over present arrangements.[81] Not to do so would invite more criticism. Delevingne would continue to oppose enlarging the agenda of the second conference, but the US delegation should be afforded the opportunity to state its case, so long as other governments had the opportunity to reply. Whitehall would also launch a public relations counterattack, explaining the contributions made by Great Britain and the Empire in the battle against drug abuse.[82]

In other European capitals officials held similar discussions, with much the same result. A few states made some minor compromises, but none offered substantial concessions.[83] Instead, governments named prestigious diplomats, cabinet ministers, and eminent politicians to head their delegations. The appointment of such distinguished figures indicated the seriousness with which governments viewed the situation. The key European players intended to meet Porter head on.[84]

The most remarkable occurrence within the American delegation was the conversion of Bishop Brent. In Geneva, Brent had displayed his characteristic moralistic and intransigent tone. Assuming that the greed of colonial powers presented the main impediment to agreement, he chided the other delegations repeatedly for their lack of charity. Not anticipating the extension of the conference, Brent made commitments that required him to return home in December. He stopped in London, intending to publicize the American position with high-ranking officials. Instead he received a careful explanation of the British position, including a detailed communication from Foreign Minister Austen Chamberlain. Chamberlain and the others said nothing new, yet the scales fell from Brent's eyes. Their arguments and personal attentions won him over.

Upon arrival in the US, Brent voiced his new support for the British position. He recommended that the US delegation drop its insistence on restricting domestic production of opium in India and concurred that the civil war in China precluded a solution to the Far Eastern opium problem. Why Brent experienced this change of heart is unclear. Perhaps his experiences in Geneva made him more aware of the complexities of the question and convinced him of the sincerity of some other governments. Brent informed the State Department that before he left Geneva he had urged Porter to drop the demand for elimination of domestic Indian production. In any case, Brent subsequently left the scene. Although he remained active in international causes until his death in 1929, Brent never again engaged in the opium crusade. One suspects he absented himself out of embarrassment.[85]

Finale

When the second conference reconvened on 29 January 1925, it quickly became apparent that little had changed. The introduction of high-profile delegates, which the League Secretariat hoped would smooth over differences, accomplished little. The tone of the meetings was only slightly more conciliatory. The British delegation announced it would agree to suppression of opium smoking, but only fifteen years after China ended excess production. Porter agreed to a fifteen-year-time limit, but wanted the countdown to begin immediately. Special committees and subcommittees created in attempts to break the deadlock all failed. On 6 February the American delegation withdrew. Only the Chinese followed suit.[86]

The American withdrawal caused a cathartic reaction. Some delegates expressed shock, others anger at the US departure. Most were relieved to be rid of the troublesome Porter. All wished to wind up the two conferences quickly.[87]

On 11 February 1925 the first conference finally completed its work. The agreement instituted only minor improvements. Until China got its house in order, other governments with Far Eastern responsibilities could do little. Signatories agreed to meet within five years to consider further measures.[88]

On 19 February the second conference presented the fruits of its labor, usually referred to as the International Opium Convention of 1925. Its most significant provisions included: (1) the creation of the Permanent Central Opium Board, (2) a system of import certificates and export authorizations designed to eliminate diversion of drugs in transit from one country to another, (3) various provisions for the enhancement of domestic control measures, (4) restrictions on the trade in coca leaves and marijuana, (5) controls on processed drugs such as crude cocaine and ecgonine, and (6) procedures to add new drugs to the list of controlled substances.

The treaty suffered from several important lacunae. As discussed previously, the Board received a weak mandate. Governments could exempt themselves from import/export controls when dealing with non-signatory nations. The treaty did not clearly define procedures for adding new substances to the list of controlled drugs. Nor did it make clear whether synthetic drugs, a new but potentially large category of substances, could be recommended for control. Finally, signatories did not have to accept recommendations for amendments to the roster of controlled substances; governments could refuse to add any drug to their domestic control list. Most importantly, for those wedded to the supply-control paradigm, the treaty placed no limitations on agricultural production, manufacturing by pharmaceutical companies, or consumption. States remained free to make and use as much as they liked, provided they reported accurately to the Permanent Central Opium Board.[89]

Half a loaf

In the realm of drug control, the governments of the world, in conjunction with the fledgling League of Nations, created a going concern between 1919 and 1925. The drug question became a permanent feature of international relations. The League structure provided opportunities to create new expectations for international behavior. Many nations appeared ready to pay more than lip service to the ideal of international drug control. In the course of the Geneva negotiations states agreed to publicize statistics that some considered confidential trade information; to restrict, albeit ever so slightly, the commerce of their nationals; and, theoretically, to limit their own sovereignty through the powers delegated to the Permanent Central Opium Board. Control advocates hoped that, assuming states were both willing and able to enforce its provisions, the new treaty would reformulate international normative standards.

Yet the control regime suffered from numerous defects. Many governments whose good will would be necessary to make the system work chose not to ratify the International Opium Convention, the United States and several producer countries chief among them. The Permanent Central Opium Board entered existence burdened by many handicaps. Any state that wished to escape statistical and import/export requirements could take advantage of loopholes. It therefore remained to be seen whether governments would adhere to the norms for international behavior established by the treaty. Moreover, in the maneuvering leading up to the plenipotentiary negotiations in Geneva, the bias in favor of supply control swept the field. As a result, investigation of alternative conceptions about the drug problem languished for decades. Questions about the relationship between regulation and illicit trafficking also received short shrift. The unwisdom of this lopsided emphasis on restricting access became evident over time.

The League Secretariat also achieved less than it had hoped. League officials shepherded a treaty through the torturous negotiation process, but proved incapable of influencing governmental policy. The Opium Section's expanded responsibilities did portend an increase in budget, personnel, and prestige. Nevertheless, Drummond and his staff suffered a major disappointment in the American rejection of the 1925 treaty. The opportunity to broker a coup slipped from the secretariat's grasp.

The United States played a key role in determining the trajectory of events. On the one hand, American pressure propelled other governments farther than they would have travelled on their own. Even Great Britain, the most favorably disposed of the other powers toward stringent controls, launched a full policy review only when pressed. Other governments would likely have done little had Washington been less persistent.

Conversely, the American insistence on an extreme policy regarding production hindered the gradual progress typical of international negotiations. Congressman Porter possessed neither the power to impose his will nor the inclination to compromise. Considering how much other governments bent over backwards to meet the Americans, a less strident stance on the part of the US delegation would certainly have resulted in more stringent control measures. Although no one could ensure that more rigorous regulations would have been accepted by the majority of states, subsequent events indicate that compliance would not have been greatly lessened. Only six years later, with a more accommodating American delegation, another treaty introduced much wider-ranging controls.

Yet the most profound revelations of the early 1920s concerned the scope of the drug problem. World production of raw materials and manufactured substances exceeded by staggering multiples even the most liberal estimates of legitimate need. Medical experts still understood little about what caused addiction or how to treat it. Turmoil in the Middle Kingdom and environs ensured continued Asian trafficking. Experience to date suggested that attempts to curb non-medical use would likely result in more smuggling. The breadth of the problem was matched only by the depth of ignorance about it. That the emerging rules governing the international drug trade considered sundry material interests (such as the preservation of the free market and the interests of manufacturers) only complicated the issue further. At best, the global campaign to eliminate drug abuse appeared likely to prove a drawn-out affair.

3 Completing the edifice – 1925–31

The League has tried often, but always in vain
To stop people taking a sniff of cocaine,
And doctors have told us that addicts are seen
In a terrible state from the use of morphine;
But profits substantial will always be made
By Switzers engaged in the drug making trade;
Though horrified Rachel her garments may rend,
Still – Hoffmann LaRoche will win out in the end.[1]

By 1931 the basic elements of a remarkably resilient international control regime lay in place. States clarified how much they would inconvenience themselves and their citizens in the name of drug control. Although governments rejected schemes that threatened fundamentally to alter international economic relationships, they did agree to increased restrictions on the manufacture, trade in, and distribution of addicting substances. Control advocates aimed to limit manufacture to legitimate needs, to ensure affordable supplies by retaining an open market, and to eliminate illicit trafficking. Despite contravening evidence, decision makers considered demand for drugs merely a function of supply. Neither depression, war, nor revolution could overturn this supply-control paradigm.

In the process of fashioning the regime, relationships of power and influence shifted. With an increasing stake in the outcome, pharmaceutical companies developed avenues for participating in international negotiations. Organizational changes in key governments streamlined the policy-making process while simultaneously creating positions of bureaucratic power. International control authorities, increasingly aware that they wielded a small stick, acted cautiously. The ability to influence events exercised by the original advocates of drug control diminished. Individuals could still have a powerful, unpredictable impact on events, but their universe of operation became more circumscribed as regulatory structures solidified. As the cost of not adhering to international rules rose, recalcitrant states reconsidered policy options.

The first surge of the international control impetus peaked in 1931. The regime's principles, goals, and structural limitations changed little over the succeeding four decades. After 1931, the success of the drug regime would depend on the ability of control advocates to marshal the forces at their disposal.

Post-Geneva maneuvers

The publicity generated by the acrimonious 1924–25 Geneva negotiations attuned states to the importance of the drug issue. Increased international cooperation and enhanced enforcement at home, even if only cosmetic, were the order of the day. Governments could no longer ignore the drug question without some risk to their domestic and international standing.

Canada utilized its participation in drug negotiations to advance its case for international stature. The government ratified the treaty quickly and urged other nations to follow suit.[2] As part of its campaign to foster an independent Canadian voice in world affairs, Ottawa pressed Drummond for a seat on the OAC. Although the Secretary-General demurred at first, citing the political imbalance that would result, the Canadians achieved their goal during an expansion of the OAC's membership in 1934. By that time Canada had emerged as the *primus inter pares* of consuming states.[3]

The momentum generated by the International Opium Convention propelled some states to revise, however grudgingly, their drug control arrangements. The Swiss diminished their reputation for less-than-ethical drug trading by instituting more stringent domestic controls over imports, exports, and distribution.[4] As part of a plan to assuage western fears about Tokyo's penetration of China, Japanese civilian authorities created an intragovernmental opium committee in hopes of better supervising the drug trade.[5] By 1929 even the previously obstructionist French tightened domestic enforcement regulations. Paris feared international censure in response to revelations concerning extensive drug trafficking.[6] The Dutch grudgingly followed suit, despite their misgivings about the likelihood that imposing controls would foster illicit traffic.[7]

Hitching the team

In London, the internal debate about British opium policy continued. The Home Office promoted rapid ratification of the International Opium Convention at home and abroad. Delevingne continued to advocate reducing both Indian exports and colonial imports of opium. The Foreign Office, attuned to the public relations aspects of the issue, maintained its support for the Home Office position.

The Indian Government, concluding that the political costs attendant to continued (albeit limited) opium exportation outweighed the economic advantages, revised its policy. In 1925 the Government of India announced that it would end opium exports to any state or colony acting as a center of the illicit traffic, even if that government produced valid import certifications. Macao and Persia fell under the interdict that same year. In 1926 the Indian Government declared a gradual reduction of all non-medicinal opium exports. Although the government did not set a firm date for discontinuing the quasi-medical trade, Indian exports dropped precipitously in succeeding years. The policy change improved relations with the United States and deflected negative publicity toward other colonial powers.[8]

The opium question nevertheless remained a major sticking point in Imperial relations. The Colonial Office refused to restrict opium supplies further, citing the likelihood of increased smuggling, hoarding, and speculation. Colonial Office officials unsuccessfully challenged the primacy of the Home Office on drug matters. The Colonial Office then announced that, as India reduced opium exports, colonial administrations would purchase their requirements on the open market. The Persians, notorious among producing states for circumventing control measures, captured most of the business.[9] The Home and Foreign Offices, appalled at this turn of events, could only batten down the hatches for the inevitable storm of negative publicity.[10]

To avoid future embarrassments, the government decreed a formal arrangement for the fashioning of British-Imperial drug policy. In April 1927 the Cabinet created a permanent Interdepartmental Opium Committee. Meeting on an ad-hoc basis over the next twenty years, the Interdepartmental Opium Committee provided a vehicle for coordinating Great Britain's disparate interests.[11]

America in the doldrums[12]

In the United States international drug policy remained hostage to Congressman Porter and America's allergy to the League. Porter maintained his uncompromising position, calling for the elimination of all opium and coca production exceeding medical and scientific requirements. He also insisted on the superiority of the 1912 Hague treaty, notwithstanding the clear advances contained in the 1925 International Opium Convention. Most observers (including the State Department) considered Porter's behavior unfortunate and his views untenable. Yet, as long as Porter remained Chairman of the House Foreign Affairs Committee, the State Department feared a public altercation.[13]

Unable to escape the dilemma, the United States marked time for the remainder of the decade. The federal government complied with some provisions of the International Opium Convention and quietly sent observers to some OAC meetings as part of a low-profile accommodation with the League, but the State Department did not challenge Porter's objections to the 1925 treaty.[14] Washington instead promoted bilateral agreements to share drug trafficking information, a poor substitute.[15] The United States reasserted itself only in 1930–31 after Porter's death, a restructuring of the national drug control apparatus, and the emergence of forceful new personalities. The other players nevertheless moved cautiously, aware that the sleeping giant might awake unexpectedly.

Return to normalcy in Geneva

After the imbroglio surrounding the Geneva plenipotentiary meetings, the League dealt with drug issues in a more routinized manner. As the stature of the OAC increased, states with less direct interest in the drug question clamored for official representation on the Committee. Despite objections from Delevingne, the number of governments represented grew, rendering the OAC's proceedings increasingly unwieldy.[16] The OAC consolidated the nascent drug control regime by investigating the opium situation in the Far East, publicizing illicit diversions in western states, and examining statistics.[17] All parties refrained from introducing major new initiatives, preferring instead to gauge the effect of the International Opium Convention.

Considerable arm-twisting by the League secretariat and the British government brought the International Opium Convention into force on 25 September 1928, only three and a half years after the delegates quit Geneva. All the major manufacturing countries, except the United States, adhered before 1930. Although several key producing countries deferred ratification, the regime enjoyed relatively widespread acceptance. Advocates of the new control system hoped the laggards would meander into the fold.[18]

The inaugural board

With the 1925 convention activated, the League invited governments to nominate candidates for the Permanent Central Opium Board (PCOB, or Board). The treaty required Board members to possess relevant professional experience (diplomacy, industry, business, governmental administration, or medicine), impartiality, and independence – nominees could not depend directly upon a government for their livelihood. Yet the selection process quickly became embroiled in political calculations; states maneuvered to promote their interests regardless of the Board's pretensions to impartiality.

Governments differed over the selection process. Many states advocated open election of Board members, because the resultant horse-trading would enable them to exchange their votes for support on other issues. Delevingne advocated closed-door negotiations to choose a limited slate of candidates. He wanted to secure an expert, independent Board that would oblige all players to follow the same rules. An autonomous Board would benefit those states, like Britain, that had cast their lot with the new regime. Delevingne also feared that the United States would not cooperate with a Board that operated as a body of government representatives. After much cajoling Delevingne won the point.[19]

The US position complicated matters. Washington refused to participate in the nomination process, but the State Department hinted that it would like to see an American serve on the Board. The FPA, through private channels developed by Helen Moorhead, proposed Herbert L. May. Desirous of American participation, Delevingne induced the New Zealand delegation to nominate May.[20]

In December 1928, a closed-door subcommittee chose eight Board nominees. The outcome reflected the geographical, social, cultural, and political realities of the day. Since the Board would meet several times each year, anyone not resident in Europe or North America would spend an inordinate amount of time travelling to and from

---

Herbert L. MAY (1877–1966). United States. A lawyer, he retired at an early age after operating his family's chain of drugstores. Member of the PCOB, 1928–64, and longtime participant in FPA activities. The soul of discretion, from whom never was heard a discouraging word. Mild-mannered, generous, moderate in all things, May often acted as a discreet go-between in intra- and inter-governmental negotiations.

Geneva. Consequently, the League named five Europeans and one American to the board. The expertise required further limited the pool of candidates to western-trained specialists: six Board members hailed from Great Powers, a seventh from India. The principal western states, whose pharmaceutical industries would be affected by the regime, placed persons on the Board sensitive to those concerns. Despite its pretensions concerning political independence, the Board has since inception included an American, a Frenchman, and a Briton. India and, to a lesser extent Germany, have enjoyed nearly continuous "representation" as well. Such was the price for securing the endorsement of the key players. By exercising their muscle in the selection process, governments instilled in Board members healthy respect for the prerogatives of states.[21]

Early Board meetings[22]

The PCOB first tackled fundamental issues of policy and procedure. The most pressing questions involved defining and implementing the Board's mandate, the relationship between the Board and the OAC, and the association between the Board's secretariat and the larger League organization.

Board members debated how best to fulfill their commission. A keen understanding of the Board's weaknesses informed the discussions. Although the International Opium Convention empowered the Board to impose penalties, members acknowledged that publicity comprised their only useable weapon. Exercising sanctions, especially an embargo, could backfire, because the Board relied on government goodwill to enforce punitive measures. A single state could undermine an embargo by selling to a pariah nation (and make a handsome profit into the bargain). Such an outcome seemed entirely plausible; many governments had not ratified the 1925 Convention. The Board concluded that a "high visibility" approach, including open meetings, extensive press coverage, and public embarrassment of recalcitrant states might be counterproductive. They decided instead to exercise discretion. Governments entrusted the Board with sensitive information, including proprietary commercial data of use to competitors. If the Board did not operate confidentially, governments might withhold information or refuse cooperation altogether. Better, the Board concluded, to hold closed meetings and operate behind the scenes, through private channels and low-profile contacts. Board members calculated that the *threat* of publicity was a more valuable tool than publicity itself, because once an infraction became public governments might stiffen rather than moderate their behavior. In a worst-case scenario, the Board could always increase the pressure on a recalcitrant state.[23]

The Board also struggled to define its role in relation to the OAC. Although they desired to cooperate, Board members also wanted to maintain a distinct profile. Issues included how much confidential information to share with the OAC, whether the Board should be represented at OAC meetings, and which body should take responsibility for exposing infractions. Faced with multiple uncertainties about those issues, Board members could not devise a general policy. They refrained from comment about their relation to the OAC, hoping to work out an acceptable arrangement over time.[24]

The most immediate controversy concerned organizing the Board's secretariat. Crowdy and Drummond wanted to integrate the Board secretariat into the Opium Section in hopes of averting clashes over authority, bureaucratic rivalry, and lapses in responsibility. Additionally, a unified secretariat would most economically utilize limited administrative resources. Delevingne opposed amalgamation. His experience indicated that political intrigue permeated the secretariat. He wished to insulate the Board from a similar fate.[25] Delevingne also wanted to divorce the Board secretariat from the League in hopes of securing American cooperation. Board members also wished to retain an independent secretariat. They too held reservations about whether the Opium Section could handle confidential documents discreetly. The Board owed its existence to the International Opium Convention, unlike the OAC, which the League created. At the same time, the Board possessed no ability to raise funds, and thus depended on the League for operating expenses. The Board, in short, wished to be in, but not of, the League. League officials objected to funding an organization over which they exercised no control. The problem demanded attention at the first Board meeting.[26]

The two parties reached an uneasy compromise. The Board retained the right to draw up a budget, within certain limits, and to hire its own Secretary on approval of the Secretary-General.[27] At the same time, the Board agreed to concessions that impinged on its independence. Most importantly, the League would allocate the total budget allotted to the Board. All Board officials except the Secretary would be supervised by the Opium Section. Documents would be controlled by the general League Registry, with secret material held by the Opium Section. The first of many clashes, the agreement represented only a truce.[28]

Although seemingly minor, such issues profoundly influenced subsequent international drug control efforts. In ensuing years internecine turf battles hindered substantive work as factions maneuvered to enhance their bureaucratic positions. In addition to deflecting resources from their assigned tasks, the unsettled administrative arrangements encouraged parties to pursue revision through treaty manipulation. Negotiations concerning the amendment of existing treaties or the creation of new agreements afforded opportunities for each side to strengthen its position. The friction also reinforced the prevailing emphasis on supply control. Rather than questioning the assumptions underpinning the international regime, the Board, the OAC, and their respective secretariats highlighted their contributions to the existing system. Requiring the support of governments to safeguard their bureaucratic position, the international drug control organs rarely challenged state prerogatives or prevailing conceptions of the problem.

The view at decade's end

By the end of 1929, drug control proponents had achieved many of their objectives. India had curtailed opium exports. A landmark treaty, the 1925 International Opium Convention, enjoyed growing acceptance. An independent semi-judicial control body, the Permanent Central Opium Board, had commenced operations. Government statistical returns provided a clearer picture of world supply and demand. Many states had strengthened domestic enforcement. Even the United States, though still refusing to sign the 1925 agreement, cooperated in large measure with the international regime.[29]

Despite such hopeful indicators, the drug problem appeared no nearer resolution. Persia and other states filled the void left by the Indian withdrawal from the quasi-medicinal market. In addition to continued overproduction of opium inside China, statistical returns indicated that Chinese imports of manufactured drugs had skyrocketed. The European colonial powers continued to tolerate (and profit from) opium smoking through government monopolies. As western European governments pressured pharmaceutical companies to conform to more stringent control standards, unscrupulous operators moved to states that had not ratified the International Opium Convention. Traffickers became more sophisticated in their operations, colluding with political and/or military power brokers to avoid prosecution. Drug abusers and their suppliers acted as inventively as the diplomats and bureaucrats; those wishing to circumvent the system altered their routes of acquisition to fit the new pattern.[30]

Committed to a supply-side strategy, control advocates proceeded to the next logical step. Since reduction of agricultural production appeared unlikely, attention focused on schemes to curb surplus manufacture. Nevertheless, all the impediments that had dashed previous control attempts remained in place.

Larger geopolitical issues propelled drug control advocates to renew their efforts. Success in the realm of drug control might provide the key to solving the paramount issue of the day, disarmament. Many recognized the similarities between the two problems. Proponents of both drug control and arms control held similar beliefs about the nature of the problems and they proposed comparable solutions. Those with a stake in creating a successful international drug regulation system hoped they could provide a model for arms control negotiations.[31]

Yet at precisely the moment when a new consensus favoring manufacturing controls might have emerged, the world economic situation disintegrated. With the collapse of the New York stock market in October 1929, nations slipped inexorably into a depression that undulated around the globe. Prices, industrial production, and international trade dropped steadily. In such an atmosphere, nations were loath to forgo any export opportunity. States dependent on imports to meet their medical requirements were likewise chary that curtailing supplies might raise prices, thereby sapping monetary reserves. Producer governments feared a diminution of demand for their (currency earning) raw materials. The worldwide economic downturn made the control advocates' task all the more problematic, yet it also offered an opportunity to foster international cooperation.

Controls on manufacture revisited

Once it became clear that the International Opium Convention was garnering widespread acceptance, interested parties revisited the issue of direct control over manufacture.[32] Alfredo E. Blanco, a rogue officer in the Opium Section, acted as an important catalyst. Frustrated by states' unwillingness to apply more stringent control measures, he concocted the "Scheme of Stipulated Supply." Its provisions were simple: governments would declare (annually, for instance) the quantity of each narcotic substance they required and from what country (or countries) they would obtain the drugs. Pharmaceutical firms would limit manufacture to orders received. Consequently, the excess available for illicit traffic would disappear. Suppliers would be guaranteed a market while purchasers ensured adequate supplies.

As a member of the ostensibly neutral secretariat, Blanco could not advocate the scheme himself. In late 1927 he recruited Charles K. Crane, an American businessman who had dabbled in opium policy, to

Alfredo E. BLANCO (1877–1945). Born in Lancashire but of Spanish nationality. Served in Chinese Maritime Customs for a quarter century. Longtime officer of the International Anti-Opium Association of Peking. Served in the League's Opium section, 1922–28. Founded the Anti-Opium Information Bureau in 1928. Small, stocky, and tough, a former prizefighter. Blanco's pugilistic tendencies were not limited to the ring. He was combative, impatient, and a strong advocate of all manner of control measures. Willing to entertain new ideas, yet often unable to distinguish between the plausible and the implausible. After he left the League Secretariat, Blanco operated as the gadfly of international drug control through the Second World War.

publicize it.[33] Crane bombarded the State Department, foreign governments, and the League with communications trumpeting the Scheme of Stipulated Supply. Crane eventually disclosed Blanco's authorship. This violation and other clashes between Blanco and Crowdy forced Blanco's resignation in 1928. Undaunted, he remained in Geneva, creating a one-man lobbying operation called the Anti-Opium Information Bureau. During the 1930s Blanco's Bureau generated considerable publicity about the drug issue, causing both headaches and opportunities for drug control officials.[34]

Detractors easily unearthed the Scheme's defects. The plan made no provision for medical emergencies or war. Small states would find the paperwork too onerous. Most importantly, states might fall prey to, or be unable to take advantage of, fluctuations in price. Concerns about costs for the ethical drug trade again clashed with the need to restrict supplies in order to curb the illicit traffic. The OAC rejected the plan in 1929, but Blanco continued to promote it through the Anti-Opium Information Bureau.[35]

Delevingne seized the opportunity to resurrect his design for direct manufacturing controls. Returning to the bottleneck idea, he promoted a quota arrangement negotiated by the small number of countries whose pharmaceutical firms manufactured the world's medicinals. With the support of secretariat members opposed to Blanco, the OAC adopted a draft that embodied the main tenets of Delevingne's position. The plan called for governments to estimate their medical requirements. Those needs would then be divided among manufacturing states according to an agreed-upon formula. The League called for new plenipotentiary negotiations and in May 1930 approved both the

OAC's plan and Delevingne's request for a preliminary conference of manufacturing states to negotiate a quota arrangement.[36]

Delevingne did not rely on the vagaries of inter-governmental negotiation to produce a quota agreement, a strategy that had failed him in 1923–24. In the spring of 1930, he instigated direct discussions among the European pharmaceutical houses. Transnational cartel agreements already existed among some European pharmaceutical firms; Delevingne reasoned that if manufacturers could settle among themselves, governments would go along.[37]

The manufacturers' representatives met privately throughout the summer, but failed to produce a quota arrangement. European pharmaceutical firms could not agree on the crucial issue of what percentage should go to each company. The protracted negotiations forced postponement of the preliminary conference of manufacturing states until October. In the interim the giant across the Atlantic suddenly awoke.[38]

America stirs

Shifts in domestic and international currents propelled the American ship of state out of the doldrums during the summer of 1930. In early June, Congress approved a Porter-sponsored reorganization of the federal drug control apparatus. The bill separated narcotics enforcement from the moribund Prohibition Bureau and consolidated domestic and international policy-making functions. The new agency, the Federal Bureau of Narcotics (FBN), entered existence as a part of the Treasury Department on 1 July. Porter did not live to see it – he died on 27 June. President Herbert Hoover appointed Harry J. Anslinger as Commissioner of the FBN, a position he would hold for 33 years. Anslinger's influence cannot be overestimated; he played a

Harry Jacob ANSLINGER (1892–1975). United States. FBN Commissioner, 1930–62, American CND representative, 1946–70. In his day, the most influential actor in international drug control circles. Likeable and a good storyteller, Anslinger could alternately charm or bully as it served his purpose. The consummate bureaucratic strategist, he developed a fiefdom that, with the demise of Stuart Fuller, even the State Department could not penetrate. His single-minded devotion to supply control comprised at once his best and worst attribute.

Stuart Jamieson FULLER (1880–1941). United States. Assistant chief of the Far Eastern Bureau of the State Department with extensive consular experience. In charge of international narcotics affairs for the State Department, 1932–41. Earned a deserved reputation as a firebrand. He distrusted Europeans and the League secretariat equally. Tutored Anslinger in the ways of bombast.

central role in international drug control matters through the late 1960s.[39]

With the death of Porter, the State Department reclaimed supervision of international drug policy. Since 1928 the sedate John K. Caldwell of the Far Eastern Affairs Division had dealt with international narcotics matters. Caldwell's chief attribute was his ability to propitiate Porter. Upon Porter's demise Caldwell recommended that the United States take a more constructive role. The State Department agreed, and named Stuart J. Fuller as Caldwell's assistant and heir apparent. Fuller's personality mirrored Porter's – forceful and energetic. His superiors hoped that Fuller would exercise his zeal with regard for the Department's wider interests.[40]

Reports from Europe about negotiations among the major pharmaceutical firms alarmed American manufacturers. They did not wish to see a European cartel endowed with the imprimatur of a League-sponsored international agreement. When the British Government invited the United States to send a representative to the preliminary conference of manufacturing states, American pharmaceutical houses clamored for acceptance. The new federal drug control apparatus, populated by bureaucrats in need of a constituency, willingly obliged.

Caldwell, Fuller, Anslinger, and officials of the Public Health Service met with manufacturers' representatives in October 1930, shortly before Caldwell travelled to London for the preliminary conference of manufacturing nations. The American firms expressed opposition to any quota plan, voicing objections characteristic of the anti-control thesis. Although they exported relatively small amounts of opiates and cocaine, manufacturers wanted to retain competitive access to the world market. The European companies would no doubt design a cartel for their sole benefit. Most importantly, since smugglers could always pay more than legitimate wholesalers, merely limiting the quantity of drugs manufactured would not end diversions into the illicit traffic. Without instituting strict controls over distribution (as existed in the United States) a cartel would simply raise the price and reduce the supply to legitimate consumers. The American manufacturers argued that other nations should enact controls similar to those in the United States. Since federal law barred domestic pharmaceutical companies from exporting to countries lacking adequate enforcement, persuading other nations to establish US-style distribution controls would also enhance opportunities for export. American firms emphasized the importance of supplying medical requirements at an affordable price, recognizing leakage into the illegal market as an inevitable concomitant.[41]

The manufacturers' concerns dovetailed with the existing elements of American drug control policy. The United States could continue to pursue elimination of excess agricultural production as its ultimate goal. In the meantime, federal officials could urge other states to imitate American domestic arrangements: retain a free market in raw materials and finished products, supervise distribution closely, and criminalize illicit use. By accentuating stringent American enforcement standards, Washington could simultaneously assume a high moral tone, level the playing field for American manufacturers, de-emphasize the importance of the 1925 International Opium Convention, and maintain pressure on producing states. In return for incorporating the requirements of American manufacturers into United States policy, federal officials secured a powerful and supportive constituency.

The preliminary conference and its aftermath[42]

The "Preliminary Conference on the Limitation of the Manufacture of Narcotic Drugs" assembled in London on 27 October 1930. Despite Delevingne's efforts to restrict the meeting to the principal manufacturing states, political considerations required him to expand the invitation list. Italy, an insignificant manufacturer, was invited to assuage its Great Power pretensions. To keep peace at home Delevingne acquiesced in the attendance of the Indian Government, still represented by the pertinacious Campbell. The Soviet Union received an invitation in the hope that the courtesy would elicit statistics from Moscow. The USSR held a unique position among states; it possessed ample capability both to produce and to manufacture narcotics. The Soviet government claimed it limited production and manufacture to domestic requirements, but non-cooperation with the League allowed no verification of the assertion.[43] Special conditions also necessitated the presence of the Turkish government. Turkey, which had possessed no appreciable manufacturing capacity a few years earlier, became the favored location for unscrupulous operators when enforcement of the 1925 International Opium Convention curtailed their activities in western Europe. Almost all drugs manufactured in Turkey found their way into the illicit traffic. Although Delevingne did not wish to reward the Turks with a slice of the licit pie, he had to take into account their capability to upset the system.

The Preliminary Conference, the culmination of Delevingne's carefully laid plans, came to naught. The European manufacturers never reached an agreement about dividing the export trade and in any case allotted no share to the Americans, Japanese, or Soviets – a situation unacceptable to those governments. In the unlikely event that those obstacles could have been overcome, Turkish representatives delivered the final blow when they demanded one-third of the entire quota. The brazen attitude of the Turks drove home the futility of further negotiations. The Preliminary Conference broke up on 11 November 1930.

Despite ample evidence that his plan could not succeed, Delevingne stubbornly forged ahead. He continued to negotiate with pharmaceutical companies and governments, vainly hoping to strike upon an acceptable quota formula. In anticipation of the upcoming plenipotentiary convention, Delevingne redoubled his efforts at the January–February 1931 OAC meeting. He rammed through a draft treaty that featured a quota arrangement as its centerpiece.[44]

At that same session Rachel Crowdy abdicated the Poppy Throne. Confounded by the intractability of the drug question and recognizing that Delevingne's maneuvers portended more trouble, she terminated her service as Head of the Opium Section. Crowdy was among the first who, after devoting some considerable portion of their lives to the subject, departed in frustration. She steered clear of the issue for the remainder of her life.[45] Drummond named Erik Einar Ekstrand, a bland Swedish diplomat, to replace her. The appointment signalled the League's desire to lower the secretariat's profile, for Ekstrand could be expected neither to give nor take offense. By selecting such a guileless character, however, the League relinquished the opportunity to exercise a leadership role.

Government preparations for the 1931 conference

Remembering Delevingne's contributions to the débâcle of 1924–25, Whitehall wished to avoid a similar outcome in 1931. The Foreign Office, calculating that Delevingne's technical expertise outweighed his interpersonal idiosyncrasies, decided against naming a politician to head the delegation. Unaware of the disparity between Delevingne's hopes and reality, Foreign Office officials permitted him to draw up the delegation's instructions. Delevingne formulated several fallback positions if the draft treaty ran into difficulty, but failed to frame a contingency plan in case the conference rejected the quota approach altogether. Delevingne's scheme included the creation of a "Control Authority" that would superintend the quota system. As the repository of many unresolved issues, the constitution of the Control Authority, its duties, and its relation to the PCOB remained unclear. Satisfied that Delevingne had provided the flexibility necessary to avoid another fiasco, the Foreign Office approved the instructions. As the British delegation set out for Geneva, its chief still believed his cherished quota scheme would prevail.[46]

Across the Atlantic, the State Department prepared for the plenipotentiary convention by canvassing the interested parties. The FPA, pro-League organizations, and anti-opium societies continued to urge greater international cooperation, but gave little indication about what policy to follow. American pharmaceutical companies objected to the OAC's quota plan and the still-circulating Scheme of Stipulated Supply. They instead exhorted the US delegation to secure controls over distribution. The State Department wished to avoid another Porteresque débâcle. Attempting to incorporate the desires of all constituencies, the US delegation's instructions placed a premium on flexibility. Although American objectives included the usual items (limiting raw material imports and re-exports, reducing manufacture in other countries, strengthening distribution regulations), the delegation remained free to support any proposal that promised to enhance control. Neither the OAC's quota plan nor the Scheme of Stipulated Supply received an endorsement. The US remained neutral about creating a new Control Authority or conferring additional duties upon the PCOB, preferring to see how those issues played out in Geneva.[47]

In Ottawa, the OAC's quota plan and Blanco's Scheme received an even more chilly reception. Colonel C. H. L. Sharman, named Chief of the Narcotics Division (part of the Department of Pensions and National Health) in 1927, assumed the principal role in developing Canadian policy. Like all drug diplomats, he had to balance his country's principal concerns: securing an adequate, affordable supply of medicaments, controlling illicit use, and safeguarding his country's options for economic development.

Canada's status as a British Dominion and its proximity to the United States placed Sharman in a unique position. In the negotiations preparatory to the 1932 Ottawa conference on inter-Imperial preferential

Charles Henry Ludovic SHARMAN (1881–1970). Canada. Born in England, but emigrated after observing the RCMP during Queen Victoria's Diamond Jubilee. Veteran of the Boer and Great Wars. He served as head of the Canadian Narcotics Service, 1927–46, and represented Canada on the OAC and CND, 1934–54. Elected to the DSB, 1948–58. Anslinger's soulmate, the two thought and behaved very much alike.

tariffs, London indicated its desire to include narcotics in the scheme. Reducing the duty on manufactured drugs would enable British firms to increase production while lowering the cost to Imperial consumers. European and American pharmaceutical firms, spying a chance to access imperial markets, requested permission to manufacture narcotics in Canada.

Sharman rejected all solicitations. He feared that increased British manufacturing capacity would generate more illicit trafficking in Canada. The cost of increased enforcement outweighed the potential savings at the customs house. Sharman also rebuffed the foreign pharmaceutical firms. He did not rule out domestic manufacture altogether, but wished to reserve the right for Canadian houses. Assurances from the FBN strengthened Sharman's resolve. Harry Anslinger pledged that in case of shortage, medical emergency, or war, the United States would provide Canada's requirements at a reasonable price.

Not wishing to increase the world's already excessive manufacturing capacity and assured of adequate supplies, Sharman adopted a classic consumerist position. He authored instructions calling for the greatest limitation of manufacture commensurate with the right of nations to buy at free market prices. Sharman repudiated the OAC's quota plan and Blanco's scheme, preferring to vest supervision in the vaguely defined Control Authority. With no manufacturing industry to protect, he called for controls over all derivatives of addicting substances. Like the other principal actors, Sharman built maneuvering room into his instructions. The Canadians would not present a stumbling block.[48]

Other governments sent their delegations to Geneva with comparable instructions. Manufacturing states such as Switzerland, Germany, France, and Japan did not wish to forgo any opportunity to increase market share. Producing countries, led by Turkey and Yugoslavia, hoped to strike a bargain by emphasizing their capacity to saturate the market with raw opium and/or morphine. Consuming states, like Canada, aimed to safeguard their ability to buy at a competitive price. Wishing to avoid the contentious atmosphere that had often marked international drug negotiations since 1924, delegations generally placed a premium on flexibility.[49]

The 1931 conference: producing compromise[50]

An impressive fifty-seven nations attended the "Conference on the Limitation of the Manufacture of Narcotic Drugs," which met in Geneva from 27 May to 13 July 1931. As the delegations arrived, the European economy imploded again; the Austrian *Creditanstalt* collapse initiated a financial and political crisis that spread quickly. Additionally, final preparations for the World Disarmament Conference had begun. Although economic, administrative, and medical concerns animated drug negotiators, they could not ignore such larger issues. The impediments to a drug control agreement were great. At the same time, the prospect of forging a model accord and the consequences of further deterioration in international relations kept delegates at the negotiating table.

Despite herculean efforts, Sir Malcolm Delevingne could not resurrect his beloved quota plan. Many delegations rejected the quota principle outright, claiming infringement of free trade. Other states would agree to quotas only if the treaty simultaneously instituted price controls to preclude gouging. Manufacturing states would not accept that provision. A few governments declared qualified support for the quota scheme, but also announced their intention to construct manufacturing facilities. The Turks used their manufacturing capacity as a bargaining chip; they would close domestic factories if western pharmaceutical firms promised to buy their raw opium from Ankara. With the realization that the OAC's draft treaty might actually increase both production and manufacture as nations scrambled to grab a percentage of the licit business, support for the quota plan quickly disintegrated.[51]

The Conference then pursued proposals for indirect limitation. A rough draft emerged, and several weeks of hard bargaining ensued. The final document represented a composite of divergent interests. The treaty borrowed elements of Delevingne's original, included stringent proposals championed by the United States and Canada, provided loopholes for manufacturing states, enhanced the position of the League secretariat, and even incorporated components of the Scheme of Stipulated Supply.

Principal provisions of the 1931 treaty

The provisions concerning estimates of need comprised a key element of the 1931 treaty. Signatories were to submit estimates for manufactured drugs by 1 August of the preceding year. States could revise the estimate in case of medical emergency. Signatories did not have to designate in advance where they would buy their supplies, thus allowing them to shop for the lowest price. The treaty required countries to cease import and/or manufacture when they exceeded their annual estimate.

Responsibility for superintending the estimates devolved in part on the treaty's version of the Control Authority, named the Drug Supervisory Body (DSB or Body).[52] The 1931 treaty required signatories to forward estimates to the DSB for examination. To create the most comprehensive assessment of global requirements, the Body was empowered to produce estimates for all countries and territories, *including those not adhering to the treaty*. This stipulation, unique among international regimes of the time, putatively endowed the DSB with great power.

Yet governments carefully circumscribed the DSB's mandate. The delegates vetoed a proposal to submit all import/export orders to the Body *before* execution, which would have granted the Body *direct* control over the trade. Instead states reported imports and exports *after* executing the order, allowing the Body only *indirect control*. The treaty also denied the Body authority to frame estimates unilaterally. Before reducing a country's allotment the DSB had to secure that government's agreement. The Body possessed no enforcement power; it could only publicize findings. The Board assumed responsibility for disciplinary action in the manner prescribed by the 1925 International Opium Convention. Governments wished the Board to retain a central role in the control regime since that organization had already demonstrated a propensity to exercise its limited mandate cautiously.

Another important issue concerned the question of derivatives. By the early 1930s pharmaceutical firms were producing an increasing number of drugs that mixed various substances with an opium-based analgesic. Codeine, a derivative of morphine, was the most common example. Control advocates feared that manufacturers would import large amounts of morphine and claim they converted it into codeine, while actually diverting the morphine into illicit channels. Opponents argued that codeine did not possess the same addictive potential as other substances and that restriction would provide no incentive for physicians to prescribe codeine instead of more potent drugs such as morphine or heroin.

The United States and Canada, the principal advocates of derivatives control, won the point, but only at a price. The German delegation vetoed all attempts to include codeine in the treaty.[53] Berlin's representatives relented only when the Conference agreed to create two separate levels of control. The final version of the treaty required states to submit estimates for preparations that included even small amounts of morphine, heroin, and cocaine. The treaty also applied to those substances all the import/export controls of the 1925 International Opium Convention. The treaty, however, applied less rigorous provisions to codeine.

From 1931 on, the notion that abuse potential might allow for graduated levels of control became an important feature of the international regime. On the one hand, multiple control levels allowed for regulation of drugs that might otherwise escape scrutiny entirely. On the other hand, the potential disparity encouraged pharmaceutical manufacturers to seek a type of *comparative international regulatory advantage*: a company could gain market share if its drug were exempted from controls imposed on competing products. Restricted to the licit drug market after 1931, this tiered regulation system (known as "schedules of control") encouraged pharmaceutical manufacturers to insinuate themselves into the process of implementing and modifying the regime.

Delegations from manufacturing countries also weakened the role given to international health authorities in the treaty.[54] The key issue concerned amendments to the list of controlled substances. Participants understood that as the pace of pharmaceutical research and development quickened, increasing numbers of drugs would come to market. Herbert May advocated the principle that all manufactured drugs be considered guilty until proven innocent.[55] He believed the League Health Committee should test substances for addiction potential and determine whether they were liable to control *before* manufacturers received permission to market them, even in the home country. Pharmaceutical companies feared an adverse decision would result in the loss of research and development investment. Delegations from manufacturing countries insisted that governments retain the right to approve new drugs for the domestic market. Consequently, the treaty empowered the League Health Committee to determine only whether a drug should be included in the international control provisions. Special exemptions further limited the scope of the Health Committee's authority.

Assessment: limited successes[56]

In pursuit of its long-term goal, the US delegation achieved some success, albeit at the price of some unintended side-effects. Caldwell inserted language into the treaty that enacted a modicum of indirect limitation over agricultural production. The provision required governments to restrict raw material stocks held by pharmaceutical manufacturers to a six-month supply (twelve months in exceptional cases). As in the 1925 International Opium Convention, however, the 1931 document exempted government stocks from regulation. This important loophole allowed state administrators, whether in pursuit of personal gain or national advantage, to circumvent the intent of the provision.

The US delegation achieved a similar result in its attempt to level the playing field for American exports. Article 15 required signatories to create a "special administration" to regulate the licit trade in drugs and suppress the illicit traffic. The provision did not prescribe the nature of the special administration; states could make whatever arrangements they deemed appropriate. Ostensibly, Article 15 encouraged other states to emulate the American control apparatus. In conjunction with domestic statutes, the 1931 treaty gave Anslinger important leverage at home and abroad. He held the power to determine from which states US firms could buy raw material and to which countries American manufacturers could export. In ensuing years, however, the Commissioner also used Article 15 to defend his bureaucratic position. For three decades Anslinger blunted attempts to reorganize the FBN by invoking international obligations supposedly incurred under Article 15 of the 1931 Convention.

In the creation of the Drug Supervisory Body the United States achieved further objectives. The US avoided directly acknowledging the League by vesting some control authority in the DSB, an organization created by treaty rather than by the League of Nations. Moreover, the US recognized the legitimacy of the Permanent Central Opium Board without openly validating the 1925 International Opium Convention. Such contortions enabled the delegation to satisfy all major domestic constituencies.[57]

The Canadian delegation likewise reported home a job well done. The treaty preserved the free market, imposed restrictions on derivatives, strengthened international control mechanisms, and delineated clearly between licit commerce and illicit trafficking. Although recognizing that all hinged on whether states lived up to their obligations,

Sharman urged ratification, asserting that the treaty represented "a very long step in advance."[58]

The League also secured notable gains. The treaty granted the Secretary-General, the League Council, and the OAC specific duties; all three entities received much-desired recognition. The Opium Section obtained control over the Drug Supervisory Body's secretariat. Additionally, the Chief of the Opium Section would serve as the DSB's Secretary. This "dual monarchy" arrangement, introduced originally to provide the League with some statutory prerogatives, proved crucial to the survival of the international drug control apparatus a decade later.[59]

The Permanent Central Opium Board fared equally well. The Board retained pride of place in the control system, notwithstanding the duties assigned to the Drug Supervisory Body. The Board also expanded its mandate and protected its administrative and statutory independence.

Similarly, pharmaceutical firms preserved their ability to make a profit and pursue research and development. Manufacturers could buy and sell freely as long as they engaged in legitimate transactions (i.e. those sanctioned by the import/export certification system and which did not exceed annual governmental estimates). The balance of regulatory power remained with national authorities and the relatively malleable Board; less politically pliable organizations such as the League Health Committee and the DSB occupied roles of secondary importance.

Not all voices praised the treaty, however. Delevingne, still smarting from the defeat of his quota scheme, tasted only sour grapes. Complaining that the new document represented a negligible advance over the 1925 Convention, he gave it a lukewarm endorsement. He recommended coordinating ratification among the major manufacturing countries so that none should gain commercial advantage owing to regulatory inequalities. The Dutch also expressed concern that the agreement might increase protectionism and raise prices, resulting in more illicit traffic.[60] Although Blanco considered the treaty an important advance, he nevertheless recognized its shortcomings. During the 1930s he contended that revenue earned from the drug trade motivated both governments and pharmaceutical companies to avoid stringent controls.[61]

Producing states found much more to dislike in the new agreement. The Yugoslav delegation withdrew, complaining that no provision had been made to compensate producers for losses incurred when raw material orders declined. Citing similar concerns, the Turks refused to sign the agreement. What action other producing states, especially Persia, might take remained uncertain. Many western observers suspected, however, that producing countries were merely posturing in hopes of maximizing orders for raw opium under the new regime.[62]

Watershed

With the successful negotiation of the 1931 Limitation Convention, the regime coalesced into coherence.[63] After three decades of haggling, states had delineated the boundary between the licit drug trade and illicit traffic. To the moral obligations of the 1912 treaty and the control provisions of the 1925 pact, the 1931 agreement added a requirement to estimate need, attached a paper trail to manufactures, imports, and exports, and increased vigilance on the part of national and international authorities. Narcotics were assumed guilty until proven innocent, with the most intrusive regulatory measures aimed at agricultural producer nations. Control would be effected through "schedules" based on addictive propensity, as determined by governmental representatives with advice from medical experts, testimony from pharmaceutical companies, and input from the research community. This combination brought manufacture by legitimate pharmaceutical companies into line with medical and scientific needs rather quickly. The regime's structure also encouraged pursuit of comparative international regulatory advantage by creating predictable worldwide marketing rules – regulatory barriers kept out unscrupulous manufacturers but did not impede commerce among "ethical" firms. The drug regime's norms and rules reflected larger international principles that favored state sovereignty and free trade. National authorities acted as the principal regulators while international bodies were relegated to exercising indirect, after the fact, control. At the same time, formalizing the rules created incentives leading to clandestine production, manufacturing, marketing, and sales. Suppliers materialized wherever individuals desired illicit substances and could procure the means to pay for them.

A changing of the guard also signalled the end of an era. Several actors who played important roles in creating the system had departed or would soon retreat from center stage. Brent died in 1929, Porter in 1930. Crowdy washed her hands of the drug business in 1931. Delevingne retired that same year, although he remained active in various capacities until 1948. Nevertheless, the buffeting of the past decade and advancing age sapped his spirit; Delevingne's later years were marked by increasing timidity. Caldwell moved to other duties in 1932, Drummond retired in 1933, and Campbell left the stage in 1934. Fatigued by the complexities of the issue, publicists including LaMotte, Buell, and Gavit[64] moved to other topics.

Moreover, the domestic anti-opium constituencies so influential in first bringing the issue before governments found themselves marginalized by the very bureaucracies they helped create. As states incorporated the drug issue into the policy-making and policy-implementation apparatus, the original groups advocating control retreated to the background. National bureaucracies, international organizations, and pharmaceutical companies supplanted mission-ary organizations, temperance workers, and anti-opium zealots at the center of the decision-making process. After 1931, government bureau-crats marshaled the old-line forces to support their initiatives, rather than the reverse. As a consequence, the leverage exercised by women and women's groups diminished. The waning influence of Elizabeth Wright, a leader of American anti-opiumists during the 1920s, exempli-fied the trend. Harry Anslinger kept Wright at arm's length, except when he needed her to whip up support for the FBN or his latest project. The other notable woman, Helen Moorhead, continued to play an important role precisely because she conformed to both the increasingly bureaucratized atmosphere that suffused the drug regime and the gender expectations of the era.

Yet the pioneers bequeathed an important legacy to their successors. Despite evidence of its limitations, an emphasis on controlling supply would remain the principal focus of the regime. The negotiations of 1930-31 exposed the weaknesses of the supply-control approach when applied to the manufacturing portion of the equation. An abundance of raw materials enabled unscrupulous manufacturers to move opera-tions to the least restrictive regulatory environment. In the 1930s states would tighten the manufacturing bottleneck no further, concentrating instead on the huge overage of agricultural production. Officials hardly considered why people used and abused drugs, assuming that elimination of excess supplies would automatically solve the addiction problem.

In replacing the old guard, the new generation operated under a somewhat different calculus. The apparatus they inherited compelled them to balance, however imperfectly, competing political, economic, medical, and enforcement considerations. The moral, ethical, and religious concerns that animated many of the original drug controllers took a back seat to more worldly interests. Not questioning the basic assumptions animating the drug control system and cognizant of their own bureaucratic requirements, this second generation pursued good drugs, bad guys, commercial advantage, and control "at the source" in a complex international environment. As the world descended into the increasingly troubled 1930s, they faced unprecedented possibilities, contradictions, and challenges.

Part III

Work in progress

4 Against the tide – 1931–39

> [In Japanese-occupied Manchuria] even the resources of modern advertising have been called upon to push the opium business. The money coined for circulation among the people bears a beautiful poppy in full bloom, so that the idea of opium will be brought continually to mind.[1]

> The uncertainty of the international situation and the apprehension of difficulties in obtaining supplies have caused almost all countries, and especially those which depend on other countries for their drug supplies, to increase their morphine reserve stocks.[2]

The successful conclusion of the 1931 Geneva conference initiated a decade of intense activity in the field of international drug control. Control officials and their allies set about implementing the regime's strictures in all corners of the globe. They aimed to eliminate unauthorized shipments by pharmaceutical manufacturers, crack down on illegal factories, curb the bounteous overproduction of raw materials, and interdict illicit trafficking. Armed with the provisions of the 1925 and 1931 treaties and bolstered by the international authority vested in the PCOB and the DSB, regime supporters believed the judicious application of diplomatic pressure would elicit compliance from laggard states. Despite the obstacles facing them, control advocates expected to make steady progress toward eliminating drug abuse.

Yet the constraints imposed by numerous factors, most beyond their control, dashed those hopes. As the 1930s unfolded, the framework within which control advocates had planned to operate unravelled. Some governments ignored their obligations, while others baldly rejected them. Totalitarian states challenged the international order, upsetting the fragile peace constructed during the 1920s. The prospect of war cast a shadow over efforts to foster international cooperation.

As the stature of the League of Nations diminished, the drug control organs also suffered. Moreover, the various national and international agencies charged with implementing the regime often concentrated on bureaucratic survival. In so doing they squandered opportunities to reconsider fundamental issues facing the control regime, despite ample evidence suggesting that the system was flawed. Conflicts proliferated within and between states, domestic constituencies, international control organs, transnational organizations, and multinational pharmaceutical companies, to say nothing of traffickers and addicts. Governments initiated massive stockpiling and other programs as a precaution against the shortages likely to occur in the event of war. Under such circumstances, it became increasingly clear that effective drug limitation would not soon be realized. Indeed, by the end of the decade, the survival of the system painstakingly constructed over the preceding thirty years appeared to be in doubt.

The Bangkok Conference

Ratifications to the 1931 Limitation Convention were delayed as drug diplomats travelled to Bangkok for a meeting concerning opium use in the Far East.[3] The negotiations highlighted again the chicken-or-egg nature of the Asian problem. Governments could not enforce domestic regulations to curb opium use until drug smuggling ended. Drug smuggling could not be stopped unless excess production were eradicated. Yet the profitability of drug smuggling stimulated production. States agreed that eliminating non-medical opium use remained a desirable goal, yet none had implemented effective controls. Prohibiting use, as the Americans had done in the Philippines, proved no more successful than the government monopolies employed by the other colonial powers.[4] The European colonial powers produced another inconsequential treaty. The Bangkok negotiations had their most profound impact an ocean away. For many Americans, the impotence of such efforts highlighted the need for US leadership.

America takes the offensive

In addition to the extant constellation of factors that supported renewed US participation, new constituencies favoring increased international effort emerged in the early 1930s. Because the 1931 Limitation Convention enhanced prospects for a level playing field, American pharmaceutical firms supported new diplomatic initiatives.[5] An increase in international discord, especially in the Far East, highlighted the links between drugs and larger geopolitical concerns. Most importantly, the bureaucratic interests of the nascent federal drug-control apparatus necessitated sustained international effort.

In the summer of 1932, the Commissioner of Narcotics feared for his agency and his job. Harry Anslinger, a Republican, recognized the failing fortunes of the GOP: a Democratic administration might replace him. Corruption scandals rocked the Bureau. Although the FBN had arrested some important drug smugglers, illicit trafficking remained a serious problem. Press criticism of the FBN mounted. The international arena presented Anslinger with opportunities to demonstrate the agency's effectiveness.[6]

The State Department's Stuart Fuller also desired Anslinger's survival. Unlike many OAC representatives, who combined diplomatic and domestic administrative powers, Fuller possessed no authority to implement control measures at home. He needed a collaborator who could secure the cooperation of medical practitioners, enforcement agencies, and the pharmaceutical industry. Anslinger and Fuller embarked on a wide-ranging offensive designed to bolster the FBN's position.

The Commissioner moved first to enhance international police cooperation.[7] During the 1931 conference, Anslinger instigated secret meetings between high-ranking enforcement officials. Designed to increase information exchanges and to coordinate the apprehension of suspects, contacts increased markedly. Select upper-echelon government officials knew about these coordinated efforts. Fearing intelligence leaks, the participants did not notify the League secretariat.[8] Enforcement efforts coordinated at the secret meetings resulted in notable drug-related arrests. Although Anslinger could not publicize this achievement, he made sure that his superiors and their counterparts abroad understood its value.[9]

The Commissioner also enhanced overt international control operations. Largely at Anslinger's behest, the OAC created a Subcommittee on Illicit Traffic, which summarized trends in drug smuggling.[10] By documenting and then threatening to expose transgressions, Anslinger and like-minded officials could increase pressure on recalcitrant states.[11] Even when publicly identifying offenders produced no improvement, the Illicit Traffic report garnered domestic support for the FBN by highlighting American anti-drug efforts.

The US position as a key manufacturing and consuming state gave American officials another sort of leverage over producer nations.[12] The Commissioner could prohibit drug imports from countries he deemed centers of illicit trafficking. At the 1931 Conference Anslinger made such a threat when he warned Turkish representatives to reduce overproduction and illicit trafficking of manufactured drugs. Fuller recruited the American Ambassador to make representations to the Turkish government. Anslinger also arranged for congressman Fiorello LaGuardia to introduce a bill requiring all shipments from states not party to the 1912 Hague treaty to be searched for illicit drugs.[13] Dismayed at the prospect of Turkish goods rotting on American docks and possessing large quantities of opium to dispose of, Ankara ratified the 1912 and 1925 treaties and closed several illicit factories. American drug officials claimed an important victory, and took away from the experience an abiding faith in the efficacy of pressure tactics.[14]

If governments did not bow to Anslinger's behind-the-scenes maneuvers, Stuart Fuller utilized the OAC to apply public pressure. Throughout the 1930s, Fuller arrived in Geneva prepared to blast nations not fulfilling their international commitments. Rarely did a session pass without some state coming under his withering verbal barrage. He also introduced clever innovations, such as tracking precursor chemicals as an indicator of illicit manufacture. Fuller's diatribes spurred some governments to satisfy the Americans before matters became public; others did so only after suffering embarrassment. Even when his outbursts accomplished nothing, American newspapers reported the story home in glowing terms.

Yet the keystone of Anslinger's strategy to defend his domestic position lay in promoting the 1931 Limitation Convention. Article 15 required states to create a "special administration" for applying the convention, regulating licit drugs, and fighting illicit trafficking. A non-binding protocol urged states to place supervision in the hands of a single government agency.[15] Owing to the diversity of governmental structures, the treaty avoided specific provisions for internal administration. Adherents could devise whatever arrangements suited them. In fact, governments located their drug control agencies in a variety of ministries.[16] Anslinger, however, placed a self-serving interpretation on Article 15. He claimed the treaty compelled the United States to maintain an independent drug control agency and that Treasury was the only logical Department within which to locate the "required" agency. If the United States ratified the 1931 Limitation Convention, Anslinger could use the "obligation" purportedly imposed by Article 15 as a bulwark against domestic assaults.

Anslinger therefore fomented domestic support for the Limitation Convention. Major interest groups, including pharmaceutical concerns, anti-opium organizations, religious groups, and even labor memorialized the government in support of the treaty. The Senate approved it unanimously on 28 April 1932. Only Nicaragua moved more quickly to adhere.[17]

After ratification, Stuart Fuller orchestrated a major effort to encourage other states to follow suit. In addition to noting the treaty's intrinsic benefits, he pointed out that a fully functioning drug regime might provide an example for disarmament negotiators. Fuller also exhorted the League secretariat to promote ratifications. Drummond complied readily.[18]

American control advocates also introduced initiatives designed to fulfill longer-term objectives. The FPA's Moorhead churned out publications concerning operation of the regime, including reports on events in Asia and the need to control marijuana.[19] Fuller queried all diplomatic posts, requesting information about manufacturing and production capabilities, shipping regulations, warehousing, drug legislation, enforcement procedures, and penalties.[20] Anslinger and Fuller used this information to pinpoint soft spots in foreign drug-control arrangements. Fuller also supported a League-sponsored initiative to draft a model code for implementing the 1931 Convention.[21] The State Department, at Moorhead's behest, allowed an American representative to participate in the 1933 PCOB elections.[22] In conjunction with the OAC, State Department and FBN personnel participated in efforts to formulate a treaty for the suppression of drug trafficking.[23] Finally, Moorhead discreetly began a lobbying effort aimed at limiting agricultural production. Although American officials recognized that project would probably take years, they hoped to design an agreement that would bring world production in line with legitimate need.[24]

This concerted effort soon redounded to Anslinger's benefit. Following the 1932 election, the FBN came under scrutiny. Franklin Roosevelt's transition team, in an attempt to rationalize government operations, considered transferring the FBN's responsibilities to the Justice Department. Anslinger and Moorhead orchestrated an impressive campaign to defeat reorganization, marshalling support from the pharmaceutical industry, pharmacists, physicians, politicians, private citizens, public interest groups, and government officials. Anslinger and Fuller even arranged statements of support from the League and foreign governments.[25] Anslinger's allies repeated his disingenuous claim that treaty obligations required maintenance of the bureaucratic status quo. The consolidation plan died in April 1933 amidst a host of other projects arousing less opposition. The fledgling Federal Bureau of Narcotics had survived the first of many attempts to reorganize it out of existence. Anslinger and Fuller took to heart the lessons learned and redoubled their efforts to maintain a high international profile.[26]

Ratification and ramifications[27]

Ratification of the 1931 Limitation Convention carried implications beyond the realm of drugs. European manufacturing governments endured complaints from pharmaceutical companies, distributors, pharmacists, and physicians about the increased paperwork and expense required to implement the treaty. To placate those constituencies in a time of economic depression, officials had to ensure implementing the treaty would not unduly prejudice domestic commerce or exports. Rising to the occasion, Delevingne[28] arranged concurrent ratifications by the four principal European manufacturing states (France, Germany, Great Britain, and Switzerland). That strategy assuaged fears that exports would gravitate to the least restrictive jurisdiction, tied the Continental powers to the new agreement, and mollified the Americans.[29] Geneva received the requisite number of ratifications in April 1933.

Drummond brought the treaty to life quickly for several reasons. Supporters of disarmament wanted to activate the treaty rapidly in hopes of providing a model for faltering arms negotiations. The League issued a report indicating how the principles embodied in the 1925 and 1931 drug control treaties could be applied to the arms question.[30] By 1933 Germany and Japan began severing ties to the League.[31] Control advocates and observers of the world scene hoped those powerful countries might maintain international links through an enhanced drug regime. Secretariat politics also impelled Drummond and his supporters to move rapidly. Drummond wanted to determine the administrative structure and appoint key personnel before his replacement as Secretary-General, Frenchman Joseph Avenol, took office on 1 July 1933. Drummond feared, correctly, that Avenol's authoritarian management style and bureaucratic philosophy would create administrative tension and reduce effectiveness. By the time the Limitation Convention entered into force on 13 July 1933, the key arrangements were completed. Drummond named E. E. Ekstrand, Director of the Opium Section, as Secretary of the Drug Supervisory Body. The Opium Section took responsibility for administrative support of the DSB. Only six weeks after the Convention came into force, the Drug Supervisory Body convened its first session.[32]

Close on the heels of implementing the 1931 treaty came new five-year appointments to the Permanent Central Opium Board. League officials and governmental representatives feared that Germany and Japan might not put forward any candidates, thereby tacitly withdrawing from international cooperation. In an extraordinary maneuver, the

League reappointed the entire Board, (including its Japanese and German members) *en masse*. By mid-October 1933, League officials and drug control authorities had done their utmost to discharge their specific obligations and to serve the greater international good.[33]

Those efforts, working against powerful currents, achieved minimal results. Tokyo and Berlin withdrew from the World Disarmament Conference, which disbanded in 1934. Both states also quit the League. The Japanese suspended ratification procedures for the 1931 Convention, but retained representation on the OAC and the Board. Berlin recalled its OAC representative and ordered the German PCOB member to resign,[34] but maintained less conspicuous ties to the regime. The Reich submitted statistics to the PCOB and the DSB, participated in Anslinger's secret police discussions, and enforced the 1925 and 1931 treaties.[35]

League supporters and control officials garnered what comfort they could from this inauspicious outcome. They maintained that future arms negotiators might find the drug regime worthy of emulation, a contention that resurfaced after the next war.[36] Japan's continued representation at the OAC provided a formal channel of communication. Despite Berlin's lower public profile, Germany's continued association with the control system provided a link between Europe's most powerful nation and the international community. Drug authorities recognized the wider significance of maintaining Berlin's participation. Germany possessed the power to undermine or sustain both the drug regime and the general international order. Control officials remained keenly aware that Germany required special treatment. Eventually they had to balance their desire for stringent control with the recognition that Germany might bring down the entire control edifice.

The drug control regime in operation

With the implementation of the Limitation Convention in 1933–34, the task of drug control authorities appeared to be divided into four parts: regulating the licit trade, suppressing illicit manufacture, reducing excess raw material production, and attacking the international traffic. Each portion of the equation required a different approach. The first appeared most amenable to successful management, the second somewhat less so, and the third most problematic. No one knew the dimensions of the last. In all four cases drug controllers believed they understood how to pursue their goals. With the exception of controlling the licit trade, however, they sorely underestimated the magnitude of the task.

The licit market[37]

Regulating licit transactions, while watching for diversions, comprised one key objective. National control officials in western countries had largely succeeded in regulating the "ethical" drug business. Transactions of narcotics and coca products, including imports, transshipment, manufacture, conversion, warehousing, wholesaling, distribution, and exports were reported to authorities. In East and South Asia, control efforts concentrated on supplying smoking opium to registered users while minimizing smuggling. The PCOB and DSB oversaw the worldwide flow of drugs by gathering statistics and inquiring about discrepancies. In ensuing years, League and national drug officials endeavored to increase compliance, offered assistance for improving control, and pressured recalcitrant governments.

Most nations calculated their medicinal requirements relatively accurately. The Drug Supervisory Body identified states that submitted estimates far in excess of the norm. In some cases the Body received satisfactory explanations. More often the DSB quietly pressed governments to reduce their estimates of need.[38] By 1934–35 the PCOB determined that licit manufacture had dropped to approximately the level of legitimate demand. Although exports from pharmaceutical firms in the industrialized West decreased, many other states had initiated manufacture. The total number of factories engaged in narcotics production rose significantly.[39] The import/export certificate system enabled authorities to follow the trade and discover anomalies quickly. Established firms in Western states rarely broke the rules.

Illicit manufacturing: limited success[40]

Yet, as stringent enforcement of regulations curbed illicit manufacture in some countries, the problem moved elsewhere. With raw materials in abundant supply, entrepreneurs willing to take risks could profit handsomely by furnishing manufactured drugs to the illicit market. Questionable manufacture occurred regularly, usually in poorer countries possessing less effective enforcement mechanisms.[41] Unscrupulous manufacturers presented a threat to the legitimate market, often taking a loss-leader approach: to provide a screen for their nefarious activities, unethical manufacturers maintained some legitimate business by underselling their competitors.

Under the right circumstances, the control system worked well. Governments generally registered complaints, but pharmaceutical companies seeking commercial advantage sometimes prodded investigations as well. International control bodies and national authorities coordinated efforts, bringing recalcitrant states into line. Once a problem came to the notice of authorities, the control organs took graduated steps designed to increase pressure incrementally. The Board usually began with an unofficial personal query. If unsatisfied, the Board wrote unofficially, asking for explanations. The Board next invited a representative to hear its concerns. Information might be leaked to the press (particularly the Anti-Opium Information Bureau) to apply added pressure. If the Board remained dissatisfied, it would publish a mild rebuke. As a final step, the Board could threaten to institute an embargo. The DSB, considering its more limited mandate, used a similar graduated approach. The OAC Illicit Traffic Sub-Committee operated comparably. The full OAC also tried to deal with matters privately before resorting to public accusations, although the unpredictability of governmental representatives complicated matters. Whatever the case, applying the new international rules worked to the advantage of established manufacturing interests. Enforcing the international rules also bolstered the authority of control agencies, even if their efforts proved unsuccessful in reducing illicit manufacture.

Governments appreciated the political cover provided by the international control bodies. States could avoid direct confrontations because the Board or the Body acted as intermediaries. Governments under scrutiny could save face; complying with a PCOB or DSB request did not challenge state sovereignty like a demand by another government. Since the Board could question any government, it stood above them all.

The OAC provided a less effective venue for quiet diplomacy, acting primarily as a policy forum. The Committee determined the direction of control efforts, publicized illicit traffic cases, proposed new treaties, interpreted the international agreements in force, and made recommendations to the League and governments concerning drug control.

Publicity, or the threat thereof, was the most important tool control advocates wielded. International authorities encouraged public complaints because they created a useable record; if the Board and OAC publicized confidential information supplied by governments, states might be less forthcoming in the future. The DSB used its authority to establish estimates as a lever. The Body could request governments to decrease estimates – refusal might lead to public censure. Blanco's Anti-Opium Information Bureau comprised an important but unpredictable factor in the equation. Other members of the press often took cues from him.

Yet the regime's effectiveness depended primarily on the ability and willingness of states to comply with emerging international norms. The combined efforts of the Board, Body, and OAC succeeded when governments calculated they would gain more than they lost by cooperating. Weak countries, often located in unstable regions, required good relations with the great powers. Even granted such advantages, however, the international control organs still achieved impermanent victories. Throughout the 1930s, many recalcitrant states required constant prodding to reduce excess production, suppress illicit manufacture, submit statistics, and crack down on drug traffickers. In cases where governments calculated the benefits of noncompliance differently, the control regime proved ineffective. Most importantly, the drug problem exploded in Asia.

Trafficking and excess production: East is East and West is West [42]

Even those who assessed the regime's capacity to curb illicit manufacture optimistically recognized that surplus production and its concomitant, illicit trafficking, presented a formidable challenge. Cultivation proceeded unchecked in much of Asia and in the coca-producing regions of Latin America. Drawing on smaller successes and harkening back to the landmark 1907 Indian/Chinese agreement, control advocates hoped that diplomatic efforts could reduce oversupply.

Persia acted as one pole of the Asian problem. After India curtailed exports in 1926, Persian opium took up the slack. Persian production increased markedly, and much of it fell into the illicit traffic.[43] Seizures of Persian opium and narcotics manufactured from that opium occurred worldwide. With the advent of the Great Depression, Persia relied even more on opium exports to earn foreign exchange.[44] Teheran refused to participate in the widely accepted import/export certification system, and as a consequence drug-control authorities could only estimate the extent of the traffic. Moreover, some Persian officials profited personally from the trade, rendering them less amenable to international pressure.[45]

In 1931 conditions worsened when Japan conquered Manchuria. Tokyo created the puppet government of Manchukuo, which immediately began importing large shipments of Persian opium. The Manchukuo government sold some opium to its own citizens, some to China, and converted the rest into heroin and morphine. Manufactured drugs of Manchukuo origin soon appeared in the illicit traffic, particularly in the western United States and Canada.[46] The opportunity for profit attracted competitors; the Turks and even the Afghanis attempted to secure a piece of the action.[47]

The Persia–Manchukuo trade also presented control authorities with a thorny political problem. The traffic could be regularized, and perhaps reduced, by accepting the import certifications that Manchukuo produced for each opium shipment. But acceptance of those certificates implied recognition of the Manchukuo regime, thereby violating non-recognition policies declared by many governments and the League.

Even worse, many sources indicated Japanese complicity in East Asian trafficking. A combination of financial strain, apathy, ineptitude, and fragmented political authority among Japan's contending civilian and military factions rendered effective controls impossible. The Imperial army and navy engaged in trafficking to supplement their budgets, Japanese pharmaceutical companies competed with each other for illicit market share, millions of individuals depended on the traffic for a living, opium monopolies failed in attempts to control smuggling, and civilian authorities could not enforce their dictates. As the civilian government became increasingly impotent, Japanese diplomats could only dissimulate or lie. Tokyo falsified statistical reports to the League and blamed the opium problem on China. When combined with the massive Persia–Manchukuo trade, the picture took on appalling proportions. Blanco considered it a new form of chemical warfare.[48]

The situation in China completed the dismal East Asian picture. Opium contributed to famines, impoverishment, and insurrection. During the 1920s and early 1930s, the Kuomintang (KMT) government sporadically instituted superficial crackdowns on opium trafficking to mollify western sensibilities, but the directives had little effect. The Nationalists, in fact, depended on opium; the revenues provided a large portion of the budget and served as security for international currency stabilization loans. Opium translated directly into power in a deadly zero-sum game: if the KMT and its gangster allies did not control the traffic, their enemies would. Without drug money, supporters would go unpaid and the government would cease to function. If Chiang Kai-shek fell, China might suffer another period of civil war, fall into the Japanese orbit, or succumb to a communist takeover. Nationalist authorities generally recognized the self-destructive nature of the opium traffic, and in 1935 the KMT launched a major control campaign intended to corner the market by underselling competitors, weaken external opponents, reduce the autonomy of internal factions, and reap public relations benefits abroad. Although the program eventually envisioned suppressing the trade, for the foreseeable future the Nationalists would continue to depend on narcotics money.[49]

Response of the international organs

The depressing realities of the Asian drug traffic presented the international control bodies with a dilemma. If the PCOB and DSB exercised their mandate too forcefully, blatant noncompliance might cause the entire structure to collapse. On the other hand, to do nothing could produce a similar result. To preserve the League's premier control regime, the Board and Body tried to uphold principle in the face of deficient practice.

The League and the principal powers, foundering on the shoals of the Manchurian invasion, attempted compromise. Concerning the drug question, Secretary-General Drummond devised an ingenious proposal to accept Manchukuo import certificates without recognizing the government. The maneuver illustrated the League's debility in the face of unrepentant Japanese aggression.[50]

The DSB attempted to sidestep the Manchukuo issue by assigning Manchurian estimates of need to China. The KMT, however, submitted no estimates, so the Body could not accurately assess the situation in any case. Even in the mid-1930s, when international pressure forced Nanking to relinquish statistics, their unreliability rendered the exercise futile. Similarly, although the Body secured a decrease in Japanese estimates, Tokyo simply "cooked the books" to placate international opinion.[51]

The PCOB fared little better. In 1930 and 1931 the Board criticized the Japanese government for paying inadequate attention to the drug menace, but avoided accusations of collusion. After the invasion of Manchuria direct mention of Japanese transgressions disappeared. Fearing that an indictment would cause Tokyo to withdraw its cooperation entirely,[52] the Board remained silent. The statistical data published in Board reports indicated that Japan harbored a trade exceeding domestic requirements, but only a painstaking comparison of figures could tease out the implications.

The PCOB repeated the same pattern with China. The Board issued a mild rebuke in 1931. In 1933, the Board considered criticizing Nanking openly, but disputes between pro-Chinese and pro-Japanese Board members could not be resolved. Some acknowledged the hypocrisy of dwelling on less significant infractions among small states while remaining silent on such a blatant example as China. Concluding that improvement was unlikely no matter what action they took, the Board addressed only private representations to Nanking.[53]

The Asian situation illustrated the limited effectiveness of the international control organs. Because the Board and Body possessed no coercive power, they required government cooperation. Publicity had little effect on states willing to suffer or unable to avoid the consequences of noncompliance. In Asia, all parties simply placed the blame elsewhere. Persia, which had not ratified the 1912 Hague or 1925 Geneva agreements, was not bound by the import/export certification system. The Chinese government blamed Japan, the colonial powers, and communists for its troubles. Tokyo claimed the problem lay with an incompetent Nanking government. Aware of their impotence when faced with governments unwilling or unable to comply, the international control organs could do little. Their reports included general references to problems in Asia, but they did not allocate responsibility. The PCOB and DSB instead offered ecumenical nostrums encouraging all nations to meet their international obligations. Many members of the Board, the Body, and their secretariats wished to take a stronger line, but all recognized that direct confrontation would highlight the regime's weakness. The heady days when drug control appeared to offer hope for the world's most serious problems had passed. The control bodies became increasingly aware that the breakdown in international comity threatened their continued existence and perhaps that of the League as well.[54]

The OAC strikes out[55]

The OAC comprised an alternative, potentially more confrontative venue in which to pursue drug control. At Geneva, governmental representatives could grapple face-to-face with the complexities of the Asian situation. However, Persian intransigence, Japanese inadequacies, Chinese deficiencies, and conflicts between potential allies merely highlighted the intractability of the Asian situation.

Governments first attempted an embargo. In 1930, western manufacturing countries had imported 109 metric tons of opium from Persia. Following revelations concerning illicit Persian trafficking, western states reduced their imports to a single ton in 1931 – an impressive display of solidarity and resolve.[56] Unfazed, Persian exports to the Far East continued unabated. Teheran joined the OAC, but its representative used the forum to obfuscate the smuggling issue, negotiate for a portion of the legitimate market, and solicit foreign aid in exchange for promises to curb production.

When such economic pressure produced no appreciable results, the OAC shifted its attention to the other end of the Persia–Manchukuo axis. The security and economic interests of Britain, France, India, the Netherlands, Portugal, and Italy prompted them to accommodate Japan. Upsetting existing economic arrangements, especially those pertaining to opium, would hardly contribute to maintaining stability in Asia. Moreover, despite Japanese withdrawal from the League, Tokyo continued to attend OAC meetings and hinted that it might adhere to the 1931 Convention. A direct condemnation of Japan might destroy the opportunity to bring Tokyo under more stringent obligations. Most OAC delegations favored pronouncements that allowed the League to save face without provoking Tokyo.[57]

The United States took a more assertive position, but to no avail. The FBN feared an increase in west-coast trafficking. Moreover, the Manchurian calamity presented Anslinger with another opportunity to display his resolve. Stuart Fuller, however, proved temperamentally incapable of distinguishing between the various shades of opposition to American goals. He considered those who advocated compromise or alternative policies to be adversaries, even when their positions reflected larger geopolitical considerations, honorable intentions, or the impracticability of American objectives. At OAC sessions, Fuller criticized Britain, the League secretariat, and other states as much as the Japanese. He caused serious rifts among potential allies, debilitated the secretariat's ability to function, and fostered mutual suspicions. Moorhead did her best to rectify matters by maintaining an impressive behind-the-scenes transnational correspondence. Ultimately, tensions among allies within the international drug control community reflected increasing frustration about their inability to accomplish the regime's goals.

After the Japanese attack on China in 1937, the Nationalist government succeeded increasingly at playing the opium card in its favor. Despite misgivings about Chiang's apparent complicity in opium trafficking and doubts about the efficacy of control/suppression campaigns, western observers nevertheless regarded any measure that might curb the problem as an improvement. Most importantly, the Japanese threat to western interests caused Britain, France, and the United States to side with Chiang. Japan's civilian authorities indicated concern about the issue, but the increasingly unmanageable drug situation in East Asia confounded all efforts at control. Tokyo's irritation with publicity generated at Geneva caused Japan to withdraw from the OAC in 1939. By that time, more pressing concerns occupied the western powers.[58]

South of the border [59]

The course of drug control in Asia mirrored larger breakdowns in international relations. Although the Soviet Union had joined the League in 1934 and adhered to the 1925 and 1931 drug conventions, those actions reflected only a change in Stalin's tactics; a resurgent Nazi Germany had become too threatening to remain isolated from potential allies.[60] In 1935 Hitler renounced the rearmament clauses of the Versailles treaty and Mussolini invaded Ethiopia. In 1936 Germany reoccupied the Rhineland and the Spanish Civil War erupted. With each event the League's prestige plummeted; it appeared incapable of action. Drug control authorities, increasingly aware of their own limitations in Asia, recognized as well the need to shore up the League's sagging reputation. Latin America seemed the best place to achieve both goals.

Many Latin American governments had not cooperated with the international drug regime. Few submitted the full complement of statistics required by the control organs. Several states had not ratified one or both of the Geneva treaties. Coca production continued unchecked, and various countries became transit centers for opiate smuggling. Illicit drugs found their way to North America, prompting complaints from Anslinger and Sharman. South American coca states resisted controls for economic, social, and cultural reasons. The worldwide depression heightened the importance of exports. Coca represented a vehicle for achieving independence; many viewed imposition of international restrictions as a type of boycott. Upland Peruvians hoped a national monopoly might help their country modernize. Proponents of a peculiarly Andean socio-medical approach to high-altitude living conditions stressed the beneficial physiological aspects of coca use. Supporters of indigenous Andean culture against the encroachment of coastal elites defended the societal value of coca.[61]

Moreover, Latin American states paid little attention to the League generally. With the US failure to accept the League, the incentive to join an organization that might rein in the colossus to the north never materialized. Six Latin American governments that had enlisted quit the League between 1936 and 1938.[62] Geneva's sagging prestige in the political sphere impelled the secretariat to promote the League's "technical" activities. Control officials recognized an opportunity to increase compliance with the international drug regime, foster greater Latin American cooperation with the League, and encourage closer ties between Geneva and Washington.

The international control organs and their allies employed their usual multi-faceted, graduated approach. Helen Moorhead instigated behind-the-scenes negotiations and fostered public contacts. The PCOB and DSB publicized (obliquely) the poor reporting record of Latin American states after private representations produced no results. The OAC and the League urged Latin American states to cooperate more fully. The OAC invited Uruguay and Mexico to join its ranks in 1931, and added Peru in 1937.

Yet the response remained disappointing. Secretary-General Avenol despatched a team of high-ranking secretariat members, including Opium Section chief Ekstrand, on a public relations junket to South America in 1938. Ekstrand met with officials to explain what the international control organs required. The combination of publicity and personal exchange produced some success. By mid-1939, the OAC, PCOB, and DSB noted that Latin American states had improved their compliance. Officials realized, however, that continued pressure would be necessary. Without reminders, governments might slip back into their old habits. The overarching goal of increasing Latin American participation in League activities met with little success. Peru, in fact, left the League in 1939, only two years after joining the OAC.[63]

Illicit trafficking: tricky business

In conjunction with efforts to cajole cooperation from recalcitrant Asian and Latin American states, control advocates attempted to combat trafficking. Implementing the 1925 and 1931 agreements had caused a significant rise in international drug trafficking, especially by increasingly sophisticated organized crime syndicates.[64] Drug officials reasoned that disrupting distribution networks would eliminate addiction by cutting off users from illicit sources of supply. In addition to negotiating bilateral agreements, governments considered a treaty that would impose uniform penalties on traffickers, punish those who facilitated smuggling into foreign jurisdictions, and enhance extradition arrangements.

Begun in 1929, the negotiations proceeded slowly. The colonial drug powers did not want an agreement that might undermine the principle of extraterritoriality or criminalize large numbers of their Asian subjects. They also suspected a back-door attempt to suppress opium monopolies. Coordination of sundry national legal systems presented another impediment. The majority of states, however, expressed interest in an anti-trafficking accord. Many governments, not suffering noticeably from the drug scourge, nevertheless were uncertain about how to fulfill their treaty obligations.[65] The League, in need of a diplomatic success, managed a quiet but persistent campaign to bring the negotiations to a successful conclusion. A plenipotentiary convention was set for June 1936 in Geneva, and the League made sure to invite the United States.[66]

The State Department had for years expressed little enthusiasm for an anti-trafficking treaty, although not for the same reasons as the European powers. Stuart Fuller maintained that if states fulfilled the obligations of existing accords, a new agreement calling for stiff penalties and improved extradition procedures would be unnecessary. In his mind, Fuller lumped together a heterogeneous collection of states (including the Netherlands, Portugal, the United Kingdom, and Japan) into an "old obstructive bloc" and concluded that they engineered a draft to protect their profits; the proposed treaty, for example, excluded raw materials and smoking opium. Fuller never appreciated the administrative difficulties, especially the problems presented by smuggling, faced by colonial administrations. Fuller also believed that the secretariat colluded with those favoring the status quo; he detected bias on the part of the Opium Section in favor of states wishing to defeat far-reaching control measures.[67]

Most importantly, the basis for negotiation of the anti-trafficking treaty threatened the FBN's position. The draft assumed that governments treated drug infractions as criminal offenses, yet the US Supreme Court had only allowed the Harrison Act to stand because of its status as a revenue measure. Prevailing constitutional opinion reserved drug-related law enforcement to the states. If the US ratified an anti-trafficking treaty along the lines of the League's draft, the statutory basis of the FBN's enforcement power would disappear.[68]

The League invitation, however, arrived in February 1936, just as another attempt to reorganize the FBN reached its height.[69] Criticism of Anslinger's failure to apprehend traffickers, allegations of corruption, and faltering support from Treasury Secretary Morgenthau caused the Commissioner to suffer a nervous breakdown in 1935. In January 1936, while Anslinger was on medical leave, Morgenthau proposed creating a single entity within Treasury to deal with all the Department's enforcement responsibilities. His plan called for the Narcotics Commissioner's post to be abolished. Legislation along similar lines was introduced into the House.

Anslinger once again activated his defenders to defeat the proposed reorganization.[70] Physicians and pharmacists, fearful of a return to the days when they suffered the brunt of enforcement activities, supported Anslinger because he concentrated FBN efforts on catching street dealers and illicit traffickers. Pharmaceutical companies, accustomed to the FBN's procedures and hopeful that Anslinger could facilitate exports, argued in favor of the status quo. The WCTU, anti-narcotics groups, and missionary organizations also mobilized in favor of Anslinger. Helen Moorhead wrote articles and inspired editorials supporting the FBN. In February 1936 she secured meetings with State and Treasury Department officials (including Morgenthau) at which she stressed the FBN's role in fulfilling America's international obligations. They found her arguments sufficiently persuasive to re-draft the bill. Anslinger's supporters made great use of the contention that treaty obligations *required* maintaining the bureaucratic status quo, as if no other arrangement would meet those responsibilities. The Commissioner's interpretation of the 1931 Convention once again proved crucial to his bureaucratic survival.

The threat to the FBN caused Fuller and Anslinger to reconsider their opposition to the upcoming anti-trafficking convention. It would hardly do to reject the League's invitation at the same time that the FBN claimed international cooperation as a key *raison d'être*. Fuller asked League officials whether the United States would be allowed to broach issues not included in the draft treaty. He wanted to avoid repetition of the 1924–25 débâcle, when American proposals never received what they considered a fair hearing because delegates ruled them outside the competence of the Conference. If Fuller could secure a blank check from the League, going to Geneva offered important benefits. Anslinger and Fuller could use the forum to pursue their traditional long-term goals and possibly to obtain a treaty basis for police-related federal drug-enforcement activities. They thought it more likely that the convention would rebuff their demands. In that case, US representatives could play the familiar part of moral crusader for the benefit of domestic constituencies.[71]

The Opium Section, hoping to secure American participation, appeased the United States. Ekstrand authorized a note, sent out in the name of the Secretary-General, stating that the conference agenda would not be limited to provisions in the draft. Fuller and Anslinger could offer any proposals they liked, and the Conference would be bound to consider them. The State Department promptly announced its intention to attend. Shortly thereafter, the Treasury Department's reorganization scheme died in Congress. Although rumors continued that Secretary Morgenthau might attempt a reorganization of Treasury's enforcement agencies by executive order, vigilance on the part of Anslinger's supporters ensured that the FBN would be exempted from the plan.[72]

The 1936 Conference[73]

At the 1936 Illicit Trafficking Conference, matters proceeded as the American representatives had predicted. Shortly after the forty-two delegations opened negotiations, Anslinger and Fuller proposed including raw materials and smoking opium in the treaty's provisions. They wanted to criminalize all non-medical production and distribution, and perhaps individual use as well. When several delegations offered the standard objection that such an alteration lay outside the competence of the Conference, Fuller produced the letter from the secretariat stating otherwise. Delegates opposed to the American proposal then pounced on Ekstrand, complaining that the secretariat had no right to make such a promise. Having nevertheless to abide by the ruling, the conference gave the American proposals a superficial hearing before rejecting them.

Unwilling to compromise and having demonstrated US resolve, Anslinger and Fuller petitioned Washington to withdraw. The State Department, unwilling to countenance a repetition of the 1924–25 fiasco, ordered them to remain. The American delegation did not participate, and privately disparaged the proceedings. Exasperated by what they viewed as a sham, the US representatives refused to sign the final document. Upon returning to Washington, Fuller recommended against future participation in League-sponsored conventions unless the United States received prior guarantees about the scope of the deliberations.[74]

Although other delegations viewed the proceedings differently,[75] the 1936 Convention ultimately represented a negligible advance against illicit trafficking. Its provisions proved too general for most pro-control governments and too specific for those wishing to avoid further obligations. Although the treaty required only ten ratifications to activate, lack of enthusiasm delayed its entry into force until October 1939. World War II rendered the Illicit Trafficking convention unworkable until hostilities ended. Even then, however, the treaty never gained widespread acceptance, garnering less than three dozen ratifications in four decades.[76] Those governments interested in pursuing traffickers negotiated bilateral agreements with like-minded states.

Dissipation of the international effort

The lackluster results achieved in Asia and South America, and the lukewarm reception of the 1936 Illicit Trafficking Convention augured ill for control advocates. Although Western pharmaceutical firms had curtailed excess manufacture, clandestine factories cropped up in Eastern Europe and Asia. Unscrupulous manufacturers simply moved operations closer to their raw-material sources, into countries that could not or would not close them down. Excess production, still impossible to estimate owing to conditions in Persia and the Far East, supplied a burgeoning illicit traffic. The international control organs proved capable of regulating the legitimate trade, but they could not eliminate the most significant cases of illegitimate manufacture. Attempts to enact a uniform anti-trafficking standard did not gain widespread acceptance, although many states imposed harsh penalties on offenders and cooperated in extradition cases. The secret police meetings and the OAC's Illicit Traffic Sub-committee acted as important fora for the coordination of drug-enforcement activities, but a plethora of political, economic, bureaucratic, social, and cultural considerations hindered the work. German, Italian, and Japanese participation could not be taken for granted. Without their cooperation the task became all the more difficult. By 1936–37, the poor prognosis produced a climate of frustration, renewed attention to alternative approaches, and fostered interest in the most grandiose project of all – instituting controls over agricultural production.

Family feud[77]

During the second half of the 1930s, control officials and their allies increasingly fought among themselves. As the League's fortunes declined, the financial and administrative anomalies created by the 1925 and 1931 treaties became increasingly contentious. Fractured relations within the drug control community resulted, and some even questioned the efficacy of the supply-control approach.

As the decade progressed, failure to avert conflict, the withdrawal of several Great Powers, and economic depression emptied the League's coffers. As the Opium Section tightened its belt, some talented officials moved to greener pastures, the workload increased, and the delivery of services suffered. Disputes over secretarial support broke out between the PCOB and DSB and Secretary-General Avenol.

Lack of American financial support exacerbated the difficulties. The State Department and the Secretary-General engaged in a drawn-out dispute concerning American contributions to League drug control expenses. Fuller attempted to earmark appropriations specifically for the PCOB and DSB, in part to reinforce the independence of those two bodies from the League. The State Department also allocated funds for certain expenses incurred by the Opium Section, but wished to send them direct to the Secretary-General rather than to the League's general fund. Avenol refused to accept disbursements allocated to a particular entity. He feared that governments might contribute only to League-sponsored activities of which they approved. As a result the United States, champion of aggressive measures to combat the international drug menace, remained in arrears throughout the decade. Deprived of a significant portion of their budgets, the international control services found it all the more difficult to carry out their duties.[78]

Ironically, Stuart Fuller, predisposed to view the secretariat's actions in the worst light, interpreted those difficulties as further evidence of Geneva's bias against substantive control measures. The secretariat's natural aversion to criticism of governments, which increased as the League's fortunes waned, also aroused his ire. Joint representations by the United States, Canada, and Britain compelled Avenol to allocate more resources to the drug control services, but the Secretary-General resented the intrusion into the League's administrative affairs.

Some insiders openly questioned the control strategy that underpinned the regime. Acrimony increased at the OAC's sessions whenever the topic surfaced. In 1936 the PCOB ignited a firestorm by suggesting that control measures had largely failed. Governments that emphasized a law-enforcement approach, most notably Canada and the United States, considered the statement a stab in the back. They insisted on removing the offending passage from the published report. Ironically, the Board amended its objective assessment to placate those most interested in supporting its independence from governmental interference. Yet, even in such instances, control officials kept disputes in the family. The outside world knew little of the difficulties that racked the drug regime.[79]

New frontiers[80]

Desperate to make some headway, the OAC discussed a variety of new projects. In addition to technical regulatory improvements, OAC members contemplated extending the scope of control to marijuana, qat, and precursor chemicals. Discussion of such topics indicated the entrenched nature of the supply-side paradigm, even when existing efforts were failing.

A new technique for narcotics manufacture caused the most immediate concern. In the early 1930s, responding to the opportunities created by the new international rules, Hungarian chemists devised a cost-effective method to extract morphine directly from poppy straw. The refuse from poppy plants cultivated for their oilseed could be utilized, thus eliminating the labor-intensive process of incising and scraping poppy heads individually. Because the new method required large amounts of straw to produce a small quantity of morphine, the OAC believed the danger of increased illicit traffic to be negligible. The potential for refined morphine to escape state control caused more concern. Most importantly, the process posed a threat to established producing and manufacturing states. If others duplicated the Hungarian method, the licit market might be flooded with competitors. Indeed, by 1937, German and Polish firms manufactured significant amounts with the new procedure, the Swiss, Danes, and Soviets had produced experimental batches, and the process had been patented in a half-dozen other countries. OAC representatives groused about the new method, but could do little more than keep an eye on it.[81]

As the Hungarian discovery demonstrated, the international control regime, by its very existence, affected technological developments and drove research agendas. Utopian solutions to the drug problem illustrated most clearly how the regulatory system drove "technological fix" thinking and market incentives. Harry Anslinger instigated a research program to develop a fully synthetic narcotic. Anslinger hoped that US firms could invent a morphine equivalent without recourse to raw opium, thereby destroying the licit market for producing countries. Any opium production would then become, by definition, illicit. American, British, Swiss, and German firms also searched for a non-addicting analgesic. The profit potential attracted pharmaceutical companies. The control system would reward handsomely a painkiller that did not induce dependence by imparting a decisive comparative regulatory advantage – such a wonder drug would not suffer any of the restrictions imposed the existing products. Control officials supported efforts to concoct a "magic bullet" in hopes that their job would be made easier.[82]

In a sure sign that the supply-control consensus was fraying, the OAC revisited demand-side issues. The OAC asked states to compile information about the size of their addict populations, but since no common definition of addiction existed the effort produced little useable information. The United States argued that addicts could only be cured by institutionalization. By the late 1930s, however, many observers (including some OAC representatives and Blanco) had come to question the drug regime's emphasis on law enforcement. Several states advocated employing some combination of social hygiene approaches including psychological treatment, dispensary clinics, follow-up visits after residential care, and prevention efforts targeted at specific audiences. Anslinger, facing calls to transfer FBN responsibilities to the Public Health Service, put down the insurrection with support from Sharman. Using public bluster and private pressure, they blocked all OAC attempts to consider etiological issues.[83] Some states pursued alternative regulatory strategies, but quietly and in moderation. Fully invested in the supply-control paradigm, the control apparatus pursued instead the ostensibly tangible goal of production limitation.[84]

The brass ring[85]

Despite the numerous problems to be overcome, the preferred avenue out of the labyrinth was negotiation of a production control treaty. Each constituency argued for control measures (or lack thereof) configured to their advantage. European colonial powers insisted that any effort to prohibit opium use would fail until the illicit traffic ended. Despite an ingenious clandestine campaign by Moorhead to persuade the British government to modify its position, London shied away from any agreement that imposed a fixed date for elimination of opium smoking and the monopolies that supported them.[86] Beyond the chicken-or-egg debate concerning illicit trafficking and legalized non-medical use, states also expressed other reservations about a production-limitation treaty. Manufacturing powers wished to ensure that adequate supplies would be available at reasonable cost; if a drastic reduction were achieved, raw material prices might skyrocket as buyers scrambled for supplies. Pharmaceutical companies insisted that governments ensure sufficient stocks would be available to offset high prices or shortages caused by a bad harvest or a war. Some manufacturing states wanted clauses guaranteeing their right to initiate domestic cultivation. Producing states adopted tactics to inhibit substantive agreement, fearing that production controls would cause economic hardship and cultural upset. Nevertheless, they continued to negotiate in hopes that a cartel or quota scheme might be hatched that would guarantee each a portion of the lucrative licit market.

Deliberations concerning a production-control treaty consumed increasing portions of the OAC's time in the late 1930s. In June 1939, the OAC produced a partial draft and tentatively scheduled a conference for 1940. By that time, in addition to the intrinsic reasons for negotiating an accord, any possibility to foster international cooperation seemed worth pursuing. Hostilities precluded further negotiations, but the idea remained alive. After World War II, production limitation would comprise a major item on the international agenda.

Prelude to war

In addition to pursuing any possibility for international cooperation, however, prudence required all to prepare for the worst. By 1938 the global political situation had deteriorated to the point where war seemed likely. The drug situation mirrored those larger developments. As the decade came to a close, drug officials, no less than others, paid close attention to German behavior. After 1933 Berlin cooperated quietly with the control regime, but refused to have official dealings with the League. The government submitted statistics to the Opium Section on the basis of treaty obligation only. At Berlin's request, the League sent opium documents to German officials privately. The officer in charge of German narcotics enforcement attended the secret-police gatherings held under cover of OAC sessions. After the *Anschluss* in March 1938, German authorities cracked down on the illicit trade in Austria. Sharman and Anslinger praised Nazi enforcement measures, noting that one suspected trafficker, who had previously operated unfettered by Austrian authorities, was thrown into an internment camp "where he will undoubtedly remain for the rest of his life."[87] In 1939 Berlin persuaded Rome to send a representative to the secret-police meeting, even though Italy had ceased formal cooperation with League activities the previous year.

Ominous signs, however, also emanated from the Third Reich. As early as 1936, the DSB ascertained that some governments, particularly Germany, were accumulating large excesses of government stocks. The only plausible explanation was preparation for war. In an effort to become medicinally self-sufficient, German pharmaceutical firms copied the Hungarian method for extracting morphine from poppy straw and stepped up research on synthetic narcotics. German drug companies refused the League permission to publish statistics about the manufacture of certain substances, claiming that the information might be of commercial value. Berlin's currency export restrictions compelled some Eastern European governments to build up their own narcotics reserves by purchasing sizeable quantities from German firms.[88]

Control officials could only treat Germany gingerly and hope for the best. When Italy withdrew from the League in December 1937, the Board and Body attempted to ensure Rome's continued compliance. Italy's importance was of secondary concern; international officials worried primarily that Berlin might emulate Rome's example. If the Third Reich openly defied the regime, the entire system painstakingly constructed to limit manufacture and track legitimate trade might collapse. The DSB, in hopes of maintaining the flow of vital information, agreed not to publish statistics about some drugs manufactured by German firms. Mild-mannered Herbert May, elected again to the PCOB in 1938, declined the Chairman's position. A Jew, he feared his acceptance might provoke the Germans to withdraw cooperation from the international organs.[89]

The League's dire straits exacerbated tensions inherent in the drug control structure. After his election as Secretary-General in 1933, Joseph Avenol instituted organizational changes designed to centralize decision-making. His desire to exercise control over secretariat matters increased as the international situation deteriorated – Avenol feared deviations from his increasingly pro-French policies might jeopardize the limited scope of action the League still enjoyed.[90] The PCOB and DSB, on the other hand, wanted to downplay their relation to the League. In 1938, the Board Secretary resigned, followed in close succession by the expiration of the Board's five-year term. Disputes between the Board and Avenol over administrative and financial control erupted into open conflict. The League followed the least controversial course by re-electing most of the existing Board. The new Board installed its candidate, genteel Englishman Elliott Felkin, as Secretary. League–Board relations remained chilly. The Secretary-General fared better when Ekstrand retired as Chief of the Opium Section in 1939. Avenol ensured that Ekstrand's replacement on the Poppy Throne, former assistant and fellow Swede Bertil Renborg, maintained the "dual monarchy" by retaining his titles as head of the League opium secretariat and the DSB secretariat. The distinction soon became crucially important.[91]

Amidst such internal and external turmoil, it seemed prudent to choose preservation over bold leadership. The Board, for example, opted not to alter its timid *modus operandi*. Disputes over unresolved

---

Arthur Elliott FELKIN (1892–1968). Great Britain. Great War veteran, served as secretary to the British peace conference delegation, and later on staff of the Reparations Commission before joining the League secretariat in 1923. PCOB Secretary 1938–53. Unpretentious, Felkin carried on dutifully through bureaucratic upset, world war, and personal illness brought on by overwork. Prudence personified, he represents the epitome of diplomatic discretion. Example: Felkin's papers, at King's College, Cambridge, remain closed at his order until the year 2017.

Bertil Arne RENBORG (1892–1980). Sweden. Well-travelled commercial and consular representative for his country, finally alighted upon the Opium Section in 1929. Rose to Chief of Section in 1939, only to preside over the OAC's demise. Renborg's mediocre diplomatic and administrative skills proved inadequate in extraordinary times. After 1945 he suffered the bureaucratic equivalent of a man without a country. Bounced from one post to another, including a stint as postmaster at UN headquarters in New York during the early 1950s and then as a correspondent for Swedish newspapers. Produced a high heat-to-light ratio.

bureaucratic–administrative matters resulted in compromises that, coincidentally, helped the control regime survive the coming war. Nevertheless, the conflicts paralleled the larger tensions of the day, weakening all parties and hindering drug control efforts.

The prospect of war in Europe forced control organs and the League secretariat to prepare for catastrophe. The PCOB and DSB inquired discreetly, through Helen Moorhead, whether the US government might grant the two bodies asylum in case of war. The Opium Section, unable to detach itself from the League in such a manner, could only ready justifications for continued operation in the event that its parent organization ceased to exist.[92]

In Washington, extraordinary times called for equally extraordinary measures. In the mid-1930s, the government included opium and cannabis on a short list of important raw materials essential to the national defense.[93] Opium was vital for its medicinal properties. Hemp was essential for many uses, including marine cordage, and was the only domestic substitute for a variety of tropical fibers. Prudence dictated that adequate supplies of coca/cocaine should be secured as well. Anslinger faced a frightening prospect: it might become necessary to cultivate and process large amounts of controlled substances on American soil. In a series of brilliant strokes, Anslinger maneuvered through the strategic materials dilemma, cementing his reputation as a tough drug cop, enhancing the FBN's bureaucratic status by ensuring supplies of vital war items, and avoiding the excess production and trafficking that might have accompanied unrestricted cultivation.

The Commissioner took a gradiated approach with all three drugs. His preferred solution was to keep them at arm's length by securing adequate supplies from abroad. Creating stockpiles comprised his fallback position. As a last resort, he made plans for domestic agricultural production.

In the case of cocaine, the first and second alternatives appeared sufficient. Anslinger, Fuller, and Herbert May discussed measures to ensure adequate supplies with Maywood Chemical Works, the country's only importer of coca. The FBN also increased coca imports to 800,000 pounds per annum.[94] In cooperation with the Agriculture Department, Anslinger arranged for the cultivation of thousands of coca plants in Puerto Rico as a ready reserve.[95]

Calculations about marijuana/hemp proved more complex. Anslinger eventually concocted the 1937 Marihuana Tax Act, a complicated document that enabled the federal government to regulate marijuana without suffocating the hemp industry. The FBN monitored distribution of seeds, cultivation, purchase of the product, and disposal of waste. The 1937 Tax Act, in conjunction with wartime regulations, made possible a massive wartime hemp-growing program under strict government control. During the war American farmers cultivated hundreds of thousands of acres of hemp, while the FBN's efforts appeared to prevent any illicit traffic.[96]

The Commissioner considered a variety of options to ensure an adequate supply of opium, including domestic cultivation of poppy plants. If American pharmaceutical companies could emulate, as had German firms, the Hungarian method for extracting morphine, the United States would not need to rely on long supply lines for its raw materials. Yet Anslinger could only countenance opium cultivation on American soil if it were strictly licensed by the government. Otherwise, he feared that unregulated producers would foster a domestic illicit traffic (a tacit admission of the futility of supply control efforts). As in the case of marijuana, constitutional constraints did not allow the FBN simply to promulgate regulations. The federal government possessed no authority to license opium growers. In fact, on the few occasions when individuals attempted to raise poppies, the FBN could only urge local authorities to pass anti-cultivation statutes. Once again, Anslinger hoped to use an international agreement to circumvent a domestic dilemma. He initiated discussions with Canada and Mexico concerning a treaty that would require each country to prohibit poppy cultivation except under government license. In exchange for such an agreement, Anslinger promised to supply all Mexican and Canadian narcotic needs, even in time of war, at a reasonable price.

The Commissioner's plans fell through, however, owing to opposition from usually reliable quarters. By 1939 Anslinger could no longer count on the unstinting support of the State Department. Stuart Fuller became ill in 1938, and never fully recovered. George Morlock, a more circumspect individual, took over Fuller's duties. Morlock's tendency to consult superiors cramped Anslinger's style. The State Department, long concerned about Anslinger's penchant for cowboy diplomacy, expressed reservations about the poppy cultivation plan: that illicit production and trafficking might occur; that the government would, in effect, create the kind of opium monopoly it had long condemned; that such an agreement might not be allowed by the extant international treaties. The State Department vetoed large-scale production without prior approval by the President. Anslinger still wished to pursue experimental production, but pharmaceutical companies refused to participate unless they could manufacture the volume necessary to make the program cost-effective.[97] Finally, rumors of reorganization once again swept the Treasury Department.[98] Lacking Fuller's patronage and requiring industry support, Anslinger dropped plans for domestic cultivation. Instead, the Commissioner redoubled his stockpiling efforts. By 1940 he had acquired over 600,000 pounds of opium (the equivalent of four years' supply).[99]

Conclusion

In the summer of 1931 many control advocates believed that the international drug regime might play an important part in shaping the world's emerging political and economic landscape. The Limitation Convention produced that year resolved one aspect of a thorny problem. States agreed to impose limitations on the manufacture, trade, and dissemination of a range of drugs. It only remained to apply the treaty on a worldwide scale, and to address the related issues of agricultural production and quasi-medical use. Early successes indicated that diplomatic pressure applied to recalcitrant states could produce compliance with those objectives. The drug regime provided a shining example of international cooperation, under the aegis of the League, that nations would do well to emulate. The control system even appeared to offer a solution to the outstanding question of the day, arms control.

By the end of the decade, such aspirations had died amidst widespread political and economic turmoil. East Asia, embroiled in war, belied all attempts to impose order. Latin American states, operating under an alternative cultural and economic calculus, offered passive and sometimes active resistance to the system. Persia and Japan disregarded the regime brazenly (and other states less so). German aspirations in Europe threatened the foundations of the regulatory edifice erected by the drug conventions and the League. Governments favoring stringent control measures and the international organs proved unable to counter the actions of those unwilling to abide by the rules. Moreover, implementing the regime engendered unexpected outcomes that created further problems. The economic incentives inherent in the illicit drug trade, created in large measure by the imposition of international controls, fostered excess production, illegal manufacture, and illicit trafficking. The treaties of 1925 and 1931 had not eliminated the phenomena associated with non-medical drug use, but simply relegated them to the illegal side of the ledger. Technological innovation produced a new manufacturing method in Hungary. Although intended as a means to compete in the licit market, the poppy straw process inadvertently undermined the control system and aided German preparations for war.

Although the inability fully to activate the regime in practice led some to question its basic assumptions, the system's emphasis on supply-control and law enforcement remained intact. The bureaucratic interests of national and League control authorities, in conjunction with an increasingly unstable international political climate, choked off debate. The very process of creating successful drug control bureaucracies privileged professionalism and specialist expertise at the expense of voluntarism and conceptual diversity; the regime's structure circumscribed opportunities for alternative voices to be heard.[100] Consequently, consideration of etiology, demand-related issues, the social consequences of control, and the practical effects of regulation languished.

Events in the United States, the world's most remorseless advocate of stringent drug control measures, reflected the untidy state of affairs existing at decade's end. By 1939 the Commissioner of Narcotics was simultaneously pursuing a League-sponsored treaty to curtail agricultural production in far-off lands, a regional agreement that would allow him to commence poppy cultivation at home, and a global acquisition program that amassed the world's largest cache of licit opium yet assembled. Uncertain what the future held, all players had begun hedging their bets by the mid-1930s. As the world descended into war, the dictates of prudence caused even the regime's most ardent supporters to prepare for the collapse of the system.

5 Preservation, perseverance, promise – 1939–46

The League in one form or another is going to live. . . . We may be a side-show while the bombs are bursting; but the history of international organization will most assuredly be resumed. Pressure of daily problems must not make us forget to keep an eye on the future.[1]

Opium is such a slippery snake that it usually gets away unless nailed down absolutely.[2]

As in all other areas of human endeavor, those individuals and agencies associated with the drug regime witnessed great upheaval during the war years. The balance of power among the principal actors shifted substantially. Alongside those changes, however, the immutable continuities that originally propelled the issue into the international arena remained intact.

The war strengthened the influence of some individuals and organizations while diminishing that of others. Herbert May and Helen Moorhead continued quietly but substantially to influence those holding formal policymaking responsibility. Commissioner Anslinger enhanced his position considerably, insinuating the FBN into the emerging American national security apparatus. The DSB and PCOB successfully walked a tightrope, although key players in their secretariats did not emerge from the ordeal unscarred. The influence of Bertil Renborg and those wedded to the League waned. The ability of European colonial powers to resist the more extreme manifestations of the control impetus declined precipitously. American and British pharmaceutical companies contributed to the war effort and their own profits by utilizing the existing control mechanisms.

Between 1939 and 1946 battles for influence over the regime's machinery and direction took place. Certain aspects of the dispute took on an intensely personal color, but profound differences of national and bureaucratic interest underlay the conflict. A small but powerful group of control advocates made good use of their advantages to launch a wide-ranging campaign. By war's end they had succeeded to a degree unimaginable only a few years earlier. Because of their efforts, the postwar era offered renewed promise that supporters of the control regime might yet achieve their ultimate goals.

At the same time, the fundamental factors driving drug diplomacy changed little. States still had to provide for legitimate medical need at reasonable cost. Wartime demand increased cultivation and spurred technological development. The drug question could not be separated from the prevailing economic, political, social, and cultural milieu. State and non-state actors continued to pursue sundry interests through the control regime. The war did not affect the attitudes that underpinned support for and opposition to the system. The ruling supply-control paradigm remained unchanged as well. It would take more than global conflagration to upset the precepts that animated the drug regime's proponents.

Altered stakes

Rather than sounding the death knell for the League's technical services, the war altered their value. On the one hand, negotiating treaties, exploring new topics, and some routine operations were suspended. At the same time, collection of statistical (especially economic) data could provide important clues to a belligerent's weaknesses, trading patterns, and productive capacity. Moreover, many individuals retained faith in the supra-national ideal. They hoped to maintain some form of international cooperation, under the aegis of the League or not, as a basis upon which to build the post-war order.

The drug apparatus occupied a unique position in those calculations. In addition to greatly increased military requirements, civilian needs would also multiply as blockade, shortages, sickness, and noncombatant casualties took their toll on the populace. Control advocates feared the disruption of trading patterns would foster increased production and manufacture. A recrudescence of the drug trafficking and addiction that had caused concern during the Great War seemed likely. Even belligerents understood the need to avoid such a catastrophe. Additionally, whatever shape the postwar settlement took, nations would require international cooperation to control the flow of drugs. It made sense, especially to those connected with the present regime, to retain at least some of the existing structure. The association of the OAC and the opium secretariat with Geneva, and the "in but not of the League" position of the PCOB and DSB, provided control advocates several avenues to preserve the regime. Although that flexibility proved crucial to survival, the plurality of allegiances also created conflict.

The assets of the drug regime also possessed an immediate significance. By following the licit trade, tracking the illicit traffic, and collecting statistics, international authorities could acquire information concerning a belligerent's supply of critical medicaments. In the global logistical contest that raged far beyond the battlefields, such information might prove crucial in denying the enemy means to alleviate the most fundamental suffering caused by war.

Plugging the dike[3]

In the early months of the war, international control officials and their allies attempted to carry on normally. They hoped to preserve their position above the fray, thereby eliciting the cooperation of all states, including belligerents. Many governments supported continued operation of the system. Most states submitted statistics for 1939 and estimates for 1940. The PCOB, DSB, and OAC assembled in Geneva in May 1940, just as German forces attacked in the west. The League instituted organizational changes that replaced the Opium Section with a more independent "Drug Control Service." Renborg received a promotion of sorts; he reported directly to the Secretary-General. Renborg remained head of the DSB secretariat and Secretary of the OAC. The accolades soon took on more than ceremonial importance. By the time the OAC finished abbreviated deliberations on 17 May, the Dutch had surrendered and German armies had split the Allied armies in half. Within a month Hitler's legions paraded down the streets of Paris, and on 22 June the French signed an armistice. With such an unexpected turn of events, all pretense of normal League operations ceased. Only the question of survival remained.

Exodus[4]

During the summer of 1940, turmoil reigned in Geneva. Rumors of a German invasion abounded. Berne vacillated in its support for continued League operations on Swiss soil. Secretary-General Avenol exhibited an increasing affinity for the New World Order. He attempted to force remaining British nationals out of the secretariat, considered transferring operations to Vichy, and even contemplated handing the League over to the Germans.[5]

Facing the prospect of the League's imminent demise, the United States took action to save the organization it had always spurned. On 11 June, in an attempt to salvage the League's technical work, Princeton University extended an invitation to transfer the "non-political" services to its Institute for Advanced Study. President Roosevelt approved the plan, despite its election year ramifications in a still-isolationist America, because federal officials hoped to acquire information about German economic penetration of the Western Hemisphere. After much vacillation, Avenol agreed to transfer the technical services while retaining the titular seat in Geneva. Key personnel evacuated Geneva and by mid-August 1940, the Economic, Financial, and Transit departments commenced operations at Princeton. Avenol resigned on 31 August, abandoning Acting Secretary-General Sean Lester to his fate in an increasingly vacant Palais des Nations.[6]

The League's drug officials did not participate because the overlapping relationships between the PCOB, DSB, and OAC secretariats precluded a straightforward removal. Since Princeton issued its invitation to the *League's* technical services, whether the offer applied to the semi-independent DSB and PCOB secretariats remained unclear. By the time Princeton officials understood the distinction and extended a specific invitation to the PCOB and DSB, Germany's occupation of France rendered travel impossible. Moreover, the connection of the Drug Control Service (formerly the Opium Section) to the OAC created a sticky dilemma. The United States would not welcome any entity connected with the League's political work. Since budgetary retrenchments had necessitated reductions in staff, remaining Drug Control Service members often performed work for more than one of the control organs. It seemed impossible to differentiate between the PCOB, DSB, and OAC secretariats.

During the fall of 1940, prospects for salvaging the international control system depended on Washington and Geneva. Officials in London, enduring the Blitz, could offer little assistance. Whitehall expressed its desire to remove the drug services and their sensitive files from Geneva, but could do little more. PCOB President Sir Atul Chatterjee and DSB Chairman Delevingne, suffering from unreliable communications, indicated their approval of any scheme that would preserve the control apparatus. Colonel Sharman also watched from the sidelines, relying on Anslinger for information. The other principal drug powers were occupied by or allied with Germany. Producing states, smelling an opportunity for profit, shed no tears at the prospect of the control system's demise.

American officials adopted differing positions about the proposed transfer. Commissioner Anslinger realized that the war presented an opportunity to reshape the control regime. He hoped to preserve the PCOB and DSB while refashioning or destroying altogether the OAC. Therefore, Anslinger wished to convey only those staff necessary to run the Board and Body. As far as he was concerned, operations pertaining to the OAC could rot in Geneva. The State Department, including an ailing Stuart Fuller, desired all League-related entities to remain intact, but in Switzerland. Herbert May and Helen Moorhead wanted the entire Drug Control Service transferred to the United States, but recognized the political expediency of bringing over one individual at a time. Leon Steinig had already arrived in August. A key secretariat member, Steinig received special permission to emigrate because his status as a stateless Austrian Jew made it unsafe to remain in Geneva.[7] May wished to bring over Board Secretary Elliott Felkin next. Once those two bodies had commenced operations, the services of Renborg and other secretariat members would become necessary.

Officials in Geneva also considered their options. Renborg had been agitating for removal since mid-May. Board Secretary Felkin arrived at a similar conclusion after Avenol inaugurated a last-ditch attempt to liquidate the League in August 1940. Sean Lester, the diminutive Irishman who took over as Acting Secretary-General on 1 September 1940, was of two minds. On the one hand, he wished to keep his head-quarters operational. The postwar world would require the League or

---

Leon STEINIG (1898–1982). Born in Hapsburg Galicia, Steinig lost his Austrian nationality after the *Anschluss* and eventually became an American citizen. Educated in Vienna and Geneva, he counted Sigmund Freud among his friends. Brilliant international lawyer with impressive grasp of technical and commercial issues, but devoid of managerial skills. Key player in drafting drug treaties between 1931 and 1953. Central figure in DSB secretariat 1931–45 and director of DND 1946–52. Named to the PCOB/INCB 1963–74 after several years as special technical advisor to the International Atomic Energy Agency. A devotee of Talleyrand, Steinig fell out of grace only to make a comeback of sorts, a feat not accomplished by any of his predecessors or successors.

some similar entity, and Lester believed his primary job was to keep the organization alive. Conversely, removal might save the Drug Control Services, one of the League's few remaining functional operations. In early September Herbert May produced an acceptable compromise. He proposed that the DSB and PCOB set up "branch offices" in the United States. Most of the personnel would transfer "temporarily," but the official seat would remain in Geneva. That arrangement allowed Lester and the State Department to pretend that the Drug Control Services operated from the League's headquarters while at the same time transferring the functional nucleus to the United States.

To close the deal, the international control organs sacrificed a measure of independence and collective operation. The State Department insisted that the Board and Body avoid activity that might be interpreted as political, including criticism of governments. Both organizations agreed to produce annual reports without the usual commentary and to suspend their quasi-judicial functions while operating in America; no questioning of governments or embargoes would be pursued. To remove taint of League association from PCOB and DSB operations, the Branch Offices would operate out of Washington rather than Princeton. American officials also indicated that secretariat members should refrain from engaging in any OAC-related activities. Lester and Renborg assented, but continued to press for acceptance of OAC-related functions. The Washington location did offer certain advantages: most states maintained diplomatic representation there, which would facilitate communications between the control organs and governments.

Even after agreement, the US government nevertheless distanced itself from the control organs. The State Department would not issue an invitation to the DSB and PCOB, but simply allowed their continued existence by granting visas to key personnel. No announcement of the transfer would be made; the two bodies could simply inform governments of their temporary address change after the November elections. President Roosevelt quietly approved the transfer on 13 September 1940.[8]

The principal obstacle to executing the agreement concerned acquisition of transit permissions. Secretariat members had to pass through pro-Nazi Spain, which balked at providing travel visas. Behind-the-scenes maneuvers by Moorhead and May and official protests by London and Washington proved ineffective. Anslinger, however, played a trump card that he would utilize repeatedly in subsequent years. The Commissioner intimated that future Spanish requests for drugs might be refused if visas were not forthcoming. With medicine in short supply and Anslinger sitting atop a huge stockpile, the threat constituted a powerful incentive. Spanish authorities relented, and in ensuing months secretariat personnel arrived in Washington one-by-one.[9]

The once-robust Opium Section had been reduced to a skeleton, yet the nucleus survived. Eight staff members transferred to the United States, while three remained in Geneva. In February 1941, the Washington Branch Office opened for business. Stuart Fuller died the same week. As if to highlight their tenuous position, Felkin, Steinig, and Renborg could offer only personal condolences. In their official capacities they represented a discredited international organization ensconced on inhospitable soil in the midst of a global war.[10]

Operations in the United States

Inadequate financial resources loomed as the most immediate problem facing the new arrivals. In spring 1941, Acting Secretary-General Lester grudgingly accepted the State Department's formula by which Washington contributed funds earmarked for the Drug Control Service rather than to the League's general budget. In ensuing years, contributions from other states dropped, rendering Washington's subsidy even more vital.[11]

The PCOB and DSB struggled through constitutional, logistical, and political problems as well. Unable to carry out elections scheduled for 1942–43, both bodies quietly extended their terms indefinitely, hoping that governments would acquiesce in light the circumstances. Unable to generate a quorum for meetings, members created interim committees to act in the name of the PCOB and DSB. Censorship regulations hindered communications, especially with Geneva. The Branch Office printed documents in Canada to circumvent State Department restrictions on producing League publications in the United States.[12]

In sum, the move to Washington, although it ensured the control agencies' survival, also entailed considerable loss of freedom. Ensconced on US soil, dependent on federal money, and hemmed in by American policies, the control organs possessed only limited ability to maneuver. For the remainder of the organs' babylonian captivity, the wishes of the US government would comprise the preponderant factor in international control officials' calculations.

The Branch Office commenced operations in February 1941. Renborg, in his capacity as DSB Secretary, and Board Secretary Felkin informed governments of the "temporary change of address." To maintain the fiction that the League's headquarters remained in charge,

Joseph DITTERT (1916–). Switzerland. Rose through the ranks of the Board secretariat to become Secretary, 1967–76. Retiring almost to the point of shyness, but nevertheless a wily practitioner of "quiet diplomacy." Chief instigator of the quiet campaign to strengthen the 1971 Psychotropic Convention.

the Geneva office gathered estimates and statistics from Sweden, Switzerland, the Baltic republics, occupied territories and Axis allies in Europe; all others communicated with the Washington office. Additionally, the State Department insisted that all OAC-related communications (seizure notifications, annual government reports, changes in laws and regulations, and other non-statistical data) should be sent to Geneva.

Caught between the desire to cooperate and wartime concerns, governments responded in a variety of ways. In Geneva, the enterprising Joseph Dittert coaxed statistics from many occupied countries, and even some states allied with the Axis. The League's host country, however, suspended compliance in 1943 as German pressure on Berne increased. After D-Day, Swiss authorities agreed to communicate data, but only privately. Felkin tried unsuccessfully to secure reports from the USSR. The Soviets had ceased all cooperation after Moscow's expulsion from the League in 1940, and no amount of explaining could convince them of the PCOB's independence from Geneva. Information from Latin American governments arrived sporadically. Felkin suggested that British colonies save time by submitting statistics direct to Washington, but Whitehall insisted on examining the data first. Nevertheless, to meet the submission deadline London took the expensive step of cabling British and colonial estimates for 1942. Few governments sent OAC-related reports to Geneva. The Home Office, for example, ignored a circular requesting an updated list of drug factories. London did not want to reveal its new manufacturing capabilities to the enemy (nor to the Americans). Yet even the Germans and Italians assured Felkin privately that they were compiling statistics and would transmit them "when conditions allowed."[13]

The great divorce

Steinig, as *de facto* head of DSB operations, and Board Secretary Felkin adjusted to their new surroundings. Both recognized the importance of keeping a low profile. They remained hopeful that the statistical work (*sans* commentary and follow-up action) could be continued, thereby maintaining at least the appearance of control. Beyond that, they exploited any opportunity to expand operations that did not ruffle their skittish hosts. Nevertheless, Felkin and Steinig understood that such opportunities would be limited; as Felkin noted, "beggars can't be choosers."[14]

Renborg found Washington's restrictive environment more problematic. Although titular head of the DSB, his principal tasks were tied to the existence of the OAC. Not possessing the technical skills of Steinig or Felkin, Renborg concentrated on diplomatic and administrative matters. Since ascending to the Poppy Throne in 1939, Renborg had insisted upon the indivisibility of the Drug Control Service in part to protect his own position. If the work became separated into its technical and political spheres, Renborg's presence in Washington might become superfluous. Yet promoting OAC-related activities was bound to cause conflict with American officials.

Renborg quickly ran afoul federal authorities. He suggested launching a campaign against excess coca cultivation in South America, which conflicted with complicated US-Peruvian drug control negotiations. Supply lines from South America appeared secure, and Anslinger preferred importing coca to domestic cultivation. He had to purchase Peruvian leaf while avoiding price hikes that might stimulate excess production, illicit trafficking, and perhaps clandestine procurement by Axis powers. Anslinger feared Renborg's machinations might provoke Peruvian producers to eschew cooperation. Renborg also pursued a Brazilian proposal for a new hemispheric drug control treaty. Anslinger and Sharman expressed their displeasure, believing that any new agreement would include provisions weaker than those already instituted. Renborg even discussed convening an OAC meeting on American soil. The State Department, Anslinger, and Sharman expressed vehement opposition. The redoubtable Blanco, still in Geneva, was making embarrassing inquiries concerning the official status of the control bodies ensconced in Washington, and American authorities did not welcome any manifestation of League activity.[15]

Renborg's activities caused growing difficulties between himself and the other principals.[16] Felkin distanced himself because he feared the statistical work might be jeopardized. Anslinger and Sharman soon soured on Renborg, eliminating all but essential contacts with him. Renborg complained to Lester about isolation and lack of cooperation. He floated the prospect of moving the Drug Control Service to another country, which only exacerbated his predicament. Lester had resisted the move to Washington partly because he feared dissension among the

Drug Control Service's principal officers. The overlapping jurisdictions between the PCOB, DSB, and OAC secretariats and the restrictions placed on operations in the United States were bound to create tension. After reading Renborg's letter, Lester's assistant Thanassis Aghnides noted, ". . . our worst fears seem to be surpassed!"[17]

Renborg's behavior forced others to choose between cooperating with or abandoning the League. In addition to League officers, officials residing in London favored Geneva. The Foreign and Home Offices, DSB Chairman Delevingne, PCOB President Chatterjee, and OAC President J. H. Delgorge (a member of the Dutch government-in-exile and head of the Netherlands drug control service) did not comprehend the growing division in North America, but in any case their interests necessitated supporting the League. Moorhead, May and Steinig, while recognizing Renborg's deficiencies, tried to steer a middle course. The State Department, Sharman, Anslinger, and Felkin wrote off the OAC. They ignored Renborg when they could not circumvent him.

In the autumn of 1941, the factions split openly over recodifying the regime. If the six existing treaties[18] could be consolidated into one document, control advocates hoped that the new agreement could be inserted into the anticipated postwar settlement, much as ratification of the 1912 Hague treaty had been included in the Paris peace accords. It might also prove possible to insert language in a consolidated drug treaty that would eliminate non-medicinal opium use and instigate controls over raw material production. All agreed that Leon Steinig alone possessed the expertise necessary to draft the treaty's provisions. May and Moorhead approached the Acting Secretary-General in hopes of getting Steinig released from some regular duties to free up time for drafting a unified treaty. Renborg and Lester, however, insisted that such a task should be overseen by the OAC. Sharman and the Americans recognized that turning over codification to the OAC would probably kill substantive reform, to say nothing of the obvious political impossibility of such a scenario.[19]

Relations deteriorated thereafter. Although rebuffed time and again, Renborg continued to propose schemes designed to enhance his position. Lester eventually found it necessary to remove Renborg from Washington. After Renborg travelled to London in December 1943 for a DSB meeting, Lester ordered him to Geneva. Unable to acquire travel visas, Renborg remained in administrative limbo in England. During 1944 he pleaded unsuccessfully for permission to return to Washington. Fearing, correctly, that events would pass him by, Renborg attempted to keep abreast of the situation by demanding information from Steinig. They exchanged increasingly vitriolic letters and by the time Renborg secured visas for Geneva in early 1945, his estrangement was complete. Felkin and Steinig threatened to quit if forced to work with him again.[20]

The division between Renborg and his compatriots represented more than a mere organizational turf battle. In following his own bureaucratic interests, Renborg's machinations imperiled the delicate arrangements that enabled the international drug control organs' continued existence. Without American backing, the system would quickly disintegrate. Moreover, by keeping the League's flame alive, Renborg threatened to upset the emerging plans of Harry Anslinger and his allies. They recognized the opportunities that the war afforded for a reconfiguration of the control regime, which might be blocked by continued recourse to the League structure. That the breach featured a contest among personalities, all of whom had contributed to keeping the regime afloat, only added to its tragic nature. Competition between the factions would play an important role in shaping the contours of the post-war control regime. The long-term consequences of that battle resonate to the present day.

Anslinger commandeers the catbird seat[21]

Hostilities in Europe presented Harry Anslinger with multiple opportunities and challenges. On the one hand, he exercised considerable leverage over allied nations, neutral states, and the international drug control organs. The Commissioner used his power to pursue the supply-control agenda in ways not possible in peacetime. At the same time, Anslinger had to take into account the medical requirements of other governments, consider the interests of American pharmaceutical firms, treat with arrogant producing states, and calculate how to avoid aiding the German war effort. Nevertheless, after the frustrations of the 1930s, the Commissioner jumped at the chance to promote his international agenda through unilateral action.

Following the war's outbreak Anslinger became a defacto global drug czar, at least in relation to the licit trade in manufactured substances. The Commissioner controlled his own fate with regard to raw materials; the federal government possessed a massive stockpile, retained access to producing regions, and had made preparations for domestic cultivation. American manufacturing capacity suffered no war damage and distribution channels to much of the world remained open. Governments wishing to acquire vital medicaments had few options; after the occupation of Western Europe, only Great Britain retained the potential to impinge upon the American hegemony over manufactured substances. Even some members of the Commonwealth, however, could not obtain sufficient supplies without appeal to the Americans.

Anslinger used his power to pursue a variety of mutually reinforcing goals. Domestic law precluded the Narcotics Commissioner from authorizing exports to states that had not ratified the 1912 Hague treaty. Anslinger instigated legislation that added the 1931 Limitation Convention (which, he claimed, required maintenance of the FBN) to the list.[22] Armed with the new statute, the Commissioner informed recalcitrant states that they would receive no drugs, nor would US firms buy opium or coca, until they adhered to the treaties and submitted statistics to the PCOB and DSB. As noted in the case of the Spanish travel visas, Anslinger also applied direct pressure on governments in order to achieve specific goals. During 1940, he banned exports to Mexico until authorities suspended an experimental ambulatory treatment program that involved the free distribution of morphine to registered addicts. When Chile commenced domestic opium production in 1942, the Commissioner embargoed drug exports and cajoled Britain into similar action. Anslinger pressured pharmaceutical giant Hoffmann-LaRoche to ensure that its Argentinean subsidiary did not sell medicines to Axis powers or their intermediaries.[23]

Other issues, however, proved less amenable to straightforward calculations about how best to advance the control agenda. The war in Europe disrupted normal supply channels for raw materials and manufactured drugs. Governments soon began ordering large quantities of narcotics from the United States. On the one hand, the increased business benefitted pharmaceutical companies, one of the FBN's key constituencies. Yet Anslinger had to keep an eye on competition from Great Britain, the only major manufacturing state free of Axis control. In 1940 the Home Office had approved additional manufacturing licenses, and allowed pharmaceutical firms to make as much as they could sell in hopes of earning desperately needed foreign exchange.[24] Anslinger wanted to limit exports to legitimate need. Any excess could fall into the illicit traffic or into Axis hands.

The drug requirements of the Axis powers constituted a principal concern for the Commissioner. If Germany and Italy could not meet their needs, all efforts should be made to deny them crucial raw materials by buying up excess supplies, regardless of the expense. If, on the other hand, the Axis proved to be self-sufficient, a "preclusive buying" program would simply drive up the price and deplete American resources.

Related uncertainties concerning raw material supplies further complicated Anslinger's task. Exploiting the circumstances, producing states attempted to raise prices. The Commissioner tried to play them off against one another by threatening to buy from the lowest bidder. In May 1941, however, the German offensive against Yugoslavia and Greece cut off supplies from southeastern Europe. Further Turkish exports to the west appeared in doubt. Only India, which conducted its primary trade with Great Britain, and the Iranians, whom Anslinger detested, remained as reliable sources of supply. Anslinger believed it necessary to continue augmenting the American stockpile because, despite the government's large reserves, no one could foretell what course the war might take. He wished, of course, to keep prices as low as possible for American manufacturers. As a hedge, the government held in reserve its plans for the domestic cultivation of poppies and coca. Anslinger, however, would only consider unleashing the production genie in his own back yard as a last resort.[25]

In order to anticipate demand from abroad, manage his reserves, determine what price to pay for raw materials, hinder the illicit traffic, and avoid inadvertently aiding the Axis, Anslinger sought to amass as much information as possible. US officials abroad transmitted whatever data they encountered, especially anything concerning Axis-controlled production, manufacturing, consumption, and imports. The American consulate in Geneva used the diplomatic bag to send "technical material" accumulated by the PCOB to the Washington Branch Office. Anslinger no doubt received a copy as well. A. E. Blanco, still attempting a rapprochement with Washington, forwarded any scrap of information he could scour from sources available in Geneva.[26]

The Commissioner also applied direct pressure on the PCOB and DSB to divulge confidential information. Shortly after the outbreak of war, the Commissioner asked for privileged information that would help him determine the legitimacy of export applications submitted by Latin American governments. The secretariat complied with his request, but expressed qualms about compromising their confidential relationship with governments. In October 1940, at the same time Anslinger was applying pressure to secure transit visas for Elliott Felkin, the Commissioner requested from the PCOB complete statistics concerning South American countries. Uneasy with the breach of confidentiality but in no position to decline, Felkin circumvented the problem cleverly. He sent the data privately to Herbert May, noting that, as a member of the PCOB and DSB, May could share the statistics privately with whomever he liked. After the arrival of the DSB and PCOB in Washington, the Commissioner pressed those bodies to divulge all statistics they collected. The Washington Branch Office existed at the sufferance of the US government, and the Commissioner expected benefits in return for his support of DSB/PCOB operations. That his demands created difficulties for the ostensibly independent DSB and PCOB mattered little to Anslinger.[27]

Thus, long before Pearl Harbor Harry Anslinger took advantage of the war to promote enhanced drug control measures worldwide. In the process Anslinger developed a hierarchy of objectives that he hoped to pursue. Certain problems appeared most amenable to the direct approach, particularly those pertaining to the institution of more stringent control measures. Countries dependent on the United States would be in no position to resist if Washington assigned the drug issue a high priority. Other problems, such as preclusive buying to forestall the Axis and calculations about the legitimate requirements of other states, could only be managed according to the best information available. A third category, most notably the continued intransigence of producing countries, would have to await the end of hostilities. Little could be done until war-related demand subsided. American entry into the war provided Anslinger with the opportunity to set his plans in motion.

Anslinger accelerates

After Pearl Harbor, Harry Anslinger took advantage of the new situation on several fronts. The FBN's unique capabilities contributed to the creation of an American espionage capability. The United States acted as the arsenal of the world's licit drug supply. Anslinger provided advice concerning economic warfare against the Axis. Most important for subsequent developments, the Commissioner headed a team of dedicated control advocates that constructed the postwar international drug control system. In so doing Anslinger and his compatriots simultaneously made important contributions to the war effort, buttressed the FBN's bureaucratic position, achieved several of the control advocates' longstanding objectives, and refashioned the international regulatory organs to their liking.

The Commissioner helped his own cause as well as the country's by playing a key role in the creation of the Office of Strategic Services. Almost alone within the US government, FBN agents had amassed extensive experience in conducting clandestine operations overseas. Bill Donovan, creator of the Office of Strategic Services, needed such expertise, and Anslinger gladly loaned agents to the new organization. By supporting American intelligence operations Anslinger not only made a vital contribution to the war effort, but also insinuated his agency into the midst of the emerging national-security bureaucracy. Those connections provided an added layer of protection in the event of further reorganization attempts.[28]

After Pearl Harbor the Commissioner continued to exercise strict control over distribution of raw material and manufactured drugs. A 1942 presidential order enhanced his authority to grant priorities and make allocations. Smaller pharmaceutical firms applied for manufacturing permits in hopes of gaining a foothold in the lucrative trade but Anslinger refused to expand the number of companies handling opium, citing increased enforcement problems. (The decision no doubt pleased the existing manufacturers that supported Anslinger.) Anslinger also continued to use his control over supplies of manufactured drugs to promote adherence to the international regime. For example, shortly after American entry into the war he approved drug shipments to the USSR, in part because he hoped the Soviets might in return prove more forthcoming with information.[29]

Preclusive buying[30]

Anslinger's most delicate dilemma remained calculations about the international market. By early 1942 he reckoned that the government possessed enough opium to meet American and Allied needs, military and civilian, for three years. He believed it unnecessary to continue purchasing large amounts of opium, preferring instead to buy only enough to replace current usage. Additionally, Anslinger feared that if hostilities ended too soon he would be unable to absorb increased agricultural production stimulated by the war, and the excess would leak into the illicit traffic. If, on the other hand, supplies were cut off completely, the federal government stood ready to begin large-scale cultivation in the United States. In hopes of securing cooperation and lower prices, the Commissioner pressured producing states, especially in Latin America, to restrict cultivation and made sure they understood the US capability to supply its own need.

In 1942, however, economic considerations intervened to overrule Anslinger's judgment. The war had disrupted the economies of neutral nations, including Turkey, Iran, and Afghanistan. To encourage sympathy for the Allied cause, the State Department wanted to purchase all available opium. Anslinger acquiesced after the Office of Production Management, the Board of Economic Warfare, the Defense Supplies Corporation, and the State Department indicated their desire to purchase. By late 1942 all federal officials agreed that the American stockpile was sufficient to meet any contingency.

Yet the question of preclusive buying to forestall Germany created further difficulties. Anslinger and George Morlock, who replaced Fuller at the State Department, believed that Germany and Italy possessed sufficient capacity to meet their needs. The Axis powers controlled poppy-growing regions in Yugoslavia, Bulgaria, and the USSR. In addition, Poland, Hungary, and Germany had perfected techniques for extracting morphine from poppy straw. The Germans were also developing synthetic substitutes for morphine and cocaine. Continuing to buy large amounts of opium would merely encourage price gouging, especially from the Turks, who could sell to both sides.

The British government, however, claimed that Germany possessed insufficient supplies. Supported by the American Board of Economic Warfare, the Foreign Office and the British Ministry of Economic Warfare insisted that all Turkish production should be snapped up. By early 1943 Anslinger became suspicious of London's claims. It appeared that British pharmaceutical firms were manufacturing increasing amounts of narcotics and encroaching on American exports, especially in Latin America. Colonel Sharman concurred, complaining that London earmarked insufficient supplies for Canada because British companies could get a better price elsewhere. An Edinburgh firm even considered starting up manufacture in Argentina. The British continued large purchases of Turkish opium, but Anslinger declined to follow suit.

The preclusive buying imbroglio increased Anslinger's distrust of the British. London's assertions of sympathy for American principles of drug control appeared less than genuine. Determined to utilize the leverage the war afforded him, Anslinger took aim at the one of the most contentious points on the American agenda. He confronted Britain and the other colonial powers over government-run opium monopolies and legalized opium smoking.

The inner circle goes on the offensive

Confident of victory in the military struggle, an "inner circle," consisting of Anslinger, Sharman, Morlock, May, Moorhead, Felkin, and eventually Steinig, began to lay plans for the post-war world.[31] They had soured on the cumbersome League/OAC apparatus, which produced endless compromise. Instead, this small group of like-minded experts championed an assertive post-war agenda, which centered on ending non-medical drug use and creating a more effective international control mechanism. Their goal, eliminating excess supplies, remained unchanged. Through persistent effort, they achieved their principal objectives by subduing the resistance of colonial empires, overcoming the lethargy of friendly governments, and outmaneuvering Renborg's bureaucratic machinations.

Engineering the emancipation proclamation

The Asian war presented Commissioner Anslinger and the "inner circle" with a particularly notable opportunity. As American forces advanced against the Japanese, they would probably occupy territories formerly controlled by the European colonial powers. Under standard military government procedures, US forces were obliged to resurrect the prewar arrangements for civil administration, including legalized opium smoking and government-controlled distribution monopolies. Instead, the Commissioner proposed regulations prohibiting opium use. If American forces could impose such a policy, the European powers would find it difficult to reestablish monopolies when colonial administrations regained control. One of the main roadblocks to the principal long-term American goal – limitation of agricultural production to the world's legitimate needs – would be removed. Ever politically astute, Anslinger realized the strategy also fit nicely into the Roosevelt administration's general anti-colonial policy.

The issue of joint occupation, however, threatened to derail the Commissioner's plans. The United States had already agreed to enact uniform occupation policies in conjunction with the Combined Chiefs of Staff. After the invasion of North Africa, the French reopened a government-operated hashish monopoly and US authorities could only declare the shops out of bounds to American personnel. If the precedent stood, attempts to close down Far Eastern opium monopolies would come to naught. To rectify the situation allied military authorities would have to issue monopoly-prohibition regulations. That outcome could only be achieved by altering the longstanding policies of the British, Dutch, and French governments.[32]

Additionally, Renborg's machinations appeared to threaten substantive progress. In September 1942, Felkin, Renborg, and May consulted with the heads of the PCOB, DSB, and OAC. They concluded that the European colonial governments might be willing to suppress opium smoking. Renborg won approval of his plan to pursue the issue through League-sponsored negotiations. He began laying the groundwork, which provided Renborg a reason to expand OAC-related activities. Anslinger and Sharman, fearing the "old political run-around," denounced the initiative. They would not allow the European colonial powers to block their designs by using the moribund League/OAC structure.[33]

In conjunction with Moorhead and May, Anslinger embarked on a risky confrontational strategy intended to make his domestic and international adversaries blink first. At a private meeting with British and Dutch representatives, Anslinger pressured the two colonial powers to suppress opium smoking and opium monopolies. The Commissioner intimated a consensus existed within the US government concerning suppression, even though the State Department had yet to formulate a policy on the matter. He created the illusion of support by recruiting Sharman (whose country had no military personnel in the Pacific) and other Commonwealth delegations to express sympathy for the initiative, even though none received instructions from their governments to endorse it. He also secured assurances from the Chinese, worthless in reality but useful for public relations, that they would prohibit opium use.[34]

Anslinger's performance forced the issue. Perturbed by his cowboy diplomacy, the State Department nevertheless consulted the Treasury, War, and Navy Departments. All favored implementing a ban, but they hesitated to present the colonial powers with an ultimatum. Throughout the summer of 1943 American officials waited nervously for replies from London. Moorhead, sensitive to the British need to save face, used her contacts to foment domestic sentiment favoring suppression. Finally, in September 1943 the State Department submitted an aide-memoire requesting adoption of a common policy enacting suppression of all non-medical opium use. The note hinted that the United States might take unilateral action if not satisfied with its allies' responses.[35]

Anslinger's unauthorized representations, however, had already succeeded: the British and Dutch acquiesced without a fight. Before receiving the September American aide-memoire, both governments concluded independently that they had little choice but to comply with what they assumed were official American wishes. Even the British Colonial Office, although continuing to grouse about the smuggling likely to ensue, recognized the handwriting on the wall. Neither government could afford the negative publicity Americans would attach to resuming the monopolies, especially since doing so would draw unfavorable comparisons with the Japanese. Both also feared that the United States might delay or terminate plans for returning civil administration to the previous colonial masters. The two governments were not sanguine about China's ability to clean up its portion of the problem, but Washington was in a position to force the issue with the colonial powers. By the time the American aide-memoire appeared in September, both were already calculating how to maximize the favorable publicity they hoped would accompany the policy change. They decided upon simultaneous announcements, made on 10 November 1943. Both declared their intention to suppress opium smoking and government monopolies, but equivocated on quasi-medical use such as opium eating. The British also noted, without specifically mentioning China, that excess production would have to be eliminated to ensure the new policy's success. French authorities issued a similar declaration in 1945.[36]

Despite subsequent quibbling about drawing up occupation regulations and belated attempts by Renborg to acquire control over implementation of the policy, the "inner circle's" gamble produced an impressive victory. By applying direct pressure, Anslinger and his allies bypassed Renborg and the League/OAC structure, thereby circumventing British and Dutch attempts to obfuscate the issue. Ever mindful of his domestic position, the Commissioner made sure to get credit for the accomplishment. The House of Representatives noted his achievement in the Congressional Record, and congratulatory notes flowed in.[37]

Strategic pursuit

Flushed with success, Anslinger, Sharman, Moorhead, and May attempted to follow up their victory by encouraging similar "voluntary" renunciations among other producing states. Moorhead hosted informal dinner meetings designed to build support among key American decision makers. The range of policy options that crystallized during this period, and thinking about how to employ them systematically, featured prominently in postwar drug diplomacy. The US strategy involved employing a carrot-and-stick approach, combining economic and political pressure with incentives to comply. The State Department urged non-compliant states to ratify the existing drug conventions and to eliminate excess production. Recalcitrants could be threatened with retaliatory legislation, including inspection of goods entering the United States, a strategy that had succeeded previously. Producers would be reminded that the United States could fill its raw material needs from compliant suppliers. The ultimate technological trump card would be deployed if necessary: US pharmaceutical firms could step up research and development of synthetic narcotics, which might eliminate the need for licit opium production altogether.

Conversely, US representatives might offer financial aid and crop substitution assistance to compliant producers.[38] The initiative, launched in 1944, yielded a mixed response. The Yugoslavian government-in-exile, willing to placate Western powers in hopes of reinstating itself, quickly agreed. Great Britain demurred, wishing to protect what it considered a purely domestic matter – Indian and Burmese domestic production for quasi-medical use. Teheran groused that crop substitution assistance promised in the past had not materialized, but nevertheless introduced legislation to eliminate poppy cultivation. Even if the measure passed, however, few believed it would be enforced; control officials worried constantly about Iran's postwar behavior. Moscow declared that its state-run monopoly over production and distribution obviated the need for a special declaration. By mid-1945, this lackluster response prompted State Department officials to refrain from further overt pressure. Control advocates hoped instead to secure compliance through the emerging United Nations Organization.[39]

The new world organization[40]

In mid-1944 maneuvering concerning the postwar international structure began in earnest. The "inner circle" expanded to include Steinig, who had broken with the exiled Renborg by then. Although they differed on particulars, all agreed a new drug control organization was necessary. They concluded the OAC should not be resurrected because it had proved too susceptible to political considerations (i.e. considerations that blocked the aims of stringent control advocates). Renborg's grip on the OAC's administrative machinery also militated against reincarnating the old structure. The "inner circle" hoped to place personnel amenable to their views in key positions, thereby avoiding the "partisan" behavior they decried in the League secretariat. Felkin had proved his value to PCOB operations, as had Steinig on a variety of technical matters. With the support of his "inner circle" compatriots, Steinig aimed to replace Renborg on a reconstructed Poppy Throne.

After the Dumbarton Oaks conference pronounced that an Economic and Social Council (ECOSOC) would deal with their issue-area, the "inner circle" campaigned to ensure that the new control body would report directly to ECOSOC. They argued that the mixture of economic, medical, social, cultural, and agricultural factors comprising effective drug control necessitated an independent organization. Yet police, administrative, and economic considerations focusing on supply control figured predominantly in their calculations. If drug control were subsumed within a larger health or social-issues organization, stringent control advocates feared that doctors would pursue ill-advised (i.e. lenient) schemes. To avoid questions about etiology and treatment that challenged their conceptions about the drug problem, Anslinger and Sharman wanted enforcement officials to represent governments. They deprecated the efforts of physicians and others who might espouse a medical or social approach to the problem.

The "inner circle" contended with Renborg, who espoused a unified structure for the international regime. He proposed subordinating the PCOB and DSB to a revitalized OAC. The Board and the Body would continue their functions, but report to the OAC instead of to the Secretary-General. One secretariat would provide all services. Many governments liked that streamlined design. The existing structure, comprised of three separate entities with overlapping responsibilities and problematic secretarial arrangements, appeared byzantine by comparison. Renborg, of course, envisioned himself atop an enhanced Poppy Throne.

Renborg's ideas, in fact, held merit. In an attempt to rationalize an increasingly fractured control system, beginning in the 1980s the United Nations adopted many of the reforms first advocated by Renborg. Yet in 1945 simplification of machinery and Renborg's person came together, a package that the "inner circle" could not accept.

By tireless effort the "inner circle" succeeded in creating an independent drug control apparatus, free of Renborg's influence. In December 1945 the UN's Preparatory Commission added a Commission on Narcotic Drugs (CND) to the list of functional commissions granted the privilege of reporting directly to ECOSOC. A 1946 Protocol transferred the League's drug control responsibilities to the UN and replaced the OAC with a similarly constituted CND. Anslinger, Sharman, and Moorhead lobbied successfully for the appointment of Steinig as Director of the Division of Narcotic Drugs (DND), the UN's equivalent to the old Opium Section. With Felkin in charge of the combined PCOB/DSB secretariat, Steinig handling the DND, and a reinvigorated CND, it appeared that the principal administrative and personnel obstacles had been removed. Advocates of stringent control could now get on with the business of reducing supply to the level of legitimate need.[41]

Conclusion

The small band of dedicated control advocates had accomplished remarkable achievements during the war. Harry Anslinger supplied most of the free world with medicine, exacting compliance with the control regime's strictures in return, and bolstering his bureaucratic position as well. In liberated and occupied areas, control administrations were resurrected as soon as possible.[42] When the dreaded postwar drug-abuse epidemic did not materialize, control advocates credited themselves with preventing an outbreak. The "inner circle" also vanquished the colonial opium monopolies, a feat which they regarded as a down payment toward their ultimate goal. The PCOB and DSB emerged intact, not permanently impaired by their sojourn in America's shadow. Although the OAC died, control advocates expected its descendant to render better service to the cause.

Yet supporters of the drug regime soon discovered that the new age bore a sobering resemblance to the old. The political, economic, bureaucratic, social, medical, and etiological complications that plagued their efforts during the interwar years had survived the deluge as well. Indeed, even in the midst of global war, manufacturers and producers competed for economic advantage with the assistance of their governments, control agencies focused on bureaucratic survival, and all parties maneuvered for postwar position. To be sure, some unexpected twists lay ahead. Typical of the postwar era, former allies would become enemies, as well as the reverse. Nevertheless, advocates of the supply-side paradigm forged ahead, determined to consummate their quest.

6 Trouble in paradise – 1945–53[1]

> . . . it all seems to be a dirty game of dollars and cents and not on the higher plane of morals and public welfare on which I had imagined international discussions of narcotics to take place.[2]

In the decade after war's end, a formidable array of difficulties faced supporters of the postwar control regime. Conditions in China worsened by the month. The war had stimulated agricultural production and pharmaceutical manufacture, providing an ample reserve for the clandestine market. In addition to the massive opium crescent stretching from Yugoslavia to Southeast Asia, even previously quiescent areas of the globe threatened to become centers of illicit activity. Control advocates wanted to reconstruct regulatory arrangements as soon as possible in liberated and occupied countries because traffickers might take advantage of any weak point in the system. And those were only the most immediate problems. The war had also accelerated the development of synthetic narcotics, a class of substances not covered by the extant treaties. The existence of addicting narcotics concocted without recourse to traditional raw materials threatened to upset the calculations of control advocates, producers, manufacturers, and traffickers alike. The advent of non-narcotic addicting substances loomed as a potential problem. Finally, control advocates' longstanding goals of eliminating excess raw material as the means to curb illegal manufacture, illicit trafficking, and non-medical use remained unfulfilled.

Champions of the control regime remained undaunted by such imposing challenges. The "inner circle" perceived themselves as operating from a position of strength. They planned a multifaceted campaign that focused on reestablishing control in war-torn countries, renewing the international organs under UN aegis, regulating synthetic narcotics, exacting compliance from recalcitrant states, and eliminating excess production. The disruptions of the war had, they believed, created a golden opportunity to reshape the world according to their prescriptions.

Control advocates, however, proved unable to accomplish their more ambitious objectives. They did assist in rebuilding shattered national control administrations, they reinstated the international apparatus to working order, and engineered the regulation of synthetic narcotics. Yet hardly had the ink dried on the United Nations Charter when administrative difficulties in the international secretariats surfaced. The wartime coalition broke apart, as members of the "inner circle" pursued divergent paths toward their ultimate goal. Differing bureaucratic interests and personal ambitions contributed much to the division, producing an atmosphere of mistrust in which cooperation proved impossible. The Cold War begat numerous unanticipated political, economic, and strategic dilemmas. Unexpectedly rapid decolonization forced control advocates to treat with an increasing number of developing nations. Differing cultural viewpoints and material interests exacerbated disputes about international regulation. Although by 1953 outward appearances indicated that control advocates had made substantial progress, the regime in fact stood in disarray.

The postwar balance of power

"Inner circle" ascendant

Harry Anslinger had achieved a commanding position in the American policy-making apparatus. The prestige accorded him for supplying the free world with vital medicaments redounded to his benefit after the war. Henry Morgenthau, always suspicious of Anslinger's competence, no longer served as Treasury Secretary. Although nominally yoked to the State Department through George Morlock, Anslinger in fact set the agenda. The Commissioner aimed to marshal the resources of both the Treasury and State Departments to overcome the hindrances impeding pursuit of his cherished goal, "control at the source."

Colonel Sharman retired as head of the Canadian Narcotics Service in 1945, but retained his position as Ottawa's international representative on drug matters. Unfettered by the responsibilities of domestic enforcement, he took on the chairmanship of the fledgling Commission on Narcotic Drugs (CND). During the Commission's crucial initial sessions, Sharman directed the proceedings toward a radical supply-control agenda. In 1948 Sharman gained a seat on the Drug Supervisory Body, further cementing his influence.

Other important players continued to occupy key positions. No longer concerned about Nazi reaction, the Permanent Central Opium Board elected Herbert May as its president. May also replaced the rapidly declining Delevingne as president of the DSB. May quietly but energetically moved to recover ground lost during the war years. He concentrated the Board's efforts on increasing states' submissions of statistics. Although ailing, Helen Moorhead continued to work behind the scenes until her sudden death in 1950. Elizabeth Wright, until her demise in 1952, soldiered on as well. She agitated for increased pressure on producing states and an official role for herself in the nation's overseas anti-opium efforts.[3]

The secretariat: circle cracked

Rifts occurred in the wartime coalition as international officials pursued vital bureaucratic interests. In 1945 Elliott Felkin moved the PCOB staff and records back to Geneva as part of Sean Lester's unsuccessful attempt to reinvigorate the League. Under UN administrative arrangements, the DSB moved to Geneva as well. The PCOB and DSB secretariats fused into one entity with Felkin acting as Secretary of both bodies. Although pleased with such streamlining, Anslinger and Sharman preferred the whole apparatus to remain at UN headquarters in New York where they could supervise operations. Felkin argued that the Board's main job in the immediate postwar years lay in Europe. If control were not reestablished on that continent, the rest of the work would be rendered meaningless. Felkin also feared that the Board's independence might be compromised by continued proximity to the Commissioner's overweening influence.

Anslinger, Sharman, and their allies acquiesced in the PCOB/DSB relocation for reasons in addition to those offered by Felkin. Maintaining the Board's seat in Geneva would reinforce its independence from the UN. Much to the chagrin of control advocates, it appeared that the new world organization had inherited many of its predecessor's difficulties.[4]

Scuffles over money and turf surfaced soon after the United Nations began operations. The transfer to UN authority did nothing to resolve longstanding structural anomalies created by the 1925 and 1931 treaties. Secretary-General Trygvie Lie chafed about funding the Board and Body, organizations over which he exercised little control. In ensuing years, the UN hierarchy repeatedly attempted to extend its authority over the PCOB/DSB secretariat and exert budgetary control over the two bodies. The preferred solution came to be known as the "single secretariat" – an expanded Division of Narcotic Drugs would take over responsibility for servicing the PCOB and DSB as well as the CND. Friction between the rival secretariats persisted for another four decades, affecting the trajectory of control efforts and deflecting energy from substantive work.[5]

In addition, national control officials soon became disappointed in the man they had installed on the Poppy Throne. Notwithstanding his many talents, Steinig's managerial skills proved deficient. Even during his tenure as *ad hoc* head of the Washington Branch Office (1943–46), Steinig experienced difficulty delegating authority and retaining staff. Other members of the "inner circle" knew of those problems, but faced with the alternative (Renborg) they had little choice. When DND operations commenced in 1946–47, expanded responsibilities and an increase in staff only exacerbated the problem. Documentation for CND meetings arrived too late for proper study, sometimes being heaped upon arriving delegates. Studies, draft treaties, and other reports ordered by the CND often contained lacunae reminiscent of the League days. Steinig also refused to name an assistant, reserving all important decisions for himself. By 1949–50, concern about Steinig's health mounted as he displayed increasingly poor judgment in the performance of his duties.

Fearing that the secretariat might once again become the pawn of "obstructionist" forces, Sharman and Anslinger kept a close eye on the DND. They often communicated with Steinig by phone or appeared in person at the New York headquarters. Leaving nothing to chance, they met with Steinig before each CND session to ensure no deviations from the agenda. Steinig quickly tired of such micromanagement, and he agitated to move CND meetings to Geneva. Fearing, correctly, that Steinig hoped to create a precedent for removing the DND permanently from New York, Anslinger and Sharman resisted. By the late 1940s, relations between Anslinger, Sharman, and Steinig had deteriorated. To keep tabs on the Division's operations, Anslinger cultivated covert contacts with subordinate DND staff members. Through secret correspondence Anslinger kept abreast of the latest in office politics, sharing the information with others as he saw fit.[6]

Against dissipation

Despite such internal troubles, the principal players desired to hold affiliated branches of the international system at arm's length. Albeit for differing reasons, they viewed other non-governmental and intergovernmental organizations as threats rather than potential allies.

British, Canadian, and American officials wished to accord only a limited role to the World Health Organization (WHO). Control advocates perceived drug enforcement as primarily a police and administrative issue, and feared that physicians might pursue supposedly irrelevant questions about etiology. Soviet attempts to enhance the WHO's role in the control regime made that body appear more suspect. Anslinger and his allies limited the responsibilities of the WHO's Expert Committee[7] to determining whether substances produced physical addiction. At that point national authorities and the CND would take over the task of regulation.[8]

Steinig and Felkin also wished to circumscribe the WHO's field of action. Pharmaceutical companies were bringing to market an increasing variety of non-narcotic substances (primarily stimulants and depressants). If the WHO handed down a plethora of uncoordinated control recommendations, the likely result would be a political and administrative nightmare. Additionally, any attempt to control such substances might dilute support for the regime, thereby weakening the campaign against the drugs considered the main adversaries: opium and coca.[9]

Control officials froze out other bodies as well. UNESCO, the Food and Agriculture Organization, and the International Labor Organization, for example, received no important role in the postwar regime. Control advocates feared those agencies might divert attention toward social and economic factors contributing to addiction. They might also question incarceration as the only viable treatment strategy. Sharman and Anslinger did not even take Interpol seriously, believing it hopelessly unprofessional.[10]

The old guard: temporary debility

In the immediate postwar years, the other principal industrialized states stood in disarray, unable to challenge the North Americans' predominance. Occupying powers administered German and Japanese foreign relations. The Netherlands never regained control of its East Indian colonies. Notwithstanding promises to suppress their monopoly in Indochina, French colonial authorities continued selling opium to shore up the budget. Aware that control advocates might expose the situation, France kept a low profile on the opium issue. Great Britain granted independence to India and Burma, thereby relieving itself of its most problematic opium-producing possessions. The Home Office's Dangerous Drugs Branch also suffered frequent turnover in the immediate postwar era. Nevertheless, British officials drew on institutional memory and long experience as a manufacturing and colonial power to act as the principal loyal opposition to Anslinger and Sharman. They argued for a moderate approach to the drug question, and sometimes exposed the illogic that suffused radical control proposals. Yet the need for American reconstruction aid blunted opposition from the traditional opium powers. Although they might grouse privately about the US/Canadian-inspired global supply-control campaign, none could allow their misgivings to endanger American financial support.

Enter Moscow

The emergence of the Soviet Union as a factor in drug diplomacy balanced the temporary predominance that stringent control advocates exercised over other western players. Moscow signalled that the USSR would not eschew the drug control regime as it had during the interwar years.[11] For the duration of the Cold War, the USSR promoted its interests in the drug control arena. Soviet officials routinely claimed that socialist societies exhibited no drug abuse, thereby demonstrating superiority over the capitalist west. The Soviets also complained about anti-socialist discrimination in PCOB appointments because the 1925 treaty required candidates to be free of direct dependence upon their governments.[12] With the KMT retreat to Taiwan, Russian delegates protested exclusion of the People's Republic of China at CND sessions and plenipotentiary meetings.[13] Most importantly, as part of its general policy against independent inspections, Moscow opposed investigation of domestic production, manufacturing, or treatment facilities. The USSR would not brook any interference with its sovereignty, internal trade, or the use of drugs for such nefarious purposes as "psychiatric treatment."

This newfound Russian participation, although heartening to western control advocates, further complicated their task. They would have to take Soviet interests into account in the midst of a developing Cold War.[14] Moscow's attention to the social factors underlying abuse made it all the more imperative for western control advocates to subdue consideration of etiological questions and alternatives to the predominant enforcement paradigm. An admission that addiction might be attributable to factors other than deficiencies residing within the individual would undermine the west's Cold War position. Moreover, the threat of a "nyet" caused regime advocates to temporize, especially when considering control provisions that required on-site inspection. Yet universal compliance could be realized only if the

USSR and its satellites participated in the regime. Control advocates tolerated Soviet obstinacy and half-compliance, hoping for increased cooperation in the future. Although rarely acknowledged, the USSR and its satellites remained an uncertain factor in drug control calculations for the remainder of the Soviet era.[15]

Despite concerns about Soviet behavior and the less-than-optimal conditions obtaining in the international secretariat, the overall postwar situation appeared promising to control advocates. Commissioner Anslinger directed American international drug policy from a seemingly secure perch. Colonel Sharman enjoyed a similar position in Canada. Sharman and Herbert May occupied the key posts of DSB Chairman and PCOB President. Elizabeth Wright and Helen Moorhead continued to make their unique contributions, the former providing external pressure and the latter lubricating the international machinery from behind the scenes. Together, that group appeared capable of keeping Steinig and the DND on-task while preventing bureaucratic squabbling at the UN from derailing progress. At the CND, Sharman and Anslinger controlled the agenda, and the many states that had often blocked far-reaching measures could offer little resistance. Control advocates had also minimized the potential for international agencies and others to interfere with their supply-control strategy. Operating from a secure base, they launched a multi-pronged offensive to recapture lost ground and scale new heights.

The postwar offensive, phase one: securing the perimeter

The first phase of control advocates' postwar offensive included two goals. They concentrated on resurrecting control mechanisms in war-torn territories, the former Axis states requiring special attention. Additionally, control advocates moved quickly to impose restrictions on a new hybrid category of drugs that offered great promise but also threatened to destabilize the regime.

Reestablishing national controls[16]

Control advocates placed first priority on resuscitating national controls in liberated and occupied territories. PCOB, DSB, and CND personnel, and American and British narcotics agents crisscrossed Europe and Asia to explain reporting procedures, search for excess stocks, uncover trafficking rings, and lobby officials for increased support. By the late 1940s, most countries had reconstituted effective regulatory systems. Regime advocates kept Europe and Japan from again becoming cockpits of the world's illicit trade.

Harry Anslinger's men played the most prominent part, sometimes clashing with the State Department. Anslinger's proclivity for openly confronting governments caused consternation. State Department officials frequently softened condemnatory statements Anslinger wished to make at CND meetings, much to the Commissioner's irritation. Anslinger selectively disregarded such strictures. Moreover, FBN agents operating overseas often pursued investigations, sometimes engaging in negotiations with enforcement authorities, without the knowledge of American diplomatic officials. Never having notified US Embassy personnel of their presence or assignment, the Commissioner's operatives might appear at the doorstep demanding money to pay an informer or access to communications facilities. Anslinger's support inside and outside Washington made him untouchable; State Department officials could only attempt to keep the FBN's "operations outside normal channels" from causing major diplomatic problems.[17]

As in all aspects of East–West relations, Germany was a site of particular friction. The British, Americans, and French established safeguards, and later created a centralized drug control service as a part of their multi-zonal governmental arrangements. The USSR, however, would not coordinate administration, and refused to exchange information about the licit trade or illicit traffic. Lack of information about interzonal transactions and incomplete submission of statistics concerned PCOB and DSB officials. Yet they could do little beyond register mild protests; too strong a rebuke might jeopardize the existing incomplete Soviet cooperation. East Germany eventually submitted statistics independently, but their veracity could not be confirmed. As before the war, the control organs could only push so far without jeopardizing their mission.[18]

Stringent control advocates also succeeded in re-establishing basic controls in Japan, although their more ambitious schemes failed. Tokyo's record of deliberate subterfuge warranted special attention. Sharman, Moorhead, and Anslinger wished to inject restrictions on Japanese drug trading into the peace treaty. At various times they proposed banning Japanese narcotics exports, limiting imports, and prohibiting domestic manufacture. They even suggested supervision of Japan's domestic stocks by an internationally controlled agency, perhaps an entity created under UN auspices.

Economic considerations, however, overshadowed all such plans. Japan's penury required that it not expend funds on imported medicines that could be manufactured domestically. Similarly, occupation officials did not want to hinder Japan's capacity to earn foreign exchange through the export of narcotics. British officials voiced concerns about the United Nations becoming a kind of wholesaler in narcotics. Consequently, control advocates settled for treaty language that imposed "the most stringent control measures." They scrutinized Japanese trade carefully in succeeding years. In time it became apparent that Tokyo had indeed turned over a new leaf. Japan played by the rules, casting its lot with other manufacturing countries.[19]

Synthetic narcotics [20]

Control advocates' most successful postwar intervention concerned synthetic narcotics. Responding to incentives created in part by implementation of the control regime and wartime shortages, several pharmaceutical firms successfully developed narcotic analgesics without recourse to opium. Demerol and methadon, two coal-tar-based morphine substitutes produced by German firms during the war, figured among the most successful creations.

Control advocates recognized the new synthetics' potential to ruin the regime. The extant treaties made no provision for statistical reporting of drugs not manufactured from opium or coca base. If an unchecked trade in synthetics developed, conditions reminiscent of the early 1920s might result. Indeed, as soon as the FBN released the German formulas, numerous American companies applied for manufacturing licenses. Even Canadian firms, long barred from domestic manufacture of narcotics, pestered Ottawa for a change in policy.

On the other hand, the new drugs provided an opportunity to escape the excess-production dilemma. A regulated trade in synthetic substances, if economically competitive, would eliminate the need to tolerate opium growing. Producing states would no longer have any excuse to allow agricultural production, and control advocates assumed illicit use would dry up as a result. Western pharmaceutical firms did not block the implementation of restrictions on the new substances, in part, because they hoped to dominate the nascent but potentially lucrative market.

The CND initiated measures to control synthetic narcotics at its first meeting. The secretariat determined that the 1925 and 1931 treaties could not be amended without causing additional complications. The CND then drafted a separate agreement that required states to submit the new substances to the same estimates-of-need and statistical reporting provisions that applied to opium-based narcotics. The WHO Expert Committee would determine the addiction liability of new substances. The DSB and PCOB could then oversee the synthetic narcotic trade in the established manner.

The 1948 Synthetic Narcotics Protocol quickly gained widespread acceptance, coming into force only a year later. By moving quickly, control advocates headed off potential disaster, enhanced their position vis-à-vis traditional producing states, and strengthened their domestic pharmaceutical industries.

Yet the advent of synthetic narcotics did not drive opium from the field. Studies by the DND staff indicated that, although synthetic narcotics might eventually replace morphine, the prospects for concocting a codeine substitute appeared poor. Since the majority of licit opium was utilized for manufacturing codeine, opium-producing states would retain their position for the foreseeable future.

In the immediate postwar years, control advocates believed they had secured the rear and flanks of their position. They expected no unpleasant surprises from liberated Europe after the reimposition of regulatory mechanisms there. Even in Germany, where Cold War tensions impinged upon the regime most directly, it appeared control officials could keep the situation in hand. Although unable to achieve their most ambitious schemes in Japan, control advocates greatly diminished the likelihood of problems emanating from that previously troublesome quarter. By negotiating the 1948 Synthetic Narcotics Protocol in a prompt fashion, control advocates plugged a breach in their defenses while simultaneously strengthening their position both behind and in front of the lines. Thus fortified, they initiated a frontal assault on the bastions of supply. The clash centered on the producing countries of Latin America and Asia.

The postwar offensive, phase two: the big push

Regime advocates embarked on a radical supply-control offensive, focusing on the traditional targets: opium, coca, and, to a lesser extent, marijuana. Most illicit production still occurred in underdeveloped countries, and in any case the policy adopted by the newly active Soviet Union precluded any investigation of conditions in North Asia or Eastern Europe. At the same time, decolonization rendered many former colonies independent of European metropolitan centers. Therefore, Anslinger, Sharman, and their allies could not simply apply pressure on European capitals. They engaged instead in herculean efforts to bring recalcitrant third world states to heel. Although achieving some notable successes, practical difficulties and political considerations thwarted their attempts to impose control "at the source."

The western hemisphere: moderate success[21]

In the Americas, control advocates held the line but made little progress. Some states considered commencing licit opium production to redress trade imbalances and postwar shortages of medicine. Anslinger squelched those proposals through a combination of bullying and promises to supply medical requirements at reasonable cost. Desperate for foreign exchange and unwilling to interpret treaty provisions as an *obligation* to restrict trade, the British supported such compromise measures. Where wartime conditions had fostered illicit opium cultivation, a combination of private and public pressure produced impermanent success. The international control organs and the FBN rebuffed Latin American suggestions that the drug problem might be a domestic, demand-related phenomenon, susceptible to educational initiatives. At the same time, fear of political instability that might bring leftists to power limited Anslinger and Sharman's ability to coerce governments. Despite some cosmetic eradication programs, illicit production, especially in nearby Mexico, remained a nagging concern for control officials. Latin American governments more regularly reported statistics and took some halting steps toward imposing substantive domestic controls, but the reforms appeared largely superficial.

Nothing new on the eastern front

Anslinger employed multifaceted pressure tactics on Turkey. Ankara utilized a state-controlled agency to purchase all domestic production, which in turn marketed the opium to foreign buyers. In theory, no surplus remained to feed the illicit market. Yet recurrent seizures of Turkish opium caused concern among American officials. Anslinger dispatched FBN agents to gather information and induce Turkish authorities to make arrests. A series of high-profile seizures in 1948 caused friction because Turkish authorities believed American agents took a disproportionate share of the credit. Ankara banned further incursions by FBN operatives. At Anslinger's behest, the State Department reluctantly requested Ankara to reconsider, but Turkish authorities held firm.

Undaunted, Anslinger engaged in undercover initiatives during the early 1950s. He cajoled the Consular Service into gathering information on Turkish production, but most reports indicated that leakages were not significant. Anslinger nevertheless attempted to bluff Ankara by threatening to expose infractions in the CND. Because his agents had indicated that the local police might be corrupt, Anslinger circumvented officials in Ankara and Washington by working directly with Turkish military authorities. Although such tactics achieved some short-term successes and provided additional leverage in International Opium Monopoly negotiations (see pp. 172–82), Turkey remained a potential trouble spot in ensuing decades. Moreover, as State Department officials slowly grasped the extent of clandestine FBN activities around the globe, they began to realize that Anslinger's propensity for "independent action" portended dangerous consequences.[22]

The Indian government stood up to American pressure. Non-medical opium use persisted in India, and Anslinger and Sharman complained that opium bought legally continued to leak into the illicit traffic. In 1946 Elizabeth Wright inspired Congressional legislation proposing sanctions similar to those threatened against Turkey in 1930. The imports of any state that did not curtail non-medical usage would suffer special attentions from Customs officials. Indian officials threatened to retaliate. The State Department feared a trade war, and worried especially that essential raw material imports might be jeopardized. Commissioner Anslinger, aware that he might again require Indian opium in an emergency, defused the situation. He shunted the issue to the CND, thereby insulating it from Wright and an unpredictable Congress. The matter died amidst the increasingly audacious actions perpetrated by India's neighbors along Asia's southern tier.[23]

Reports from Southeast Asia depicted an exceptionally dismal situation. Burma, both before and after independence in 1947, exerted little control over opium-growing areas. Agricultural experts reported that redressing the situation would require massive investments in infra-structure, uprooting entrenched social habits, improvements in medical services, and an extensive program of crop substitution and agricultural education – in short, a practical impossibility. In Thailand, govern-mental corruption figured prominently in reports detailing a burgeon-ing opium trade. The nascent Indonesian Republic utilized opium stocks captured from the Japanese to finance resistance to the Dutch. Indonesian officials at the highest levels connived in the trade because it earned crucial foreign exchange that kept the government alive during its most difficult years. Concerning French Indochina, the State Department's Southeast Asia desk conceded that reports read "like Radio Moscow at its worst." The French government monopoly, ostensibly selling opium to effect a "cure" of existing addicts, in fact pro-vided one-third of the Indochinese budget in 1947. Wartime shortages of licit opium imports had spurred local production. In addition to the colonial government, French military and intelligence forces became

> Charles VAILLE (1911–). France. Fought with the Resistance. Pharmacist and civil servant, rose to position of Inspector General of Health. Represented Paris at the CND, 1950–59. DSB member 1958–62. Charming, yet ruthless in his pursuit of national and/or personal advantage. Almost singlehandedly sired the 1953 Opium Protocol. Singleminded in his concentration on narcotic substances and supply control.

involved in trafficking to supplement their coffers. Commissioner Anslinger wanted to expose the situation at the CND, but State Department higher-ups overruled him; the emerging Cold War precluded attacks on allies. Anslinger instead made private representations that resulted in the appointment of Charles Vaille to head French drug-control efforts. In ensuing years the wily Vaille exerted a profound influence on drug diplomacy.[24]

Paradoxically, events in China illustrated the best and worst possible outcomes. Chiang's dependence on opium revenues not only fatally weakened the Nationalist government, but continued after the communist victory in 1949. As KMT forces retreated to China's southern border area, they financed continued anti-PRC operations by participating in the region's opium traffic. On the other hand, Mao's victorious government banned all traffic in opium and made the decree stick by applying increasingly draconian suppression measures. The campaign drastically curtailed opium abuse nationwide.[25]

Attempts to impose control in far-flung regions ran up against unalterable political, economic, social, and cultural realities. Despite considerable effort, control advocates' gains proved disappointing. The Iranian front, however, proved most bedeviling of all, prompting further recourse to international treatymaking.

The Iranian conundrum[26]

A combination of geostrategic factors, western medical requirements, and continued Iranian intransigence provided the final blow to the initial postwar drug control offensive. Fears that Teheran would return to its prewar behavior proved well founded. In 1945–46 Elizabeth Wright agitated for a public campaign to pressure the Iranian government, and hounded State Department officials in hopes of securing a special investigative mission for herself. By 1947–48 reports indicated that Iran produced as much as 4 million pounds of opium annually (global "legitimate" needs were around 750,000 pounds at that time). In addition to exports, wartime dislocations had caused a surge in domestic Iranian addiction. In response, Anslinger banned American imports of Iranian opium in 1948. Even the British CND representative, usually reserved in his judgments, noted the "astonishing effrontery" with which Teheran's CND delegation dispensed "barefaced lies" concerning Iran's conduct. The PCOB, with characteristic understatement, referred to repeated deficiencies in Iranian statistical reports as "disquieting."[27]

Yet larger strategic and economic considerations tempered attempts to cajole Iran. The American ambassador in Teheran vetoed Wright's proposed mission, fearing her intervention might further destabilize an already shaky parliamentary system. As had observers in other producing countries, the Embassy in Teheran questioned the feasibility of, and the costs associated with, the magnitude of changes necessary to effect a significant decrease in opium cultivation.

By late 1948 increasing East–West tensions further complicated the picture. Not wishing to drive Iran into the Soviet camp, and mindful of the country's oil reserves, the British Foreign Office and the US State Department vetoed the strong condemnations that control advocates proposed to make in the CND. Iranian officials hinted that if their government fell they could be replaced by a pro-Soviet administration. The new regime, in order to cement a trade pact, might accept a recent offer from Moscow to buy two years' worth of Iranian opium production. Apparently, the Soviet Union also appreciated the value of preclusive buying.

In 1949 Cold War tensions caused Commissioner Anslinger to begin rebuilding the strategic drug stockpile liquidated after the war. In the wake of the Berlin Crisis and the detonation of a Soviet atomic bomb, it appeared prudent to prepare for casualty rates, especially civilian, much higher than any experienced previously. Anslinger required a very large strategic reserve. British and French officials came to similar conclusions and instituted their own stockpiling programs.

Owing to fluctuations in supply, prices, and the American procurement budget, Anslinger knew he could not meet the country's dramatically increased requirements without recourse to Iranian opium. Making a virtue out of necessity, he changed tactics; perhaps Teheran would reduce excess production if sizable licit purchases were in the offing.

Once the Commissioner indicated an interest in buying Iranian opium, factions within the Iranian government emerged, each peddling its own cache. American officials and pharmaceutical companies supported various contenders, leading to chaotic cross-negotiations. Such horse-trading only increased Anslinger's loathing for Iranian officials.[28]

Yet the outbreak of war in Korea in 1950, in conjunction with a poor harvest in Turkey, made it imperative to augment American stocks with Iranian opium. At the same time, it appeared that negotiations concerning an International Opium Monopoly (see pp. 172–82) might succeed. Commissioner Anslinger did not want to tip off the Iranians concerning the country's requirements, fearing exorbitant prices. He also wished to conceal the size of American needs from the Russians.

Faced with such a dilemma, Anslinger launched a campaign to talk down the price of opium. During 1950–51 he made numerous pronouncements hinting that the United States might buy large quantities in exchange for cooperation in negotiations concerning an international opium limitation agreement. The Commissioner also trotted out an old war horse: legislation instigating customs inspections of imports from recalcitrant nations. Anslinger announced as well that cost-competitive breakthroughs in the manufacture of synthetic narcotics might soon become a reality. Yet his efforts proved ineffective, producers having heard it all before.[29]

After an attempt to trade wheat for opium fouled over concerns that it might set off a destructive commodity price war, Anslinger resorted to purchasing large lots through US pharmaceutical firms. Unable to wait for the conclusion of international opium limitation negotiations and unwilling to make direct purchases publicly, the Commissioner's strategy enabled him to obscure the opium's ultimate destination. American manufacturers, however, soon began to speculate in "opium futures." They offered to buy large quantities at a low price in hopes of reselling at a profit later on. During 1950–52 Anslinger made several multi-million-dollar purchases through such intermediaries. Both the US Embassy in Teheran and the Iranian Embassy in Washington became embroiled in the negotiations. Increasingly upset at the specter of diplomatic missions engaged in commercial transactions, especially of such a sensitive item, the State Department forbad the practice in mid-1952. From then on Commissioner Anslinger met his needs through commercial channels or FBN operatives acting as purchasing agents.

As a final recourse the Commissioner once again made quiet preparations for growing poppies on American soil. During the 1950s the federal government acquired over 50,000 pounds of poppy seeds, storing them in secure sites around the country. To Anslinger's relief, it never proved necessary to commence cultivation.[30]

The clandestine Iranian–American maneuverings of the early 1950s illustrated the dilemmas Anslinger and other policy-makers faced. On the one hand, as a part of the International Opium Monopoly and 1953 Opium Protocol negotiations (see pp. 172–82), the US government publicly advocated low prices as a means to achieve production limitation. Yet, in order to protect a vital American interest (supply of medicines in wartime), the Commissioner quietly bought up large Iranian opium stores. His actions risked supporting higher prices for licit opium, thus destroying the ongoing limitation negotiations. Anslinger's purchases also achieved another important goal; buying excess opium removed it from the illicit traffic. At the same time, however, the American buying campaign might stimulate more agricultural production.

It is difficult to assess whether the secret American purchasing program increased Teheran's willingness to strike a production limitation deal or stiffened its resistance. In either case, American actions sent a signal to producing states: goals other than the much-touted "control at the source" competed for attention in Washington and other western capitals. If they acted skillfully and took advantage of fortuitous circumstances, producers were not doomed to ever-increasing encroachment upon their prerogatives.

Attempt to regroup

By the end of 1948, although achieving many of its objectives, the initial postwar anti-drug campaign had ground to a halt. Control advocates engineered a smooth transition to UN authority, regulation of synthetic narcotics, and reconstruction of national control agencies. Moreover, despite prolonged death throes, Far Eastern opium monopolies were disappearing. Control authorities also prevented significant expansion of illicit agricultural production in the western hemisphere. Finally, the world's opium vortex, China, dealt with the issue on its own terms. Control advocates could not take credit for that achievement, but had reason to feel cautious optimism concerning China's self-cleansing.

Yet, despite those successes, opium and coca production continued far in excess of world legitimate need, and political-economic considerations stymied control officials' attempts to make headway. In their quest to eliminate the "drug scourge," control advocates had to deal with not only traditional producing and manufacturing countries, but also a new cohort of post-colonial states, all within the context of a developing Cold War.

Moreover, control advocates encountered additional obstacles of their own making. Administration of the international regime had become increasingly unwieldy. With the addition of the 1948 Synthetic Protocol, eight major multilateral agreements existed.[31] Some had achieved wide acceptance, while others languished. Since the provisions of the various treaties differed, a complex web of obligations and loopholes existed between states. Officials charged with implementing drug control yearned for rationalization.

To overcome the deadlock, Harry Anslinger and his allies modified their grand design. They planned to create a new treaty incorporating the provisions of all previous agreements into one document. Dubbed the "Unified Convention" or "Single Convention," Anslinger and his allies hoped the new treaty would serve a dual purpose. Consolidating existing agreements would create a truly universal regime. Additionally, the Commissioner aimed to inject more stringent production control provisions into the Single Convention. With like-minded officials holding key positions (Sharman on the CND and DSB, May on the Board, Steinig at the DND) stringent control advocates could overcome opposition to their designs. They realized opponents would utilize delaying tactics to lengthen the process, but they believed that a careful advance could not be thwarted.[32]

Commissioner Anslinger guided the proposed "Single Convention" through the initial bureaucratic shoals. In 1948–49, ECOSOC approved a CND recommendation to negotiate a new consolidated treaty.[33] The secretariat took responsibility for creating an initial draft for governments' consideration. Everything seemed to be going according to Anslinger's plans. By 1950 or 1951, he hoped, the CND would possess a variety of carrots and sticks with which to goad recalcitrant states into acceptable behavior. The Single Convention would serve as the tool to formalize his achievement.

Paradise lost

At the same 1948 CND meeting where Anslinger launched the Single Convention on its journey, the Chinese representative suggested, as an immediate measure, negotiating an interim agreement limiting opium production. In need of Washington's support for its faltering effort against the Communists, Nanking hoped to placate American public opinion. In the fleeting moments of the 1948 CND session a recommendation endorsing a feasibility study passed by one vote (over the objections of the British, Canadians, and Americans, who wished to concentrate on the longer-term project). Like many CND recommendations, it seemed likely to languish in the wake of more important initiatives, especially the new Holy Grail – the Single Convention.

Yet this seemingly innocuous recommendation led to one of the most extraordinary episodes in the history of international drug control. DND director Steinig perceived, in the call for an interim opium limitation agreement, the opportunity to propel himself onto the world stage. He launched a campaign to create not merely an interim agreement, but an "International Opium Monopoly."

The notion that an international agency could act as the world's opium wholesaler appeared deceptively attractive. Anslinger himself had proposed a variant of the idea for the Japanese peace treaty. In theory, a monopoly would provide producer states a guaranteed market at an acceptable price, supposedly eliminating the incentive for illicit trafficking. Manufacturing states would have access to adequate supplies at reasonable cost. Consuming states could continue to acquire medicaments from the manufacturer of their choice, ensuring no prejudice to free market principles. Steinig's version of the Monopoly envisioned an independent "Agency." The Agency would set prices, buy from producing states, and sell to manufacturers, thereby eliminating excess production. Steinig envisioned himself as Director of the Agency. If successful, Steinig could engineer an impressive coup: he would create an independent base of power, while at the same time obviating the need for Anslinger's cherished Single Convention. Steinig would demonstrate that he, rather than the Commissioner (the self-proclaimed "world's expert"), possessed the acumen necessary to resolve the drug puzzle.

Steinig's dream, however, took on even more grandiose proportions. He hoped to parlay his success at brokering the International Opium Monopoly into an opportunity to do the same for nuclear material. In the post-Hiroshima world, discussions about the control of atomic energy featured regularly in the press, academic exchange, and at the United Nations. Harkening back to interwar arms-control negotiations, Steinig recognized the similarities between the drug and atomic questions.[34] In September 1949, just as Steinig's campaign entered high gear, the Soviet Union exploded an atomic bomb. The need to control fissionable material appeared more imperative than ever. Steinig believed himself in the right place, at the right time, with the right answer.

Yet Steinig's gambit failed, resulting in disastrous consequences for the international drug regime. With megalomaniacal determination, he pursued his goal until he destroyed his career. Many of his disciples within the DND suffered a similar fate, damaging the reputation and proficiency of the secretariat for years. Steinig's actions inadvertently led to a fatal weakening of Colonel Sharman's domestic position and caused Commissioner Anslinger anxious moments as well. Charles Vaille filled the ensuing power vacuum with counterproductive maneuvering. Instead of an international monopoly, an abortive new treaty emerged from the wreckage. Almost singlehandedly, Leon Steinig set back the control agenda by a decade.

Steinig ascendant

During most of 1949, as Steinig attempted to arrange an agreement among producing states, few took the scheme seriously. Control officials in industrialized countries believed it unlikely that producers would accept the quotas necessary to make a monopoly work. The Iranians would surely scuttle any potential deal by demanding too large a piece of the licit pie. Then, in September (the same month that the Soviets successfully tested a nuclear device), the Nationalist government in China collapsed. Although Communist officials cracked down on opium abuse at home, they also spied an opportunity to acquire some much-needed foreign exchange. Beijing astounded everyone by offering to sell one million pounds of opium on the open market. Chinese officials claimed (probably correctly) that they had seized the opium from retreating Nationalist forces, and made no pronouncements about any offerings in the future. Commissioner Anslinger forbad opium imports from the PRC. In addition to his concern about flooding the market with China's massive productive capabilities, he did not wish to make any move that might suggest support for the Communists. Other manufacturing states followed suit, rejecting China's bid to enter the licit market.[35]

The prospect that China might actually become a competitor, the fear that American aid might be cut if they did not cooperate, and the promise of massive (if clandestine) buying by the United States provided powerful incentive for the "Big Four" opium exporters (Turkey, Iran, India, and Yugoslavia) to negotiate. To everyone's surprise, two weeks of bargaining in late 1949 produced an agreement. Each party would take a percentage of the licit trade, the Turks and Iranians receiving the lion's share. Steinig received high marks for his negotiating acumen, and for the first time it appeared that the International Opium Monopoly might become a reality.[36]

In early 1950 Steinig pursued his vision with vigor. In order to operate the International Monopoly, the supervisory Agency would have to purchase opium from producing states and warehouse it until sale. Such an outlay of funds in advance of sales would require consider-able capital. Steinig approached the International Bank for Recon-struction and Development (IBRD) about securing a loan, and received a guarded but positive initial response. Officials in the US State Department and the Canadian Department of External Affairs also began to take notice of the scheme. With the advent of the Russian bomb, any opportunity to put the atomic genie back in the bottle appeared worth pursuing.[37]

Most national drug control officials, however, took a dim view of the International Monopoly's prospects. The obstacles blocking prohi-bition of excess production remained formidable. Additionally, the issue had become a personal matter with Sharman and Anslinger. For over a year, Steinig expended his energies primarily on the Inter-national Opium Monopoly. He spent little time preparing a first draft of the Single Convention and even postponed the 1950 CND meeting on his own authority in hopes of presenting a completed Monopoly plan to the Commission. The secretariat appeared in danger of becoming master rather than servant. Unable to overrule their respec-tive foreign services, Anslinger and Sharman bided their time.

By the summer of 1950 Steinig's grand scheme began to unravel. The IBRD determined that they could not lend the full $9 million the Agency required for initial opium monopoly purchases without govern-ment loan guarantees. Paris, London, Washington, Ottawa, the Hague, and Brussels all declined. In the last week of June the Korean war erupted and Afghanistan announced its desire to enter the export trade again. Multinational pharmaceutical firms, fearing a restrictive agreement would result in higher prices, urged governments to reject the International Opium Monopoly. Anslinger and Sharman took up the refrain, claiming that only low prices could drive out illicit pro-duction. They reasoned that farmers would turn to alternate crops if a better return appeared in the offing. European officials also feared higher prices, since their national health services would have to absorb the increased costs.

Events came to a head in August 1950 when representatives of the principal manufacturing states met with their producer counterparts.[38] Despite Steinig's efforts to broker a deal, the parties could not agree on several key issues. Manufacturers wanted to pay considerably less than producers were willing to accept. Manufacturing states desired a strong Agency, possessing inspection powers to ensure that over-production did not occur. Producing states would not countenance such a violation of their sovereignty. The PCOB, which under certain versions of the scheme took on enforcement responsibilities, expressed doubt about the plan's feasibility. Nor could the parties agree about how to resolve currency payments. Finally, since drugs manufactured from poppy straw and synthetic processes did not come under the agreement, the scheme appeared of limited value to manufacturers (although its potential to reduce excess agricultural production still appealed to control advocates). Undaunted, Steinig continued long after it became evident he had failed. He upbraided anyone who obstructed his efforts, thereby alienating most CND representatives.[39]

Counterattack

At the Sixth CND session (April–May 1951), the British, Dutch, Canadians, Americans, and French combined to deal Steinig a mortal blow. The Commission terminated discussion of the International Opium Monopoly. French representative Charles Vaille then introduced an alternate "interim agreement." He proposed controls over opium production similar to those placed on manufacturing in the 1931 treaty. The idea was at least as unworkable as Steinig's scheme, but it served one basic purpose: to provide the opposition with an alternative. The CND approved Vaille's plan as a basis for drawing up a treaty to limit opium production. Under normal circumstances, the CND then would direct its secretariat to produce a draft for consideration at a later meeting. The Commission's members, however, no longer trusted the Steinig-controlled Division of Narcotic Drugs. They called instead for a plenipotentiary conference to draft articles and negotiate a treaty. Over Steinig's objections ECOSOC approved a plenipotentiary meeting to enact the Vaille Plan, scheduling the convention for May 1953.[40]

Incensed by Steinig's intransigence, CND representatives decided to end his reign on the Poppy Throne. Anslinger and Sharman even considered Bertil Renborg, so desperate were they to be rid of Steinig.[41] The wheels of UN administration, never to be rushed, finally produced the desired result in May 1952. Steinig was replaced by Gilbert Yates, late Secretary of the Economic and Social Council, and one of the UN's most experienced administrators.[42]

Although it appeared unlikely that the 1953 plenipotentiary convention would produce any substantive improvement, CND members could not afford quietly to bury the proposal. As late as February 1953 Steinig's supporters were still attempting to cancel the upcoming plenipotentiary negotiations. Failing that, they hoped that the meeting called to enact the Vaille Plan would self-destruct, thereby leaving the International Opium Monopoly as the only remaining contender.[43]

Gilbert E. YATES (1907–72). Great Britain. Took first-class honors in history at Edinburgh. Entered the Health Ministry in 1930, and served in the Near East during the war. Named ECOSOC Secretary in 1946 and served as DND Director, 1952–62. Retired to Directorship of the Association of the British Pharmaceutical Industry, but soon regretted leaving the international civil service. Returned to the UN as the Secretary-General's special representative to Malta a few years later and acted as a consultant to UNDCP, 1971–72. Described by his wife as an analytical, reflective bon vivant who enjoyed travelling, wine, and food. Indicative of his general approach to management and bureaucratic diplomacy, Yates hired pretty women for his secretarial staff in order to make his messages as appealing as possible.

Fallout

The brouhaha surrounding the International Opium Monopoly created consternation in several capitals. Two key national control officials came under increased scrutiny, resulting in an important power shift within the international drug regime. For Harry Anslinger and Clem Sharman, things would never be the same.

In the years after the war, Colonel Sharman acted as a more or less independent agent. Sharman had long ago become estranged from his top assistants in the Narcotic Division (part of the National Health and Welfare Department – DNHW). Upon his retirement as head of the domestic service in 1946, his superiors asked him to continue handling the international work until a replacement could be trained. Seven years later the DNHW had not yet designated a successor and Sharman seemed in no hurry to give up his position. Communication with his old office receded to virtually nil. Sharman operated instead as an ad-hoc appendage of the External Affairs Department, which openly professed its inadequate understanding of the subject. External Affairs exercised little control over the Colonel, trusting in his internationally recognized expertise.

Sharman's behavior during the International Opium Monopoly feud caused concern in Ottawa. During 1950–51 Sharman engaged in intemperate attacks on the UN secretariat, complained loudly that the Monopoly negotiations ignored the interests of consuming states, and nearly refused to attend the 1951 CND meeting in protest. External

Affairs expressed concern that a clash with the United States or Great Britain might be imminent, and that Canada appeared to be impeding progress on an issue in which the country had traditionally taken a leading role. The DNHW feared that its interests were beholden to a man who had lost touch with the domestic enforcement apparatus. Yet no one in Ottawa possessed the technical expertise, to say nothing of the prestige, necessary to replace Sharman. Throughout 1951–52, officials in Ottawa slowly worked up the courage to challenge Sharman.

Matters came to a head in 1953. The DNHW informed Sharman that Kenneth Hossick, Sharman's successor as head of the Narcotic Department, would attend the 1953 CND session as "advisor" and heir apparent. The two men, who had worked together for 18 years, despised each other. Hossick actually cared little about international negotiations, but relished the opportunity to knock Sharman from the pedestal. The two fought incessantly at the 1953 CND session, resulting in Hossick's refusal to serve on delegations headed by Sharman. The plenipotentiary gathering called to render the Vaille Plan into a treaty convened a month after the 1953 CND session adjourned. To make sure that no embarrassments occurred, External Affairs appointed a member of Canada's permanent mission to the UN as titular head of delegation. Sharman refused to serve as deputy under such circumstances, and attended the 1953 conference as a representative of the DSB. The Canadian delegation, populated by neophytes, contributed little to the conference.

By mid-1953 Ottawa ended Sharman's reign as an independent prince. His power to direct events outside the limited confines of the DSB had been broken. The other players waited to see who would replace one of the regime's longest-serving officials.[44]

Anslinger worried throughout 1950–53 that the controversy surrounding Steinig's monopoly, although hidden from the public, might nevertheless unhorse him.[45] He had little to show for his postwar diplomatic efforts beyond the 1948 Synthetic Narcotics Protocol. The Anslinger-inspired Single Convention remained, at best, years from completion. The Commissioner had also taken a prominent part in torpedoing the International Opium Monopoly, to the chagrin of many in the State Department. Efforts to bring producer states to heel remained only partially successful, and illicit trafficking appeared on the increase. FBN agents abroad periodically created international incidents while pursuing drug traffickers, to the perturbation of the State Department. To cement his position with the new Republican administration and repair relations with the State Department, Anslinger required demonstrable progress in his long-standing attempts to institute "control at the source." The Vaille Plan presented the only opportunity for scoring a quick victory.[46]

Sound and fury: the 1953 opium protocol[47]

As the time approached for rendering it into an international agreement, many became painfully aware of deficiencies inherent in the Vaille Plan. The negotiations would turn on whether producing states agreed to onerous provisions: limiting agricultural production, reporting accurately their crop plantings and yields, buying and storing securely all opium, and allowing the PCOB authority to conduct inspections and impose embargoes. In exchange, a small number of producing states would compete (without benefit or hindrance of quota) for the worldwide licit opium export trade. Realizing that many of those same issues had sunk the International Opium Monopoly negotiations, officials in London practically gave up on the proceedings. Even if producing states agreed to substantive restrictions without loopholes (an unlikely event) their ability and/or willingness to enforce them remained doubtful. Great Britain would attend, but viewed the exercise primarily as one of damage control. The PCOB objected as well, noting that the Board did not possess the capabilities to become an investigatory and/or enforcement agency. The Canadian delegation, absent Colonel Sharman for the first time in twenty-five years, wished to ensure licit supplies at reasonable prices, even at the expense of a meaningful agreement.

The French and American delegations, however, were determined to produce an accord. For Charles Vaille, the matter entailed personal prestige; he publicly maintained the validity of his plan, although admitting privately that many of the provisions necessary to enact them were impractical. Anslinger, as well, understood the Vaille Plan was unlikely to reduce illicit production. The Commissioner needed an agreement for domestic purposes, however, and supported any provision that appeared to get tough with producers, whether feasible or not.

Other players also wished to see an agreement, regardless of its substantive provisions. The United Nations secretariat, in particular the DND's new Director, Gilbert Yates, desired a successful conclusion. Shepherding a treaty through would make a start at repairing the secretariat's shattered reputation and morale. The Swedish delegation took an unexpectedly active role owing to Stockholm's decision to appoint Renborg as its representative. Still hoping to find a place in the post-Steinig era, Renborg ingratiated himself to Anslinger and Vaille. He supported any provision that conformed to the hard-line order of the day.

Producing states approached the negotiations cautiously. On the one hand, the opportunity to corner the licit market offered great appeal. Conversely, provisions that imposed on national sovereignty had to be contested. Additionally, governments ran the risk of jeopardizing both foreign aid and large western defense-related purchases of opium. Finally, competition from narcotics derived from poppy-straw or synthetic processes threatened to undermine their position. In 1952, for example, Harry Anslinger had announced that a team of American researchers successfully synthesized morphine and codeine. Anslinger routinely produced such revelations when he thought it would improve his negotiating position. In fact, the process proved too expensive for commercial manufacture, a detail the Commissioner admitted only to Vaille and Sharman. Nevertheless, producing states knew that a technological advance might eliminate licit demand for their product. Under such circumstances, it appeared wise to make accommodations and keep prices reasonable.

Iran, usually the most recalcitrant of producer states, occupied a particularly weak position in early 1953. Since coming to power in 1951 the Mossadeq government had attempted to break the monopoly exercised by the Anglo-Iranian Oil Company over the country's oil production. With American backing, major oil companies imposed a boycott on Iranian petroleum exports. By the spring of 1953 Mossadeq desperately needed cash, economic assistance, and American support. As a result, Iranian delegates were more pliable than at any previous plenipotentiary gathering.

The Soviet bloc refused to participate in the proceedings. Comprehending that any agreement with teeth would require parties to allow on-site inspections, they did not wish to set a precedent that might influence arms negotiations or peace talks in Korea. Stalin's death in early 1953 made the USSR's representatives even more cautious than usual.

As the 1953 Opium Protocol negotiations opened, Vaille took center stage. He maneuvered to have himself elected Chair. From that position Vaille directed the proceedings with ruthless efficiency. He ruled legitimate amendments out of order, forced votes on problematic and confusing provisions before delegations could examine them, and ran roughshod over opponents. The drafting committee prepared many provisions hastily, as Vaille insisted on maintaining a brisk pace. Although a relative newcomer to international drug negotiations, Vaille apparently understood the likelihood of stalemate if he allowed delegations to dissect the draft article-by-article.

Nevertheless, the conference bogged down at several points. Attempts to define such fundamental concepts as "opium," "stocks," "territory," "imports," and "exports" required considerable attention. After much wrangling, the delegates decided to place poppy straw under control, despite the fact that the principal states utilizing that method for morphine extraction were not present. The British insisted that the USSR and Bulgaria would have to be added to the original list of four exporters (Yugoslavia, Turkey, Iran, and India) if the agreement were to have any chance of success. Canada, wishing to expand the list of exporters as much as possible, supported the British delegation. Adding Bulgaria to the list prompted protests from the Greek delegate, who insisted on including his country as well. The conference agreed to this expansion, but drew the line when Vietnam petitioned for inclusion. Producing states, abetted by consuming states such as Canada, watered down inspection and embargo provisions.[48]

Despite such hindrances, Vaille produced a treaty from scratch in only five weeks. The 1953 Opium Protocol contained the most stringent drug-control provisions yet embodied in international law. The agreement extended to raw opium the reporting provisions placed on manufactured drugs in the 1931 treaty. Aimed primarily at producing states, signatories would submit to the DSB estimates concerning the amount of opium planted, harvested, consumed domestically, exported, and stockpiled. Year-end statistics would be reported to the PCOB. The treaty also gave the Board responsibility for making inquiries into discrepancies, conducting inspections, and imposing embargoes. As with earlier treaties, the Body was empowered to fix estimates and the Board could take investigatory and punitive action even in the case of states not party to the Protocol. In a victory for Anslinger, symbolic of the general trend, the Protocol also stipulated that opium use should be restricted to medical and scientific needs. Although signatories were allowed a fifteen-year grace period before the provision had to be enforced, the treaty nevertheless shattered the "quasi-medical use barrier" for the first time.

In exchange for accepting such burdens, producers received a monopoly on licit sales. Parties to the treaty agreed to buy opium only from the seven states named in the text.[49] Against the wishes of consuming states such as Canada, the Protocol did not allow any additions to the list of approved opium exporters.

Producing states also inserted several loopholes into the treaty. On-site inspections, euphemistically dubbed "local inquiries" by the drafters, could only be carried out with the approval of the target country. Embargoes imposed by the Board could be appealed.

Producing governments were allowed to accumulate very large stocks before triggering investigatory action by the PCOB. Military stores, as usual, did not have to be reported. Production for domestic consumption remained unregulated and a provision for submitting supplementary estimates-of-need allowed some room to maneuver. An escape clause allowed states to disregard the treaty's provisions in an emergency. Most importantly, Article 21 stipulated that three of the seven producing states had to ratify in order to activate the treaty. Originally intended to prevent price gouging by ensuring that importing states were not limited to one or two sources, producers found that Article 21 could be turned to their advantage.

Notwithstanding such lacunae, the 1953 Opium Protocol represented a potentially serious threat to producing states' prerogatives. If they could not finesse the treaty's provisions, a stark choice remained: either commit wholeheartedly to the illicit traffic (a course wrought with problematic consequences) or struggle for market share of a declining licit trade. Coca producers recognized the threat to their interests as well. The precedent set might next be applied to them. Ironically, the dilemma made both the coca and opium powers uncharacteristically enthusiastic participants in the next round of international negotiations. They would modify their traditionally obstructionist tactics by taking on the mantle of revisionism.

Conclusion

The decade after war's end represented a time of great successes for proponents of drug control. Having preserved the regime's foundation, they restored it to functional operation in the second half of the 1940s. Control advocates also made headway on several fronts, particularly in the realm of synthetic narcotics. They remained committed to the more far-reaching prescriptions of the supply-side approach developed a generation earlier: elimination of excess raw material supplies coupled with independent inspections to ensure compliance.

Many of the components control advocates devised to enact their designs, however, failed to operate as the creators expected. The United Nations disappointed those hoping for a more virtuous successor to the League. The CND proved less amenable to obfuscation only so long as control advocates micromanaged the proceedings. Continued bureaucratic infighting impeded cooperation between the DND, PCOB, and DSB secretariats. Moreover, the scandals of the Steinig Directorship exceeded anything perpetrated under the League.

The negotiations surrounding the International Opium Monopoly and the 1953 Opium Protocol left a bad taste in the mouths of governmental representatives and weakened the bureaucratic positions of key players.[50] Steinig's actions also derailed fast-track consideration of the Single Convention. It took years to rekindle interest, and by then a recast constellation of external factors and *dramatis personae* altered the outcome. In the meantime the 1953 Protocol only added to the multiplicity of treaties. The episode highlighted the impact a single person could have on the trajectory of events, especially if able to manipulate an entrenched bureaucracy. Helen Moorhead's death in 1950 left the system without the human grease that lubricated negotiations – for the past quarter-century she had helped participants reconcile their desires to the demands of feasibility. The void presented equally eloquent testimony to the effects wrought by a unique individual's absence.

Control advocates also could not escape the political, economic, social, and cultural milieu in which drug diplomacy operated. The Soviet bear came out of hibernation, but Moscow's increased attentiveness to the drug question created more problems than it solved. The Cold War warped attempts to impose more stringent limitation by creating countervailing pressures favoring increased agricultural production and pharmaceutical manufacture. Fears that drug-control measures could cause economic hardship or political upheaval, which in turn might drive strategically located producer states into the Soviet camp, hindered the efforts of control advocates. Moreover, some western operatives worked at cross-purposes to the regime by becoming involved in drug trafficking to support local anti-communist activities. Latin American coca-producing states and opium-using regions of Asia still registered little appreciation that a problem existed. The logic that required elimination of traditional substances from society and economy seemed impenetrable to cultures in which such drugs were deeply embedded. Producer states also gained a greater appreciation that global geopolitical circumstances could work to their advantage – it was possible not only to stand up to the control apparatus but to manipulate it as well.

Thus, despite the best efforts of control advocates, the conclusion of the initial postwar campaign to implement control "at the source" remained in doubt. The 1953 Opium Protocol included the most stringent provisions yet embodied in an international treaty. It comprised the maximum infringement that producing states would accept. Many consuming and manufacturing countries voiced reservations about the agreement as well. Would governments ratify the new treaty? If so, could they implement its provisions effectively? In short, would the tenets of the supply-control thesis work, if actually put to the test? Whether the 1953 Opium Protocol represented a stepping stone to greater achievements, the culmination of the regime, or a soon-to-recede high-water mark in the annals of international drug control would depend on the next round of drug diplomacy.

7 The long march to the Single Convention – 1953–61[1]

... it might be desirable from a medical or scientific standpoint to [enact new control measures] but politically impossible so to do.[2]

With political and military disturbances taking place in several of the countries of South-east Asia, effective control over poppy cultivation and concerted action against illicit traffickers are not feasible.[3]

In retrospect it is apparent that the 1953 Opium Protocol represented the high tide of the original drug-control impetus. A small company of hard-core advocates had forced through a tough document. Their efforts capped a decades-long campaign to curb excess agricultural production by way of global agreement. Calls to ratify the treaty caused governments, the international control organs, and other interested parties to consider whether control "at the source" was an achievable and desirable goal, especially in light of the complications brought on by geopolitical considerations such as the Cold War and decolonization. Many questioned the feasibility of attempting to impose strict new regulations on nations unable or unwilling to comply.

The prospect of the Opium Protocol entering into force caused participants to reconsider the regime's objectives. For some, limitation of cultivation remained a practical impossibility. Others concluded precisely the opposite. Still wedded to the supply-control paradigm, governments cast about for alternative methods to implement that goal. As drug abuse worsened in some western countries, domestic constituencies arose to challenge predominant assumptions about the nature of the problem. Furthermore, some perceived a new threat in psychotropic substances. States would have to consider whether those drugs should be deemed liable to control as well.

As a result of such factors, the focus of the control regime began to splinter between 1953 and 1961. Governments evinced a new willingness to consider competing visions about the scope and purpose of the system. A protracted battle ensued between shifting coalitions of governments and non-state actors. The struggle culminated in a contest between the 1953 Opium Protocol and the still-unfinished Single Convention. Recognizing that one of those two documents would serve as the new cornerstone of the control regime, all parties strove to promote outcomes favorable to their interests.

The international organs: view from the top

After the turmoil of the early 1950s, the international organs and their secretariats resumed the pursuit of statutory obligation and bureaucratic interest. Personnel changes caused reshuffling in the PCOB and DSB hierarchies, but both bodies continued to exercise their mandates with reserve. Gilbert Yates re-formed the DND secretariat, simultaneously strengthening and weakening that organization in the process. This never-ending internal dynamic sapped the meager residual strength residing within the international organizations, which in turn led to timidity. External factors further exacerbated the feebleness of the control agencies. Economic, political, and social conditions in much of the world precluded dealing effectively with the drug problem, at least by the organs charged with primary responsibility for doing so. By the early 1960s, the Board, Body, and DND suffered from a paucity of ideas, initiative, and influence.

PCOB and DSB: staying the course

By the mid-1950s the PCOB and DSB settled into routine operations. Originally feared by some and welcomed by others as independent expert bodies that would confront recalcitrant states, the Board and Body long ago opted for a strategy of quiet diplomacy. In certain respects the strategy succeeded. The PCOB and DSB provided a valuable service by compiling the statistics that underpinned regulation of the licit trade. They also uncovered trouble spots, although infractions received, at best, mild rebukes. Manufacturing states supervised their pharmaceutical firms so well that, with a few exceptions, illicit trafficking by reputable companies disappeared. PCOB and DSB reports differed little from one year to the next. The CND and ECOSOC did not find much in them worthy of comment.

Yet the unconsidered effects of imposing control structures became increasingly apparent. The illicit trade grew steadily during the 1950s. The very effectiveness of the international regime had driven unauthorized manufacturing underground – where no one could estimate its size or staunch its growth. Such problems lay at the periphery of the PCOB/DSB mandate. The 1925 and 1931 treaties did not indicate clearly the responsibilities of the Board and Body with respect to the illicit traffic. The PCOB might have acted assertively, excoriating governments that tolerated illicit production, manufacture, and traffic, perhaps even threatening sanctions against the principal offenders. Instead, the Board worked unobtrusively with governments in hopes of securing increased cooperation.

Personnel factors contributed to that restraint. Enfeebled by arthritis, DSB President Sharman served out his last term (1953–58) without distinction. The Board's guiding light, Herbert May, turned 80 in 1957. Although still energetic, he could hardly carry on indefinitely. In 1953 Sir Harry Greenfield succeeded May as the Board's President. An old India hand with experience in colonial opium administration, Greenfield was not unsympathetic to the plight of producing states. Greenfield also possessed connections to the (British) pharmaceutical industry. His ties to producers and manufacturers predisposed Greenfield to steer a moderate course. The Board's other emerging leader, international law professor Paul Reuter of France, also opted for caution. His academic background gave Reuter insight into why governments did not wish to give the Board coercive powers. He favored operating within the system, which in the case of the Board meant tortuous behind-the-scenes work to achieve incremental improvements in compliance. PCOB/DSB Secretary Elliott Felkin retired in 1952, to be replaced by his assistant Louis Atzenwiler. A cautious man who had

Sir Harry GREENFIELD (1898–1981). Great Britain. Indian civil servant 1919–47, rose to Chairman of the Central Board of Revenue (a position that required considerable familiarity with opium-related issues). After retirement promoted Chamber of Commerce, international trade, charities, various Royal Societies and educational institutions. Elected to PCOB in 1948, served as PCOB/INCB President 1953–75. An affable aristocrat, but considered a lightweight by many national control officials. Under his Presidency the Board settled into a postwar routine marked by the judicious pursuit of "quiet diplomacy."

Louis ATZENWILER (1903–). Switzerland. Joined the League
staff in the mid-1920s. After a long career in the PCOB secretariat,
served as Secretary of the Board 1952–63. Somewhat gruff, a
plain, honest man. Stalwart in defense of the Board's separate
secretariat.

risen through the ranks, Atzenwiler was not given to grand designs. He
concentrated on improving the quality of statistical submissions and
defending his semi-independent secretariat against encroachment by
the Secretary-General's lieutenants. Criticizing governments too
harshly could engender calls for more supervision of the Board. A hostile
takeover of the PCOB/DSB staff by the DND secretariat might well
result.[4]

Most importantly, both members and staff realized that the Board
and Body stood powerless in the face of governmental impotence or
indifference. Instituting embargoes against producing states would
probably have little effect – cutting off imports of manufactured drugs
would not reduce clandestine exports of raw materials. Although the
1953 Opium Protocol appeared to offer a solution by giving the Board
more enforcement authority, members expressed doubts about the
plan's feasibility.[5] Any serious attempt to infringe on the sovereignty of
one state might reduce support for the regime elsewhere.

Difficulties in carrying out even basic duties reinforced this cautious
attitude. When the Board hinted that receiving statistics from the
People's Republic of China and other Communist states would
greatly aid its work, Anslinger vehemently objected. Support for the
Nationalist government remained strong in the United States, and the
Commissioner had no intention of alienating such a powerful constituency. Unwilling to risk the ire of Anslinger, the Board acquiesced in an
absurd situation by accepting statistics submitted by Taiwan for the
entire country.[6]

With successive Board elections, finding candidates possessing both
the expertise and the willingness to serve proved increasingly difficult.
To remedy that problem, and to increase administrative efficiency, the
notion of creating a "personal union" between the Permanent Central
Opium Board and the Drug Supervisory Body gained popularity. The
plan called for the four Members of the DSB to be chosen from those
currently serving on the eight-person PCOB. DND Director Yates
found the proposal attractive because it might help him gain control
over the PCOB/DSB secretariat.[7]

As a consequence of such complications, the international control organs attempted only incremental reforms. Board/Body members and staff offered suggestions on successive drafts of the Single Convention. The Board and Body also attempted to inject language into the Single Convention that would enhance their authority to deal with the illicit trade. That maneuver, however, brought the two bodies into conflict with Gilbert Yates and the CND, who considered drug trafficking to lie exclusively within their bailiwick.[8] In any case, no one contemplated fundamental changes that would give the international control organs a truly independent power base.

The division on the march

At the United Nations, new DND chief Gilbert Yates acted to strengthen both his own position and that of his agency. In 1953–54 he redoubled the effort originated by Steinig to move the DND away from New York. Anslinger feared, correctly, that Yates hoped to subsume the PCOB/DSB secretariat into the DND, thereby threatening to bring those bodies under the nefarious influence of UN bureaucratic politics. Yates circumvented the CND, Anslinger's stronghold, by shepherding a resolution through ECOSOC. Anslinger protested, marshalled his domestic constituencies, and even appealed to the Secretary-General, but the State Department would not support him. In mid-1955 the DND moved to Geneva, to Commissioner Anslinger's continuing annoyance.[9]

Having escaped outside interference, Yates purged the DND staff.[10] Incompetents and holdovers loyal to Steinig went first. Yates then eliminated Anslinger's moles, depriving the Commissioner of unofficial information sources. By 1958 over half the professional staff had been replaced. As a result, the Division suffered a shortage of experienced personnel just as preparatory work related to the Single Convention reached its peak.

Yates also stepped up the Secretary-General's longstanding campaign to take over the PCOB/DSB secretariat. He took a conciliatory approach, utilizing his considerable personal skills to lobby Board members directly. Yates persuaded the majority that administrative efficiencies could be achieved, without prejudice to the Board's independence, by a DND takeover of the PCOB/DSB secretariat. A few holdouts fought tenaciously to protect the status quo. Board Members Herbert May and Paul Reuter defended the Board's prerogatives, claiming that to subsume the secretariat would endanger the Board's independence. Louis Atzenwiler resisted as well, both because he believed in the principle and because he did not wish to lose his own position. Anslinger and Charles Vaille, in their attempts to garner support among producing states for the 1953 convention (see pp. 202–4), opposed the "single secretariat" as well. Together they stymied Yates's efforts to engineer an internal coup.[11] Yates ultimately turned to the Single Convention, hoping to insert language requiring a single secretariat into the treaty. As had occurred on many previous occasions, this bureaucratic squabble distracted parties from dealing with policy matters.

Plagued by internal friction and the insolubility of the tasks assigned to them, the PCOB, DSB, and DND foundered. By the early 1960s they became hidebound organizations, conservative in approach and espousing limited objectives. No leadership emanated from the international organs, which frustrated stringent control advocates.

The western powers: something old, something new

The later 1950s also witnessed a shift in the power relationships between the principal western states involved in drug diplomacy. Anslinger became increasingly isolated at home and abroad, causing US influence to dissipate. The Canadian government replaced Sharman's zeal for control "at the source" with a policy that reflected Ottawa's traditional interest in cooperation and moderation. Charles Vaille emerged as a powerful force in the international arena, promoting the 1953 Protocol with vigor. A resurgent Great Britain forged a new coalition of manufacturing states that adopted a more clement attitude toward the drug question. By the early 1960s these parties promoted competing visions of how the control regime should be structured.

Anslinger besieged

At home, Anslinger faced increasing challenges. As the 1950s progressed, a gradually rising groundswell of opposition to the FBN's policies and practices emerged. Rumors of corruption within the FBN surfaced again. Despite increasingly draconian penal legislation enacted at the FBN's insistence, drug use appeared to rise. Reliable statistics on the extent of addiction did not exist, primarily because the FBN refused to compile them. Anslinger preferred to manipulate the number of addicts reported according to his immediate need to demonstrate crisis or success. As conditions worsened, especially among inner-city minorities, a growing number of physicians, academics, and public health officials expressed concern. Little more was known about the nature of addiction than in the 1920s. Anslinger's influence over the country's drug research program slanted work toward a quixotic effort to develop non-addicting analgesics. In the realm of treatment, the Commissioner held an equally tight rein. He ridiculed schemes that de-emphasized "civil commitment" (lockup) of addicts. Proposals contemplating ambulatory treatment triggered violent opposition from Anslinger and his dutiful lieutenants. Yet the federal narcotics prisons at Lexington and Fort Worth produced dismal results. Almost all addicts relapsed after release. Criticism from physicians, lawyers, and researchers reached unprecedented proportions by the late 1950s.[12] Legislators repeatedly proffered proposals to reorganize the FBN. Within the executive branch, the State, Justice, and HEW Departments challenged Anslinger's predominance in forging domestic and international policy.[13]

Abroad as well, the Commissioner was losing his ability to direct events. Vaille's emergence as the pre-eminent advocate of radical supply control, British attempts to form a moderate coalition of European manufacturing states, and increased vigor on the part of producing states all shifted the initiative away from Anslinger. Most importantly, difficulties with his closest ally and the UN apparatus left Anslinger isolated as never before.

Sharman's retirement spelled the end of the special relationship between Canada and the United States. After Sharman turned over domestic responsibilities to Kenneth Hossick in 1946, trouble soon erupted. Hossick took a more open-minded approach to such issues as treatment. A series of incidents created a permanent rift between Anslinger and Hossick.[14] The previously copious communications between Washington and Ottawa on drug matters ceased abruptly.

The DND's move to Geneva, which symbolized the Commissioner's lessened influence, galled Anslinger. To regain leverage, Anslinger demonstrated his disapproval by boycotting the 1956 CND meeting. In Anslinger's place, an ad-hoc team of State Department and FBN personnel represented the United States. Hoping to placate Anslinger, the CND voted to meet the following year in New York. Anslinger chaired the 1957 session, but could not prevent the CND from holding its 1958 meeting in Geneva. Anslinger again absented himself, instructing his substitutes to insist on convening the 1959 meeting in New York. Despite American threats of non-cooperation in police matters that further alienated other delegations, the maneuver failed. In a cost-saving move, the UN General Assembly ordered all functional commission meetings to remain in place for the ensuing five years. The CND would meet in Geneva until at least 1963.[15]

Anslinger still refused to attend. Increasingly beleaguered, the Commissioner believed it unwise to leave the country for too long a period of time. Without constant vigilance, some Congressional committee or group of "eggheads" might stir up trouble. Additionally, by 1960 his wife had become terminally ill, and Anslinger naturally wished to stay near her.

In Anslinger's stead, American representation at CND meetings fell to an uncoordinated group of State Department and Treasury personnel. George Morlock retired in 1955, taking with him most of the State Department's institutional memory. Mistrust between delegates and an overriding fear of incurring the Commissioner's wrath caused near-paralysis. Anslinger adjusted the roster each year, attempting to reduce State Department influence, but his maneuvers only further damaged the delegation's performance. Other representatives commented on the lack of American initiative, the British noting that Anslinger appeared to be directing his surrogates by "remote control." Thus, from the mid-1950s through the early 1960s, a period during which the struggle between proponents of the 1953 Opium Protocol and the Single Convention reached its height, Harry Anslinger absented himself from the intricate negotiations that determined the outcome.[16]

Despite victories on several minor issues,[17] a disingenuous campaign against Communist China designed to deflect attention from his agency's deficiencies, and continuing exertions to link FBN activities to American Cold War efforts,[18] from the mid-1950s onward the Commissioner found himself on the defensive. Under assault at home, increasingly isolated from his colleagues on the CND, he lost control of the agenda. As the decade closed Anslinger retreated into a bunker mentality that dissipated the American capacity to influence events.

Collegiality returns to Canada[19]

In Canada, a heightened sensitivity to the drug question accelerated Colonel Sharman's eclipse.[20] In 1954, the federal government placed more power in the hands of department heads. Sharman's performance during the brouhaha surrounding the Opium Monopoly and the 1953 Opium Protocol displeased Deputy Minister of Health G. W. Cameron. In 1955, Cameron permanently replaced Sharman with Hossick. Sharman served on the Drug Supervisory Body until 1958, but his influence waned quickly. Suffering progressive debility as old age set in, by the early 1960s his arthritic hands could barely manage a short letter to his old friend, Harry Anslinger.

Robert E. CURRAN (1903–78). Canada. After a decade as a solicitor in Winnipeg, he served in the Royal Canadian Navy's Judge Advocate General's office during the war. Joined the Department of National Health and Welfare in 1945 as a legal adviser. Rose to Special Assistant to the Deputy Ministers in 1963. Served as principal Canadian figure in international drug negotiations during the later 1950s and 1960s. Curran possessed an impressive eye for the acceptable. More than any other he can claim title as father of the 1961 Single Convention.

With Sharman's decline, the formation of Canadian policy reverted to a more collegial style. The External Affairs Department took a more active role, attaching its own representatives to CND delegations. In addition to Hossick, the DNHW assigned its legal adviser, Robert Curran, to grapple with the intricacies of the Single Convention. As in the United States, Canadians concerned about drug abuse called for a wider variety of approaches to the problem. Addiction scares in the 1950s prompted several investigatory commissions to examine the nation's drug control system.[21] As concern mounted, other Departments became involved in aspects of Canadian drug policy. The Canadians nevertheless utilized a team-oriented approach that emphasized cooperation between agencies.

After regaining control over its international policy, Ottawa adopted positions that bore a typically moderate hue. In keeping with its role as a leading consumer state, Canada de-emphasized draconian measures to reduce agricultural production, especially if that appeared likely to increase prices. Consequently, support for the 1953 Opium Protocol waned, even though Ottawa had been among the first to ratify it. Canadian representatives preferred the Single Convention because that treaty consolidated the extant international agreements. The Single Convention also held the potential to gain widespread acceptance; Ottawa wished to promote international harmony rather than radical schemes.

DNHW officials assumed the leading roles on international matters. Hossick participated steadfastly in the international work, although colleagues did not rate his performance as particularly distinguished. Curran proved the most influential Canadian of the post-Sharman era. He toiled for several years to produce a workable draft of the Single Convention. Curran's methodical dedication contributed substantially to the success of that document.

France: Vaille's day in the sun [22]

In Paris, Vaille turned the disastrous negotiations of the early 1950s to his advantage. His ability to forge an agreement, even if it proved unworkable, saved face for all those connected with the control regime. Despite his rough tactics, other key players (including the UN secretariat) were indebted to Vaille for pulling their chestnuts out of the fire. Since the 1953 Protocol did not prejudice the interests of France's domestic manufacturing industry, he retained support at home. In addition to serving as Paris's representative on the CND, the government allowed Vaille to occupy the French seat when ECOSOC discussed drug-related issues. This unique position conferred upon Vaille an extra measure of influence: in a venue populated by non-specialists, he could shepherd favored resolutions toward approval and deprecate CND pronouncements with which he disagreed. A forceful debater, Vaille used his pharmacological expertise to confound opponents. Only Samuel Hoare, a former CND member who acted as Britain's ECOSOC representative throughout the 1950s, could challenge Vaille successfully.

Vaille possessed one overarching goal for the remainder of the decade: to bring the 1953 Opium Protocol (or its equivalent embodied in the Single Convention) into force. Vaille engaged in labyrinthine maneuvers to achieve his aim. In addition to the personal attachment Vaille exhibited for his Plan, he truly believed a production limitation scheme for raw materials could work. Vaille maintained that the technical difficulties were surmountable, if only the political obstacles could be overcome. As had so many before him, he refused to recognize that the two were inextricably linked.

Britannia's new tack [23]

For British officials, the negotiations surrounding the Opium Monopoly and the 1953 Opium Protocol had demonstrated that the Americans, French, and perhaps even the Canadians could not be trusted to take what London considered a reasonable attitude. The Foreign Office did not believe that the Opium Protocol could be implemented, maintaining that, until governments proved willing and able to observe current obligations, more stringent regulations would only alienate states from the system. The Home Office objected to many of the 1953 Protocol's stipulations, especially those that might increase prices for Britain's pharmaceutical industry. Physicians, pharmacists, and pharmaceutical companies vigorously opposed increased regulatory burdens, and no domestic constituency arose to challenge the government's enforcement and treatment policies.

Under such circumstances, British officials pursued a new course of action. They rallied other European manufacturing states to the cause of regulatory moderation. The Single Convention represented an opportunity to eliminate the excesses of the 1953 Protocol while consolidating the numerous treaties in force. Although little cooperation could be expected from France's Vaille, British officials recruited the Swiss, Dutch, Italians, and Belgians for their cause. Most importantly, West Germany's diplomatic reinstatement created an opportunity to shift the balance of power toward centrist manufacturing states. That country's burgeoning pharmaceutical industry would no doubt insist that Bonn take a role in shaping the international regime. Additionally, drug trafficking in Asia remained a concern, primarily because certain British colonies lay astride key smuggling routes. Hong Kong, in particular, acted as a conduit for the illicit trade from Southeast Asia. British officials hoped to forge a coalition of manufacturing states that would ensure adequate supplies of raw materials at reasonable prices, avoid undue restrictions on the licit international trade, and seek ways to reduce illicit trafficking.

As the principal industrialized states reconsidered their policies during the later 1950s, the control impetus faltered. The influence that Anslinger and Sharman exercised during the immediate postwar period dissipated amid internal turmoil and external challenge. Vaille picked up the standard, but it remained to be seen how far he could carry it. Great Britain, Germany, the Netherlands, Switzerland, and Japan recovered from their war-related debility to question the wisdom of following the 1953 Opium Protocol to its logical conclusion. This reversion to a multiplicity of opinions reflected the atmosphere in which drug diplomacy had traditionally been conducted; the United States along with its trusty Canadian ally could no longer dictate the agenda.

Producing states: raising the stakes

Events in producing states mirrored those occurring among the industrial giants, as governments reconsidered their options during the later 1950s. For some, the imposition of controls approximating those in the Opium Protocol appeared inevitable. Even more draconian measures might be in the offing if they did not cooperate. Others sought to reverse the trend, fearing increased infringement on the rights of producing states. Many hoped to find a third way, one which allowed producers to take more responsibility for controlling drugs while at the same time addressing the full range of issues that contributed to the problem. Regardless of which strategy they adopted, producing states demonstrated an increasing sophistication in their efforts to turn the control apparatus to their ends.

India opts in[24]

By the mid-1950s India decided to throw in its lot with the legitimate trade, thereby making its peace with the control regime. New Delhi gradually suppressed domestic quasi-medical opium use, and discontinued sales of smoking opium abroad. The government permitted opium cultivation for export to pharmaceutical firms overseas, but instituted procedures to guard against diversions. As a result, India secured an increasing share of the world export market during the 1950s, despite the inferior quality of the country's opium (as compared to that produced in Turkey, Iran, and Yugoslavia).[25] India's willingness to play by the rules ensured that New Delhi would also maintain an important position as legitimate supplier of last resort. The potential for crop failure in other countries, unpredictable increases in demand stimulated by Cold War strategic stockpiling programs, and concern that other producing states might fall under international sanction worked to India's advantage. New Delhi participated conscientiously in CND meetings, and generally acted as the most accommodating of the major producing states. In 1954, for example, India became the first producer nation to ratify the 1953 Opium Protocol, thereby enhancing its reputation in the west.

Iran kicks the habit[26]

The most startling turnaround in policy took place in Iran. In 1955 Teheran announced a comprehensive anti-opium campaign.[27] The government banned poppy cultivation and suppressed opium smoking. To everyone's surprise independent reports indicated that this time the government, backed by the Minister of Health and the Shah, meant what it said. Within a few years Iran reported that opium had become scarce and that the number of addicts had decreased. The Iranian representative at CND meetings gained a new respect among his colleagues. In 1959 Teheran even ratified the 1953 Opium Protocol, despite the self-imposed ban on opium cultivation that precluded Iran from exercising its prerogatives as one of the seven exporters named in the treaty.

Although pleased with Iran's actions, control advocates nevertheless remained wary. In a depressing turn of events that highlighted the relationship between control, demand, and supply, the Iranian ban fostered smuggling *into* the country, primarily from Turkey and Afghanistan. Iran solicited technical assistance for its enforcement efforts, and requested foreign aid subsidies for crop substitution and economic development. In 1959–60 Teheran hinted that, if sufficient international support were not forthcoming, the government might reconsider its prohibition policy.

Afghanistan muddies the waters[28]

Mixed signals from Afghanistan further complicated the picture. In 1955, Kabul, which had ignored the 1953 conference, petitioned to add Afghanistan to the list of producers named in the Opium Protocol. The Afghan request set all sides scrambling, setting off internecine disputes within several western governments and producing howls of protest from neighboring countries, especially Iran. In 1957 Kabul suddenly reversed itself. The government banned opium production, and promptly requested technical aid to carry out the task. Most observers expressed incredulity at this abrupt change, but reports confirmed that Afghan efforts appeared to be serious. Speculation about Kabul's motives varied. Many opined that the Afghan government hoped to emulate Iran's success in securing technical assistance and the development funds that often followed. British officials believed Kabul planned to use foreign aid to create effective domestic control, develop an improved infrastructure, and then re-enter the licit trade as a competitive player.

The Iranian and Afghan episodes reflected a shift in the balance of power between producing and manufacturing states. By cooperating with the regime's stipulations, producer governments could play the opium card in exchange for financial support. Western states had long opposed any sort of assistance, noting that producer nations should not receive a payoff for complying with treaty obligations. By the mid-1950s, however, the intractability of the problem and increasing dissent at home caused manufacturing powers to reconsider. They could no longer ignore producers' pleas without appearing indifferent to the plight of ostensibly sincere governments. To make further progress against illicit cultivation and trafficking, western nations would have to help foot the bill.

Turkey defiant[29]

At the very time that Iran and Afghanistan appeared to fall into line, the Turkish government became more obstinate. Through the mid- and late-1950s evidence accumulated that Turkish opium supplied a sizeable proportion of the global illicit market, although Ankara denied all charges.

At the same time, Turkish opium increasingly dominated the licit market. The Iranian opium ban and manufacturers' dislike of Indian opium combined to Ankara's advantage. Yugoslavia, the only other significant exporter to the west, produced a comparatively small amount of opium. Incredibly, by the late 1950s, manufacturing firms experienced a *shortage* of licit opium available for purchase. To keep prices high, the Turkish Opium Regie concealed the amount of opium it had for sale and smugly encouraged buyers to order while supplies lasted.

Ankara also tried to divert attention from Turkish transgressions by playing up other aspects of the drug problem. Ankara's CND representatives regularly charged that the traffic in synthetic narcotics necessitated stricter controls, or, preferably, outright prohibition. Since synthetic narcotics competed with Turkish opium in the licit marketplace, such pronouncements did not impress the representatives of western manufacturing states. In fact, little evidence could be found to substantiate charges of an extensive international traffic in synthetic narcotics.[30] Turkish officials also raised alarms about the dangers of psychotropics, cannabis, and even qat, a substance little known outside the southern Red Sea basin.[31] Had the charges come from a more disinterested corner, they might have been taken more seriously. Leading states on the CND, however, interpreted the Turkish alarums as an effort to deflect attention toward secondary concerns. Control advocates succeeded for the most part in focusing attention on what they considered to be the important problem – opium. By doing so they kept the pressure on Turkish authorities but also missed the opportunity to take preemptive action against other dangerous drugs.

Southeast Asia: the black hole

As the 1950s progressed, the news from Southeast Asia worsened. The Golden Triangle and environs, encompassing southern China, Vietnam, Laos, Burma, and Thailand, emerged as an area of uncontrollable illicit production, trafficking, and, for the first time, heroin manufacture. Whereas in previous decades regime advocates could at least confront a recognized entity responsible for the issue, by the mid-1950s governments openly admitted that they exercised no effective control over significant portions of their territory. Civil war and governmental corruption, both of which relied on opium trafficking, stymied efforts to make headway. That key western states, in particular the United States, did not recognize the governments of mainland China and North Vietnam only exacerbated the problems. No solution could be found as long as Washington would speak only to Taipei about Chinese conditions, especially considering the fact that American-backed forces in the area comprised a principal engine behind the region's illicit activity.[32]

Latin America: sleeping giant

Latin American compliance improved in some respects, but concerns about the region lingered. Many states cooperated at least superficially, submitting statistics, promoting police cooperation, and taking halting steps toward domestic enforcement. Modernizers, public health officials, military authorities, some nationalists, and those who deprecated indigenous cultural mores usually supported enhanced regulatory measures. On the other hand, coca production remained uncontrolled, opium cultivation recurred sporadically, and illicit trafficking might surface anywhere in the region. Profiteers, defenders of traditional upland culture, and those who resented overweening US influence challenged the international control system's tenets. Attention paid to the region diminished under competition from more pressing issues. PCOB members considered themselves fortunate; if Latin America reemerged as a center of the illicit trade, little could be done about it. Control advocates, concerned about other issues and discouraged by previous failed attempts to bolster the regulatory regime in Latin America, let sleeping dogs lie.[33]

Alternative medicine

As officials concerned with the drug question surveyed this picture, it appeared none too encouraging. To be sure, the principal manufacturing countries, including the previously wayward Japan, had imposed adequate restrictions on the trade. Many consuming states did so as well. Yet uncontrolled production continued to plague control efforts. The 1953 Opium Protocol, if it ever came into force, might or might not curb that problem. In the meantime, however, clandestine manufacture (particularly of heroin) proliferated, and illicit trafficking increased. Faced with a seemingly intractable set of problems, officials reconsidered alternate methods for implementing the traditional supply-control strategy.

Regional control efforts [34]

Since illicit production could not be eliminated, it appeared all the more necessary to prevent drugs from exiting their areas of origin by curbing increasingly sophisticated international trafficking organizations. Beginning in the mid-1950s, regional enforcement activities proliferated. Efforts focused first on southeast Asia, later on southwest Asia, and spread from those beginnings. Governments and the UN created regional offices and convened meetings within geographic zones designed to enhance police cooperation. Interpol, clamoring for a larger role in drug enforcement, insinuated itself into this emerging mid-level stratum. Subsets of the international control regime became a permanent feature of the system. That phenomenon allowed for a level of cooperation (among states not at odds for other reasons) not previously attained, but also engendered a plethora of new acronyms, organizations, and bureaucratic allegiances. Despite governments' desires to simplify the regime, a sentiment exemplified by support for the Single Convention, the machinery and diplomacy of international drug control became more complicated.

Foreign aid [35]

The issue of foreign aid became more significant after the mid-1950s. Many producer countries began to request "technical assistance," consisting of training for administrators, police, and other specialists in order to fulfill their international obligations. Some developing nations hoped that securing technical assistance would demonstrate the need for large aid projects such as crop substitution, infrastructure improvements, and public health initiatives. Just as some viewed drug exports as a path to modernization, many technocrats believed the drug war provided an opportunity to revitalize third-world economies and societies. Manufacturing and consuming states wanted to avoid linking narcotics enforcement to the increasingly competitive market for large foreign aid projects, but producers won the essential point. As long as the ultimate regulatory goal remained control "at the source," producer states would not have to shoulder the burden alone. Once antinarcotics money became available, pressure to increase aid and expand programs soon followed. By the early 1960s, aid programs had become a permanent fixture of the international drug system.

Yet an assortment of bureaucratic, political, economic, and practical complications retarded attempts to reach the goal by such alternate routes. Competing geostrategic imperatives and conflicts between neighboring governments diminished enforcement efforts. Foreign aid could support only selected projects, and in any case cultivating illicit drugs yielded a higher return per acre than competing agricultural products. Such limitations ensured that production control would remain the centerpiece of the regime's supply-side ethos.

Psychotropics: double standard[36]

As the 1950s drew to a close, a new problem came to light. Synthetically produced, non-narcotic substances such as barbiturates, tranquilizers, amphetamines, and certain hallucinogens (referred to in the aggregate as "psychotropics") entered into therapeutic use with increasing frequency. Physicians and psychiatrists hoped to ameliorate heretofore untreatable maladies with such substances. Pharmaceutical companies, intent on recovering research and development costs and reaping profits, aggressively marketed the new compounds. The typical euphoric response to new drugs occurred, reinforced by western predisposition to favor products of the scientific–medico-industrial complex.

Pharmaceutical firms and physicians originally downplayed the addiction liability of psychotropics, but experience indicated that the substances carried serious abuse potential. Scandinavian countries issued some of the first warnings, complaining that lax controls in other European states fostered a burgeoning traffic in amphetamines. Producer states soon took up the cause, seizing the opportunity to turn the tables on manufacturing countries. Led by Turkey, the producers demanded international control over the manufacture and distribution of psychotropics comparable to those imposed on opiates and coca products.

Manufacturing states, although divided on many other drug-control issues, presented a combined front concerning psychotropics. For several years they defeated attempts to discuss the matter at the CND. Unable to avoid the issue indefinitely, manufacturing states then blocked recommendations calling for control over the substances. The weight of evidence presented by the WHO and others eventually forced western industrialized states to concede that psychotropics might indeed present a hazard. Nevertheless, their representatives watered down CND resolutions to the point of impotency. CND representatives from manufacturing countries utilized the same anti-control arguments they had so often rejected when proffered by producer countries – that no definitive proof existed concerning ill effects, that psychotropics should not be pronounced guilty without a fair trial period, and that nations should be free to determine what level of control suited them. The irony was not lost on consumer and producer states. The CND, so quick to institute controls over narcotic substances, refused to take similar precautions with psychotropics. Bowing to their domestic pharmaceutical interests, blind to the cultural bias that privileged "modern" western drugs, and not wishing to let producer states off the hook concerning the "real problem," manufacturing states shunned the chance to nip a potentially serious matter in the bud.

Promoting the 1953 Protocol[37]

All international drug control activity from the mid-1950s through the early 1960s took place in the shadow of one central question: Would nations support a significantly more stringent regime as exemplified by the 1953 Protocol? Those answering in the affirmative wished to bring the Protocol into force quickly. Those opposing the Opium Protocol hoped to delay its activation indefinitely. Both sides recognized that the still-unfinished Single Convention would play a key role in the fate of the 1953 Protocol. Already on the drawing board for almost a decade, the Single Convention became a pawn in the battle between those favoring substantive production limitation and those preferring the status quo.

The 1953 agreement received mixed reviews from the international community. Western manufacturing states accepted the treaty fairly quickly. By the end of the decade, only the British and Dutch had not ratified. Many consuming states also adhered. Latin American states ignored the treaty, hoping it would die of neglect. Eastern Bloc governments shunned it, claiming that it infringed on state sovereignty.

Given the 1953 Protocol's lukewarm reception, the opium producing states held the key to its fate. The Protocol required ratification by three of the seven producing states named in Article 21 before the treaty could come into force. India ratified in 1954. After the American-backed reinstatement of the Shah, Iran announced its intention to ratify as well. For several years Teheran withheld adherence in hopes of securing a better foreign aid package. Under pressure to ratify from Anslinger and others, the Iranian government finally complied in 1959.

Yet proponents of the treaty proved unable to secure the crucial third ratification. The Protocol's inspection provisions precluded adherence by Bulgaria or the Soviet Union. The remaining three candidates dragged their feet. Despite pressure from the French and American governments, Greece and Yugoslavia demurred. They would not ratify unless Turkey did so. With Teheran's self-imposed withdrawal from the licit trade, Ankara possessed the power to wreck the 1953 Protocol. Turkey could remain outside the agreement and flood the market with opium. Manufacturing states might denounce the treaty if a substantial commercial advantage could be gained by dealing with the Turks. Consequently, the Yugoslavs and Greeks did not wish to have their hands tied. Turkish officials preferred the Single Convention because it promised to supersede all previous treaties, including the 1953 agreement. Ankara hoped to eliminate the Opium Protocol's onerous provisions by watering down the Single Convention.

To maintain pressure on Turkey, Vaille worked to eliminate a "soft" Single Convention as an escape hatch. Vaille assumed the chairmanship of the CND in 1954–55, and during that period he delayed progress on the Single Convention. At the same time, Vaille fortified the Single Convention with provisions similar to those embodied in the Opium Protocol. In the Single Convention's third draft Vaille retained the essence of the 1953 Protocol by inserting meaningful inspection and enforcement provisions and by limiting the number of authorized producing states.

Recognizing Turkey's pivotal position, Vaille also attempted to reduce Ankara's opposition to the 1953 Protocol by supporting other Turkish initiatives. Vaille acted energetically to secure funding for technical assistance. He seconded Turkish diatribes against synthetic narcotics, and attempted to include provisions aimed specifically at outlawing those drugs in the Single Convention.[38] He also supported Ankara's attacks on cannabis, khat, and psychotropic drugs. Vaille hoped that by demonstrating solidarity he could convince Ankara to acquiesce in the 1953 Protocol's restrictions.

Vaille and Anslinger also supported giving producer states a greater voice in the international control organs. Both a Greek and a Yugoslav gained seats on the PCOB in 1958, in large part because of support from Vaille and Anslinger. New appointments to the DSB were made that same year, and once again (keeping in mind the ECOSOC resolution calling for a personal union between the Board and Body) the Greek and Yugoslav filled two of the four DSB seats. Turkish attempts to place a member on the PCOB failed, but Vaille and Anslinger engineered the election of Ankara's CND representative as one of the Commission's officers. Vaille capped his efforts by successfully maneuvering to have himself elected to the DSB, in direct contradiction of the personal union ordered by ECOSOC.[39] By giving producer states more ownership of the system and by demonstrating that they could count on friends in high places, Vaille and Anslinger hoped they would accept the burdens imposed by the 1953 Opium Protocol.

Events beyond his control, however, dashed Vaille's efforts. The Fourth Republic fell in 1958, to be replaced by Charles de Gaulle's new constitution. Vaille received a promotion to the position of Inspector General of Health. Although Vaille intended to continue representing France at the CND, his new superiors had different ideas. They took a dim view of his machinations in support of the Opium Protocol, and in any case his new duties precluded long absences from Paris. Shortly before the 1959 CND session Vaille was replaced by Dr. J. Mabileau, deputy head of the French Pharmaceutical Service. Although Mabileau proved to be a diligent worker, he did not display the forcefulness of his predecessor. Vaille served out his 5-year term on the DSB, but could not nudge the Body to act more boldly. Although he continued to participate in the French inter-ministerial committee on narcotics matters, he no longer spoke for France at CND and ECOSOC sessions. Vaille's influence receded precisely when the 1953 Protocol most needed his protection. Sensing the change indicated by Vaille's unexpected absence at the 1959 CND session, producing states quickly abandoned any pretense of supporting the Opium Protocol. Turkey, Yugoslavia, and Greece rejected the 1953 Treaty, favoring instead rapid completion of the Single Convention.

The Single Convention: drafting for position[40]

In the midst of all its other activities, throughout the 1950s the CND oversaw the tortuous process of creating a Single Convention. ECOSOC had called for a consolidation of existing treaties in 1948. It took 13 years to produce the final document (slow even by UN standards) and in the meantime two additional treaties had come into existence. Although originally intended simply to rationalize inter-national control efforts, the Single Convention became embroiled in the debate over the 1953 Protocol.

The Single Convention's first draft, produced by the secretariat during the early 1950s, bore the stamp of Leon Steinig. In addition to consolidating the extant treaties, it included many of International

Opium Monopoly's essential features. In 1955 governments rejected that effort as hopelessly tainted.

The CND produced a substantially altered second draft in 1956. Once again, that document not only rationalized control arrangements but also broke new ground. Vaille and Anslinger, desiring insurance in case attempts to activate the 1953 Protocol failed, incorporated most of the Protocol's provisions into the text. The second draft, however, proved too confusing to act as a serviceable document because it contained many conflicting clauses. An inexperienced DND secretariat proved unable to corral the draft's multiple trajectories.

In 1957–58 the CND composed a third effort that eliminated many of its predecessor's shortcomings. Canadian Robert Curran played the crucial role in fashioning a useable document. He eliminated most of the alternative provisions and rendered the rest into footnotes. Governments pronounced this streamlined third draft acceptable as a basis for negotiations.

Nevertheless, CND representatives remained divided on key issues. Producer states attempted to weaken the articles dealing with control over cultivation, but achieved only minor success. In conjunction with some consuming states beginning to experience problems with psychotropic substances, producers also argued for language that would control such drugs as amphetamines and barbiturates. Representatives of manufacturing states, sensitive to the interests of domestic pharmaceutical companies and blinded by their faith in western medicine, would not countenance such suggestions. Provisions concerning PCOB/DSB responsibilities and independence also produced controversy. Some wished to enhance the authority of those international organs while others wanted to weaken them. Nor could states agree on whether to incorporate language replicating the 1936 anti-trafficking treaty into the Single Convention.[41] Differences in national legal systems and reluctance to reduce restrictions on extradition impeded those wishing to enact a universal enforcement regime. All sides viewed the upcoming plenipotentiary negotiations as an opportunity to revise the Single Convention in their favor.

The 1961 conference[42]

In January 1961, seventy-three delegations assembled in New York to negotiate the Single Convention. As at previous plenipotentiary meetings, a relatively small group of representatives, those with expertise and/or a special interest in the issue dominated the proceedings. Several influential groupings wishing to revise the text utilized classic anti-control arguments to varying degrees of success, while the defenders of the third draft's more onerous provisions suffered defeat. The negotiations resulted in a moderate treaty that served as a new foundation for the control regime, but the 1961 Conference proved as incapable as its predecessors of devising permanent solutions.

Actions of the key players

Producing states took the lead in the revision effort. In addition to Turkey, Yugoslavia, and Greece, the coca-growing states of South America had delayed ratification of the 1953 Protocol in hopes of securing a less onerous Single Convention. Other developing nations, many of which cultivated cannabis for its hemp fiber, followed suit. During the course of the 1961 negotiations, delegations from producer countries fought consistently to loosen controls the draft placed on opium, coca, and cannabis. They argued that manufactured substances, especially synthetic narcotics, should be controlled at least as strictly as raw materials. Producer states also sought to weaken the authority of the international control bodies, evade reporting requirements, eliminate on-site inspections, and generally blunt provisions that they viewed as a threat to national sovereignty. Finally, producing states engaged in a counteroffensive intended to turn the tables on manufacturing states. Producers took advantage of the platform provided by the 1961 convention to publicize their demands for the imposition of controls over psychotropic substances.

Great Britain led a group of western European manufacturing states that assisted the producers by arguing for a simple consolidation of the status quo. Switzerland, West Germany, the Netherlands, Italy, and Japan generally supported British efforts to strip the treaty of provisions extending control over cultivation. Britain and its allies feared that an overly zealous treaty would discourage ratifications, as had happened with the 1953 Protocol. Without wide acceptance the Single Convention would simply add to the plethora of treaties already in existence. The British-led group also objected to the third draft's closed list of producers (similar to the seven states enumerated in the Opium Protocol). The licit opium shortage of the late-1950s had propelled prices upward, and manufacturers did not wish to become beholden to a small group of suppliers for their raw material. In opposition to the producers, neither the British nor their allies wished to see restrictions placed on the new psychotropic drugs that appeared therapeutically promising, highly profitable, and culturally acceptable.

The Soviet bloc also objected to provisions that went beyond mere consolidation. As usual, Moscow and its allies would not allow any interference in internal matters. The third draft's authorization of on-site inspections, notwithstanding provisions requiring prior governmental approval, proved too much for the Eastern bloc. Similarly, the USSR objected to the closed list of producers, arguing that developing countries should not be barred from exploiting their resources as they wished.

The positions of Vaille and Anslinger, the two principal supporters of an unadulterated third draft, suffered from important weaknesses. Vaille no longer exercised direct oversight over France's international drug policy. Mabileau tried to follow Vaille's lead, but superiors in Paris wished to skirt the issue.[43] Anslinger's ability to direct American policy waned as well. During 1960 his wife's condition deteriorated, and Anslinger spent progressively less time at the office. He moved his wife home to Pennsylvania in hopes of making her final days more comfortable, a relocation that further reduced the Commissioner's contact with Washington. At the FBN, Anslinger's failure to delegate responsibility left the agency without direction. Officials at the State Department did not share Anslinger's affinity for the 1953 Protocol. They expected the Single Convention to achieve its original aim, consolidation of the regime, without making forays into controversial regulatory territory. As a result, the US delegation suffered from a lack of coordination. The Treasury and State Department members did not work together, and failed to cooperate with the French as well. In a situation where only aggressive cultivation of other delegations could save the third draft, its defenders proved ill-suited to the task.

As the negotiations progressed, opponents of the third draft's more far-reaching provisions prevailed with little difficulty. Vaille and Anslinger maintained enthusiasm for the third draft only as long as provisions replicating those in the 1953 Opium Protocol remained unadulterated. Other defenders proved hard to discover. Delegates not familiar with the preliminary negotiations commented on the dispatch with which CND members dismantled their own handiwork. Most governments, interested in achieving accord rather than taking bold new steps, sided with those advocating a conservative approach.

Results of the 1961 conference

First and foremost, the conference effected a significant simplification of the control regime. Upon activation of the Single Convention, nine previous agreements would be terminated. Only the poorly subscribed

1936 Illicit Trafficking treaty remained in force, because delegations could not agree on which of its provisions to incorporate into the Single Convention. The principal pillars of the previous treaties remained intact. The Single Convention required parties to submit estimates-of-need and statistics concerning drugs imported, exported, manufactured, retained in stocks, and consumed. The import/export certification system remained in force, providing multiple avenues for discovering diversions from the licit trade. Governments were required to license manufacturers, traders, and distributors, and all who handled drugs had to maintain records of their transactions. The Single Convention retained the concept of "schedules of control" first introduced in the 1931 treaty, but expanded the number of schedules from two to four. Governmental representatives retained their place at the center of the decision-making process, with pharmaceutical interests and medical experts acting in an advisory capacity. The reconstituted regime made no attempt to alter the global liberal market-oriented order – quotas and monopolies did not fit the reigning economic paradigm.

The final version of the 1961 Single Convention also provided for administrative improvements. The PCOB and DSB would be combined into a new body, the International Narcotics Control Board (INCB). The new Board would collect estimates-of-need (formerly submitted to the DSB) and statistics of use from governments. The Single Convention preserved the Board's authority to make estimates and calculate statistics for states failing to submit them, thereby retaining the INCB's universal compass. The Board's heretofore unutilized embargo power remained intact, albeit in a somewhat weaker form. To accommodate calls for geographical diversity the treaty increased the number of Board Members from eight to eleven. The "single secretariat" issue remained unresolved, despite Yates's attempts to secure an endorsement for amalgamation. The Single Convention included only an ambiguous reference requiring the Secretary-General to provide services for the Board.

Producing states achieved several of their primary objectives. The conference eliminated provisions dealing with inspections, mandatory embargoes, and prohibition of cannabis cultivation. Opium producers also garnered enough support to insert language calling for controls over poppy straw, thereby placing one of their competitors under some limitations. Additionally, producing states ensured that the 1953 Opium Protocol would be among the treaties terminated when the Single Convention entered into force.

Producing states proved unsuccessful in fending off all new obligations. The 1961 Single Convention imposed enhanced reporting requirements. The new INCB received authority to request estimates-of-need and statistics for opium, coca, and cannabis. For the first time producer states would have to report their requirements and usage to the Board. Opium producers also had to accept language mandating a government-operated agency to license growers and to buy, warehouse, and sell the harvest. This provision effectively barred private firms from participating in the lucrative business of buying up the crop and siphoning off excess supplies into the illegitimate market. The treaty imposed somewhat less exacting requirements on coca-producing states, while cannabis-growing countries avoided serious restrictions. Additionally, the "schedules of control" outlined by the Single Convention discriminated against the interests of producers. Raw materials and simple concoctions such as heroin and cocaine suffered under the more severe restrictions of schedules I and IV. Certain manufactured (primarily codeine-based) narcotics received somewhat more lenient treatment in schedules II and III. Nevertheless, when compared with the Opium Protocol, producer states found the 1961 Single Convention a palatable alternative.

The British-led manufacturing alliance also achieved their principal objectives. The Single Convention rationalized the regime by reducing the number of treaties from ten to two. Manufacturers avoided having synthetic narcotics singled out for special restrictions and also eliminated the closed list of recognized producers. Most importantly, manufacturers defeated attempts to place psychotropic substances under control. After failing to incorporate such a provision into the treaty, producer states sponsored a resolution, to be attached to the final document, calling for limitation on psychotropics. Although not holding the force of obligation, manufacturing states worked hard to avoid censure. The anti-psychotropics resolution failed by one vote.

The USSR and its allies also advanced their interests. The Soviet bloc ensured elimination of the third draft's inspection provisions. The USSR scored political points as well, championing the rights of underdeveloped nations by opposing the closed list of producers.

The Single Convention represented a repudiation of Harry Anslinger's hopes. Fairly early in the negotiations, it became clear that stringent controls over agricultural production would be removed from the treaty. After that point, the Commissioner largely wrote off the conference. He made only a few brief appearances in New York, preferring to disassociate himself from the proceedings. His surrogates did assist in defeating the anti-psychotropic provisions introduced by producer states and also secured special language enabling the Coca-Cola company to import coca for flavoring extract.[44] For the most part, however, the American delegation floundered in Anslinger's absence, failing to achieve its objectives. For example, despite Soviet support, attempts to include a provision that required civil commitment of addicts failed. Anslinger wanted such a statement in the treaty to provide ammunition against domestic critics. The Vatican, fearful that communist countries would use the provision to incarcerate church supporters, protested vehemently. Anslinger had to settle for a resolution attached to the final document that provided only a lukewarm endorsement of his position.

Worst of all for Anslinger, the new treaty represented a threat to the FBN's existence. Upon entry into force the Single Convention would terminate the 1931 treaty, including Article 15. Anslinger had always contended that the FBN could not be reorganized or eliminated because Article 15 required an independent organization to deal with the drug issue. The Single Convention, which simply required states to "maintain a special administration" substantially weakened Anslinger's position.[45] The Commissioner recognized the threat to his Bureau. Before the ink was dry on the final document Anslinger had already initiated a new campaign to convince one more producing state to ratify the 1953 Protocol. He believed the Single Convention might still be derailed if the Opium Protocol could be brought into force quickly.

Conclusion

The 1953–61 era represented a period of transition in the history of drug diplomacy. Traditionally defensive producing areas in Asia and Latin America, buoyed by decolonization and the global Cold War struggle for influence in the third world, developed strategies for manipulating the control impetus in their favor. Spurred by the excesses and embarrassments surrounding the International Opium Monopoly and the 1953 Opium Protocol, governments exerted more control over the policy-making process. States also began to rely more on social scientific knowledge vested in professional organizations and government agencies. As a result, increasing bureaucratization slowly brought an end to the more personal, idiosyncratic cast that had often maintained in drug diplomacy heretofore. As the "old drug hands" exited the scene, an unprecedented combination of producing, manufacturing, and consuming states and non-state actors reconsidered the feasibility of pursuing control "at the source." Governments refused to impose the truly stringent limitations on agricultural production necessary to achieve the ultimate objective. Officials searched instead for other methods to corral illicit trafficking and manufacture, hoping that regional and programmatic approaches might produce better results. Even support for the supply-control paradigm itself started to fray at the edges. Those promoting alternative conceptions of, and solutions to, the problem of drug abuse began to crack the barriers erected by enforcement-oriented administrators of the old school.

The 1961 Single Convention appeared to represent the culmination of fifty years' progress in the field of international drug control. The new treaty promoted the regime's universality by providing one general document that states could accept. Deleting the more draconian aspects of the third draft would no doubt increase ratifications without weakening the existing level of control. Technical assistance programs and regional cooperative efforts provided new weapons in the "war against drugs." PCOB/DSB Secretary Louis Atzenwiler exemplified sentiments typical of the time. He retired in 1963 believing that the Single Convention represented the crowning achievement of his career. The control system appeared to be on solid ground for the foreseeable future.[46]

Yet control officials soon found themselves blindsided by an unanticipated deluge. Producing states had proven adept at avoiding the most burdensome obligations proposed by control advocates. Those not wishing or unable to comply with the regime's strictures retained the essential freedom of action they required. Moreover, control bureaucracies remained fixated on pursuing the supply-side agenda defined at the turn of the century. Few recognized the significance of the storm clouds brewing on the horizon. Within a few years, social upheaval, an expanding war in Southeast Asia, and the merchandising proclivities of pharmaceutical companies engendered an explosion of drug use. In less than a decade, the problem of substance abuse reached crisis proportions. Unprepared for the onslaught, the control regime would be shaken to its core by the events of the 1960s.

Part IV
The regime challenged

8 Crucible – 1961–73[1]

... it might not be an exaggeration to suggest that the problems posed by [psychotropics] may prove far greater than the problems which the hard narcotics at the present time are posing.[2]

... the present state of crisis, or near-crisis, provides a rare opportunity to recruit men from the relatively "hard" sciences such as economics to this area. . . . The pay offs tend mostly to be long-range in such an effort, but even in the near term you are likely to avoid a certain amount of bad advice by consorting with skeptical professors.[3]

Regardless of what we think we are trying to do, if we make it illegal to traffic in commodities for which there is an inelastic demand, the actual effect is to secure a kind of monopoly profit to the entrepreneur who is willing to break the law.[4]

In the wake of the 1961 New York negotiations, control agencies assumed matters would proceed in a routine manner for the foreseeable future. Few anticipated the surprises around the corner. The depth of Harry Anslinger's antipathy to the Single Convention, nor to what extremes he would go to defeat it, was not yet apparent. Yet even Anslinger's machinations paled in the face of an unprecedented onslaught of drug abuse. In the decade after the 1961 conference, national and international control arrangements underwent massive changes. States created new organizations to grapple with the situation, while some venerable institutions did not survive.

Yet, in the midst of such upheaval, governments, international control organs, and other parties continued the traditional maneuvering for position. Political, economic, social, and cultural factors continued to inform the policies key players pursued. Despite the novel threat posed by the new drug epidemic, the principal actors still danced to the traditional tune.

Nevertheless, by the early 1970s, a new era had dawned in the annals of drug diplomacy. The difficulties facing regime proponents appeared more problematic than ever. At the same time, a wider range of approaches offered renewed promise for deciphering the intricacies inherent in the drug question. Calculations about the supply and demand of addicting drugs (both licit and illicit) acquired an unprecedented prominence in international relations, and the crisis spawned a new international agency as well. Things would never be the same again.

The ratification race[5]

Before the New York negotiations ended, Harry Anslinger initiated a campaign to discredit the Single Convention. He charged that various treaty provisions seriously weakened the control system, but his complaints rang hollow. Anslinger's real concern was that the treaty threatened the FBN's survival. The Single Convention terminated Article 15 of the 1931 treaty, which Anslinger had used repeatedly to justify maintaining the FBN as an independent fiefdom within the Treasury Department. Anslinger would reach retirement age in 1962, and the Commissioner did not wish his impending departure to provide an excuse for dismantling the edifice he had painstakingly erected. Increasing domestic opposition to his punitive methods, continued disputes with the State Department, longstanding interagency enmities, and lack of support from the White House posed an unprecedented threat to the FBN. If the treaty came into force with US support, an important statutory impediment blocking the FBN's foes would evaporate.

Beginning in March 1961 the Commissioner embarked on an aggressive campaign to protect his agency while promoting a more stringent international regime. He aimed to activate the 1953 Protocol by securing the adherence of a third producing state. He simultaneously deprecated the Single Convention at every opportunity. If the Opium Protocol came into force with the backing of the United States, Anslinger hoped that support for the 1961 treaty would fade.

Anslinger first outmaneuvered the State Department. He called in all his markers, cajoling support from other government agencies, colleagues abroad, pharmaceutical companies, and members of Congress. In January 1962, under pressure from members of the Senate Foreign Relations Committee influenced by pharmaceutical industry representatives, the State Department unenthusiastically acquiesced in an official rejection of the Single Convention.

Long before receiving that imprimatur, Anslinger commenced his overseas offensive. During 1961–62, he sent special representatives to Europe and Asia, touting the Opium Protocol and informing officials of the Commissioner's aversion to the 1961 treaty. Anslinger also canvassed for support at the UN, hoping to create a groundswell of opposition to the Single Convention. In 1962, armed with Washington's expressed preference for the Opium Protocol, Anslinger ended his long boycott of CND meetings held in Geneva. He led the US delegation, expending his primary energies on promoting the 1953 Protocol.

Most importantly, Anslinger pressured the Greek and Turkish governments to ratify the Opium Protocol. Turkish officials reacted coolly to the Commissioner's overtures, hoping that both treaties might languish. Anslinger's emissaries found Athens more amenable. Greek officials indicated their sympathy with the FBN's position, but hesitated to act without an official pronouncement from Washington. In the spring of 1962, after the State Department belatedly informed governments of the anti-Single Convention policy, Athens agreed to ratify the Opium Protocol. With great relish, Harry Anslinger arranged for the Greek CND representative to drop his bombshell at the May 1962 CND session.

The Greek announcement stunned CND representatives, the UN secretariat, and the PCOB. Lobbying in favor of the Single Convention had proceeded in a low-key manner, largely out of deference to the American position. Most assumed that Anslinger's nominal complaints about the Single Convention could be ironed out through negotiation. Indeed, much of the 1962 CND session dealt with measures to be taken once the Single Convention entered into force. Many control officials felt betrayed by Anslinger's coup.

Governments attempted to counteract the American offensive (quietly encouraged by State Department officials who sheepishly admitted they had lost an interdepartmental battle), but the UN Secretariat proved Anslinger's most formidable opponent. DND Director Gilbert Yates initiated a worldwide counteroffensive, canvassing UN and governmental officials on every continent and using UN publications to promote the Single Convention. At ECOSOC's autumn 1962 session, eighty-one nations approved Yates's resolution in favor of the Single Convention; only the United States voted against. In response, many states accelerated ratification procedures.

Anslinger won the ratification battle but lost the war. The deposit of Greece's ratification activated the Opium Protocol in March 1963.

Unwilling to renounce its prerogatives as a recognized exporter, Turkey adhered to the 1953 Protocol a few months later. By that time, however, the DND's efforts had ensured the success of the Single Convention. The 1961 treaty entered into force in December 1964. A number of states that had delayed adhering to the Single Convention out of deference to the United States then ratified. The Opium Protocol received few adherences after 1963.

In late 1966 the State Department won a long battle to reverse US policy. Over fifty nations had adhered to the Single Convention, and the American boycott proved increasingly debilitating. Washington could hardly pressure other states to improve compliance with international norms without itself incurring criticism. On 25 May 1967 the United States deposited its ratification with the UN. Less than a year later, the FBN ceased to exist.[6] In 1969, Anslinger stepped down as head of the American CND delegation. He died in 1975, unsure about his legacy. Noting that "policies must necessarily change," Anslinger admitted to BNDD Director John Ingersoll, "Sometimes I think my decisions were about half right, but now I am not sure which half."[7]

Sea change[8]

The controversy over the Single Convention represented the last unadulterated debate of the old regime. Since the turn of the century nations and non-state actors contended over limitation of supply, focusing primarily on addicting substances derived from agricultural products. Differing views about the merits of the Single Convention fell squarely within that longstanding paradigm. At the center of this conceptual universe lay governments, enforcement agencies, international organs, and pharmaceutical interests. Control officials rarely considered issues of demand, had little knowledge about addicts, and seldom examined the relationship between regulatory measures and illicit activity. Control advocates believed that if only the rules could be drawn properly, and if only governments carried out their obligations, the problem would recede. Those long-established conventions appeared to crumble under the weight of unprecedented events, however, as drug use exploded the world over during the 1960s.

Events in the United States provided the most spectacular demonstration of a widespread phenomenon. Heroin spilled out from the ghettoes to encumber a notable segment of the population. Massive opiate addiction in the military accompanied the Vietnamese war. Some intellectuals touted the merits of psychedelic drugs, fostering indiscriminate use among their less-disciplined followers. Cannabis-related arrests skyrocketed, and cocaine made a comeback. Young people proved particularly susceptible to the blandishments of an ostensibly countercultural movement that nevertheless traced its roots to 1920s anti-prohibitionism; consumerist industry, mass media, and other economic interests benefitted by promoting a lack of social .restraint and enshrining individual liberty over communal standards as the basis for judging conduct.[9] Drugs, new and old, enjoyed a euphoric reception of classic proportions. Many other countries experienced similarly alarming increases in drug abuse.

Moreover, abuse of psychotropic substances contributed significantly to this new epidemic. As late as the mid-1960s, many countries imposed only minimal limitations on the distribution of amphetamines, barbiturates, tranquilizers and other non-narcotic drugs. The CND, led by western states with influential pharmaceutical industries, had discouraged efforts to place the issue on the international agenda. The problem, in part, was one of definition. The extant drug control treaties defined an addicting drug as one that generated effects similar to those produced by opiates or coca products; central nervous system stimulants and depressants acted differently upon the body, *ergo* they were not considered "addictive." Yet the experience of millions of users proved otherwise. Many individuals, under medical care for physical or psychological maladies, developed dependencies to psychotropic substances. Others obtained their supplies surreptitiously and used them for pleasure. Some became addicted to multiple substances, for example, self-administering "uppers" and "downers" in a cyclical fashion that proved highly debilitating. The medical profession encountered concerns about iatrogenic illness, caused largely by the explosion of drug-based therapies, to an extent not seen since the 1920s.[10] By the late 1960s most western governments had imposed at least some restrictions on the availability of psychotropic substances, usually over the objections of pharmaceutical interests.

Yet, as pharmaceutical companies acquiesced in increased domestic restrictions, they aggressively marketed overseas. The less-developed countries of Latin America, Africa, and Asia witnessed an invasion of "detail men" as drug companies touted their products. Regulatory agencies in those nations could not cope with the onslaught of new substances.

The anomalies that arose between national control regimes fostered new categories of illicit traffic. For example, a brisk trade in amphetamines erupted between strict-limitation states such as Sweden and less fastidious neighbors. Some Latin American countries became havens for unscrupulous middlemen who took advantage of insufficient laws and lax enforcement. They imported psychotropics legally from the United States only to smuggle them back for sale on the street at great profit.[11]

Response to the new crisis

As a result of this radical departure from previous experience, the prohibitive enforcement model that underpinned the control regime came under intense scrutiny. The appeal of traditional solutions focusing on restriction of supply and punitive measures against users diminished as substance abuse surged into mainstream society. Proponents of alternative approaches, emphasizing medical, psychological, and/or sociological models, gained credibility. Criticism of an exclusively supply-side strategy reached a fever pitch. Many advocated dismantling the old regime and discarding the assumptions that informed it.

The issue rapidly became a high-profile concern in many western countries. Blue ribbon commissions, legislative committees, expert reports, and special hearings proliferated. A legacy of the regime's supply-control emphasis, the dearth of objective research on etiology, addiction, treatment, rehabilitation, the effects of drug use, and the impact of control measures, impeded informed discourse. Governments initiated programs to accumulate data upon which policy recommendations could be based. Those advocating continued emphasis on enforcement and those favoring alternative strategies often disagreed on what to do.

Nevertheless, general agreement concerning a shift in emphasis emerged. Those wishing to curb the rising tide of drug abuse recognized that a more integrated strategy offered a better likelihood of success. Investigation of new treatment modalities, expansion of rehabilitation facilities, and educational efforts seemed in order. The notion advanced heretofore that public campaigns would only increase drug experimentation, especially among the young, carried little credence in the face of rampant illicit use. Psychotropic substances came under scrutiny for their potential to cause harm. Some authorities reconsidered the similarities between alcohol and other drugs. It appeared notions of addiction might require adjustment in light of recent experience with a wider variety of substances. Moreover, such expanded efforts could not be limited by political boundaries – international coordination seemed essential.[12]

Yet curtailing excess supplies remained a key dimension of this expanded drug-control effort, albeit with a somewhat altered emphasis:

governments could no longer ignore the hazards of psychotropics. Consequently, some type of international control standards would have to be negotiated for those substances. What shape that agreement would take, and whose interests it would serve, remained to be negotiated. Beset anew by heroin from abroad, many western authorities advocated an enhanced carrot-and-stick approach toward producing states. Some believed a commitment should be made to implement significant crop substitution programs, others advocated increased attention to technical assistance, while still others preferred to emphasize enhanced regional control efforts. At the same time, western officials believed producer nations should do more to conform to international norms. A reinvigorated public pressure campaign, featuring more varied avenues of approach, figured prominently in their plans.

The new epidemic prompted a variety of responses among the industrialized nations most directly affected. Governments attempted to incorporate the new thinking about drug abuse into their existing control mechanisms. Many found it necessary to introduce major organizational or programmatic changes. On the other hand, some preferred to retain the status quo in defense of economic, cultural, and political interests. As western states reconsidered their policy options and adjusted their bureaucratic arrangements, newly reconfigured control bureaucracies grappled with the complexities of the international arena.

The United States

The most dramatic organizational changes occurred in the United States.[13] Harry Anslinger retired from his post as FBN Commissioner in 1962. Following the example of Delevingne and Sharman, Anslinger continued to represent the United States in the international arena. For the remainder of the decade he attended CND sessions as the chief American delegate and he played a role in formulating and promoting US policy. Nevertheless, the former Commissioner could not hold back the tidal wave that swept over his fiefdom. The Kennedy and Johnson administrations created several new entities within the federal government to coordinate research, enhance legal procedure, and expand treatment facilities. The Drug Abuse Control Act of 1965 regulated psychotropics through the creation of the Bureau of Drug Abuse Control (BDAC). The 1965 Act also altered the constitutional basis for federal drug control activities from the taxing power to the interstate and commerce clauses. Moreover, a continuing series of revelations concerning corruption among FBN agents further weakened the agency. In 1968, the *denouement* so long feared by Anslinger took place with little opposition. The FBN was reorganized out of existence by the creation of the Bureau of Narcotics and Dangerous Drugs (BNDD). The new agency, which also subsumed the BDAC, became part of the Justice Department. Under its director, John Ingersoll, the BNDD pursued a combination of old and new initiatives that reflected the tenor of the times.

Canada[14]

Canada completed a thoroughgoing bureaucratization of its policy-making apparatus begun in the mid-1950s. Kenneth Hossick retired in 1961. Robert Curran, Legal Counsel for the Department of National Health and Welfare, assumed Hossick's seat at the CND. He took a leading role in the "ratification race," working with CND colleagues and the UN secretariat to foil Anslinger's anti-Single Convention machinations. Curran reached retirement age in 1969, just as the Single Convention, which he had done much to nurture, came into general acceptance. The debate over the proposed treaty to control psychotropic drugs also heated up at that time. Nevertheless, the DNHW replaced Curran with Dr. Ross Chapman, head of the Department's Food and Drug Directorate. In the 1970s, Ottawa's representation in the international arena typified the shift in emphasis that occurred in many countries. Administrators with backgrounds in medicine, public health, social science, and pharmacology took a greater role in determining national and international policy.

The United Kingdom[15]

British officials concentrated on altering policy rather than on making organizational changes, largely because British physicians had retained more independence than their American counterparts in the treatment of addicts. Attempting to promote a social hygiene approach, the government launched some new research, outreach, public health, and educational programs. The Home Office also exercised closer scrutiny over physicians and pharmacists. Nevertheless, as the drug-using population increased, especially among the underclass, Britain gravitated toward a more punitive approach to individual users and tighter domestic controls.

The Netherlands[16]

The Netherlands extended its tradition of bucking the system. Dutch officials had expressed concern since the 1920s that overly stringent national and international regulations increased illegal manufacture, trafficking, abuse, and associated criminality. Beginning in the later 1960s, the Dutch polity engaged in a painstaking debate about the merits of greater control versus a more tolerant approach. Drawing on the *Opium Regie* experience and an appreciation of the special characteristics of Dutch political society, a consensus program emerged featuring: decriminalized personal use of substances viewed as relatively benign (particularly marijuana), a quasi-legal shadow market to service that demand, increased restrictions on abuse of "hard drugs," directing enforcement efforts against illicit imports, and a general emphasis on social normalization rather than ostracization of drug addicts. Dutch policy since the later 1960s served as a lightning rod for opponents and supporters of the international regime's continued emphasis on supply control, enforcement, and punishment.

The international organs

The new wave of drug abuse also broke over international control organizations. Still plagued by internal strife, the DND did not launch a coherent response for several years. The Board underwent a time of organizational transition, but retained a conservative approach to carrying out its duties. Both bodies continued to serve as battlegrounds upon which other parties maneuvered for position.

The division of narcotic drugs[17]

At the United Nations, the increasing scope of the drug question created pressure to expand CND membership. Some nations, such as Brazil and Morocco, wished to join out of concern for spiraling drug abuse and smuggling. Important industrialized states wanted representation on the CND for defensive purposes. Berne, suffering increasing disapproval for the role that Swiss banks played in protecting illicit drug profits, wished to move aggressively against critics. Germany and Japan wanted to gain a place at the table to protect their domestic industries, especially since the threat of controls loomed over the highly profitable psychotropic trade. States aligned with the Soviet Union hoped to take advantage of social turmoil in the west to point out the superiority of their socialist systems. Southeast Asian states, on the other hand, declined to join out of fear that they would endure more castigation; as matters stood they could ignore invitations to attend as observers. Originally limited to fifteen members, the CND grew to an increasingly unwieldy size.[18] Additionally, numerous non-member states, extra-governmental organizations, and other entities sent observers to CND meetings. By the early 1970s, the Commission's sessions attracted well over a hundred attendees.[19]

As this heightened interest in the CND's proceedings took hold, bureaucratic issues once again interfered with the UN's drug control efforts. The latest in a succession of budget crises forced economies upon the DND and PCOB/DSB secretariats at the same time that their responsibilities increased. Gilbert Yates unexpectedly stepped down as DND chief in 1962 and a prolonged period of instability ensued until Vladimir Kuśević of Yugoslavia took the helm in 1967. In addition to his impeccable credentials, Kuśević's connection to Yugoslavia made him a palatable choice for producing states. Kuśević also brought to the DND a medical expertise not seen since Rachel Crowdy. Most importantly, he possessed an open mind. Kuśević recognized that, in order to combat increasingly sophisticated illicit traffickers, to deal with psychotropic substances, and to take account of demand issues in reducing drug addiction, changes in the control regime's configuration and practice were necessary. By espousing a global emphasis on supply and demand, Kuśević encouraged new approaches during his five years as DND Director.

Vladimir KUŚEVIĆ (1914–). Yugoslavia. Pharmacist and biochemist. Fought with Tito. Director of Yugoslavia's pharmaceutical industry (1945–46), opium monopoly (1946–49), and pharmaceutical division of the Health Ministry (1950–67), served intermittently as Belgrade's representative to the CND. Elected to PCOB 1956–67, DSB 1960–67, and named DND Director 1967–72. Enjoyed a well-earned reputation as a frank, reliable, and impartial international civil servant. Kuśević advocated a more holistic view of the drug problem that emphasized new approaches and did not neglect the needs of developing states. Primary force behind the 1971 Psychotropic Convention and UNFDAC.

Adolf LANDE (1905–197?). Swiss after 1955. Jewish Austrian lawyer who fled across Europe to America after the *Anschluss*. Learned international law while working for the US government during World War II. Worked in turn for the DND, the PCOB, as UN consultant, for American manufacturers, and again for the UN. Specialist in international law as it applied to narcotics treaties. A brilliant, cantankerous perfectionist, Lande expressed his views in the strongest terms. Possessed a chameleon-like ability to argue whatever position appeared most likely to advance the interests of his current employer.

Affairs of the Board[20]

With little direction emanating from the DND during the mid-1960s, the struggle for leadership at the international level inevitably affected the Board. The DND's most experienced staff member, Adolf Lande, jumped ship to the PCOB/DSB secretariat. Passed over for the Directorship of the DND, Lande assumed the position of Board/Body Secretary from the retiring Louis Atzenwiler. Lande, who had previously acted as Yates's chief henchman in attempts to subsume the PCOB/DSB secretariat, suddenly became the staunchest defender of the administrative status quo. He highlighted the relatively aggressive activity of the Board, at least when compared to the rudderless DND. Under the circumstances, many national control officials, otherwise disposed to favor amalgamating the two services, supported continuation of a separate Board secretariat. Elections to Board membership became embroiled with the dispute over the Single Convention. The Board added several seats to placate those calling for wider geographical representation. When the Single Convention came into force the INCB, with slightly reconfigured powers, replaced the old Board and DSB. Nevertheless, the new Board carried out its duties in the same cautious manner as its predecessor.

New initiatives

By the late 1960s, then, governments and international agencies had attempted to institute measures to meet the new situation. The upsurge in drug use prompted all the principal players to look to the international arena. Many western states blamed their domestic difficulties on inadequate control abroad. Some focused on the threat posed by the traditionally defined dangerous drugs – opiates, coca products, and cannabis. Others considered psychotropic substances the primary concern. Socialist countries spied a golden opportunity to score political points against a corrupt capitalist west. Producer nations sought a measure of revenge; they aimed to impose controls on psychotropics that would prove burdensome to manufacturing states. The stage was set for a new round of negotiations covering psychotropics, narcotics, and assistance programs designed to help states carry out their international obligations. Governments, international agencies, special-interest groups, and pharmaceutical companies maneuvered on all three fronts simultaneously in hopes of promoting their interests.

Toward control of psychotropics[21]

Since its inception, the CND had adopted a double standard when considering the merits of potentially harmful drugs. Under the formula championed by Herbert May as part of the 1931 treaty negotiations, international regulations presumed new narcotic substances guilty until proven innocent. Controls were imposed automatically unless supporters produced evidence indicating the non-addictive nature of a drug. Psychotropics, on the other hand, operated under an innocent-until-proven-guilty standard.

Several factors accounted for this fundamental difference in approach. Most importantly, the symbiotic relationships between pharmaceutical companies, government officials, the research community, and physicians created a predisposition to view the new substances as benign agents. Despite the absence of long-term clinical experience, most preferred to believe laudatory pharmacological claims, especially when buttressed by scientific analysis. Non-narcotic drugs offered the promise of alleviating a wide range of physical and psychological maladies, creating a strong demand among practitioners. Since the new substances were intended for non-analgesic purposes, and since notions of addiction relied on a model that tied dependency to narcotic-like symptoms, most assumed that psychotropics possessed little potential for addiction.

The profit potential of psychotropics caused the pharmaceutical industry to oppose narcotics-style regulation with great vigor. At both the national and international levels, regulatory officials relied on industry cooperation. Few wished to engender resistance from drug companies that might jeopardize existing controls. Many preferred to concentrate on the traditional drugs of abuse, opiates and coca. In the international arena, representatives from manufacturing states dominated the CND's proceedings, and they promoted the interests of their domestic pharmaceutical industries vigorously. As a result, the CND took a *laissez-faire* attitude toward the new substances.

Manufacturing states proffered a number of arguments to support their position on psychotropics, drawing on a century-long tradition of anti-control arguments. They claimed that these modern, scientifically based substances did not possess the properties necessary to create "addiction." At the same time, western CND representatives discouraged UN and WHO-sponsored studies that might uncover the undesirable qualities of widely used stimulants and depressants. Manufacturing states also contended that unless substantial incidence of addiction came to light, sale of psychotropics should not be impeded. That position, precisely the opposite of the attitude taken toward narcotics, enabled rapid expansion of psychotropic use in medicine. Western CND representatives disingenuously claimed that even if psychotropics were being abused, no evidence of an international traffic existed. The issue therefore lay outside the competence of the UN control apparatus. (A lack of international smuggling had not stopped control advocates from imposing restrictions on some narcotic substances.) Finally, manufacturing states asserted that the 1961 Single Convention, like all previous treaties, only pertained to drugs producing effects similar to opiates, coca products, and cannabis. Since hallucinogens and central nervous system stimulants and depressants produced different effects, they could not be regulated by any of the extant multilateral agreements.

By the mid-1960s, however, those assertions collapsed under the weight of countervailing evidence. Broader experience with psychotropics indicated that a type of addiction did indeed occur, although it often took a form somewhat different from that produced by narcotics. As pharmaceutical companies promoted their products for as many uses as possible, the entirely predictable excesses soon occurred. Beginning in the mid-1960s, the WHO issued findings indicating that some amphetamines possessed characteristics similar to cocaine and that certain hallucinogens appeared to produce effects analogous to cannabis.

During the 1960s, calls for international restrictions on psychotropic drugs increased markedly. The negative effects caused by abuse of psychotropics had become apparent, and many governments (including those with significant pharmaceutical industries) instituted local and/or national measures to limit their availability. Yet the disparity between states' regulatory regimes created opportunities for entrepreneurs to thrive. As had occurred in the 1920s, legitimate manufacturing firms exploited markets that remained relatively open. Unscrupulous traders soon developed a brisk business supplying non-medical demand in countries with more restrictive regulations. Scandinavian states, led by Sweden, complained loudly about the lack of cooperation from manufacturing states such as Germany. In 1965, Sweden circumvented the dilatory CND by calling upon the World Health Organization's drug committees to impose controls on stimulants and depressants. Recognizing the propaganda value of the drug problem, Eastern bloc states agitated for controls as well. Producer states, which had long advocated controls over psychotropics (more to place the shoe on the other foot than out of any concern for their own citizens), delighted in the new converts to their cause. Agitation for regulation of psychotropics emanated from within as well. As abuse became more widespread, especially among the middle class, many concerned citizens, public health officials, and medical professionals called for increased restrictions on availability. Faced with a challenge of such magnitude, especially the WHO's threat to seize the regulatory initiative, CND representatives from manufacturing states could no longer ignore the issue.

Once it became clear that controls were in the offing, officials from manufacturing states exerted a predominant influence in fashioning international regulations. In August 1966 a CND subcommittee recommended a package of controls to be imposed on psychotropics. Manufacturing states engineered a report that emphasized enhanced national regulation while downplaying the need for import/export controls or international legislation. In 1967 manufacturing states scored a victory when the Board, the UN Legal Office, and the WHO pronounced that in order to control psychotropics a new treaty would have to be negotiated. In separate statements, all three bodies noted various administrative and definitional difficulties that precluded a simple application of the Single Convention to non-narcotic drugs. In 1968, the CND approved the preparation of a draft treaty for the control of psychotropic substances. The experience of creating the Single Convention "by committee" had proven so dismal that few wished to entrust the CND with generating the first draft. Owing to turmoil within the DND that Kuŝević had not yet overcome, the secretariat did not possess the requisite expertise or cohesion. Only one man, Adolf Lande, appeared capable of carrying out the task. Recently retired as Secretary of the Board, Lande had served fifteen years in the DND. He possessed experience drafting previous treaties and had produced the official UN commentary on the Single Convention.

The decision to hire Lande augured well for manufacturing states. Lande had always demonstrated an affinity toward the interests of the principal western powers. In 1968, he believed they would not agree to controls over psychotropics that approximated those embodied in the Single Convention. Lande's work reflected that assessment. To placate anticipated criticism, Lande produced two drafts. One version allowed fewer loopholes than the other, but both variants imposed considerably less stringent controls than those applied to narcotics.

With the publication of Lande's draft in late 1968, differences between states emerged clearly. A "manufacturing group," comprised primarily of western countries with significant pharmaceutical industries, opposed strict controls. The "manufacturing group" adopted a divide-and-defend position. They acquiesced in relatively severe limitations being placed on hallucinogens (less used in medical practice and considered less promising by researchers) and a small number of amphetamines considered most dangerous by the Scandinavian countries. Manufacturing states, however, insisted that no controls should be placed on more widely used depressants such as barbiturates and tranquilizers. A "strict control" coalition, consisting of Scandinavian governments, producer states, and Soviet bloc countries, argued for stringent limitation of all classes of psychotropics. International organizations maneuvered for position as well. Both the Board and the WHO hoped a new treaty would bestow stronger mandates to carry out their duties.

Pharmaceutical industry representatives recognized that a general treaty would bring certain benefits to manufacturing firms. Most importantly, a treaty would determine a *de facto* level of control that many states would not exceed. Few governments possessed the resources to investigate the bewildering array of new substances entering the market. Indeed, many had copied the four control schedules appended to the Single Convention directly into their domestic legislation. A treaty covering psychotropics would likely produce a similar result. By creating a standard regulatory environment, pharmaceutical companies achieved several goals. They could proceed with the business of developing, securing approval for, and marketing new substances in a worldwide market. At the same time, minimum barriers kept unscrupulous competitors at bay. Any manufacturer who did not play by the international rules would suffer opprobrium as an illicit supplier. Pharmaceutical companies aimed to whittle down the regulations to the minimum necessary to achieve those two goals.

To augment their strategy, pharmaceutical firms and their governmental supporters modified anti-control arguments of the past to forge a powerful least-restrictive-environment case for psychotropics. Noting that widespread use of psychotropic substances raised new issues for the control regime, they focused on a cost-benefit analysis dubbed the "utility question." Although a certain number of individuals abused the new psychoactive agents, many more benefitted from their proper use. Under medical supervision, these substances could alleviate a variety of physical and psychological maladies. Undue restriction of psychotropics would deny their benefits to many in need. Research and development of new drugs might be curtailed as well. Even if regulatory structures did not directly restrict access, the same result might occur by indirect means. Reporting requirements, administrative oversight, and distribution restrictions might drive up the cost of manufacturing and marketing psychotropic substances, thereby limiting availability to consumers. Pharmaceutical firms and their supporters insisted that each drug must be evaluated individually, and that a balance must be struck between the *proven* risk to public health and the degree of therapeutic usefulness demonstrated by that drug.

During 1969–70, the usual pre-negotiation process ensued. Manufacturing states won a key victory by expunging language from the draft that would have required governments to submit estimates-of-need to the Board. Without an estimates system, no mechanism existed to determine whether pharmaceutical firms were manufacturing in excess of "legitimate" need. States advocating strict controls over psychotropics would have to do without one of the linchpins supporting the control system devised for narcotics.

The UN scheduled the plenipotentiary conference for January 1971 in Vienna. The large number of attendees (over 300) reflected heightened concern about drug abuse, the burgeoning of national and international control bureaucracies, and the interest of those with a material stake in the outcome. In addition to seventy-five government delegations, representatives of the WHO, INCB, Interpol, intergovernmental organizations, non-governmental organizations, and the International Pharmaceutical Federation attended. The atmosphere was reminiscent of the 1925 and 1931 conferences, where the basic rules defining the narcotic control regime had been laid out. The negotiations featured much behind-the-scenes maneuvering, and reflected the overweening influence of the pharmaceutical industry and its supporters.

The 1971 Vienna Conference[22]

As in the case of previous drug conferences, lengthy pre-negotiations did not resolve many fundamental differences between participants. The

Scandinavians, producer states, and Soviet bloc nations continued to advocate stringent controls over psychotropics. Although attempts to make direct use of the Single Convention failed, they wanted to impose equivalent provisions on non-narcotic substances in the new treaty. Manufacturing states, on the other hand, remained determined to avoid stringent controls. The outcome reflected the continued power wielded by the industrialized nations that had bent the regime's contours to their purposes since the beginning.

The negotiations

The "strict control" coalition attempted to insert a variety of strong provisions into the new treaty. They advocated a full range of statistical reporting requirements on the manufacture, distribution, and consumption of psychotropics, import/export authorizations, procedures that facilitated placing new drugs under control, and schedules-of-control containing meaningful restrictions over a wide range of non-narcotic substances. As an added security, "strict control" states wished to restrict the trade in precursor chemicals – synthetic raw materials comprising the active ingredients for psychotropic drugs. Strict control states also wished to remove as much decision-making power as possible from the manufacturer-dominated CND by promoting a predominant role for the WHO in the scheduling/amendment process. The Scandinavian and producer states wanted to strengthen the Board's powers of investigation and censure, but the Soviet bloc vehemently opposed that provision.

Not surprisingly, manufacturing and producing states reversed the positions they occupied during the 1961 negotiations. The producers now harkened back to a previous treaty (the Single Convention) as a benchmark of rectitude. Western industrial powers, on the other hand, argued for the type of loopholes they had opposed in 1961.

The attitude of the United States, *primus inter pares* among manufacturing states, exemplified the approach that industrialized states applied to psychotropic substances. BNDD Director John Ingersoll's instructions contrasted greatly with those given to American delegations attending all previous plenipotentiary gatherings. The influence of pharmaceutical firms, the research community, government health bureaucrats, and physicians over an issue that had previously resided nearly exclusively with enforcement officials could not have been more apparent. The American delegation was instructed to secure a "reasonable" treaty – one that struck a balance between legal, administrative, economic, social, and scientific interests. The treaty should not unduly restrict physicians' prerogatives nor researchers' investigations. In 1970 Congress had revised American drug laws, including the regulations that dealt with placing new substances under control. In deference to the pharmaceutical industry, the 1970 law ensured that new drugs would not be restricted without receiving a fair administrative hearing. Consequently, the American delegation insisted on language that allowed states to exempt themselves from control decisions handed down by the WHO or CND.

The Americans nevertheless represented moderate opinion among manufacturing states. A group of irreconcilables including West Germany, Switzerland, the Netherlands, Belgium, Austria, and Denmark insisted on weakening the treaty at every juncture. Although securing much of what they desired, the Germans, Dutch, Belgians, and Austrians (the country hosting the conference) voted against the final document.

Despite the seminal influence they exerted over the policy-creation process at the national level, pharmaceutical companies took out extra measures of insurance. Individuals in the employ of manufacturing firms played an important, if behind-the-scenes, role in the Vienna negotiations. Lande, who had recently concluded his long career with the UN drug control apparatus by drafting the psychotropic treaty, surprised his colleagues by attending the conference as a member of the American delegation. Lande represented the Pharmaceutical Manufacturers' Association, a trade-industry group. High-ranking employees of individual American firms attended as unofficial US observers. Berne's delegation included two members who, although not identified as such, worked for large multinational pharmaceutical firms headquartered in Switzerland. Dr. Walter Wartburg, of Roche, Basle, worked incessantly, and ultimately successfully, to remove from control substances manufactured by his firm. Perhaps the most notable example of pharmaceutical company influence occurred when the secretariat noticed that a group of six Latin American countries uncharacteristically supported weakening the treaty. Their leading representative spoke poor Spanish. A quick investigation revealed that the man worked for Hoffmann-LaRoche. By such extraordinary measures pharmaceutical firms made sure to advance their interests.[23]

The provisions

In the course of the Vienna negotiations, manufacturing states prevailed on most of the essential points. Making good use of the "utility equation," they insisted on reducing the scope of reporting requirements and import/export controls over some classes of drugs. Other substances, including precursor chemicals, escaped control altogether. Manufacturing states inserted a number of provisions that made adding new substances to the "schedules of control" more difficult. The CND retained a central position in scheduling and amendment procedures. The final document also allowed governments to make reservations concerning key provisions of the treaty. At several important junctures manufacturing states, either individually or in small clusters, threatened to withhold signature of the final document if their demands were not met. Conference delegates, largely out of fear of walking away empty-handed, bowed to such pressure repeatedly.[24]

The manner in which the 1971 treaty dealt with derivatives exemplified the clout exercised by pharmaceutical firms and their governmental representatives. International drug control agreements had always included language specifying which salts, ethers, esters, and isomers of the substances in question fell under the same regulations as their parent drugs. This stipulation was crucial to proper control, because medical application of narcotics in their pure form occurred rarely. The inclusion of derivatives in the schedules obviated the need to list every possible chemical combination – an impossible task. Additionally, the inclusion of derivatives simplified the task of adding opium- or coca-based substances to the schedules at a later date. Most drugs would automatically come under control.

The schedules appended to the Psychotropic Treaty, however, included *no mention* of derivatives. The international regulatory measures outlined in the treaty, therefore, applied only to a small number of compounds (a mere 32 substances spread among four schedules).[25] The ramifications of this omission were not lost on participants. Without automatic inclusion of derivatives, the Psychotropic Treaty's provisions were nearly toothless. The technical experts responsible for creating the schedules subsequently claimed that this giant loophole represented a simple oversight; in the rush of events as the conference came to a close, they had forgotten to include a footnote pertaining to derivatives. A more plausible explanation is offered by István Bayer, longtime Hungarian CND representative who worked for the DND in 1971. He maintains that the omission resulted from a deal made by the political representatives when the technical experts were not present.[26] Manufacturing states appeared poised to reject the conference's work altogether. The schedules had to be sacrificed to secure their acquiescence. The technical experts expressed their dismay when they found out what had transpired, but little could be done at that point. Excluding derivatives – 95 percent of the substances created by pharmaceutical firms – represented an unprecedented departure from the scope of control laid down in previous treaties.

Having eviscerated key portions of the treaty, manufacturing states supported language that enhanced the Board's authority. The American delegation, in particular, wished to devolve greater power upon the Board. The United States, as part of a rejuvenated campaign against heroin trafficking and illicit opium production, had already initiated procedures to strengthen the Single Convention. Provisions improving the Board's statutory power would set a precedent for the upcoming narcotics negotiations of 1971–72.

The Vienna Treaty: summary

Although the UN public relations apparatus claimed that the 1971 Psychotropic Treaty represented a new era in drug control, insiders knew the issue remained in doubt. The treaty placed hallucinogens under fairly stringent controls, but applied considerably weaker limitations to the trade in much more widely used (and profitable) substances such as stimulants and depressants. Numerous loopholes, particularly the omission of derivatives, weakened the document further. Nevertheless, a precedent had been set; control over psychotropics received international sanction. In subsequent years, skillful manipulation by pro-control governments and the UN secretariat gradually plugged many of the treaty's gaps. Pharmaceutical firms and their supporters encountered increasing difficulties in avoiding the type of restrictions they defeated in the original text.

Similarly, the Psychotropic Convention broke modest new ground in another area, but how governments would respond remained unclear. Article 20 called upon signatories to prevent misuse of psychotropics, and to identify, treat, educate, and rehabilitate abusers. The provision was couched in deliberately vague language, thereby allowing states to avoid implementing programs unless they believed them necessary. Nevertheless, Article 20 represented a victory for those wishing to shift attention away from an exclusive emphasis on enforcement and supply. States finally admitted, at least symbolically, that the demand side of the equation required attention.

In the immediate wake of the Vienna negotiations, however, questions about the Psychotropic Treaty could not be considered. Governments returned to old ground at the behest of Washington. The United States had once again gone on the warpath concerning narcotics.

Amending the Single Convention[27]

Over there

At the same time that manufacturing states defeated attempts to erect a stringent control regime for psychotropics, the United States led a new attack on narcotics. In response to unprecedented levels of substance abuse, President Richard Nixon declared war on drugs, particularly heroin. He ordered federal agencies to undertake a comprehensive offensive against drug addiction. On the domestic front, the Nixon administration paid increased attention to all facets of the problem. New legislation increased resources devoted to law enforcement and placed amphetamines under stricter controls. The White House created a Special Action Office to coordinate research, treatment, and educational efforts. Congress increased appropriations for rehabilitation and treatment of drug abusers. Yet, as had happened so many times before, American officials found it politically expedient to locate the source of trouble abroad. Consequently, the United States initiated an aggressive international anti-narcotics campaign at the highest level.

Once again, bilateral negotiations, even when successful, proved insufficient to curb illicit trafficking. American pressure on Ankara to reduce excess production yielded respectable results.[28] Events in other opium-producing areas, however, threatened to negate the progress achieved in Turkey. In 1969 Teheran announced its intention to license domestic opium production on a limited basis, a fearsome prospect to those who remembered previous Iranian behavior.[29] Other areas of the globe, particularly, Southeast Asia, continued to produce a large over-supply of opium.[30]

Aware of the necessity for a multilateral, coordinated effort, the Nixon administration launched a campaign to toughen the international regime's restrictions on narcotics. BNDD Director Ingersoll and others did not wish negotiations surrounding the control of psychotropics to detract from what they still viewed as the main enemy – narcotics. In 1970 American officials began agitating to strengthen the Single Convention. At first they hoped to institute an outright ban on opium cultivation by claiming that development of synthetic narcotics obviated the need for natural substances. Many states objected, noting that such a policy would further strengthen industrialized countries by raising prices for consumers and depriving producing states of a profitable export item. American officials then proffered a plan to augment the regulatory and investigatory powers assigned to the INCB. The United States also wished to pursue international traffickers more vigorously by enhancing extradition procedures. To implement its program Washington proposed convening a plenipotentiary meeting for amending the 1961 Single Convention. In that way manufacturing states could tighten regulations that applied primarily to producers while avoiding increased Board supervision of psychotropic drugs. Producing states and the Soviet bloc objected vehemently to any new encroachments on national sovereignty, and many developing nations supported that position. Anticipating such opposition, American officials aggressively solicited the support of other governments throughout 1971. At Washington's behest, the UN moved rapidly to schedule a conference. Delegates assembled Geneva in March 1972 to amend the Single Convention.

The 1972 Conference[31]

At the 1972 Geneva conference, matters proceeded in accordance with American wishes. Most states recognized that, in an election year, the Nixon administration wanted to score anti-narcotics successes in the international arena. As long as the proposed amendments did not disrupt the supply of legitimate narcotics, governments were generally disposed to let the Americans have their way. Producing and Soviet Bloc governments succeeded in pruning somewhat the INCB's enhanced powers. Those states also insisted that the amended Single Convention apply equally to synthetic narcotics, a proposal to which manufacturing governments reluctantly agreed. Additionally, the treaty called on states to pursue rehabilitation and treatment as an alternative to incarceration. Nevertheless, the 1972 Protocol Amending the Single Convention symbolized an enduring emphasis on traditional conceptions of the drug problem. Led by the United States, the international control system continued to concentrate on eliminating excess supplies of narcotics, while downplaying the significance of non-narcotic substances, demand issues, and the relationship between control and criminality.

The Fund[32]

As a part of its overseas anti-narcotics campaign, the Nixon administration recognized the necessity of deploying carrots as well as sticks to motivate recalcitrant producer states. The United States expressed a new willingness to support large-scale crop-substitution programs, technical assistance to improve administration and law enforcement, regional efforts to interdict trafficking, and even coordination of educational efforts. The direct infusion of American money, however, proved unpalatable to many developing countries, owing in large part to domestic pressure to resist Washington's dictates. To circumvent such qualms, US officials proposed the creation of an anti-drug abuse fund to be managed by the United Nations. The fund, which the United States proposed to finance through government contributions, would operate independently of regular UN-sponsored aid programs.

Washington first broached the idea of an independent fund in late 1970. Other states reacted cautiously. Many western governments believed it necessary to make some sort of anti-drug gesture, but they disagreed on what course to take. London opposed in principle the creation of special funds operating outside of the regular UN budget. The world body should set priorities for granting assistance without making exceptions, even for high-profile issues such as drug abuse. Ottawa did not object in principle, but expressed concern about aspects of the proposal. Some advocated utilizing the fund to advance research on prevention, while others wanted to concentrate on law enforcement. Managerial questions also caused concern. The CND currently operated a relatively small technical-assistance program. Could the Commission and DND staff administer a large fund properly? If not, should the task fall to the UN Development Program or some other organization?

The UN proved to be the most enthusiastic supporter of the fund proposal. DND director Kuśević wished to promote a more integrated attack on drug abuse by focusing attention in roughly equal amounts on supply, demand, and the illicit traffic. Monies dedicated specifically to the elimination of drug abuse could be directed at whatever aspect of the problem seemed most likely to produce results. Kuśević hoped to expand a pilot program for crop substitution recently initiated in Southeast Asia, provide support for regional efforts to stem smuggling, direct a coordinated effort to investigate the etiology of drug addiction, and perhaps explore preventive strategies as well.

With support from the United States and the UN secretariat, the CND approved creation of an independent "UN Fund for Drug Abuse Control" (UNFDAC) in 1971. Many governments remained skeptical, but none wished to challenge the United States openly. Washington pledged $2 million for the Fund, but few contributions were forthcoming from other quarters. In hopes of embarrassing states into making further contributions, Kuśević personally donated a $5000 prize he received for outstanding work in the field of drug control. Governments nevertheless demurred, largely out of concern for the Fund's motives.

Such skepticism proved justified. The enterprise soon came to be dominated by American priorities. Washington insisted that the Fund emphasize law enforcement and crop substitution projects at the expense of undertakings designed to reduce demand. UNFDAC monies were steered toward countries where direct US pressure to curtail opium production failed. Moreover, the aid took on a political cast; the Fund favored projects that included American allies. Kuśević expressed his concern to BNDD Director Ingersoll forthrightly: "Who could in these circumstances have any doubts that the Fund is in fact an American undertaking?"[33]

The creation of the Fund added a new feature to the international apparatus. After 1971 the global drug regime resembled a three-legged stool. The CND, in which governments were represented, acted as the executive and policy-making body. The INCB exercised its oversight and quasi-judicial functions. The UNFDAC financed programs designed to achieve regulatory goals. With money to spend, the Fund became a magnet for attention. In subsequent years, the older international control organs had to accommodate this altered power configuration. Other actors, keeping in mind the US influence over Fund operations, adjusted to the new situation as well.

Conclusion

The drug control universe underwent changes of cosmic proportions during the 1960s. Driven by skyrocketing demand, illicit use of old and new substances flourished. Many rejected the ethos that informed the system – restricting access to drugs appeared as simply another manifestation of bankrupt "establishment" values. Others, recognizing the danger of unregulated availability, nevertheless questioned the assumptions underpinning the control regime. By the early 1970s, most observers, experts, and policymakers no longer supported an exclusive emphasis on supply control. For the first time, governments devoted at least some attention, money, and organizational resources to fundamental investigations about the nature of addiction, treatment programs, rehabilitation schemes, and preventive education efforts. The new sensibility manifested itself at the international level; both the 1971 Psychotropic Convention and the 1972 Protocol Amending the Single Convention included language encouraging states to address the demand side of the equation.

At the same time, however, the paradigm informing the old regime proved exceptionally resilient. With the retirement of Anslinger the last of the framers left the scene, to be replaced by a less colorful collection of bureaucrats and specialists. Yet the founders' legacy lived on: the national and international machinery they built continued to emphasize approaches in circulation since the turn of the century. Despite the increased attention paid to alternatives, governments and international organizations concentrated on longstanding supply-oriented goals: restrictions on the movement of psychotropics, tightened controls on narcotics and coca-based substances, and providing increased resources designed to assist developing nations in carrying out their international obligations. The creation of UNFDAC only reinforced this bias. The traditional calculus remained intact – western industrialized states focused control efforts toward producing countries and primary agricultural products. Developing nations, hoping that manufacturing states might finally get their comeuppance, again settled for the short end of the stick.

Nevertheless, the 1961–72 period represented, to borrow Churchill's phrase, the "end of the beginning." In 1912 the Hague Opium Treaty had created a new set of expectations concerning the international trade in drugs. Although it took two decades to implement those proscriptions, by the early 1930s manufacturing states and pharmaceutical firms had come to terms with the new covenant. They acquiesced permanently in a certain level of restriction over the trade in narcotics, although the regulatory burdens landed disproportionately on producing states. By agreeing to the 1971 Psychotropic Convention, manufacturing states again conceded an essential point – at least some non-narcotic substances were liable to abuse and should be treated accordingly. In subsequent years those advocating substantive international controls over psychotropics edged slowly toward their goal. Moreover, the events of the 1960s engendered a permanent challenge to the long-dominant supply-control paradigm. Slowly and unevenly, demand reduction came to play a role in the calculations of those formulating policy and allocating money. In the subsequent years, the differences between those competing visions came into sharp relief as control authorities and their critics faced a variety of challenges, new and old.

9   Crosscurrents – 1972–2000[1]

An unprecedented policy-related turbulence[2] characterized drug diplomacy for the remainder of the century. On the one hand, amendments to the regime enacted in the early 1970s represented only the latest adjustments to the trans-national balance of power. All parties continued promoting their interests in the usual manner. The supply-side impetus retained saliency despite, and in some ways because of, significantly altered circumstances. Conversely, a formidable counter-current arose that challenged long-dominant assumptions. Parties reconsidered traditional approaches to the drug question in light of rising awareness about demand issues, the increasing threat posed by illicit trafficking and use, and a greater appreciation of the role that social factors play in shaping perceptions about deviance and addiction. Whirling about one another, these contrary courses generated a choppy ride for all concerned.

Business as usual: theme and variations

Secretarial entrepreneurship

Maneuvers surrounding the 1971 Psychotropic Convention exemplified the continuities most clearly. Predictably, many key manufacturing states moved slowly to bring themselves under the treaty's obligations. Pharmaceutical companies led the opposition, finding allies among some medical and pharmacists' organizations and many engaged in drug research. Those groups objected to the increased restrictions on availability and use that the treaty required. The UN secretariat, by nature invested in any successfully completed treaty, embarked on its customary campaign for ratification by informally encouraging states to adhere. Largely as a result of those efforts, the Psychotropic Treaty entered into force fairly rapidly, in 1976. Resistance to the new treaty, especially among manufacturing states, abated only gradually.[3]

Yet implementation remained problematic even after nations ratified the Psychotropic Convention. The treaty suffered from debilitating loopholes that rendered it nearly sterile. In addition to "strict control" states and some producer governments, the UN secretariat wished to strengthen the treaty's provisions. In addition to concerns about psychotropic abuse, the DND secretariat hoped producer governments might offer fuller cooperation on narcotics and coca if manufacturing states suffered under increased psychotropic controls. The 1971 treaty weakened the INCB's mandate somewhat; the Board's secretariat feared that operations would be impaired, and that its independent position might be threatened. Yet all viewed the prospect of renegotiating the treaty as unpalatable.

As an alternative, the DND and INCB secretariats launched an ingenious campaign to amend the Psychotropic Convention by unofficial means. The DND and the INCB asked governments to submit information not required by treaty statute on a "voluntary" basis. A number of producing and "strict control" states obliged, and the secretariats used those initial acceptances to encourage others to follow suit. At the behest of several governments and with quiet support from the secretariat, the WHO and CND pronounced that derivatives (salts, ethers, etc.) of drugs included in the schedules also fell under international control. By the early 1980s, many governments voluntarily reported manufacturing, consumption, and trade statistics not required by the treaty. In this manner, provisions not included in the original Psychotropic Convention became part of customary international law. International civil servants active at that time count this accomplishment among their greatest achievements.[4]

Staying the course

The United States vigorously pursued its longstanding focus on reducing excess supplies of traditional dangerous drugs, but again achieved only fleeting success at considerable cost. In the early 1970s Washington successfully pressured Ankara and Paris about the "French connection," but Mexican opium producers and heroin manufacturers soon replaced them. Subsequent American administrations used high-profile diplomatic pressure to eliminate havens for producers and traffickers in Asia or Latin America, but each time the business simply moved to another conducive environment.[5]

The seriousness of the drug problem also caused a reconsideration of the psychotropics issue. Pharmaceutical companies' products suffered under increasing scrutiny from Congress and federal regulatory agencies. In 1980, the United States ratified the Psychotropic Convention, symbolizing the country's shifting attitudes. Washington even moderated its previous opposition to enacting controls over precursor chemicals,[6] and dropped its longstanding resistance to negotiating a treaty aimed at curbing trafficking.

Bureaucratic realignments reflected the heightened emphasis Washington placed on the drug issue. The Nixon administration replaced the BNDD with the Drug Enforcement Administration (DEA), an agency designed to enhance enforcement at home and abroad. The State Department paid increasing attention to the issue, creating the post of Assistant Secretary for International Narcotics Matters in 1978. Mathea Falco, the first occupant of that office, co-ordinated American anti-drug efforts with regional bodies around the globe. On the domestic front, Falco shepherded the Psychotropic Convention through the ratification process despite strong opposition from pharmaceutical companies and their allies. After Anslinger's retirement, the State Department regained leadership over the country's drug diplomacy to an extent not exercised since the early 1920s.[7]

World developments

A combination of international pressure and concerns expressed by domestic constituencies resulted in numerous national and regional regulatory initiatives. Many states tightened domestic control measures. The Co-operation Group to Combat Drug Abuse and Illicit Trafficking in Drugs (usually referred to as the Pompidou Group) initiated regular ministerial-level contacts between European countries. Governments also inaugurated regional meetings for Heads of National Law Enforcement Agencies (HONLEA) designed to enhance police and customs drug enforcement cooperation. Organized under UN auspices, HONLEA meetings originated in Asia and the Pacific during the 1970s, and spread to Africa, Latin America, and Europe in the 1980s. UNFDAC also offered assistance, primarily to developing nations. The Fund expended the majority of its resources on crop substitution, law enforcement, and technical assistance to national control agencies. Although still often viewed as an American-inspired entity, the Fund nevertheless provided a politically acceptable way for developing nations to accept western money. Other UN, regional, and nationally funded development programs offered assistance as well, often emphasizing the notion of integrated rural development, which aimed to provide economically viable alternatives to illicit drug production. Interpol utilized interest in drug enforcement to launch a major expansion of its operations. During the 1970s Interpol became an important clearinghouse for information and a sponsor of local, regional, and global drug enforcement meetings.[8]

The control system's bias toward achieving traditional ends, even if by novel means, remained largely intact. Most efforts were still directed primarily at opiates, coca, and cannabis. The focus of control efforts was still aimed at the developing nations in which those substances originated and (mostly third world) transit countries. Although psychotropics garnered more attention from control authorities over time, they nevertheless remained a secondary concern despite widespread use and great potential for addiction. Moreover, psychotropic control efforts, as with traditional drugs of abuse, remained directed primarily at eliminating excess supplies.

Revisiting old ground

The traditional control emphasis culminated in a new illicit trafficking treaty.[9] The agreement dealt with many of the issues included in the moribund 1936 treaty, but the altered circumstances of recent decades created a more receptive atmosphere among states. The 1988 Illicit Traffic Convention criminalized acts such as illicit trading in precursor chemicals, laundering of assets, and international trafficking. The accord recognized the offense of conspiracy and called upon adherents to enact legislation allowing for the confiscation of ill-gotten assets. The treaty also required parties to offer mutual legal assistance, share information, and cooperate in law enforcement efforts. The agreement included a limited but not insignificant extradition clause and a provision calling for states to enact "appropriate measures" for the eradication of illicit cultivation. With support from a coalition of states including the United States, Canada, India, and Mexico, the treaty came into force in less than two years. Some important states proved reluctant to sign on, but resistance generally eroded over time as the treaty's strictures became more widely accepted.[10]

Reaction

The increasingly restrictive trend of the 1980s prompted proponents of the anti-control thesis to redouble their efforts. Pharmaceutical companies challenged the voluntary reporting requirements invented by the UN secretariat and subsequently supported by sympathetic national control bureaucracies. Manufacturing firms argued that governments could not claim treaty obligation as a basis for collecting ever-increasing statistical information about manufactured drugs. Many observers also began to calculate the cost/benefit equation as it applied to the drug issue differently. Some worried that increasingly invasive enforcement procedures threatened civil liberties and the integrity of treatment programs. Organizations dedicated to the reduction of suffering among those enduring debilitating pain lobbied for fewer restrictions on the distribution of powerful analgesics, despite their potential for addiction. Some research scientists also complained that restrictions on availability hindered the search for new substances possessing beneficial potential. As in earlier periods, coalitions of anti-control advocates maneuvered for advantage within the customary supply-control paradigm.[11]

Countertrends

Yet, alongside such traditional pursuits, alternate currents expanded the scope of the drug question. The explosion of drug use among otherwise respectable individuals prompted renewed attention to the demand side of the equation. Governments and researchers, primarily in Europe and North America, launched initiatives to discover how many users existed and what types of substances they abused. Debates about the nature of addiction drew upon a flourishing and increasingly sophisticated literature. Drug abuse presented an increasingly serious threat to societal cohesiveness, causing a proliferation of treatment, rehabilitation, and prevention programs. Illicit trafficking emerged as a threat to national and international order. As the illegal market exploded, mushrooming clandestine manufacture in producing areas even caused environmental degradation.[12]

International currents reflected this parallel emphasis. Producing nations applauded the new attention paid to the sins of consuming states, but also acknowledged that drug abuse affected their societies as well. Domestic constituencies such as public health agencies, those engaged in counseling and treatment, academic and clinical researchers, and large sections of the public echoed the call for a more inclusive approach. Governments tilted their policies accordingly. The WHO, CND, and even the INCB began to address issues of definition, etiology, treatment, and prevention. Attention to "illicit demand," a term that had come into general use by the 1980s, signified the change in attitude. The 1988 anti-trafficking treaty included language encouraging demand reduction. The phrase "drug abuse control" replaced the older conception encapsulated in the term "drug control."[13]

The heightened cognizance of issues other than supply control resulted in a reconsideration of the system's priorities. By the late 1980s, the international community, at least on paper, arrived at a more balanced approach. A major international conference, held in 1987, produced not only the draft of the 1988 anti-trafficking treaty but also a Comprehensive Multidisciplinary Outline of Future Activities in Drug Abuse Control (CMO). The CMO placed equal stress on four categories: (1) prevention and reduction of illicit demand, (2) control of supply, (3) suppression of illicit trafficking, and (4) treatment and rehabilitation.[14] In addition to giving issues other than supply serious attention, the CMO recognized many of the problems associated with abuse of psychotropic substances. In 1990 the United Nations devised a System-Wide Action Plan that aimed to coordinate the activities undertaken by UN organs and associated agencies. That same year the UN General Assembly held a Special Session devoted to the issue and declared 1991–2000 as the United Nations Decade against Drug Abuse.[15]

Even longstanding bureaucratic arrangements succumbed to the new approach. In 1990, after a valiant rearguard action, the UN absorbed the semi-independent INCB secretariat. Although the DND, the UNFDAC, and the Board continued to be served by distinct secretarial branches, the newly designated UN Drug Control Program brought the administrative structure under one roof, fully beholden to the Secretary-General's authority. The conglomeration offered other advantages as well. Historically, it has not been unusual for one or more of the key international organs to suffer debility brought on by political difficulty, personnel problems, or programmatic atrophy. At such times, the organization(s) still functioning can pick up some of the slack, thereby ensuring at least the appearance of continued constructive operation. Such considerations are of seminal importance to an international civil service hamstrung by the vagaries of capricious governmental masters and its own self-imposed shortcomings.[16]

No watershed

The countervailing trends of the post-1972 period resulted in a more considered, multifaceted approach that simultaneously lacked decisive direction. In addition to the more even-handed balance struck between supply and demand, governments generally placed less stress on the distinctions between producing, manufacturing, transit, and consuming states. A growing recognition that all nations suffered the negative consequences of illicit drug use weakened the tendency to blame others.[17] Nevertheless, the focus of international control efforts did not change as much as the altered rhetoric might suggest. National, regional, and international control efforts continued targeting heroin, cocaine, and marijuana more than psychotropics. Producing states and developing nations that lay astride trafficking routes received the majority of attention. Treatment, rehabilitation and, to a certain extent, prevention programs emphasized traditional drugs of abuse as well. Moreover, money devoted to the drug problem remained aimed primarily at controlling supply. Development programs intended to reduce excess supplies, interdiction efforts, and law enforcement continued to consume the lion's share of funding.[18] The result was a churning of policy options; state bureaucracies, international organs, and other actors could employ or jettison various alternatives as circumstances and the socio-economic-political-cultural climate warranted.

Conclusion

As the twentieth century closed, the drug issue appeared among the most paradoxical confronting the world community. Hardly a nation on earth could claim exemption from substance abuse. In addition to a public health problem possessing international dimensions, drugs posed a threat to national, social, cultural, and economic security. However, the "drug wars" created casualties among a variety of innocent victims. Furthermore, pharmacological advances created unprecedented opportunities for relieving physical and psychological maladies. Demarcating and managing the boundaries between licit and illicit, ethical and unethical, profitable and marginal, moral and pragmatic, became increasingly problematic. Maneuvering for political, strategic, regulatory, and economic advantage occurred in an environment fraught with the sort of cultural friction, material interest, and dynamic tension between conflict and cooperation that have marked drug diplomacy since the beginning.

Conclusion

Retrospective

The expansion of world trade that began in the early modern era featured an influential exchange of substances capable of relieving pain, stimulating activity, and altering consciousness. Coffee, tea, and tobacco gained widespread acceptance, acquiring significant functions in society and providing an important impetus to world trade. Alcohol occupied a central position as well, although many viewed it as a less benign agent (at least in the hands of the lower classes). Yet opium, its derivatives, and to a lesser extent coca, became the most contentious features of this global exchange in addicting substances. A combination of factors, emanating from both Occident and Orient, marked those drugs for special attention.

Domestic and diplomatic concern about drugs accelerated during the nineteenth century. Although the Chinese were not unfamiliar with opium, the infusion of vast amounts from abroad caused the substance to become a prime symbol of foreign encroachment. Yet Chinese complaints about opium importation fell on deaf ears until a combination of domestic and geostrategic factors prompted western governments to reconsider their policies. Opium use, when introduced by overseas Chinese to a new urban underclass, heightened the drug's image in the west as an alien threat. Influential constituencies possessing a material interest in the drug issue, including temperance advocates, supporters of missionary activity, and promoters of less debilitating wares also acted as catalysts for control efforts. Geopolitical concerns provided a key stimulus. By the turn of the twentieth century, the Middle Kingdom appeared in desperate straits; curbing drug abuse became a priority for those desiring to preserve China's territorial integrity and internal cohesiveness.

By the late nineteenth century, support for international control was strongest in the United States and Great Britain. The principal missionary activity directed at the Far East emanated from the two Atlantic giants. England and America experienced most acutely western fears about encroachment by East Asians. The domestic climate linked anxieties about drugs to some of the era's principal concerns, including industrialization, technological innovation, social reform, alcohol prohibition, public health, and professionalization in medicine and government. The particular configuration of each country's commercial interests and strategic pretensions in Asia proved central to their pursuit of international drug control. Anti-control arguments developed during this initial period also shaped regulatory measures and acted as a brake on the designs of control advocates.

Between 1909 and 1931, western governments erected a supply-oriented regime that placed heavier regulatory burdens on raw materials than on the substances manufactured by pharmaceutical companies. This configuration of rules, embedded in the 1925 and 1931 treaties, reflected the material concerns and cultural biases of key constituencies. Alcohol, for example, received preferential treatment; with a few exceptions, western governments actively promoted, or at least did not discourage, exports of that debilitating substance. Producing territories, whether colonial or independent, generally resisted placing fetters on the drug trade out of revenue and administrative concerns, despite abundant evidence that substance abuse besotted a sizeable portion of their own populations. Pharmaceutical companies acquiesced in international regulations only when assured that they would receive the benefits of limited competition in return for compliance. Occidental regulators and medical practitioners favored drugs derived from technologically advanced processes invented and controlled (at least initially) by westerners; the discipline of science, they believed, produced substances superior to those of the east. That same faith in the Technological Fix shaped investigations into the etiology of drug use. Research focused on a supply-oriented solution – concocting a "magic bullet" that would relieve pain without causing addiction.

The same cultural and material concerns that shaped the regime's parameters influenced attempts to institute control measures during the 1930s. The imposition of substantive regulations endangered international free-trade principles, pharmaceutical company profits, the designs of aggressor nations, and domestic power structures, both licit and illicit. Serious efforts to curtail cultivation would require a reordering of rural society in producing states and might jeopardize the often precarious control those governments exercised, especially over back-country areas. Yet western governments pursued a supply-side strategy in large part because it placed the onus of responsibility on producing states.

Moreover, the interwar years witnessed the advent of drug control bureaucracies that infused a further constellation of interests into drug-diplomatic calculations. In the west, national regulatory agencies largely supplanted the original advocates of control. Officials espousing a stringent law-enforcement approach exhibited the most belligerent behavior. Creation of the international control organs introduced another subset of important bureaucratic actors. The Opium Advisory Committee, the Permanent Central Opium Board, the Drug Supervisory Body, their secretariats and successors carried the burden of great expectations. Yet they proved able to effect solutions only to the extent allowed by national governments, the global economic order, the machinations of traffickers, the desires of users, and other transnational influences. Hopes of creating strong supra-national organizations capable of overcoming the existing state system remained unrealized.

In the midst of World War II, the drug regime survived largely because those bureaucratic structures remained relatively intact. In addition to League of Nations officials, the British, Canadians, and Americans each hoped to derive advantage from keeping the apparatus alive. With a successful conclusion to the war in sight, Federal Bureau of Narcotics Commissioner Harry Anslinger, Canadian narcotics chief Clem Sharman, and their allies aimed to re-create the drug control world according to their designs.

In the first two postwar decades, control advocates' attempts to make headway once again ran afoul of countervailing considerations. Control officials modified their agenda to accommodate Cold War priorities. Decolonization multiplied the number of potential obstacles as the centrifugal influence exercised by imperial administrations waned. Other actors, especially anti-communist operatives in producing areas, inadvertently undermined control efforts – selling opiates conflicted with certain policy objectives but served others.[1] Producing nations resisted attempts to impose more stringent limitations that would require major upheavals in social structure, culture, and economy. Division of Narcotic Drugs Director Leon Steinig, pursuing both a noble dream and personal glory, orchestrated a spectacular bureaucratic fiasco in advocating an International Opium Monopoly. His attempts to use the Poppy Throne as a base from which to scale the heights of the nuclear arms question set back the agenda of drug control advocates by a decade, put Sharman, Anslinger, and other key players on the defensive, and spawned the abortive 1953 Opium Protocol. The respite afforded producing states an opportunity either to make accommodations with the regime's stipulations or to put up a more spirited defense against them. Manufacturing states also allowed psychotropic substances to spread with little restriction. This leniency emanated not only from cozy relations between regulatory agencies and pharmaceutical firms – as the products of western science and industry, control officials assumed that psychotropics did not warrant the zealous attention they directed toward "alien" substances derived from opium and coca.

The demand explosion that occurred in the last third of the century required all parties to reconsider their positions. Western countries acknowledged, to some extent, the importance of reducing illicit demand. Many governments in industrialized states (although not pharmaceutical companies and their allies) recognized the need to place some restrictions on the trade in psychotropic substances. Producer states perceived more clearly the threat drug abuse posed to their societies. Such alterations in attitudes and in calculations about material interest engendered, at least superficially, more cooperation in the international arena. Nevertheless, policymakers and other actors retreated into the blame game, placing the onus of responsibility for the "drug problem" elsewhere, when it suited their purposes. As the twentieth century closed, the drug question counted among the most problematic issues in the international arena.

Drug control and its discontents

The paradoxes and ironies associated with international control efforts illustrate why the drug question cannot be separated from the contexts within which it resides. Most importantly, by defining the "source" of the drug problem as "outside" (i.e. the supply-side focus), western societies relinquished much of their capability to craft a "solution" to forces beyond their control. Requiring international cooperation, control advocates' efforts stalled until World War I accelerated the pace of drug regulation: domestic sentiment shifted in favor of more restrictions and the dormant 1912 Hague agreement came to life when appended to the peace treaties and tied to the nascent League of Nations. By the mid-1930s the control regime had entered into statutory fullness, but events in both east and west undermined control efforts. World War II, whose potential to spread addiction so frightened control officials, instead consumed excess supplies. Both before and after that war, regime promoters insisted, correctly, that the drug system could provide a model to proponents of arms control. Their inability to implement the rules in practice, however, undermined attempts to transfer their proscriptions to the realm of arms. Beginning in the 1950s, Western-allied anti-communist movements supplied much of the world's growing illicit traffic. By promoting the development and dissemination of psychotropics while imposing few distribution limitations, western societies stand doubly responsible for much of the post-1950 drug problem.

Similarly, attempts to fashion effective drug control have often suffered from inauspicious timing. The British–Indian–Chinese Ten Year Agreement of 1907 appeared to be working, but the fall of the Manchus dashed hopes for a successful conclusion. In the mid-1920s, an effective treaty could be successfully negotiated only if the British government forged a consensus among its disparate constituencies. The political instability surrounding the short-lived Labour government of 1924, however, ensured that chief negotiator Malcolm Delevingne would arrive in Geneva lacking direction from his own government. In 1931, delegates to a plenipotentiary meeting intended to limit the trade in drugs had the bad fortune to meet at the very moment the world plunged into depression. Grand schemes were shelved in favor of a plan that allowed nations more freedom to promote their national industries. The control regime reached full operational status in 1933–34, just as Germany and Japan pursued policies that undermined international cooperation. A generation later, by the time that supposedly definitive instrument, the Single Convention, came into force, the first waves of an unprecedented drug abuse problem had already broken over western shores. Drug diplomacy is part and parcel of the modern world.

The consequences of control

Efforts to implement the international drug control agenda also engendered many unforeseen results. The drug regime's stipulations encouraged, however inadvertently, the development of new manufacturing processes and pharmaceutical products. The imposition of regulations spurred companies with capital invested in factories to develop new substances and manufacturing technologies.[2] For example, in the 1930s, enforcement of control measures drastically shrunk the licit pie. Western firms believed they had secured comparative regulatory advantage because they boasted advanced manufacturing processes. The Hungarians, however, invented the poppy-straw method of morphine extraction. Their discovery not only proved competitively successful, it also provided Germany a technology that ensured an adequate supply of vital medicaments in wartime.

Incentives created by the control regime's configuration influenced research agendas.[3] The company that successfully concocted a non-addicting analgesic would reap handsome rewards in the regulatory marketplace. Rather than explore questions related to the etiology of drug abuse, pharmaceutical firms, researchers, and governments concentrated on the quest for a magic potion that would kill pain without inducing dependence. Governmental control officials such as Anslinger and Sharman, who hoped to remove all legitimate need for agriculturally produced raw materials, encouraged the trend.

By imposing less restrictive regulations on psychotropics, the regime fostered their proliferation. Pharmaceutical companies, responding to opportunities offered by the relatively unfettered market, produced a variety of psychoactive substances. Physicians, searching for alternative treatments and sensitive to regulatory issues, prescribed the new drugs in increasing quantities. It only became apparent over time that many of the wonder drugs produced symptoms of addiction just as debilitating as the traditional substances.[4]

The advent of psychotropics probably created whole new categories of potential addicts as well. Individuals not inclined by temperament or body chemistry to abuse opiates, coca products, or alcohol, might nevertheless possess a predisposition to the addictive qualities of stimulants, depressants, or hallucinogens.[5]

The evolution of a formal drug control system also marginalized women's roles at the policymaking level. As bureaucracies expanded, the influence exerted by women and women's groups contracted. Notable individuals, like Rachel Crowdy, Helen Moorhead, and Elizabeth Wright continued to play important roles only in so far as they proved able to operate within an increasingly formalized system regulated by the gendered expectations of the day. For decades after the deaths of Moorhead and Wright, women contributed minimally to refining, operating, and criticizing the system.

Perhaps the most notorious outcome accompanying implementation of the international drug control regime has been the creation of a massive illicit market. By definition, specifying the parameters of the regime creates illicit demand, illegitimate production, unauthorized manufacture, and illegal trafficking. In the 1920s, control advocates assumed that, once governments made the commitment to enforce the rules, illicit supplies would soon dry up. Instead, entrepreneurs willing to accept higher risk took over the illegal trade, colluding with power brokers who benefitted from protecting the traffic. Each time the international community refined its enforcement measures, smugglers responded in kind. When pressure for tighter controls became acute in one area, unscrupulous traders relocated. Abetted by improvements in technology, transportation, communication, etc., illicit manufacture and trafficking could be carried on virtually anywhere and came to be controlled increasingly by organized (and often government-associated) crime syndicates. Impoverished or war-torn areas that could not otherwise compete in the international marketplace became havens of illicit production, infusing much-needed capital into local economies. The continued emphasis on supply-side solutions, however unintentionally, contributed to the process.[6]

Drugs and (national) security

The drug question is intertwined with fundamental issues of national, subnational, and transnational interest. The opium trade and drug use comprised a central factor in the calculations of Chinese statesmen from the early nineteenth century onward. The course of international relations in East Asia, especially during the first half of the twentieth century, cannot be understood without a thorough appreciation of the role played by opium.[7] Even after the Chinese Communists suppressed a longstanding domestic problem, Nationalist opponents in the southern border areas financed continued military operations through profits garnered from the traffic. Independent Latin American, Asian, and African countries consistently used drug production as an economic bulwark against foreign encroachment. Moreover, drug production and trafficking served as a form of political protest, denigrating the values of the world's supposed overlords.

As more sophisticated therapeutic use of drugs became common-place, states exhibited substantial interest in ensuring adequate supplies of vital medicaments. In wartime, nations have gone to great lengths to maintain sufficient stocks. The United States, for example, broke its own cardinal rules during World War II when the federal government acquired huge quantities of opium and commenced agricultural production on its own soil. In peacetime, cost usually became the overriding concern. Poorer nations, in particular, have expressed repeatedly their vital interest in securing needed medicines without making unreasonable expenditures.

In the later twentieth century, the rise of massive drug abuse and its attendant increase in illicit trafficking posed an unprecedented threat to governments, other institutions, and societies. An explosion of demand in the 1960s created opportunities for profit unseen since the heyday of the nineteenth-century India-to-China trade. The pattern reproduced throughout the century accelerated: refinements in law enforcement efforts spawned an increasingly sophisticated illicit trade. Drug production and trafficking centers shifted between Latin America, Southeast Asia, South Asia, and elsewhere on the heels of political instability and local corruption. Moreover, control efforts directed against one substance exacerbated the poly-drug phenomenon. For example, the anti-heroin initiatives of the 1970s played into the hands of South American traffickers, who took advantage of a potent product, proximity to market, and economies of scale to sell cocaine in record quantities. Attempts at suppression often fostered a more sophisticated and ruthless class of drug entrepreneurs. As profits rose, corruption of enforcement agencies and legal systems became all too prevalent in both producing and consuming countries. Money laundering emerged as a new and highly corrosive form of international criminal activity. Use of military units to interdict drug trafficking prompted concerns about degrading integrity within the armed forces.

The dynamic of drug diplomacy itself also represents a national security concern entwined with political, economic, social, and cultural implications.[8] Control efforts reflect, from one viewpoint, attempts by western industrialized states to impose their standards and values upon the rest of the world. For example, in the late twentieth century the United States promoted adoption of American-style drug control laws in other countries as vigorously as any commercial export, often threatening the domestic stability of other states in the process.[9] Moreover, the rising influence of agents such as international organizations, multinational (pharmaceutical) corporations, and illicit trafficking associations reduced the sovereign prerogatives of states worldwide. Since the later nineteenth century, many of the proffered solutions to the drug question, accommodations with the drug regime, and reactions against drug policy have gradually eroded authority structures organized on a national-territorial basis.

The history of international efforts to control psychoactive substances illuminates the intricate relationships between individuals, the social milieu, and the environment. People learned to harness naturally occurring drugs, to blend and refine them, and to invent entirely new substances. Human social interaction conferred purpose and meaning upon drug use. Attitudes toward drugs that developed over centuries caused friction when interests attached to those cultural constructs clashed in the global arena. Recognition of the drug issue's importance grew in modern times, drawing the attention of legislators, reformers, researchers, bureaucrats, industrialists, medical professionals, users, and many others. That concern culminated in the extended diplomatic activity upon which this work has focused. The pursuit of conflicting goals, influencing and influenced by material and conceptual factors, illustrates the intractability of the drug issue. Drug use and drug policies blur tidy distinctions between national and international, social and anti-social, affluence and poverty, trade and traffic, power and weakness. The demonstrated propensity of individuals to alter their state of consciousness by chemical means reinforces the point. Drug policy remains an enduring issue of contention necessitating diplomatic negotiation. We are coupled to the ecosystem, to each other, and to our own physical and psychic desires in an unbreakable embrace.

Notes

Terms and definitions

1 F. Zimring and G. Hawkins, *The Search for Rational Drug Control*, Cambridge, Cambridge University Press, 1992, ch. 2. Quote from pp. 31–2.
2 ibid., p. 32. Owing to the amorphous character of phrases like "drug abuse" or "drug problem", Zimring and Hawkins believe such terms cannot be defined and used in a principled way. See pp. 33–5.
3 The USSR occupied a distinctive position because it possessed considerable productive and manufacturing capacity. Incomplete disclosure of verifiable information about its drug industry makes it impossible to determine whether the Soviet Union should be assigned a minor or major role in each category. The term applies only to the "ethical" drug trade. Clandestine manufacture has occurred in most parts of the globe at one time or another.
4 ibid., regarding USSR.
5 Skran goes on to note that regimes "reflect shared principles and norms, and have established rules and decision-making procedures." see C. Skran, *Refugees in Inter-War Europe: The Emergence of a Regime*, Oxford, Clarendon Press, 1995, pp. 65–6. International relations specialists disagree, however, on the extent and nature of those principles, norms, rules, and procedures. Most acknowledge that regimes can foster cooperation but may also serve as centers of conflict, a theme this work emphasizes. The standard work is S. Krasner (ed.), *International Regimes*, Ithaca, Cornell University Press, 1983. A. Hasenclever, P. Mayer, and V. Rittenberger, *Theories of International Regimes*, Cambridge, Cambridge University Press, 1997, provides a helpful recent overview. They note that few contributors to the debate consider domestic factors in their calculations, an omission that limits the utility of regime theorizing for this study (p. 223). E. Nadelmann, "Global Prohibition Regimes: the Evolution of Norms in International Society," *International Organization*, 1990, vol. 44, no. 4, pp. 479–526, contributes to our understanding about deficiencies built in to the drug control system. His assessment suffers, however, because he does not recognize that the international regime was designed primarily to regulate rather than prohibit. See also J. Donnelly, "The United Nations and the Global Drug Control Regime," in P. Smith (ed.), *Drug Policy in the Americas*, Boulder, Westview Press, 1992, pp. 282–304; E. Haas, *When Knowledge is Power: Three Models of Change in International Organizations*, Berkeley, University of California Press, 1990, pp. 56–7.

Introduction

1 B. Renborg, "The Grand Old Men of the League of Nations," *Bulletin on Narcotics*, 1964, vol. 16, no. 4, pp. 8–9. See also Fitzmaurice to interdepartmental committee on inter-Imperial relations, 23 July 1931, PRO, HO 45/21786.

2 For a now-classic statement about the importance of state structures, see P. Evans, D. Rueschemeyer, and T. Skocpol (eds), *Bringing the State Back In*, Cambridge, Cambridge University Press, 1985, especially chs 1, 11. This work highlights the agency of producing and consuming states; they often acted as key players, possessing the capacity to make, break, or tacitly undermine the system. H. Milner, *Interests, Institutions, and Information: Domestic Politics and International Relations*, Princeton, Princeton University Press, 1997, pp. 260–1, discusses this phenomenon in her treatment of the reversion point, which occurs in the absence of an accommodation in policy. "The player who has the best alternative to an agreement may be the most powerful."

3 Drug-control gadfly A. E. Blanco noted sarcastically:

> The desire to limit manufacture is best illustrated by the fact that official representatives of manufacturing countries attending the Conference are frequently seen in earnest conversation with representatives of the manufacturers, or the actual manufacturers themselves, whom they, presumably, consult as to the best, quickest and most equitable manner of limiting manufacture.

AOIB, no. 15, 9 June 1931, p. 3.

In discussing interaction between states and non-state entities, Risse-Kappen defines transnational relations as "regular interactions across national boundaries when at least one actor is a non-state agent or does not operate on behalf of a national government or an intergovernmental organization." T. Risse-Kappen, "Bringing transnational relations back in: introduction," in Risse-Kappen (ed.), *Bringing transnational relations back in: non-state actors, domestic structures and international institutions*, Cambridge, Cambridge University Press, 1995, p. 3.

Depending on the criteria applied, some groupings involved in international drug control, especially enforcement officials, might be considered as functional "epistemic communities." International relations specialists define epistemic communities as collections of individuals possessing professional knowledge, expertise, and standing, and who share a worldview concerning their issue-area. I avoid entangling the narrative with digressions about whether various clusters meet the loosely drawn requirements outlined by Haas and others. The essential point is that groups of experts who share common conceptions about the nature of, and solutions to, a problem can have a substantial influence on policy creation and implementation, especially when they have access to the levers of power. P. Haas, "Introduction: epistemic communities and international policy coordination," *International Organization*, 1992, vol. 46, no. 1, pp. 1–35; P. Haas, "Do regimes matter? Epistemic communities and Mediterranean pollution control," *International Organization*, 1989, vol. 43, no. 3, pp. 377–403; E. Haas, *When Knowledge is*

Power: Three Models of Change in International Organizations, Berkeley, University of California Press, 1990, pp. 40–2.

4 For an insightful discussion about the role of intermediary institutions see M. Bulmer, "Mobilising Social Knowledge for Social Welfare: Intermediary Institutions in the Political Systems of the United States and Great Britain between the First and Second Wars," in P. Weindling (ed.), *International Health Organisations and Movements, 1918–1939*, Cambridge, Cambridge University Press, 1995, pp. 305–25.

5 This phenomenon is not unusual, although the archivally based detail provided here is exceptional. E. Haas, op. cit., pp. 97–8.

6 E. Adler and P. Haas, "Conclusion: Epistemic Communities, World Order, and the Creation of a Reflective Research Program," *International Organization*, 1992, vol. 46, no. 1, p. 380, recognizes this phenomenon.

7 F. Zimring and G. Hawkins, *The Search for Rational Drug Control*, Cambridge, Cambridge University Press, 1992, p. 30–1, 58–9; P. Stares, *Global Habit: The Drug Problem in a Borderless World*, Washington, Brookings Institution, 1996, ch. 5; P. Bean, *The Social Control of Drugs*, New York, Halstead Press, 1974, p. 5–7; D. Courtwright, *Dark Paradise: Opiate Addiction in America before 1940*, Cambridge, Mass, Harvard University Press, 1982, pp. 113–26; A. Lindesmith, *The Addict and the Law*, Bloomington, Indiana University Press, 1965, ch. 4; K. Meyer and T. Parssinen, *Webs of Smoke: Smugglers, Warlords, Spies, and the History of the International Drug Trade*, Lanham, Maryland, Rowman & Littlefield, 1998, pp. xi–xii; D. Kinder, "Shutting Out Evil: Nativism and Narcotics Control in the United States," pp. 133–4, and J. McWilliams, "Through the Past Darkly: The Politics and Policies of America's Drug War," pp. 7–8, in W. Walker (ed.), *Drug Control Policy: Essays in Historical and Comparative Perspective*, University Park, Pennsylvania, Penn State University Press, 1992; I. Chein, *et al.*, *The Road to H: Narcotics, Delinquency, and Social Policy*, New York, Basic Books, 1964, pp. 17–22, 349; R. Bonnie, and C. Whitebread, *The Marihuana Conviction: A History of Marihuana Prohibition in the United States*, Charlottesville, University of Virginia Press, 1974, pp. 175–9; R. Carroll, "The Weed with Roots in Rhetoric: Harry J. Anslinger, Marijuana, and the Making of American Drug Policy," PhD dissertation, University of Pittsburgh, 1991, ch. 6, pp. 13–17, and conclusion.

1 Drugs through the ages to 1920

1 Rather than singling out Germans for special opprobrium, this quote illustrates an attitude concerning the drug trade widely held through the early twentieth century. Muller to FO during the 1911–12 Hague negotiations, from S. Stein, *International Diplomacy, State Administrators, and Narcotics Control*, Brookfield, Vermont, Gower, 1985, p. 72.

2 J. Goodman, P. Lovejoy, and A. Sherratt (eds), *Consuming Habits: Drugs in History and Anthropology*, London: Routledge, 1995, pp. 33–4.

3 F. Zimring and G. Hawkins, *The Search for Rational Drug Control*, Cambridge, Cambridge University Press, 1992, pp. 50–1, refers to this phenomenon as the "metaphysics of uniqueness," in which each new drug is considered different from substances already known. R. Mathee, "Exotic Substances: The Introduction and Global Spread of Tobacco, Coffee, Cocoa, Tea, and

Distilled Liquor, Sixteenth to Eighteenth Centuries," in R. Porter and M. Teich (eds), *Drugs and Narcotics in History*, Cambridge, Cambridge University Press, 1995, pp. 24–51; G. Austin, *Perspectives on the History of Psychoactive Substance Abuse*, Rockville, Maryland, National Institute on Drug Abuse, 1978; M. Smith, *A Social History of the Minor Tranquilizers*, New York, Pharmaceutical Products Press, 1991, especially ch. 1; M. Kreutel, *Die Opiumsucht*, Stuttgart, Deutscher Apotheker Verlag, 1988; J. Gagliano, *Coca Prohibition in Peru: The Historical Debates*, Tucson, University of Arizona Press, 1994, pp. 8–11.

4 ibid.; P. Curtin, *Cross-Cultural Trade in World History*, Cambridge, Cambridge University Press, 1984; J. Walvin, *Fruits of Empire: Exotic Produce and British Taste, 1660–1800*, London, Macmillan, 1997; A. McCoy, *The Politics of Heroin: CIA Complicity in the Global Drug Trade*, New York, Lawrence Hill, 1991, pp. 3–8, 78–82.

5 D. Owen, *British Opium Policy in China and India*, New Haven, Yale University Press, 1934, chs 1–5; P. Lowes, *The Genesis of International Narcotics Control*, Geneva, Librarie Droz, 1966, ch. 2; M. Greenberg, *British Trade and the Opening of China, 1800–1842*, Cambridge, Cambridge University Press, 1951, ch. 5; C. Stelle, *Americans and the China Opium Trade*, New York, Arno Press, 1981, chs 1–2; McCoy, op. cit., pp. 80–96.

6 Owen, op. cit., p. 52; Lowes, op. cit., p. 26.; McCoy, op. cit., pp. 77–86; E. van Luijk, "A Lesson from history on the issue of drug legalisation: The case of the opiumregie in the Dutch East Indies, 1890–1940," 1991, unpublished paper, Netherlands Institute for Advanced Study; A. So, *The South China Silk District: Local Historical Transformation and World-System Theory*, Albany, State University of New York Press, 1986, pp. 57–8. Statistics are the best available, but nevertheless incomplete. Actual Chinese imports and consumption, to say nothing of the rest of the world, were no doubt higher.

A comparison helps to indicate the magnitude of the trade: During the 1920s, when global population and medical sophistication far surpassed that of a century earlier, the League of Nations estimated world legitimate medical and scientific requirements probably did not exceed 800,000 pounds annually (see Chapter 2).

7 J. Rush, *Opium to Java: Revenue Farming and Chinese Enterprise in Colonial Indonesia, 1860–1910*, Ithaca, Cornell University Press, 1990; C. Trocki, *Opium and Empire: Chinese Society in Colonial Singapore, 1800–1910*, Ithaca, Cornell University Press, 1990.

8 Despite disagreement with other authors about timing, So illustrates the essential point: opium played a key role in the incorporation of South China into the world economy on an unfavorable basis. So, op. cit., ch. 4. For opium's centrality to political economy and the development of capitalism in Asian colonies during the nineteenth century, see C. Trocki, "Drugs, Taxes, and Chinese Capitalism in Southeast Asia," in T. Brook and B. Wakabayashi (eds), *Opium in East Asian History*, Berkeley, University of California Press, 2000.

9 K. Meyer and T. Parssinen, *Webs of Smoke: Smugglers, Warlords, Spies, and the History of the International Drug Trade*, Lanham, Maryland, Rowman & Littlefield, 1998.

10 ibid., p. xvi, refers to the "efficient system of product standardization and delivery that brought to the China coast an increasing volume of high-quality opium." Greenberg, op. cit., p. 221; Lowes, op. cit., p. 34; So, op. cit., pp. 57–8.

11 Brook and Wakabayashi, op. cit., Part 1; Owen, op. cit., chs 6–11; Lowes, op. cit., chs 1, 3–4; J. Spence, "Opium," *Chinese Roundabout: Essays in History and Culture*, New York, Norton, 1992; A. Taylor, *American Diplomacy and the Narcotics Traffic*, Durham, NC, Duke University Press, 1969, ch. 1; Stelle, op. cit., chs 3–8.

12 P. Fay, *The Opium War, 1840–42*, New York, Norton, 1976.

13 Greenberg, op. cit., p. 104.

14 The advent of clipper ships in Eastern waters predated the Cape Horn route. In addition to fast turnaround time, the well-armed clippers could usually outrun or outfight pirates who plied opium transit routes seeking doubly illicit gain. B. Lubbock, *The Opium Clippers*, Glasgow, Brown, Son & Ferguson, 1933.

15 J. Wong, *Deadly Dreams: Opium, Imperialism, and the Arrow War (1856–1860) in China*, Cambridge, Cambridge University Press, 1998, especially ch. 16; J. Polachek, *The Inner Opium War*, Cambridge, Mass., Harvard University Press, 1992.

16 M. Lin, "The Opium Market in China, 1820s–1906," paper delivered at the Conference on Opium in East Asian History, University of Toronto–York University Joint Centre for Asia Pacific Studies, May 1997; J. Richards, "The Indian Empire and Peasant Production of Opium in the Nineteenth Century," *Modern Asian Studies*, 1981, vol. 15, no. 1, pp. 59–82; A. Seyf, "Commercialization of Agriculture: Production and Trade of Opium in Persia, 1850–1906," *International Journal of Middle East Studies*, 1984, vol. 16, no. 2, pp. 233–50; D. Headrick, *The Tentacles of Progress: Technology Transfer in the Age of Imperialism, 1850–1940*, Oxford, Oxford University Press, 1988, pp. 260–8.

17 Spence, op. cit., p. 119; S. Adshead, "Opium in Szechwan, 1881–1911," *Journal of Southeast Asian History*, 1966, vol. 7, no. 2, pp. 93–9; J. Marshall, "Opium and the Politics of Gangsterism in Nationalist China, 1927–1945," *Bulletin of Concerned Asian Scholars*, 1976, July–September, pp. 19–20; J. Jennings, *The Opium Empire: Japanese Imperialism and Drug Trafficking in Asia, 1895–1945*, Westport, Connecticut, Praeger, 1997, pp. 18–19, 78.

18 J. Goodman, *Tobacco in History: The Cultures of Dependence*, London, Routledge, 1993, pp. 117–20. Concerning alcohol, the few treaties limiting availability in parts of Africa negotiated around the turn of the century had little effect. "Wets" often claimed that restricting alcohol consumption would foment increased drug abuse. Taylor, op. cit., pp. 26–8, 124–5. American prohibition between 1920 and 1933 produced diplomatic tension precisely because it received little international support. L. Spinelli, *Dry Diplomacy: The United States, Great Britain and Prohibition*, Wilmington, Scholarly Resources, 1989. See also K. Bruun, L. Pan, and I. Rexed, *The Gentlemen's Club*, Chicago, University of Chicago Press, 1975, ch. 12; E. Gordon, *The Anti-Alcohol Movement in Europe*, New York, Revell, 1913. Even complaints from missionaries about the role that alcohol played in depopulation among indigenous peoples in the Western Hemisphere and Pacific Islands fell on deaf ears. See A. Crosby, *Germs, Seeds, and Animals:*

Studies in Ecological History, Armonk, Sharpe, 1994, ch. 8. J. Burnham, *Bad Habits: Drinking, Smoking, Taking Drugs, Gambling, Sexual Misbehavior, and Swearing in American History*, New York, New York University Press, 1993, suggests an important difference between alcohol and other drugs that affected regulatory activity. Purveying alcohol was the primary business of brewing companies, whereas pharmaceutical manufacturers' product lines usually included many substances. Brewers therefore had more to lose from controls; drug companies proved more willing to acquiesce in regulation over addicting substances both because those drugs were less vital to the business and also because not doing so might entail negative publicity that would hurt the image of other products.

19 Headrick, op.cit.; S. Karch, *A Brief History of Cocaine*, Boca Raton, Florida, CRC Press, 1998; Gagliano, op. cit., ch. 5; J. Kawell, "The 'Essentially Peruvian' Industry: Legal Cocaine Production in the 19th Century," M. de Kort, "Doctors, Diplomats, and Businessmen: A History of Conflicting Interests in the Netherlands," H. Friman, "Germany and the Transformations of Cocaine, 1880-1920," P. Gootenberg, "Reluctance or Resistance? The Export of Cocaine (Prohibitions) to Peru, 1900–1950," all in P. Gootenberg (ed.), *Cocaine: Global Histories*, London, Routledge, 1999; M. de Kort and D. Korf, "The Development of Drug Trade and Drug Control in the Netherlands: A Historical Perspective," *Crime, Law, and Social Change*, 1992, vol. 17, pp. 131–2; J. Spillane, "Modern Drug, Modern Menace: The Legal Use and Distribution of Cocaine in the United States, 1880–1920," PhD Dissertation, Carnegie Mellon University, 1994, ch. 3; B. Hansen, "America's First Medical Breakthrough: How Popular Excitement about a French Rabies Cure in 1885 Raised New Expectations for Medical Progress," *American Historical Review*, 1998, vol. 103, no. 2, pp. 373–418.

Spillane's estimates outline the enormous increase of the trade. Imports of coca leaf into New York alone rose from approximately 25,000 pounds in 1884 to at least 1.3 million pounds in 1905 (pp.160–4). US prices dropped from $440 per ounce in 1884–85 to $8 per ounce in 1887. Between 1892 and 1916 prices fluctuated between $6.50 and $2 per ounce (pp. 147–9). American consumption increased 500 percent between 1890 and 1910, exceeding 200,000 ounces in several years (p.170). Between 1886 and 1901, the number of factories producing crude cocaine in Peru rose from two to twenty-one (pp. 145–6). Profits in the early years reached stratospheric levels: Java leaf valued at 50 Netherlands Guilders could render cocaine worth 725NLG (de Kort, op. cit., pp. 6–7).

20 N. Zinberg, *Drug, Set, and Setting: The Basis for Controlled Intoxicant Use*, New Haven, Yale University Press, 1984; A. Brandt and P. Rozin (eds), *Morality and Health*, New York, Routledge, 1997, especially D. Courtwright, "Morality, Religion, and Drug Use," pp. 231–50; Burnham, op. cit.; G. Harding, *Opiate Addiction, Morality, and Medicine*, New York, St. Martin's, 1988; S. Holloway, "The Regulation of the Supply of Drugs in Britain Before 1868," ch. 4, E. Hickel, "Das Kaiserliche Gesundheitsamt and the Chemical Industry in Germany during the Second Empire: Partners or Adversaries?," ch. 5, and C. Acker, "From all-purpose Anodyne to Marker of Deviance: Physicians' Attitudes towards Opiates in the US from 1890–1940," ch. 6, all in Porter and Teich, op. cit.; S. N. Tesh, *Hidden Arguments: Political Ideology and Disease Prevention Policy*, New Brunswick, Rutgers University

Press, 1988; P. Haas, "Introduction: epistemic communities and inter-
national policy coordination," *International Organization*, 1992, vol. 46, no. 1,
pp. 7–12; H. Friman, *Narcodiplomacy: Exporting the US War on Drugs*, Ithaca,
Cornell University Press, 1996, pp. 20–2; McCoy, op. cit., pp. 7–9;
V. Berridge and G. Edwards, *Opium and the People: Opiate Use in Nineteenth
Century England*, London, Allen Lane/St. Martin's Press, 1981, chs 1–13, 16–
17; V. Berridge, "Drugs and Social Policy: The Establishment of Drug
Control in Britain, 1900–30," *British Journal of Addiction*, 1984, vol. 79, p. 18;
T. Parssinen, *Secret Passions, Secret Remedies: Narcotic Drugs in British Society,
1820–1930*, Philadelphia, Institute for the Study of Human Issues, 1983,
chs 1–7; Friman, op. cit., and de Kort, op. cit., in Gootenberg, op. cit.;
M. de Kort, "Drug Policy: Medical or Crime Control? Medicalization and
Criminalization of Drug Use, and Shifting Drug Policies," in H. Binneveld
and R. Dekker (eds), *Curing and Insuring: Essays on Illness in past times: the
Netherlands, Belgium, England, and Italy, 16th–20th centuries*, Hilversum,
Verloren, 1993, pp. 203–18; de Kort and Korf, op. cit.; P. Giffen,
S. Endicott, and S. Lambert, *Panic and Indifference: The Politics of Canada's
Drug Laws*, Ottawa, Canadian Centre on Substance Abuse, 1991, ch. 2;
Spillane, op. cit., chs 1–2; D. Courtwright, *Dark Paradise: Opiate Addiction in
America before 1940*, Cambridge, Mass., Harvard University Press, 1982;
D. Musto, *The American Disease*, Oxford, Oxford University Press, 1987,
ch. 1; Musto, "Patterns in US Drug Abuse and Response," in P. Smith
(ed.), *Drug Policy in the Americas*, Boulder, Westview Press, 1992, ch. 2;
H. Morgan, *Drugs in America: A Social History, 1800–1980*, Syracuse, NY,
Syracuse University Press, 1981, chs 1–6; S. Barrows and R. Room (eds),
Drinking: Behavior and Belief in Modern History, Berkeley, University of
California Press, 1991, especially D. Herd, "The Paradox of Temperance:
Blacks and the Alcohol Question in nineteenth-century America" (ch. 16),
and J. Gusfield, "Benevolent Repression: Popular Culture, Social Structure,
and the Control of Drinking" (ch. 18); D. Kinder, "Shutting Out Evil:
Nativism and Narcotics Control in the United States," in W. Walker (ed.),
Drug Control Policy: Essays in Historical and Comparative Perspective, University
Park, Pennsylvania, Penn State University Press, 1992; P. Bean, *The Social
Control of Drugs*, New York, Halstead Press, 1974. Such concerns were not
limited to western industrialized countries. For the Peruvian debate, see
Gagliano, op. cit., ch. 6. For Japan see Jennings, op. cit., pp. 5–15. For
interesting parallels to the emerging refugee problem, see C. Skran, *Refugees
in Inter-War Europe: The Emergence of a Regime*, Oxford, Clarendon Press,
1995, especially pp. 21–9.

21 For the classic description of moral entrepreneurs, see H. Becker, *Outsiders:
Studies in the Sociology of Deviance*, New York, Free Press, 1997. For helpful
categorizations about attitudinal approaches to drug control, see Zimring
and Hawkins, op. cit., pp. 8–15, 77–9; Courtwright, op. cit., in Brandt and
Rozin, op. cit.; P. Stares, *Global Habit: The Drug Problem in a Borderless
World*, Washington, Brookings Institution, 1996, ch. 3; Tesh, op. cit.;
G. van de Wijngaart, *Competing Perspectives on Drug Use: The Dutch Experience*,
Amsterdam, Swets & Zeitlinger, 1991, ch. 6.

22 F. Lyons, *Internationalism in Europe, 1815–1914*, Leyden, A. W. Sijthoff, 1963;
W. Kuehl, *Seeking World Order: The United States and International Organization
to 1920*, Nashville, Vanderbilt University Press, 1969; P. Weindling, "Intro-

duction: Constructing International Health between the Wars," in
P. Weindling, (ed.), *International Health Organisations and Movements, 1918–
1939*, Cambridge, Cambridge University Press, 1995, ch. 1; Lowes, op. cit.,
pp. 1–9.

23 Stein, op. cit., pp. 9–16; Owen, op. cit., ch. 11; Lowes, op. cit., pp. 58–78;
Berridge and Edwards, op. cit., chs 14–15; Harding, op. cit., chs 4–5; van
Luijk, op. cit.; B. Johnson, "Righteousness Before Revenue: The Forgotten
Moral Crusade Against the Indo-Chinese Opium Trade," *Journal of Drug
Issues*, 1975, vol. 5, pp. 304–26; J. Brown, "Politics of the Poppy: The Society
for the Suppression of the Opium Trade, 1874–1916," *Journal of Contemporary
History*, 1973, vol. 8, no. 3, pp. 97–111; I. Tyrell, "Women and Temperance
in International Perspective: The World's WCTU, 1880s–1920s," in
Barrows and Room, op. cit., ch. 10; J. Papachristou, "American Women
and Foreign Policy, 1898–1905, *Diplomatic History*, 1990, vol. 14, no. 4,
pp. 493–509; J. Reed, *The Missionary Mind and American East Asia Policy,
1911–1915*, Cambridge, Mass., Harvard University Press, 1983; K. Lodwick,
Crusaders Against Opium: Protestant Missionaries in China, 1874–1917, Lexington,
University of Kentucky Press, 1996; Meyer and Parssinen, op. cit., ch. 3.

24 Tokyo instituted a monopoly on Taiwan in 1896, but missionary sentiment
played no role there. Considerations of profit and protection of Japan from
the contagion of drug abuse predominated. Jennings, op. cit., pp. 17–28.
See also Trocki, op. cit., in Brook and Wakabayashi, op. cit.; Meyer and
Parssinen, op. cit., pp. 90–2.

25 Observing China's deterioration, the Japanese recognized the danger opium
presented and its symbolic role as an indicator of foreign intentions.
B. Wakabayashi, "From Peril to Profit: Opium in Late-Edo to Meiji Eyes,"
in Brook and Wakabayashi, op. cit.; Jennings, op. cit., pp. 11–13.

26 Stein, op. cit., ch. 2; Owen, op. cit., chs 10–11; Burnham, op. cit.; Gordon,
op. cit., ch. 8.

27 Lowes, op. cit., pp. 9–16; Stein, op. cit., pp. 16–22, 28–30; Owen, op. cit.,
pp. 329–35; R. Newman, "India and the Anglo-Chinese Opium Agreements, 1907–14," *Modern Asian Studies*, 1989, vol. 23, no. 3, pp. 525–35;
Meyer and Parssinen, op. cit., p. 20.

28 Although not dealing specifically with the drug question, the themes discussed in A. Kleinman and J. Kleinman, "Moral Transformations of
Health and Suffering in Chinese Society," in Brandt and Rozin, op. cit.
pp. 101–18, suggest that Peking's demarches on the international front
were congruent with traditional Chinese cultural views, which conceived of
illness as emanating from a disjunction of proper relationships between
individuals, groups, society, setting, etc.

29 Newman, op. cit., pp. 535–60; Lowes, op. cit., pp. 78–84; Taylor, op. cit.,
pp. 22–4; Stein, op. cit., pp. 22–6; Owen, op. cit., pp. 335–54; Lodwick,
op. cit., pp. xii–xiii, 116–30; Meyer and Parssinen, op. cit., pp. 41–61;
N. Miners, "The Hong Kong Government Opium Monopoly, 1914–
1941," *Journal of Imperial and Commonwealth History*, 1983, vol. 11, no. 3,
pp. 283–4.

30 Using the average of the years 1901–1905 as a base for calculation.

31 Taylor, op. cit., pp. 135–6; Meyer and Parssinen, op. cit, pp. 144–5.

32 Marshall, op. cit.; Meyer and Parssinen, op. cit.

33 H. Traver, "Opium to Heroin: Restrictive Opium Legislation and the Rise of Heroin Consumption in Hong Kong," *Journal of Policy History*, 1992, vol. 4, no. 3, pp. 307–24; Meyer and Parssinen, op. cit., pp. 84, 144.

34 Taylor, op. cit., ch. 2; A. Taylor, "Opium, American–Chinese Relations, and the Open-Door Policy," *South Atlantic Quarterly*, 1970, vol. 69, pp. 79–95; Musto, op. cit., pp. 24–35; Lowes, op. cit., chs 5–6; Stein, op. cit., pp. 30–49.

35 Great Britain, France, Japan, Germany, Russia, Portugal, and the Netherlands.

36 Taylor, op. cit., ch. 3; Musto, op. cit., pp. 35–7; Lowes, op. cit., chs 7–8; Stein, op. cit., pp. 50–60; Jennings, op. cit., pp. 62–5.

37 Taylor (1969), op. cit., pp. 82–96; Lowes, op. cit., ch. 9; Stein, op. cit., pp. 60–7; Friman, 1996, op. cit., pp. 11–15; Friman, op. cit., in Gootenberg, op. cit.; Hickel, op. cit., in Porter and Teich, op. cit.

38 Taylor (1969), op. cit., pp. 83–4.

39 States attending included Great Britain, France, Japan, Germany, Russia, Portugal, the Netherlands, the United States, China, Siam, Italy, and Persia.

40 Taylor, op. cit., pp. 96–111; Lowes, op. cit., pp. 176–82; Stein, op. cit., ch. 5; Musto, op. cit., pp. 49–53. For the sake of clarity in discussing this and subsequent treaties, I consider only the key provisions.

41 Musto, op. cit., chs 3, 5–8; Taylor, op. cit., pp. 129–32.

42 ibid., pp. 111–22; Lowes, op. cit., pp. 182–6.

43 Stein, op. cit., ch. 6; Parssinen, op. cit., ch. 9; Miners, op. cit., pp. 275–80; V. Berridge, "War Conditions and Narcotics Control: The Passing of Defence of the Realm Act Regulation 40B," *Journal of Social Policy*, 1978, vol. 7, no. 3, pp. 285–304; M. Kohn, *Dope Girls: The Birth of the British Drug Underground*, London, Lawrence & Wishart, 1992; Friman, 1996, op. cit., pp. 22–4; Friman, op. cit. and M. Kohn, "Cocaine Girls: Sex, Drugs, and Race in Early Modern London," in Gootenberg, op. cit.; Berridge, 1984, op. cit.; Giffen, Endicott, and Lambert, op. cit., pp. 103–4; de Kort and Korf, op. cit., pp. 127–8; de Kort, op. cit., in Gootenberg, op. cit.

44 For Germany, see article 295 of the Versailles treaty; Austria, Article 247 of the St. Germain treaty; Hungary, Article 230 of the Trianon treaty; Bulgaria, Article 174 of the Neuilly treaty; Turkey, Article 280 of the Sèvres treaty.

45 Taylor, op. cit., pp. 141–5; Stein, op. cit., pp. 114–22; Lowes, op. cit., pp. 186–9. For the Hague Opium Convention, see LN Treaty Series, Vol. VIII, p. 187.

46 J. Slinn, "Research and Development in the UK Pharmaceutical Industry from the Nineteenth Century to the 1960s," in Porter and Teich, op. cit., pp. 168–76; Berridge, 1978, op. cit., p. 293; Jennings, op. cit., pp. 39–46; de Kort, op. cit., in Gootenberg, op. cit.; Friman, 1996, op. cit., pp. 18–19, 41–3; Spillane, op. cit., ch. 3; C. Acker, "Addiction and the Laboratory: The Work of the National Research Council's Committee on Drug Addiction, 1928–1939," *Isis*, 1995, vol. 86, pp. 167–93; J. Swann, *Academic Scientists and the Pharmaceutical Industry: Cooperative Research in Twentieth-Century America*, Baltimore, Johns Hopkins Press, 1988, ch. 1; V. Harden, *Inventing the NIH: Federal Biomedical Research Policy, 1887–1937*, Baltimore, Johns Hopkins Press, 1986, chs 4–5; Parssinen, op. cit., ch. 10; Stein, op. cit., pp. 106–14.

47 Meyer and Parssinen, op. cit., Introduction. Note that drug trafficking represents the point "where profits and power converge" (p. 12). In exchange for protection, drug traffickers provide power brokers (primarily politicians and/or the military), money, information, and connections to clandestine procurement networks. This phenomenon occurred not only in China. J. Sandos, "Northern Separatism During the Mexican Revolution: An Inquiry into the Role of Drug Trafficking, 1910–1920," *Americas*, 1984, vol. 41, no. 2, pp. 191–214.
48 In addition to examples cited earlier, see Spillane, op. cit., pp. 379–80; E. Nadelmann, "Global Prohibition Regimes: the Evolution of norms in International Society, *International Organization*," 1990, vol. 44, no. 4, pp. 503–13.

2 Laying the foundation – 1919–25

1 J. Gavit, *Opium*, New York, Brentano's, 1927, p. 1.
2 Charter OAC members included China, France, Great Britain, India, Japan, the Netherlands, Portugal, and Siam. In 1922 the OAC invited Germany and the United States to participate although those governments were not members of the League. Germany accepted, calculating that compliance with emerging international norms benefitted pharmaceutical exports more than the accompanying limitations hindered them. H. Friman, *Narcodiplomacy: Exporting the US War on Drugs*, Ithaca, Cornell University Press, 1996, p. 24. The US relationship with the OAC is discussed below. The Committee's membership steadily increased, reaching 30 in 1938. LNd C.32.1939.XI. (12 January 1939). See also T. Burkman, "Opium in China and the League of Nations," paper delivered at the Conference on Opium in East Asian History, University of Toronto–York University Joint Centre for Asia Pacific Studies, May 1997.
3 Crowdy's appointment epitomized the period's promise and limitations for women. Her position entailed considerable visibility, and her distinguished career entitled her to respect; she provided an example of what women might accomplish. Yet Crowdy oversaw the section that dealt largely with "women's issues." Gendered conceptions of the age could not countenance females taking part in, for example, discussions about disarmament or high politics. C. Miller, "Women in International Relations? The Debate in inter–war Britain," in R. Grant and K. Newland (eds), *Gender and International Relations*, Bloomington, Indiana University Press, 1991, ch. 6; Miller, "Lobbying the League: Women's International Organizations and the League of Nations," PhD dissertation, St. Hilda's College, Oxford, 1992, pp. 12–28, 88–96 *passim*.
4 The League Health Committee created a subsidiary body, the "Opium Committee," to consider drug-related issues, but to avoid confusion I disregard the distinction. LN documents cited refer to the Opium Committee (of the League Health Committee) by its proper title.
5 Sweetser to Drummond, 16 October 1922, SP, Box 31, File: "Drummond, Sir Eric."
6 Sperling minute, 17 May 1923, and Fletcher minute, 18 May 1923, PRO, FO 371/9242.

7 W. Kuehl and L. Dunn, *Keeping the Covenant: American Internationalists and the League of Nations, 1920–1939*, Kent, Ohio, Kent State University Press, 1997, chs 5–7; T. Diebel, "Struggle For Cooperation: The League of Nations Secretariat and Pro-League Internationalism in the United States, 1919–1924," UN Library, Geneva, unpublished thesis, 1970, pp. 21–8, 75–80, 118–22, 137–44; K. Meyer and T. Parssinen, *Webs of Smoke: Smugglers, Warlords, Spies, and the History of the International Drug Trade*, Lanham, Maryland, Rowman & Littlefield, 1998, pp. 15–16.

8 A. Rovine, *The First Fifty Years: The Secretary General in World Politics, 1920–1970*, Leyden, A. W. Sijthoff, 1970, pp. 27–51; Diebel, op. cit., chs 1–3; Joseph Dittert, interviews, Geneva, 21 April, 26 April, and 3 May 1993; Louis Atzenwiler, interviews, Geneva, 30 April and 1 May 1993.

9 P. Weindling (ed.), *International Health Organisations and Movements, 1918–1939*, Cambridge, Cambridge University Press, 1995.

10 F. Walters, *A History of the League of Nations*, London, Oxford University Press, 1952, pp. 183–5; Gavit, op. cit., ch. 3; W. Willoughby, *Opium as an International Problem*, Baltimore, Johns Hopkins University Press, 1925, ch. 3; R. Buell, "The International Opium Conferences with Relevant Documents," *World Peace Foundation Pamphlets*, 1925, vol. 7, nos 2–3, pp. 47–53; Burkman, op. cit.

11 Delevingne championed early information-gathering efforts. He made sure to condone not only medical but also "other legitimate uses" of opium. That formulation allowed him to protect colonial interests. Delevingne promoted the certification scheme in hopes of leveling the playing field for British pharmaceutical firms. Gilchrist to Secretariat, 14 March 1922, LNA, R710 12A/19019/10346; Delevingne to Drummond, 22 April 1921, LNA, R710 12A/12305/10346; Reports of the first three OAC sessions, LNds A.38.1921.XI. (3 September 1921); A.15.1922.[XI]. (15 August 1922); A.15(a).1922.XI. (2 September 1922).

12 The Opium Committee recommended a maximum annual per-capita allowance of 450 milligrams for opium and 7 milligrams for cocaine. The Mixed Sub-Committee advocated 600 milligrams of opium. C. Terry and M. Pellens, *The Opium Problem*, New York, Bureau of Social Hygiene, 1928, 700–06. For full text see reports of the League Health Committee and its opium sub-committee: LNds C.8.M.2.1922.III, p. 1; C.366.M.217.1922.III, pp. 9–11; C.402.1922.III, pp. 1–2; C.594.F.374.1922.III, pp. 9–10; C.588.M.202. 1924.II. See also OAC fourth session report, LNd A.13.1923.XI. (16 June 1923), Annex 6.

13 Weindling, op. cit.; Miller (1992), op. cit., pp. 109–111; G. Harding, *Opiate Addiction, Morality, and Medicine*, New York, St. Martin's, 1988, ch. 7; Kuehl and Dunn, op. cit., pp. 51–2.

14 A. Taylor, *American Diplomacy and the Narcotics Traffic*, Durham, NC, Duke University Press, 1969, pp. 146–57; G. Ostrower, "The United States and the League of Nations, 1919–1939," in *The League of Nations in Retrospect*, Berlin and New York, Walter de Gruyter & Co., 1983, p. 130, calls the standoffish US policy "silly"; Kuehl and Dunn, op. cit., ch. 7; Diebel, op. cit., ch. 2; Crowdy to Sweetser, 6 July 1922, SP, Box 14, File: "Opium Question, LaMotte Article"; Second OAC session minutes, LNd C.416.M.254. 1922.XI. (21 June 1922), p. 6.

15 Crowdy to Tufton, 14 November 1922, FO, *The Opium Trade*, part XVIII
 (July–December 1922), No. 30; Taylor, op. cit., p. 150; Geddes to FO, 26
 January 1923, PRO, FO 371/9242; Delevingne to Wellesley, 21 March
 1923, PRO, FO 317/9242. (I usually delete file numbers from PRO documents because most citations are from bound volumes arranged in chrono-
 logical order, obviating the need for superfluous references.)
16 Taylor, op. cit., pp 149–51; W. McAllister, *A Limited Enterprise: The History of*
 International Efforts to Control Drugs in the Twentieth Century, PhD dissertation,
 University of Virginia, 1996, p. 49; Meyer and T. Parssinen, op. cit.,
 pp. 128–30; Delevingne to Newton, 23 April 1923, Newton to Delevingne,
 16 May 1923, PRO, FO 371/9247; Delevingne to Wellesley, 30 January
 1923, PRO, FO 371/9241. Delevingne revoked the license of T. Whiffen,
 the largest British morphia manufacturer, for its part in the illicit traffic.
 T. Parssinen, *Secret Passions, Secret Remedies: Narcotic Drugs in British Society,*
 1820–1930, Philadelphia, Institute for the Study of Human Issues, 1983,
 ch. 10.
17 Diebel, op. cit., p. 70–4, 80–4; M. Leffler, *The Elusive Quest: America's Pursuit*
 of European Stability and French Security, 1919–1933, Chapel Hill, University of
 North Carolina Press, 1979, pp. 41–2.
18 Executive Committee minutes, 14 December 1922; Chamberlain to
 McDonald, 16 March 1923, FPAA, Micro 48, Reel 1; G. Ostrower, *Collective*
 Insecurity: The United States and the League of Nations in the Early Thirties, Lewisburg, Bucknell University Press, 1979, p. 31; Kuehl and Dunn, op. cit.,
 pp. 66–7; D. Dennis, "From Isolationism to Internationalism: 75 Years of
 the Foreign Policy Association, 1918–1993," 1994, unpublished manuscript,
 pp. 52–3; Taylor, op. cit., pp. 151–2.
19 Diebel, op. cit., pp. 99–118, quote: p. 118; Ostrower, 1983, op. cit., pp. 130;
 Kuehl and Dunn, op. cit., pp. 50–1, 127–38.
20 US Surgeon-General from 1912 to 1920, during the 1920s Blue served as
 "Assistant Surgeon-General at large," working in Europe on public health
 issues. His significant international profile signalled Washington's serious
 intent.
21 Taylor, op. cit., pp. 152–3.
22 This formulation allowed the Indian delegate to save face. He could equally
 assert that quasi-medical opium use was "not illegitimate."
23 Taylor, op. cit., pp. 153–6; fourth OAC session report, LNd
 C.37.M.91.1923.XI. (26 January 1923).
24 Executive Committee minutes, 7 March 1923, FPAA, Micro 48, Reel 1.
25 Taylor, op. cit., pp. 157–8.
26 McAllister, op. cit., p. 64.
27 Drummond to Tufton, 11 May 1923, PRO, FO 371/9242.
28 PRO, FO 371/9242 (May 1923).
29 OAC fifth session minutes, LNd C.418.M.184.1923.XI. (1 August 1923);
 McAllister, op. cit., pp. 66–8; Taylor, op. cit., pp. 162–3; Kuehl and Dunn,
 op. cit., p. 53.
30 Taylor, op. cit., pp. 167–70; Terry and Pellens, op. cit., pp. 675–6;
 Willoughby, op. cit., pp. 465–6.
31 C. Acker, "Addiction and the Laboratory: The Work of the National
 Research Council's Committee on Drug Addiction, 1928–1939," *Isis*, 1995,
 vol. 86, 167–193; Acker, "Social Problems and Scientific Opportunities:

The Case of Opiate Addiction in the US, 1920–1940," PhD dissertation, University of California at San Francisco, 1994, ch. 3. L. Grinspoon and J. Bakalar, *Marihuana, The Forbidden Medicine*, New Haven, Yale University Press, 1993, and L. Grinspoon, *Marihuana Reconsidered*, Cambridge, Mass., Harvard University Press, 1977, discuss how controls placed on marijuana in the later 1930s terminated promising lines of medical research.

32 "Once the drug problem became defined predominantly as a challenge to law and order rather than public health, this underlying approach became largely self-sustaining." P. Stares, *Global Habit: The Drug Problem in a Borderless World*, Washington, Brookings Institution, 1996, p. 46.

33 "The proceedings of the Opium [Advisory] Committee, and still more of the conferences which it organized, were the scene of violent language and hasty action to a degree unknown among other organs of the League." Walters, op. cit., p. 185.

34 PRO, FO 371/9240 (October–December 1923); Taylor, op. cit., pp. 168–72.

35 Taylor, op. cit., p. 180. For an overview of Latin American reticence to participate in the drug regime, see W. Walker, *Drug Control in the Americas*, Albuquerque, University of New Mexico Press, 1989, pp. 35–51.

36 To further complicate matters, a running argument developed about employing heroin in medical practice. The United States favored prohibition. Health officials and medical societies in many other countries nevertheless insisted on its efficacy in a small number of cases. Delevingne pressed UK authorities to accept a ban, but they resisted. The disagreement continued into the 1950s. See PRO, HO 45/24817 and HO 45/24818; sixth OAC session minutes, LNd C.397.M.146.1924.XI. (30 August 1924), pp. 53–55; PAC, RG 29, Vol. 224, 320–5–9, Part 7 (August 1953–March 1954).

37 Powers invited were Britain, China, France, India, Japan, the Netherlands, Portugal, and Siam. All attended.

38 Delevingne's strategy also appeared to reap dividends in the United States. Brent expressed a heightened opinion of the League once a date had been set for the first conference. Brent to Sweetser, 23 October 1923, SP, Box 30, File: "Brent, Bishop Charles H."

39 Terry and Pellens, op. cit., pp. 687–92; Willoughby, op. cit., ch. 4; Gavit, op. cit., pp. 169–77.

40 *Report of the Opium Preparatory Committee*, LNd C.348.M119.1924.XI. (17 July 1924); McAllister, op. cit., pp. 75–80; Taylor, op. cit., pp. 171–9; Willoughby, op. cit., ch. 5.

41 Neville's proposals discomfited other representatives. Cadogan noted, "as usual, drastic and impractical." FO Minute, 28 March 1924, PRO, FO 371/10323.

42 In fact, the Versailles Treaty linked the drug question and the reparations issue directly. Part VIII, Annex VI, required the Germans to deliver medicines, including narcotics, as a part of the reparations settlement. The French did not wish to relinquish those deliveries without compensation. Additionally, the cross-border transfers complicated the task of determining medical requirements, stocks, quantities manufactured in each country, etc. Drummond to Reparation Commission, 19 March 1924, PRO, FO 371/10323.

43 Foreign Office officials viewed the French as the principal obstructionists. Given the import of the issue, the Foreign Office instructed the British Ambassador to discuss the matter with M. Herriot. See minuted comments of Cadogan, Collier, Waterlow, and others, 25–29 August 1924, PRO, FO 371/10326:F2881/20/87.

44 OAC sixth session report and minutes, LNds A.32.1924.XI. (16 August 1924) and C.397.M.146.1924.XI. (30 August 1924); Campbell's reports, IOA, L/E/7, 1324(21); Taylor, op. cit., pp. 176–7.

45 Delevingne to Waterlow, 13 May 1924 and interdepartmental conference records, 2 June 1924 (dated 21 June), PRO, FO 371/10324.

46 Minutes of 21 July–9 August 1924 attached to correspondence concerning the dispute, PRO, FO 371/10325: F 2463/20/87.

47 Cabinet Papers, C.P. 414(24), 24 July, 1924; C.P. 425(24), 31 July 1924; C.P. 450(24), 18 September 1924; C.P. 459(24), 30 September 1924; C.P. 463(24), 11 October 1924; all in PRO, CAB 24/168; Delevingne to Waterlow, 2 August 1924, PRO, FO 371/10326; Collier and Newton minutes, 17 October 1924, PRO, FO 371/10327.

48 PRO, FO 371/10327 (15–17 October 1924).

49 FO minute, 21 October 1924, PRO, FO 371/10328.

50 Taylor, op. cit., pp. 177–80; D. Musto, *The American Disease*, Oxford, Oxford University Press, 1987, pp. 121–204.

51 D. Courtwright, *Dark Paradise: Opiate Addiction in America before 1940*, Cambridge, Mass., Harvard University Press, 1982, ch. 5; C. Acker, "From all-purpose Anodyne to Marker of Deviance: Physician's Attitudes towards Opiates in the US from 1890–1940", in R. Porter and M. Teich (eds), *Drugs and Narcotics in History*, Cambridge, Cambridge University Press, 1995, ch. 6; D. Kinder, "Shutting Out Evil: Nativism and Narcotics Control in the United States", in W. Walker (ed.), *Drug Control Policy: Essays in Historical and Comparative Perspective*, University Park, Pennsylvania, Penn State University Press, 1992, pp. 125–7; H. Morgan, *Drugs in America: A Social History, 1800–1980*, Syracuse, NY, Syracuse University Press, 1981, ch. 7.

52 E. LaMotte, *The Opium Monopoly*, New York, Macmillan, 1920, and *The Ethics of Opium*, New York: The Century Company, 1924. In addition to haranguing religious and prohibitionist groups, Wright, LaMotte, Hobson, and others memorialized the US and foreign governments. Taylor, op. cit., p. 178, n. 17; W. Pittman, "Richmond P. Hobson and the International Limitation of Narcotics," *Alabama Historical Quarterly*, 1972, vol. 34, pp. 181–93; PRO, FO 371/11714 (February–November 1924).

53 Representative Hamilton Fish, no shrinking violet, complained, "Steve hogs all the publicity." *The Reminiscences of Herbert L. May*, OHRO, pp. 16–17.

54 FPA Minutes, 5 November 1924 and 19 November 1924, FPAA, Micro 48, Reel 1; Sweetser to Crowdy, 7 June 1924, SP, Box 14, File: "Opium Conference and Protest."

55 M. de Kort, "Doctors, Diplomats, and Businessmen: A History of Conflicting Interests in the Netherlands", in P. Gootenberg (ed.), *Cocaine: Global Histories*, London, Routledge, 1999; M. de Kort, "Drug Policy: Medical or Crime Control? Medicalization and Criminalization of Drug Use, and Shifting Drug Policies", in H. Binneveld and R. Dekker (eds), *Curing and Insuring: Essays on Illness in past times: the Netherlands, Belgium, England, and Italy, 16th–20th centuries*, Hilversum, Verloren, 1993, pp. 210–17; M. de Kort and

D. Korf, "The Development of Drug Trade and Drug Control in the Netherlands: A Historical Perspective," *Crime, Law, and Social Change*, 1992, vol. 17, pp. 127–8, 137.

56 J. Kawell, "The 'Essentially Peruvian' Industry: Legal Cocaine Production in the 19th Century" and P. Gootenberg, "Reluctance or Resistance? The Export of Cocaine (Prohibitions) to Peru, 1900–1950," in Gootenberg, op. cit.; J. Gagliano, *Coca Prohibition in Peru: The Historical Debates*, Tucson, University of Arizona Press, 1994, ch. 5.

57 P. Giffen, S. Endicott, and S. Lambert, *Panic and Indifference: The Politics of Canada's Drug Laws*, Ottawa, Canadian Centre on Substance Abuse, 1991, ch. 5.

58 Byng of Vimy to Thomas, 29 January 1924, PRO, FO 371/10323.

59 Even those present found the Geneva negotiations confusing. What follows is a streamlined account that covers the main themes. The negotiations generated worldwide publicity. In addition to scores of articles in the popular press, professional publications, and academic journals, major works in print within three years included Willoughby, op. cit.; O. Hoijer, *Le Trafic de l'opium et d'autres stupéfiants*, Paris, Editions Spes, 1925; Buell, op. cit.; FPA, *International Control of the Traffic in Opium: Summary of the Opium Conferences Held at Geneva, November, 1924, to February 1925*, New York, Foreign Policy Association, 1925; J. J. Pila, *Le Trafic des stupéfiants et la Société des nations*, Paris, 1926; M. Liais, *La Question des stupéfiants manufacturés et l'oeuvre de la Société des nations*, Paris, Société anonyme du recueil sirey, 1928; J. Gastinel, *Le Trafic des stupéfiants*, Aix-en-Provence, 1927; L. Lewin and W. Goldbaum, *Opiumgesetz (Gesetz zur Ausführung des internationalen Opiumabkommens vom 23. I. 1912), nebst internationalen Opiumabkommen und Ausführungsbestimmungen*, Berlin, Stilkes Rechtsbibliothek. Nr. 75., 1928; Terry and Pellens, op. cit.

Accounts by governmental representatives:

Netherlands: W. Van Wettum , "Les Conférences de l'opium à Genève (3 novembre 1924–19 février 1925) et leurs résultats mis en regard de ceux de la conférence de la Haye (1912)," *Grotius*, 1926, pp. 63–78.

India: Campbell's letter to *The Times* (London), 12 December 1924; published and confidential reports of the Indian delegation, 27 May 1925 and addendum of 16 November 1925, IOA, L/E/7, 1406(4696) and L/E/7, 1395(3343).

Great Britain: Delevingne's widely circulated report, 13 May 1925, FO, *The Opium Trade*, Volume XXII (January–December 1925), No. 13.

United States: Bishop Brent's "Appeal to My Colleagues" and Porter's statement accompanying US withdrawal, both in Buell, op. cit., pp. 159–68.

60 Minutes and annexes of the First Opium Conference, LNd C.684.M.244. 1924.XI.; Taylor, op. cit., pp. 181–4; Buell, op. cit., pp. 87–93; Willoughby, op. cit., chs 6–12; Gavit, op. cit., ch. 7.

61 J. Jennings, *The Opium Empire: Japanese Imperialism and Drug Trafficking in Asia, 1895–1945*, Westport, Connecticut, Praeger, 1997, pp. 28–32, 39–40, 46–52, 70–3.

62 Drummond to Chamberlain, 19 December 1924, PRO, FO 371/10331.

63 Numerous references in PRO, FO 371/10329 (November–December 1924).

64 LNd C.760.M.260.1924.XI. *Records of the Second Opium Conference, Geneva, November 17, 1924–February 19th, 1925, Volumes I and II*. For other general

accounts see Taylor, op. cit., pp. 184–209; Buell, op. cit., pp. 100–19; Gavit, op. cit., ch. 8; Willoughby, op. cit., chs 13–23; Musto, op. cit., pp. 202–3; S. Chatterjee, *Legal Aspects of International Drug Control*, The Hague, Martinus Nijhoff, 1981, ch. 4; records of the Indian delegation to the second conference, IOA, L/E/7, 1368(5349).

65 Delevingne to Anderson and attached minutes, 22 November 1924, PRO, FO 371/10329.

66 Delevingne to Waterlow and attached minutes, 26 November 1924, PRO, FO 371/10329.

67 PRO, FO 371/10329 (November 1924).

68 Cecil to Chamberlain, 1 December 1924, and Howard to FO and attached minutes, 3 December 1924, PRO, FO 371/10329; PRO, FO 371/10330 (11–16 December 1924); Cabinet Committee on Opium Policy, 16 December 1924, OP (24) 2nd Minutes, PRO, CAB 27/256.

69 Annex 2 of LNds A.32(a).1924.XI. (16 August 1924) *Measures Suggested by the Advisory Committee as a Basis for the Deliberations of the Second Conference, November 1924* and A.32(b).1924.XI. (16 August 1924) *Note Explanatory of the Proposals Contained in Document A.32(a).1924.XI.*

70 FO minute by Collier accompanying a clipping from the Manchester Guardian, 28 November 1924, PRO, FO 371/10329.

71 Most states wished to keep their military requirements and reserves secret. To meet this concern language was inserted that excepted government stocks and usage from reporting requirements.

72 Geneva Opium Convention, 1925, Chapter VI, Article 19.

73 J. Barros, *Betrayal from Within: Joseph Avenol, Secretary-General of the League of Nations, 1933–1940*, New Haven, Yale University Press, 1969, pp. 3–4.

74 Hurst to Delevingne, 13 June 1924, PRO, FO 371/10324; for a parallel case see discussions about the World Court in Diebel, op. cit., ch. 5; Kuehl and Dunn, op. cit., ch. 8.

75 UNDCPA, Narcotics Division, Inventory 80-1, Series G. XVIII, Item #31, file 4/3/1 (23269), ?1956–7?; Delevingne to Hurst, 10 June 1924, PRO, FO 371/10324; Crowdy to Sweetser, 6 July 1922 and 18 November 1922, SP, Box 14, File: "Opium Question, LaMotte Article"; Walters, op. cit., p. 185. For more discussion of these references see McAllister, op. cit., p. 103. See also Miller (1992) op. cit., pp. 90–1, 134–82, 193–4.

76 Article 20 of the 1925 Convention: "The Council of the League of Nations shall, in consultation with the board, make the necessary arrangements for the organization and working of the board, with the object of assuring the full technical independence of the board in carrying out its duties under the present convention, while providing for the control of the staff in administrative matters by the Secretary-General. The Secretary-General shall appoint the secretary and staff of the board on the nomination of the board subject to the approval of the (League) Council."

77 McAllister, op. cit., pp. 104–5.

78 Drummond-Sweetser correspondence, 11–13 May 1925, SP, Box 14, File: "Opium Conferences and Protest"; Drummond to Chamberlain, 19 December 1924, PRO, FO 371/10331; Drummond to FO and attached minutes, 12 January 1925, PRO, FO 371/10966.

79 Drummond to Selby and attached minutes, 20 December 1924, PRO, FO 371/10331.

80 McAllister, op. cit., pp. 106–8; 10 December 1924, OP (24) 1; 11 December 1924, OP (24) 2 and OP (24) 3; 12 December 1924, OP (24) 1st Conclusions; 15 December 1924, OP (24) numbers 4–7; 16, December 1924, OP (24) 2nd Conclusions; all in PRO, CAB 27/256; Grindle to Waterlow and attached minutes, 10 January 1925 and Waterlow minute, 19 January 1925, PRO, FO 371/10966.

81 Paris and The Hague pressed London to sign, hoping to forestall an American move to reconsider the opium-smoking question. French Ambassador to FO, 18 December 1924, PRO, FO 371/10330; French Ambassador to FO, 20 December 1924, PRO, FO 371/10331.

82 Inter-departmental Conference minutes, 19 December 1924, PRO, FO 371/ 10966; FO minute, 23 December 1924, PRO, FO 371/10330; Cabinet Committee on Opium Policy, Conclusions of Interdepartmental Conference, 8 January 1925, PRO, CAB 27/256, OP (24) 8; report on inter-departmental meetings, 14 January 1925, IOA, L/E/7, 1350(284); Amery to Canadian Governor-General, 7 January 1925, PAC, RG 25, Vol. 1388, File 1925–8, Part 1. For the public relations initiative, see Delevingne to FO, 22 December 1924, and Howard to FO including attached minutes, 16 December 1924, FO, PRO 371/10330.

83 For example, Germany strengthened export controls on drugs shipped to China. Friman, op. cit., p. 31.

84 McAllister, op. cit., p. 108; Taylor, op. cit., pp. 192–3.

85 Taylor, op. cit., pp. 191–2, 210; Brent to Chamberlain and attached minutes, 11 December 1924, and Chamberlain to Brent, 19 December 1924; PRO, FO 371/10330; A. Zabriskie, *Bishop Brent: Crusader for Christian Unity*, Philadelphia, Westminster Press, 1948, ch. 7.

86 Taylor, op. cit., pp. 193–6, 200–02.

87 Taylor, op. cit., pp. 202–04; Gavit, op. cit., pp. 203–05; Willoughby, op. cit., pp. 344–52; Buell, op. cit., pp. 111–13.

88 Willoughby, op. cit., chs 9–12; Gavit, op. cit., ch. 7; Chatterjee, op. cit., pp. 113–17.

89 Willoughby, op. cit., chs 18–23; Gavit, op. cit., chs 8–9; Chatterjee, pp. 117–28; Taylor, op. cit., p. 209.

3 Completing the edifice – 1925–31

1 From: FBNA, ACC 170-71-A-3554, Box 10, File 0355 (Geneva Convention). First stanza of anonymous poem, undated. Probably written in 1930 or 1931 by an FBN wag. References are to Rachel Crowdy and Hoffmann LaRoche, a Swiss-based pharmaceutical giant. By the 1920s Hoffmann had established operations in several countries and was the most ubiquitous manufacturer of addicting drugs.

2 The Canadian delegation took credit for quietly brokering the most widely acceptable agreement that circumstances permitted. Riddell to Mackenzie King, 20 February 1925, PAC, RG 25, Vol. 1388, File 1925–8, Part 1.

3 Riddell to Skelton, 25 January 1926, PAC, RG 25, Box 1440, File 1926-8-C; R. Veatch, *Canada and the League of Nations*, Toronto, University of Toronto Press, 1975, ch. 4.

4 FO to Sperling, 18 August 1925 and following documents, PRO, FO 371/ 10970:3946/106/87; Cecil to Austen Chamberlain, 18 September 1925,

and following documents, PRO, FO 371/10970:4641/106/87; Sperling to Collier, 17 September 1925, and following documents, PRO, FO 371/10970:4657/106/87.

5 J. Jennings, *The Opium Empire: Japanese Imperialism and Drug Trafficking in Asia, 1895–1945*, Westport, Connecticut, Praeger, 1997, pp. 73–5; W. McAllister, "A Limited Enterprise: The History of International Efforts to Control Drugs in the Twentieth Century," PhD dissertation, University of Virginia, 1996, p. 118.

6 A. Taylor, *American Diplomacy and the Narcotics Traffic*, Durham, NC, Duke University Press, 1969, pp. 231–2; K. Meyer and T. Parssinen, *Webs of Smoke: Smugglers, Warlords, Spies, and the History of the International Drug Trade*, Lanham, Maryland, Rowman & Littlefield, 1998, pp. 118–19; Bramwell minute, 5 January 1931, PRO, FO 371/14769.

7 M. de Kort, "Doctors, Diplomats, and Businessmen: A History of Conflicting Interests in the Netherlands," in P. Gootenberg (ed.), *Cocaine: Global Histories*, London, Routledge, 1999; M. de Kort and D. Korf, "The Development of Drug Trade and Drug Control in the Netherlands: A Historical Perspective," *Crime, Law, and Social Change*, 1992, vol. 17, pp. 127–8.

8 FO, *The Opium Trade*, 1910–1941, 5:XXII, 1925, nos 10, 14, 18, and 6:XXIII, 1926, nos 5–9, 11. The Indian Government announced a 90 percent reduction of exports, from 1 million pounds in 1927 to 120,000 pounds in 1935. Domestic opposition to the opium trade, organized by the Indian National Congress, contributed to the government's policy change. G. Blue, "Opium for China: The British Connection," in T. Brook and B. Wakabayashi (eds), *Opium in East Asian History*, Berkeley, University of California Press, 2000.

9 Crosby to FO, 2 September 1927, PRO, FO 371/12533; IOpC meetings, 28 March 1928 and 19 February 1931, PRO, HO 45/20413.

10 Grahame to FO, 9 November 1927, PRO, FO 371/12533; BLI to FO, 4 May, 1 June, and 15 June 1928; Delevingne to Strang, 18 May 1928; Delevingne to Mounsey, 17 December 1928, all in PRO, FO 371/13260. For disputes between the Government of Burma and the IO, HO, and FO, see R. Maule, "The Opium Question in the Federated Shan States, 1931–36: British Policy Discussions and Scandal," *Journal of Southeast Asian Studies*, 1992, vol. 23, no. 1, pp. 14–36.

11 FO, *The Opium Trade, 1910–1941*, 6:XXIII, 1926, nos 1, 4, 17, 20, and 6:XXIV, 1927, nos 6, 8; PRO, FO 371/11715 (November–December 1926); PRO, FO 371/12526 (February–July 1927); PRO, HO 45/20413 (December 1926–June 1927); HO to FO, 29 June 1929, and Strang to Cadogan, 9 July 1929, PRO, FO 371/13976; CO to FO, 20 May 1930, PRO, FO 371/14772.

12 Taylor, op. cit., ch. 8; W. Walker, *Drug Control in the Americas*, Albuquerque, University of New Mexico Press, 1989, pp. 53–6, 60–2.

13 In other countries, accounts of the Geneva negotiations usually followed the line taken by governments. In the United States, however, many commentators recognized that Porter's actions did more harm than good. Even Wright and Brent, members of the American delegation, expressed regret at the US withdrawal. See Taylor, op. cit., pp. 204–08, for American press opinion. Willoughby penned the strongest book-length defense of the official US position. See W. Willoughby, *Opium as an International Problem*,

Baltimore, Johns Hopkins, 1925, ch. 25. See also J. Gavit, *Opium*, New York, Brentano's, 1927, ch. 9; *The Reminiscences of Herbert L. May*, OHRO, p. 18; R. Buell, "The International Opium Conferences with Relevant Documents," *World Peace Foundation Pamphlets*, 1925, vol. 7, nos 2–3; Warnshuis-Buell correspondence, 15 and 23 April 1925, LC, BP, Box 43, File: Geneva Conference on Opium and Drugs, 1925. British accounts of US press opinion stressed the numerous publications that deprecated Porter's position. Howard to FO, 23 February and 2 March 1925, PRO, FO 371/10966; FO, *The Opium Trade, 1910–1941*, 5:XXII, 1925, nos 2, 4, 5.

14 W. Walker (ed.), *Drugs in the Western Hemisphere: An Odyssey of Cultures in Conflict*, Wilmington, Scholarly Resources, 1996, pp. xvii–xviii; W. Kuehl and L. Dunn,*Keeping the Covenant: American Internationalists and the League of Nations, 1920–1939*, Kent, Ohio, Kent State Univ. Press, 1997, pp. 137–41, 146; G. Ostrower, "The United States and the League of Nations, 1919–1939," in *The League of Nations in Retrospect*, Berlin and New York, Walter de Gruyter & Co., 1983, pp. 130–1.

15 McAllister, op. cit., p. 121.

16 Rogers minute, 8 August 1927 and Delevingne to Mounsey, 19 August 1927, PRO, FO 371/12532; Delevingne to Cadogan, 2 December 1926, PRO, FO 371/13260; Strang to Cadogan, 9 July 1929, PRO, FO 371/13976; Croft to Cadogan, 16 August 1929; Bramwell minutes, 16, 17, 18, and 22 January 1930; Secret Provisional Minutes, Second Private OAC Meeting, 8 February 1930; Delevingne to Cadogan, 22 March 1930; Delevingne to Cadogan, 10 April 1930, all in PRO, FO 371/14762; Bramwell minute, 24 May 1930; Harding to FO, 12 June 1930; Carr to Orde, 9 December 1930; all in PRO FO 371/14763; Sharman–Amyot correspondence, 14–17 May 1930, PAC, RG 25, Vol. 1554, File 1930-8B, Part 1.

17 OAC reports to the League Assembly, LNds A.20.1926.III [i.e.,XI] (29 July 1926); C.521.M.179.1927.XI (12 October 1927); A.23.1927.XI (12 July 1927), etc. The League studied conditions in Persia including the possibilities for crop substitution. Commission of Enquiry into the Production of Opium in Persia, LNd C.580.M.219.1926.XI (December 1926). The League also sponsored a Commission of Enquiry in Opium Producing Countries. LNd C.635.M.254.1930.XI (two volumes, February and November 1930). Herbert May surveyed conditions in Asia for the FPA in 1926–27. See: May, op. cit., pp. 19–32; FPA Executive Board minutes, 3 March 1926, FPAA, Micro 48, Reel 1; BLI to FO, 2 September 1927, PRO, FO 371/12533; Delevingne to Cadogan, 28 February 1929, PRO, FO 371/13976.

18 PRO, HO 45/20965 (September–November 1925); PRO, HO 45/20968 (March–June 1927); PRO, HO 45/20969 (February–October 1927); PRO, FO 371/12530 (January–December 1927); PRO, FO 371/13257 (February–June 1928). The FPA, through May and Moorhead, lobbied Washington in a vain attempt to alter US opposition to the 1925 Convention. See Howard–FO correspondence, 2 February and 16 March 1926, PRO, HO 45/20967; Buell–Moorhead correspondence, 12–13 January 1927, BP, Box 10, File: H. H. Moorhead; FPA Executive Board minutes, 18 June 1927, 11 May 1927, 14 March 1928, 12 June 1929, all in FPAA, Micro 48, Reel 1.

19 FO Minute, 22 June 1928, PRO, FO 371/13256; Delevingne to Mounsey, 10 July 1928, PRO, FO 371/13257; PRO, FO 371/13258 (July–August 1928); Delevingne to Cadogan, 21 May 1928; FO memorandum, 24 August 1928; HO memorandum, 23 November 1928; HO memorandum, 7 December 1928, all in PRO, FO 371/13260; IOpC, 7th meeting, 22 October 1928, PRO, HO 45/20413; Crowdy to Avenol, 1 August 1928, LNA, R3272, 12A/6281/3085; Hall memo, 5 December 1928, LNA, R3272, 12A/6398/3015; Executive Committee minutes, 28 June 1928, FPAA, Micro 48, Reel 1.

20 May had distinguished himself by producing an even-handed review of the Far Eastern opium situation for the FPA. The British supported him in part because of his Republican connections. May op. cit, pp. 33–4; Executive Committee minutes, 14 November 1928, FPAA, Micro 48, Reel 1; FO Minute, 30 October 1928, Hall memo, 29 June 1928; Hall to Crowdy, 15 November 1928; Hall to Drummond, 3 December 1928; Hall to Crowdy, 4 December 1928, all in LNA, R3272, 12A/6398/3015; Sweetser to Crowdy, 26 October 1928, LNA, R3272, 12A/6999/3015; PRO, FO 371/13258 (November–December 1928).

21 McAllister, op. cit., pp. 122–5; H. Friman, *Narcodiplomacy: Exporting the US War on Drugs*, Ithaca, NY, Cornell University Press, 1996, pp. 25–6.

22 Minutes of the first three PCOB meetings, all held in 1929, LNA, Dossiers 12A/13524/3015; 12A/13525/3015; 12A/13547/3015; 12A/13548/3015; 12A/13975/3015; 12A/15108/3015, all in Box R3274; LN to FO, 23 January 1931, PRO, FO 371/15528; Joseph Dittert, interviews, Geneva, 21 April, 26 April 1993; Louis Atzenwiler, interview, Geneva, 1 May 1993.

23 The leading proponent of the open approach was Herbert May. Physician Otto Anselmino, closely tied to the German pharmaceutical industry, championed the more limited view of the Board's mandate. McAllister, op. cit., pp. 125–7.

24 First Board Report, LNd C.176.M.99.1929.XI. (9 May 1929); OAC twelfth Session Report, LNd A.16.1929.XI. (9 July 1929), pp. 6–7.

25 Other observers also noticed a deterioration in the impartiality of the secretariat. They feared League service was becoming merely a stop on the career path for officials who retained national loyalties. Moorhead's report to FPA, 13 June 1928, FPAA, Micro 48, Reel 1.

26 Delevingne to Cadogan, 31 January 1928; Drummond to Cadogan, 10 April 1928; Delevingne to Mounsey, 1 May 1928; FO minute, 5 May 1928; FO minute 13 June 1928, all in PRO, FO 371/13258; FO minutes, 7 June 1928, PRO, FO 371/13256; Drummond memos, 21 January and 23 March 1928; Crowdy to Drummond, 27 March 1928, LNA, R3272, 12A/3015/3015.

27 Selecting the first Board Secretary also engendered controversy. See McAllister, op. cit., p. 129.

28 LNd C.176.M.99.1929.XI. (9 May 1929). The Board Secretary gradually gained supervisory control over his staff, although hiring decisions could not be made without the approval of League officials.

29 FO, *The Opium Trade, 1910–1941*, 5:XXIII, 1926, nos 16, 21 and 6:XXIV, 1927, nos 1, 7; Taylor, op. cit., ch. 8.

30 Taylor, op. cit., pp. 230–2; Meyer and Parssinen, op. cit., ch. 5; de Kort, op. cit., in Gootenberg, op. cit.; FO, *The Opium Trade, 1910–1941*, 6:XXV, 1928, nos 3, 8, 11, 16, 19, 20, 22–25; 6:XXVI, 1929, nos 6–7; 6:XXVII,

1930, nos 1–5, 7, 14–16, 19–23, 25–27, 51, 53, 62, 74, 76–77; Constantinople Chancery to FO, 17 October 1929, PRO, FO 371/13973; AOIB, nos. 1–26 (1928–39).

31 W. McAllister, "Parallel Tracks: Similarities Between the Questions of Arms and Drugs, 1919–1939," unpublished paper, 1997. "Analogies between the Problem of the Traffic in Narcotic Drugs and that of the Trade in and Manufacture of Arms" LNd C.280.1933.XI.(4 May 1933); L. Morgan, *A Possible Technique of Armament Control*, Geneva Studies, vol. 11, no.7, Geneva, 1940; LNd C.608.1931.IX. (25 September 1931); Morgan, "Armaments and Measures of Enforcement," *World Organization*, Washington, American Council of Public Affairs, 1942, pp. 121–57; O. Ewing, "The Narcotic Battle at Geneva," 1931 (undated), AP, Box 10, File 11, 3–4. For discussions during 1924–25, see H. Forbes, *The Strategy of Disarmament*, Washington, Public Affairs Press, 1962, pp. 67–8; Campbell to FO, 11 December 1924, PRO, FO 371/10330.

32 McAllister (1996), op. cit., p. 133; Taylor, op. cit., pp. 224–8; FO, *The Opium Trade, 1910–1941*, 5:XXIII, 1926, nos 10, 16, 21, 6:XXIV, 1927, nos 1, 7, and 6:XXV, 1928, no. 18; PRO, FO 371/11715 (September 1926–January 1927).

33 Ryan to Fletcher, 29 July 1927, PRO, FO 371/12532.

34 As an independent player with expert knowledge and a sarcastic wit, Blanco did not mince words; he embarrassed governments that he thought took inadequate drug control measures. For British reaction to Blanco's early broadsides see AOIB to FO, 2 April 1929, PRO, FO 371/13972; AOIB to FO, 11 May and 4 November 1930, PRO, FO 371/14770; Perrins to Bramwell, 24 October 1930, PRO, FO 371/14758. See also McAllister (1996), op. cit., pp. 134–5.

35 Taylor, op. cit., pp. 227–30; undated black binder (probably 1929 or 1930) in NA, RG 59, Lot file 55D607, box 3; PRO, FO 371/13259 (February–August 1928); LN to FO, 3 January 1929, PRO, FO 371/13973; Cecil to Henderson, 12 October 1929, PRO FO 371/13972; AOIB to FO, 23 October 1929, PRO, FO 371/19378; AOIB to FO, 3 November 1929, PRO, FO 371/19378; BLI to FO, 27 December 1929, PRO, FO 371/14758; LN to FO, 14 May 1930, PRO, FO 371/14770; Perrins to Sharman, 14 July 1928, PAC, RG 29, Vol. 601, File 324–7–3.

36 Twelfth OAC session minutes, LNd C.33.1929.XI. (2 February 1929); Thirteenth OAC session minutes, LNd C.121.M.39.1930.XI. (15 April 1930); LN to FO, 21 September 1929, PRO, FO 371/13972; LN to FO, 24 September 1929; Cadogan to Delevingne, 10 December 1929; Delevingne to Orde, 16 December 1929; all in PRO, FO 371/19378.

37 IOpC meeting, 5 March 1930, PRO, HO 45/20413; J. Slinn, "Research and Development in the UK Pharmaceutical Industry from the Nineteenth Century to the 1960s," in R. Porter and M. Teich (eds), *Drugs and Narcotics in History*, Cambridge, Cambridge University Press, 1995, pp. 169–71.

38 PRO, FO 371/14770 (June–September 1930); PRO, HO 45/14686 June–September 1930); PRO, HO 45/14687 (June–December 1930); Everett to Caldwell, 5 July 1930, NA, RG 59, LF 55D607, Box 10, File: "Cannabis"; Taylor, op. cit., pp. 233–6. Continental manufacturers lowered prices in an attempt to undersell British competitors, thereby increasing the percentage

they could claim in quota negotiations. Johnstone to Strutt, 8 April 1931, PRO, HO 45/21785.

39 For Anslinger's early career and the creation of the FBN, see J. McWilliams, *The Protectors: Harry J. Anslinger and the Federal Bureau of Narcotics, 1930–1962*, Newark, University of Delaware Press, 1990, pp. 13–48; D. Musto, *The American Disease*, Oxford, Oxford University Press, 1987, pp. 206–14; J. Jonnes, *Hepcats, Narcs, and Pipedreams: A History of America's Romance With Illegal Drugs*, New York, Scribner, 1996, pp. 83–5; Walker (1989), op. cit., pp. 63–70.

40 Taylor, op. cit., pp. 270–1.

41 Record of conference, 7 October 1930, FBNA, ACC 170–71–A, Box 10, File 0355 (Geneva Convention); O. Ewing, "The Narcotic Battle at Geneva," 1931 (undated), AP, Box 10, File 11. Ewing acted as attorney for Merck & Company, Mallinkrodt Chemical Works, and New York Quinine and Chemical Works, the principal manufacturers of opiates in the US The American Drug Manufacturers' Association, some of whose members produced specialty drugs from alkaloidal base, also sent a representative to the meeting. For evidence of earlier government collaboration with American pharmaceutical companies to protect manufacturer's interests, see P. Gootenberg, "Reluctance or Resistance? The Export of Cocaine (Prohibitions) to Peru, 1900–1950," in Gootenberg, op. cit.

42 Participants included France, Germany, Great Britain, India, Italy, Japan, the Netherlands, Switzerland, Turkey, the US, and the USSR Preliminary Conference report, LNd C.669.M.278.1930.XI. (2 December 1930); Taylor, op. cit., pp. 236–40; PRO, FO 371/14770 (July–September 1930); PRO, FO 371/14771 (September–October 1930); PRO, FO 371/14772 (October–December 1930); PRO, HO 45/14686 (June–September 1930); PRO, HO 45/14687 (June–December 1930); AOIB, nos 1–12 (1928–30).

43 HO to FO, 2 September 1930 and Patterson to FO, 11 September 1930, PRO, FO 371/14771; Strang to FO, 29 September 1930, PRO, FO 371/14773; M. Conroy, "Abuse of Drugs Other than Alcohol and Tobacco in the Soviet Union," *Soviet Studies*, 1990, vol. 42, no. 3, pp. 447–80.

44 Fourteenth OAC session minutes, LNd C.88.M.34.1931.XI. (2 volumes, 7 February and 1 May 1931); Cecil to Henderson, 30 September 1930, PRO, FO 371/14769; Delevingne to Avenol, 12 December 1930, PRO, FO 371/14763; Drummond to FO, 10 December 1930, PRO, FO 371/14772; Macfarlan & Co. to Perrins, 31 December 1930, PRO, HO 45/21785; Delevingne to Orde, 16 March 1931, PRO, FO 371/15526; Merck to other pharmaceutical firms, 18 February 1931, and attached letters, PRO, HO 45/21785:582132/8; Hall to Delevingne, 1 April 1931, PRO, HO 45/21785; Executive Committee minutes, 10 April 1931, 13 May 1931, FPAA, Micro 48, Reel 1.

45 Crowdy–Sweetser correspondence 21 June and 7 July 1928, LC, SP, Box 30, File: Crowdy, Dame Rachel; Crowdy–Hall correspondence, 29 March and 12 April 1930, LNA, R3240 (Section 12), Dossier #30955.

46 PRO, HO 45/21785 (January–April 1931); PRO, FO 371/15523 (February–May 1931); IOpC meeting, 13 May 1931, PRO, HO 45/20413; McAllister (1996), op. cit., pp. 142–3.

47 Taylor, op. cit., pp. 242–3; Russe to Merck, 1 January 1931; Russe to Caldwell, 20 March 1931; summary of discussions at informal conference

between American manufacturers and the American Delegation, 9 April 1931; Ewing to Anslinger, 1 May 1931, all in FBNA, ACC 170-71-A-3554, Box 10, File 0355 (Geneva Conference); Gilbert to SD, 11 February 1931, AP, Box 10, File 13; Executive Committee minutes, 12 June and 13 November 1929, FPAA, Micro 48, Reel 1; Nash to Ekstrand, 18 March 1931, LNA, R3164, Dossier# 26771; LaGuardia to Stimson, 18 March 1931, AP, Box 3, File 9; MacCormack report to President's Commission on Law Enforcement, 4 March 1931, PRO, FO 371/15530.

48 Amyot to Skelton with accompanying report by Sharman, 8 September 1930, PAC, RG 25, Vol. 2622, File 8–AE–40, vol. 1; Skelton to Sharman, 12 May 1931, PAC, RG 25, Vol. 2623, File 8–AE–40, part 2; PAC, RG 29, Box 602, File 325–2–5 (January–May 1931).

49 For Latin American developments and a similar conciliatory attitude toward the 1931 negotiations, see Walker (1989), op. cit., pp. 56–60, 70–3.

50 Records of the Conference on the Limitation of Manufactured Drugs, (2 Volumes), LNd C.509.M.214.1931.XI.; American delegation report, Department of State Conference series No. 10, 15 September 1931; Taylor, op. cit., 243–53; Ewing, "The Narcotic Battle at Geneva," 1931 (undated), AP, Box 10, File 11; Taylor, op. cit., pp. 253–61; PRO, FO 371/15523 (June 1931); PRO, HO 45/21786 (June–July 1931); HO to FO, 27 July 1931, PRO, FO 371/15524; Delevingne to Cadogan, 28 July 1931, PRO, FO 371/15526; PAC, RG 25, Vol. 2623, File 8–AE–40, part 2 (June 1931); PAC, RG 25, Vol. 2623, File 8-AE-40, part 3 (July–October 1931); AOIB, nos 13–17 (1931); Jennings, op. cit., p. 75; S. Chatterjee, *Legal Aspects of International Drug Control*, The Hague, Martinus Nijhoff, 1981, pp. 142–67; May, op. cit., pp. 36–39; Woodward to Anslinger, 24 June 1931, AP, Box 3, File 9; Small to Eddy, 25 July 1931, NLM, LSP, MS. C. 333, Box 2, File: EDDY; Small to White, 25 July 1931, NLM, LSP, MS. C. 333, Box 4, File: WHITE; Wood to Copeland, 5 February 1932, AP, Box 3, File 8.

51 McAllister (1996), op. cit., pp. 145–9.

52 It is likely that other factors influenced the DSB's configuration and mandate. The American delegation probably expressed an unwillingness to recognize the Board directly because of its relation to the 1925 Convention. The League secretariat no doubt supported delegating administrative responsibilities to the Opium Section instead of the PCOB. Crowdy's departure may have made the arrangement more palatable to those concerned about secretariat activism.

The OAC, the PCOB, the League Health Committee, and the Office International d'Hygiène Publique (an international health organization that predated the League and in which the US participated) each named one person to the four-member DSB.

53 Since German pharmaceutical firms fabricated the largest share of the world's codeine, any restrictions on the free flow of codeine would affect German firms most severely. McAllister (1996), op. cit., p. 151.

54 The medical experts of the League Health Committee, charged with recommending new drugs for control, had for several years attempted to impose broad restrictions that encompassed as many substances as possible. Pharmaceutical companies devised several compensatory strategies. One tactic consisted of developing numerous analogous derivatives. Another involved encumbering a competitor's drug with more onerous (or at least similar)

restrictions. PRO, HO 45/17002 (1928–1930); PRO, HO 45/17003 (1930–37); HO to FO, 8 January 1929; Cadogan minute, 16 January 1929; Delevingne to FO, 20 February 1929; FO minute by Cadogan, 18 June 1929, all in PRO, FO 371/13973; Small to Anslinger, undated (probably 1931), AP, Box 9, File 2; McCoy to Anslinger, 29 November 1930 and Woodward to Merck, 16 March 1931, AP, Box 3, File 9.

55 LNd C.168.M.62.1931.XI.(6 February 1931), p. 22; May, op. cit., pp. 36–9.
56 Historical and Technical Study, LNd C.191.M.136.1937.XI. (October 1937).
57 US delegation report, Department of State Conference series No. 10, 15 September 1931.
58 Sharman's report, 29 October 1931, PAC, RG 25, Vol. 2623, File 8–AE–40, part 3.
59 Hall memo to Ekstrand, "Place of the Opium Advisory Committee, of the Secretariat, and of the Permanent Central Opium Board in the Limitation Convention," 18 June 1931, LNA, DSB files (Washington Office), Box C.1804, File #8 (Lande and Ekstrand, 1931–45).
60 Delevingne's report, FO, *The Opium Trade, 1910–1941*, 6:XXVIII, 1931, no. 20; Delevingne to Cadogan, 28 July 1931, PRO, FO 371/15526; Conant to Small, 29 August 1931, NLM, LSP, MS. C. 333, Box 1, File: CO; de Kort, op. cit., and H. Friman, "Germany and the Transformations of Cocaine, 1880–1920," in Gootenberg, op. cit.
61 See, for example, AOIB, no. 15, 9 June 1931, p. 3.
62 Sharman to Skelton, 13 July 1931, PAC, RG 25, Vol. 2623, File 8–AE–40, part 3; Delevingne's report, FO, *The Opium Trade, 1910–1941*, 6:XXVIII, 1931, no. 20.
63 The drug control regime's development was in many respects typical. For applicable generalizations see D. Puchala and R. Hopkins, "International Regimes: Lessons from Inductive Analysis," pp. 86–91, O. Young, "Regime Dynamics: The Rise and Fall of International Regimes," pp. 98–111, R. Keohane, "The demand for International Regimes," pp. 141–71, all in S. Krasner (ed.), *International Regimes*, Ithaca, NY, Cornell University Press, 1983; E. Haas, *When Knowledge is Power: Three Models of Change in International Organizations*, Berkeley, University of California Press, 1990, pp. 89–92, 97–8, 172–4. For examples of comparable regimes see Puchala and Hopkins, op. cit., pp. 79–81; C. Skran, *Refugees in Inter-War Europe: The Emergence of a Regime*, Oxford, Clarendon Press, 1995, pp. 66–84; E. Nadelmann, "Global Prohibition Regimes: the Evolution of Norms in International Society," *International Organization*, 1990, vol. 44, no. 4, pp. 484–6.
64 "When I gave six solid months to [the opium question], in the writing of my *Opium*, and a lot more time in other ways too numerous to mention, I did my bit, and I have devoted considerable energy ever since to get and keep my feet out of the mess. Fly-paper is no name for it!" Gavit to Blanco, 4 May 1933, AP, Box 10, File 9.

4 Against the tide – 1931–39

1 Remarks of Stuart Fuller, sixteenth OAC session, 2 November 1933, LNd C.661.M.316.1933.XI (5 December 1933), p. 15.

2 DSB annual report, LNd C.379.M.292.1939.XI (30 December 1939), p. 5.
3 The first Geneva treaty of 1925, concerning the suppression of opium use in Far Eastern territories, required signatories to convene a follow-up meeting. W. McAllister, "A Limited Enterprise: The History of International Efforts to Control Drugs in the Twentieth Century," PhD dissertation, University of Virginia, 1996, p. 162.
4 Herbert May, in fact, recommended abandoning prohibition in the Philippines in favor of a Dutch-style monopoly.
5 Anslinger and Fuller also supplied valuable information to pharmaceutical firms about overseas markets, production, prices, and foreign governmental regulations. J. McWilliams, *The Protectors: Harry J. Anslinger and the Federal Bureau of Narcotics, 1930–1962*, Newark, University of Delaware Press, 1990, pp. 85–7; P. Gootenberg, "Reluctance or Resistance? The Export of Cocaine (Prohibitions) to Peru, 1900–1950," in P. Gootenberg (ed.), *Cocaine: Global Histories*, London, Routledge, 1999; Russe to Hull, 15 April 1937, and Hayes to Anslinger, 20 April 1937, AP, Box 3, File 3; NA, RG 59, LF 55D607, Box 4, File: "Coca-cola extract" (1933–38); Anslinger memo, 12 September 1933, NA, RG 59, LF 55D607, Box 8, File: "15th Session, Subcommittee on Model Code"; Anslinger to Gibbons, 3 February 1936, AP, Box 3, File 4; Bobst to Anslinger, 29 April 1936, SP, MS. C. 333, Box 2, File: "Ho-Hu"; Small memo, 18 December 1937, NA, RG 59, LF 55D607, Box 4, File: "Desomorphine." Since congressional legislation prevented the Commissioner from exporting to nations that had not adhered to the 1912 treaty, Anslinger urged nonsignatory states to ratify. Morlock to Ward, 23 December 1941, NA, RG 59, LF 55D607, Box 8, File: "US Treasury Department, Bureau of Narcotics, Regulations No. 2."
6 McWilliams, op. cit., pp. 81–3; J. Jonnes, *Hepcats, Narcs, and Pipedreams: A History of America's Romance With Illegal Drugs*, New York, Scribner, 1996, pp. 88–93, 102–3; R. Carroll, "The Weed with Roots in Rhetoric: Harry J. Anslinger, Marijuana, and the Making of American Drug Policy," PhD dissertation, University of Pittsburgh, 1991, p. 14; D. Kinder and W. Walker, "Stable Force In a Storm: Harry J. Anslinger and United States Narcotic Foreign Policy, 1930–1962," *Journal of American History*, 1986, vol. 72, no. 4, pp. 908–27.
7 Since the mid-1920s the "drug powers" had periodically exchanged information about suspected traffickers. Governments allowed enforcement agencies to communicate without prior clearance from their respective foreign ministries, enabling control authorities to act on time-sensitive leads and reduce intelligence leaks. McAllister, op. cit., pp. 163–4; H. Friman, *Narcodiplomacy: Exporting the US War on Drugs*, Ithaca, NY, Cornell University Press, 1996, p. 32; Jonnes, op. cit., pp. 93–102.
8 The secretariat never knew about the secret meetings. Louis Atzenwiler, letter, 2 December 1993.
9 SD memo, 4 April 1933, NA, RG 59, LF 55D607; Perrins to Sharman, 13 February 1931, PAC, RG 29, Vol. 601, File 324-7-3; Amyot–External Affairs correspondence, 14 and 27 October 1931, PAC, RG 25, Vol. 1554, File 1930-8B, Part 1; FO minute, 26 June 1939, PRO, FO 371/23583; Thornton to Henniker-Major, 25 May 1939, PRO, FO 371/23585; M. de

Kort, "Doctors, Diplomats, and Businessmen: A History of Conflicting Interests in the Netherlands," in Gootenberg, op. cit.

10 Prior to 1930 the OAC acted timidly concerning illicit trafficking, only criticizing governments when presented with an overwhelming case.

11 Sharman to Skelton, 22 June 1933, PAC, RG 25, Vol. 1554, File 1930-8B, Part 2. Opprobrium might be directed anywhere: Anslinger and Fuller accused British officials of inadequate enforcement in the Bahamas, causing consternation in London. IOpC meetings, 12 May 1932 and 1 November 1934, HO 45/20413.

12 A. Taylor, *American Diplomacy and the Narcotics Traffic*, Durham, NC, Duke University Press, 1969, p. 244, 305–6; Anslinger to LaGuardia, 20 September 1932, and Ewing to Conboy, 21 December 1932, AP, Box 3, File 8; Anslinger to Medalie, 22 October 1931, AP, Box 3, File 9; H. May, *The Reminiscences of Herbert L. May*, OHRO, pp. 68–72; Anslinger memo, 29 November 1938, FBNA, ACC 170-71-A-3554, Box 25, File: "0660 Yugoslavia"; Campbell to FO, 5 December 1938, PRO, FO 371/22206; Sharman to Robertson and attached letters, 22 February 1939, PAC, RG 25, Vol. 1759, File 1936-8-B, Part 4.

13 Anslinger did not originate the idea; Blanco first proposed it as part of his Scheme of Stipulated Supply. AOIB, no. 1, 11 September 1928, p. 16. See also AOIB, no. 13, 9 January 1931, p. 9; AOIB, no. 25, 20 December 1938, pp. 11–12.

14 Illicit production and trafficking resurfaced in Turkey repeatedly. Nevertheless, such immediate successes enabled Fuller and Anslinger to claim that their remonstrations had alleviated the most visible instances of illicit trafficking.

15 Recommendation 1 of the 1931 Limitation Convention.

16 For example, primary responsibility for drug control devolved upon the Health Ministry in Japan, Germany, and Switzerland, the Agriculture Ministry in France and Turkey, the Justice Ministry in the Netherlands, the Home Office in Britain, the Department of Pensions and National Health in Canada, the Interior Ministry in Egypt, and Customs in India.

17 Taylor, op. cit., pp. 258–9.

18 Taylor, op. cit., pp. 259–61; IOpC meeting, 12 May 1932, PRO, HO 45/20413; Anslinger to LaGuardia, 20 September 1932, AP, Box 3, File 8; Atherton to Simon, 25 August 1932, PRO, FO 371/16254; Orde to HO, 8 September 1932, and HO to FO, 12 September 1932, PRO, HO 45/21788; Executive Committee minutes, 10 February, 9 March, and 9 November 1932, all in FPAA, Micro 48, Reel 1; Fletcher to Leeper, 19 October 1932 and related material, PRO, FO 371/16524:F7659/437/87.

19 BLI to FO, 2 March 1935, PRO, FO 371/19372; Moorhead to Anslinger, 7 March 1935, AP, Box 3, File 5; Executive Committee minutes, 20 November 1935, 16 December 1936, 15 December 1937, 16 February 1938, 16 March 1938, and 18 May 1938, all in FPAA, Micro 48, Reel 1; Moorhead to Anslinger, 8 December 1937, AP, Box 3, File 3; Gaston to Anslinger, 18 April 1938, FBNA, ACC 170-75-17, Box 8, File 1690-10, File: "FPA, 1938–44." Moorhead included Blanco on her mailing list. SD memo, 18 March 1937, FBNA, ACC 170-75-17, Box 8, File 1690-10, File: "FPA."

20 SD to American diplomatic and consular officers, 10 June 1931, NA, RG
    59, 854.114 Narcotics/20; Wait to Customs Commissioner, 8 February
    1938, FBNA, ACC 170-71-A-3554, Box 25, File: O660 Yugoslavia.
21 Caldwell memo, 25 May 1932 and Fuller memo, 6 September 1932, NA,
    RG 59, LF 55D607, Box 8, File: "15th Session [OAC] Subcommittee on
    Model Code."
22 Taylor, op. cit., pp. 262-5; Osborne to FO, 26 September 1933, PRO,
    FO 371/17173; Sweetser memo, 29 September 1933, Wilson memo,
    29 September 1933, LN Legal Section memo, 30 September 1933, all in
    LNA, R.5056, 12A/7034/4161. Moorhead trumpeted US participation in
    the election as the crowning achievement in the FPA's ten-year effort to
    promote international drug control and closer American cooperation with
    the League. Executive Committee minutes, 18 October 1933, FPAA,
    Micro 48, Reel 1.
23 Amyot–External Affairs correspondence, 14 and 27 October 1931, PAC,
    RG 25, Vol. 1554, File 1930-8B, Part 1; Taylor, op. cit., pp. 290-1.
24 Executive Committee minutes, 10 February and 9 March 1932, FPAA,
    Micro 48, Reel 1.
25 New York *Times*, 20 April 1933, p. 12; FO, *The Opium Trade, 1910–1941*,
    6:XXIX, 1932, nos 9, 10.
26 McWilliams, op. cit., pp. 47-8, ch. 4, describes a continuous series of
    threats to Anslinger's position during the 1930s. I concentrate on the
    instances with international ramifications. Numerous references in AP,
    Box 3, File 8 (January 1932–April 1933); AP, Box 3, File 7 (January–
    April 1933); AP, Box 10, File 8, (April 1933); Fuller–Fowler conversation
    memo, 4 April 1933, NA, RG 59, LF 55D607, Box 14, File "Proposed
    Merger of BND"; Hull–FDR correspondence, 1 and 20 April 1933, Moor-
    head to Fuller, 6 April 1933, all in NA, RG 59, LF 55D607, Box 17;
    Jonnes, op. cit., pp. 103–115; Carroll, op. cit; R. King, *The Drug Hang-up:
    America's Fifty-Year Folly*, New York, Norton, 1972, chs 7–8; W. Walker,
    Drug Control in the Americas, Albuquerque, University of New Mexico Press,
    1989, pp. 77–9.
27 McAllister, op. cit., pp. 169–75.
28 Delevingne, although retired, retained responsibility for international
    drug affairs through 1934. M. D. Perrins took over domestic matters.
29 PRO, FO 371/16254 (May–November 1932); HO 45/21788 (June–
    September 1932); HO 45/21789 (November–December 1932); Delevingne
    to Orde, 6 May 1932, PRO, FO 371/16258; IOpC minutes, 12 May 1932,
    PRO, HO 45/20413; FO, *The Opium Trade, 1910–1941*, 6:XXIX, 1932,
    no. 5; AOIB to FO, 13 July 1932, PRO, FO 371/16256.
30 "Analogies between the Problem of the Traffic in Narcotic Drugs and that
    of the Trade in and Manufacture of Arms," LNd C.280.1933.XI. (4 May
    1933); *New York Times*, 9 May 1933, p. 10.
31 Concerning Germany, see C. Kimmich, "Germany and the League of
    Nations," in *The League of Nations in Retrospect*, Berlin and New York,
    Walter de Gruyter, 1983, pp. 118–27.
32 Perrins memo, 3 March 1933, HO 45/21789; Bouscharain memo, 18
    November 1932, and "Liste de suggestions relatives à une amélioration de
    la liaison entre la Section d'Information et la Section de l'Opium, 19 June
    1933," LNA, S212-19, no. 1 (1931–46); Drummond–Theodoli correspon-

dence, 26–28 April 1933, Drummond to Ekstrand and Theodoli, 1 May 1933, all in LNA, R.5107, 12B/3823/1674; DSB records, LNA, R.5107, 12B/6432/1474 (August–October 1933); DSB records, LNA R.5146, 12B/8707/8707 (October 1933); DSB records, LNA, R.5107 (September–November 1933), 12B/7704/1674; PCOB seventeenth session minutes, LNA, R.5040, 12A/6222/1405 (August 1933); Ekstrand to Drummond, 3 and 10 October 1933, LNA, R.4934, 12/7288/7288; DSB third session minutes (November 1933), LNA, R.5107, 12B/8282/1674.

33 PRO, FO 371/16250 (December 1931–February 1932); IOpC meetings, 9 March 1932 and 6 July 1933, PRO, HO 45/20413; PRO, FO 371/16258 (May–July 1933); PRO, FO 371/17173 (July–October 1933); LNd C.569.1933.XI (11 October 1933).

34 LNd C.678.1933.XI. (13 December 1933); FO Minutes, 2 and 3 January 1934, PRO, FO 371/17173:F7988/4896/87; Lyall to Strang, 28 December 1933 and FO to Strang, 2 January 1934, PRO, FO 371/18196; IOpC meeting, 9 January 1934, PRO, HO 45/20413; Lyall to Strang, 29 November 1935, PRO, FO 371/19371.

35 German Foreign Office to FBN, 3 May 1934, FBNA, ACC 170-71-A-3554, Box 29, File 1230-2 (PCOB records), File: "1934."

36 Executive Committee minutes, 14 November 1934, FPAA, Micro 48, Reel 1.

37 Early DSB reports, LNds C.462.M.198.1934.XI (17 October 1934) and C.429.M.220.1935.XI (18 October 1935); PCOB reports, LNds C.390.M.176.1934.XI (7 September 1934), C.364.M.185.1935.XI. (17 September 1935).

38 Prewar DSB meetings, LNA, boxes R.5107, R.5108, and R.5109. The Body considered confidential information in framing estimates. For example, Dr. Carrière (closely connected to Swiss drug interests) and Herbert May (privy to intelligence from the Board and the FBN) presented information indicating that a high Honduran estimate for 1934 might be connected to illicit trafficking. Consequently, the Body lowered the Honduran estimate. DSB minutes, 2nd session, 3rd meeting, 11 October 1933, LNA, R.5107, 12B/7492/1674.

39 HO memo, 5 August 1936, PRO, HO 45/21792.

40 For a case study involving Bulgaria and additional examples see McAllister, op. cit., pp. 177–84. E. Haas, *When Knowledge is Power: Three Models of Change in International Organizations*, Berkeley, University of California Press, 1990, p. 68, outlines a generalized model that is applicable here.

41 A. Block, "European Drug Traffic and Traffickers between the Wars: The Policy of Suppression and its Consequences," *Journal of Social History*, 1989, vol. 23, pp. 327–9.

42 For the Asian situation, see voluminous references in the OAC, PCOB, and DSB reports, 1931–39.

43 The USSR, although claiming innocence, at least tolerated some trafficking into Vladivostok since the 1920s. K. Meyer and T. Parssinen, *Webs of Smoke: Smugglers, Warlords, Spies, and the History of the International Drug Trade*, Lanham, Maryland, Rowman & Littlefield, 1998, p. 126. In the 1930s Persia shipped large quantities to Vladivostok that disappeared after arrival. Block, op. cit., pp. 330–1.

44 Even before the Depression, opium comprised 25 percent of all Persian non-oil exports and accounted for 9 percent of government revenue. Taylor, op. cit., p. 308.

45 IOpC meetings, 16 September 1930, 10 December 1930, 31 March 1931, 20 August 1931, 1 May 1933, 20 November 1933, all in PRO, HO 45/20413; W. Walker, *Opium and Foreign Policy: The Anglo-American Search for Order in Asia, 1912–1954*, Chapel Hill, University of North Carolina Press, 1991, pp. 43–4, 49, 58, 67, 71, 97–100; Taylor, op. cit., pp. 282–5, 306–07; May, op. cit., pp. 75–9.

46 IOpC meetings of 20 August 1931, 1 May 1933, 20 November 1933, 8 March 1934, all in PRO, HO 45/20413; FO minute, 3 May 1934, PRO, FO 371/18200; Walker (1991), op. cit., pp. 64–8, 78–82, 90–2, 114–16; Taylor, op. cit., pp. 281–6.

47 IOpC meetings, 31 August 1932 and 8 March 1934, PRO, HO 45/20413.

48 Meyer and Parssinen, op. cit., chs 4, 7 (and p. 280, for their discussion of "bureaucratic schizophrenia," which explains how governments can sincerely condemn drug trafficking while lower-level operatives condone it); J. Jennings, *The Opium Empire: Japanese Imperialism and Drug Trafficking in Asia, 1895–1945*, Westport, Connecticut, Praeger, 1997; S. Karch, *A Brief History of Cocaine*, Boca Raton, Florida, CRC Press, 1998; Karch, "The History of Japan and Southeast Asian Cocaine Industry, 1864–1944," in Gootenberg, op. cit.; Friman, op. cit., ch. 3; Walker (1991), op. cit., chs 4–6; Taylor, op. cit., pp. 281–6; AOIB, no. 25, 20 December 1938, p. 11.

49 T. Brook and B. Wakabayashi (eds), *Opium in East Asian History*, Berkeley, University of California Press, 2000, Part 2, especially A. Baumler, "Opium Control vs. Opium Suppression: The Origins of the 1935 Six-year Plan to Eliminate Opium and Drugs"; Walker (1991), op. cit., chs 3–6; J. Marshall, "Opium and the Politics of Gangsterism in Nationalist China, 1927–1945," *Bulletin of Concerned Asian Scholars, 1976*, July–September, pp. 19–48; Taylor, op. cit., pp. 281–7; Meyer and Parssinen, op. cit., ch. 6; AOIB, no. 21, 30 September 1933, p. 1; Gavit to Blanco, 4 May 1933, AP, Box 10, File 9.

50 Taylor, op. cit. 284. The Manchurian crisis further complicated League–US relations. G. Ostrower, "The United States and the League of Nations, 1919–1939," in *The League of Nations in Retrospect*, op. cit., pp. 134–40; Ostrower, *Collective Insecurity: The United States and the League of Nations in the Early Thirties*, Lewisburg, Bucknell University Press, 1979, ch. 7.

51 Jennings, op. cit., and Karch, op. cit., in Gootenberg, op. cit.; first DSB session minutes (August–September 1933), LNA, R.5107, 12B/6547/1674; second DSB session minutes, (October 1933), LNA, R.5107, 12B/7492/1674; Lyall to May, 8 January 1936, FBNA, ACC 170-71-A-3554, Box 29, File 1230-2 (PCOB records), 1936 file; tenth DSB session records, LNA, R.5108, 12B/26633/1674.

52 Even after Japan quit the League, the government submitted statistics and sent a representative to OAC sessions. The Japanese government also ratified the 1931 Limitation Convention on 3 June 1935. Six weeks later, however, Tokyo ordered the Japanese member of the Board to resign. LN to FO, 19 June 1934, PRO, FO 371/18196; HO minute, 23 July 1934, PRO, HO 45/21790; Japanese Embassy to FO, 23 February 1935 and League to FO, 7 March 1935, PRO, FO 371/19367; PRO, HO 45/21791 (March–

April 1935); LN to FO, 8 April 1935, PRO, FO 371/19368; British delegation's notes on twentieth OAC session in Coles to Makins, 30 July 1935,
PRO, FO 371/19370; Sharman's report on the twentieth OAC session,
8 August 1935, PAC, RG 25, Vol. 1758, File 1936-8-B, Part 1.

53 Seventeenth PCOB session minutes (August 1933), LNA, R.5040, 12A/
6222/1405.

54 See, for example, the timidity evident in the preparation of the Board's
report, thirty-seventh PCOB session, second meeting, 2 November 1938,
LNA, R.5046, 12A/36080/1405; thirty-eighth PCOB session minutes,
sixth meeting, 18 April 1939, LNA, R.5047, 12A/38108/1405.

55 McAllister, op. cit., pp. 190–6.

56 1931 PCOB report, LNd C.624.M.307.1932.XI. (5 September 1932), p. 13.

57 See, for example, seventeenth OAC session minutes, LNd
C.661.M.136.1933.XI (5 December 1933), pp. 13–21, 24–27, 40–2. See
also Kinder and Walker, op. cit., pp. 917–18.

58 Walker (1991), op. cit., chs 5–6; Jennings, op. cit., pp. 61–2, 88–90; numerous documents concerning joint US/UK representations to Tokyo, 1938–
39, NA, RG 59, LF 55D607, Box 34, File: "Source material for statement
of 5-20-39"; Executive Committee minutes, 20 December 1939, FPAA,
Micro 48, Reel 1. Canada's position mirrored that of the United States.
Sharman's twenty-first OAC session report, 10 August 1936, PAC, RG
25, Vol. 1758, File 1936-8-B, Part 2; Nicholson? to Customs Commissioner,
17 May 1937, FBNA, ACC 170-75-17, Box 8, File 1690-10, File: "FPA";
Sharman's twenty-third OAC session report, 31 August 1938, PAC, RG
29, Vol. 589, File 322-1-3, Part 2.

   For the chaotic drug situation in East Asia during the 1937–1945 war,
see Parssinen and Meyer, op. cit., ch. 8; Jennings, op. cit. For example, by
1941–42, illicit trafficking became so rampant in Japanese-occupied
territories that legitimate manufacturers experienced difficulty securing
adequate supplies (ibid, pp. 102–03). Matters became so turbulent that
even the staunchly anti-opium communists engaged in drug trafficking
(Meyer and Parssinen, pp. 228, 271–2).

59 For League-related activities in Latin America see DSB, PCOB, OAC, and
League Council reports, 1935–39. See also Executive Committee minutes,
12 December 1934, 9 January 1935, 13 February 1935, 10 April 1935, all
in FPAA, Micro 48, Reel 1; Moorhead to Anslinger, 19 December 1934,
FBNA, ACC 170-75-17, Box 8, File 1690–10, File "FPA"; thirteenth DSB
Session minutes (August–September 1938), LNA, R.5108, 12B/35822/
1674; Walker (1989), op. cit., pp. 79–93, 135–51.

60 Moorhead had a hand in interesting the Soviet government in ratifying the
drug conventions. Executive Committee minutes, 8 May 1935, FPAA,
Micro 48, Reel 1. For British commentary on the connection between
Soviet adherence to the drug treaties and larger security issues, FO
minute 9 December 1935, PRO FO 371/19371. The Opium
Section's Leon Steinig travelled to Moscow to close the deal. Chilton to
FO, 9 December 1935, PRO, FO 371/19371. See also K. Davis, "The
Soviet Union and the League of Nations, 1919–1933," *Geneva Special
Studies*, 1934, vol. 5, no. 1, pp. 3–23.

61 Gootenberg, op. cit., in Gootenberg, op. cit. He characterizes Peru as an
"informational resister" (p. 12 of manuscript).

62 G. Ostrower, *The League of Nations From 1919 to 1929*, Garden City Park, New York, Avery, 1996, pp. 124–5.

63 ibid.; M. Dubin, "Toward the Bruce Report: the Economic and Social programs of the League of Nations in the Avenol Era," *The League of Nations in Retrospect*, Berlin and New York, Walter de Gruyter, 1983, pp. 56–7.

64 Meyer and Parssinen, op. cit.; Block, op. cit.

65 FO minutes, 1 June 1933, PRO, FO 371/17173:F3665/3663/87; Dowson to Fitzmaurice, 27 March 1934, PRO, FO 371/18196; Hutson to Stevenson, 4 May 1934, PRO, FO 371/18199; Fitzmaurice–Harris correspondence (November 1935–January 1936), PRO, FO 371/18196:F 7539/7/87; Harris to Fitzmaurice, 13 February 1935, PRO, FO 371/19372; FO 371/20295 (January 1936); IOpC meeting, 3 April 1936, PRO, HO 45/20414. For Canadian participation and reservations, Sharman to Skelton, 20 December 1935, PAC, RG 25, Vol. 2624, File 8-AG-40, Part 1; Sharman to Robertson, 7 April 1936, PAC, RG 25, Vol. 2624, File 8-AG-40, Part 2.

66 For public negotiation records see twelfth through twenty-first OAC session reports (1929–1936).

67 Taylor, op. cit., pp. 288–91.

68 Fuller's report on the Illicit Trafficking Conference, 22 March 1938, 34, NA, RG 59, LF 55D607, Box 28; Manning to Gaston, 11 January 1938, FBNA, ACC 170-75-17, Box 8, File 1690-10, File: "FPA."

69 Jonnes, op. cit., pp. 104–7; McWilliams, op. cit., pp 89–92; Carroll, op. cit., ch. 1; Moorhead to Anslinger, 7 March 1935, AP, Box 3, File 5; AP, Box 10, File 8 (January–March 1936); Russe to Anslinger, 30 January 1936, and Hayes to Anslinger, 21 March 1936, AP, Box 3, File 4; Moorhead to Anslinger, 8 December 1937, AP, Box 3, File 3; Executive Committee minutes, 19 February and 18 March 1936, FPAA, Micro 48, Reel 1. Blanco expressed distress at the American reluctance to send representatives and promised to work for a clause requiring signatories to maintain a centralized narcotics police force. Dyar to Fuller, 26 November 1935, NA, RG 59, LF 55D607, Box 27, File: "Illicit Traffic Conference of 1936."

70 However, the Treasury Department shifted some duties to the Customs Service, causing increased rivalry between the two agencies. McAllister, op. cit., pp. 200–01.

71 Fuller's report on the Illicit Trafficking Conference, 22 March 1938, 34, NA, RG 59, LF 55D607, Box 28. Anslinger, Moorhead, and Fuller also entertained the possibility of utilizing an international accord to secure marijuana control. To bolster his domestic position and to enhance his authority over strategic material (see below) Anslinger began a campaign to regulate domestic production and use of the drug. Treaty obligation appeared the easiest way to circumvent constitutional constraints. Executive Committee minutes, 15 January 1936, 20 May 1936, 16 December 1936, all in FPAA, Micro 48, Reel 1; Anslinger to Gibbons, 3 February 1936, AP, Box 3, File 4; Carroll, op. cit., ch. 1.

72 "Brokmeyer Bulletin," 9 November 1936, AP, Box 10, file 8; Executive Committee minutes, 24 November 1936, FPAA, Micro 48, Reel 1.

73 1936 Conference minutes, LNd C.341.M.216.1936.XI. (June 1936); Taylor, op. cit., pp 291–8; Walker (1989), op. cit., pp. 93–7; S. Chatterjee, *Legal Aspects of International Drug Control*, The Hague, Martinus Nijhoff, 1981, pp. 168–96; Gootenberg, op. cit., in Gootenberg, op. cit.

74 See catty notes passed between Fuller, Anslinger, and the delegation's legal adviser, Frank Ward, in NA, RG 59, LF 55D607, Box 28, File: "Report Data"; Fuller's report on the Illicit Trafficking Convention, 22 March 1938, NA, RG 59, LF 55D607, Box 28; Fuller to Gilbert, 6 November 1936, FBNA, ACC 170-71-A-3554, Box 8, File 0355, Folder #4 (1936 Convention).

75 McAllister, op. cit., pp. 204–05.

76 Fewer governments ratified the 1936 Convention than even the ill-fated 1953 agreement.

77 For the controversy over the effectiveness and intentions of the PCOB, the DSB, the OAC, their secretariats, and the Secretary-General see numerous communications between London, Geneva, Ottawa, Washington, and Moorhead in:

League of Nations. "Essai de critique constructive des travaux du secrétariat" (undated, concerns the fifteenth OAC session, April–May 1932), Romer to Opium Section, 10 February 1936, Romer to Ekstrand, 10 June 1936, all in LNA, S. 212–19, No. 6 (Correspondence avec Mlle de Romer, 1931–46); seventeenth PCOB session minutes, LNA, R.5040, 12A/6222/ 1405 (August 1933); Renborg to Ekstrand, undated May 1938, 28 June 1938, undated July 1938, 16 July 1938, all in LNA, S. 212–20 (working papers of Renborg and Steinig, 1931–46), File 7 (1938–44).

Canada. Sharman's report on the twentieth OAC session, 8 August 1935, PAC, RG 25, Vol. 1758, File 1936-8-B, Part 1; PAC, RG 29, Vol. 589, File 322-1-3, Parts 1 and 2 (August 1935–March 1936); Sharman–Skelton correspondence, 25 July and 7 October 1939, PAC, RG 25, Vol. 1759, File 1936-8-B, Part 4; Sharman's report on the twenty-third OAC session, 31 August 1938, PAC, RG 29, Vol. 589, File 322-1-3, Part 2; Rive to Sharman and External Affairs, 19 June 1939, PAC, RG 25, Vol. 1759, File 1936-8-B, Part 4.

United States. Dyar to Fuller, 26 November 1935, NA, RG 59, LF 55D607, Box 27, File: "Illicit Traffic Conference of 1936"; Fuller's report on the twenty-first OAC session, 14 September 1936, NA, RG 59, LF 55D607, Box 33, File: "twenty-first session, OAC"; Moorhead to Merrill, 2 August 1936 and Moorhead to Buell, 16 July 1937, BP, Box 10, File: "H. H. Moorhead"; May to Fuller, 25 September 1938, NA, RG 59, LF 55D607, Box 4, File: "Coca–cola extract"; Fuller's report on twenty-second OAC session, 30 August 1937, NA, RG 59, LF 55D607, Box 33; Fuller's report on twenty-third OAC session, 24 August 1938, NA, RG 59, LF 55D607, Box 34; Tittman to SD, 1 May 1940, NA, RG 59, LF 55D607, Box 4.

Great Britain. British delegation's notes on the twentieth OAC session included in Coles to Makins, 30 July 1935, PRO, FO 371/19370; Harris to Orde, 24 July 1935, FO minutes concerning LNd C.362.1935.XI., dated 16 September 1935 and 23 September 1935, all in PRO, FO 371/ 19371.

AOIB. no. 14, 26 May 1931, p. 6; no. 16, 20 August 1931, p. 10; no. 17, 16 November 1931, p. 13; no. 23, 20 May 1935, p. 12; no. 24, 23 May 1938, p. 22.

78 American contributions for OAC-related expenditures, which commenced when Blue attended the 1923 session, were the only instance in which the United States supported an ongoing League activity. Disbursements were

hidden in the State Department emergency allocations budget until 1936, when Washington openly funded a League organ for the first time. The American share amounted to roughly 15 percent. Taylor, op. cit., pp. 264–7; W. Kuehl and L. Dunn, *Keeping the Covenant: American Internationalists and the League of Nations, 1920–1939*, Kent, Ohio, Kent State University Press, 1997, p. 141–5; Delevingne to Orde and related documents, 21 October 1935, PRO, FO 371/19373:F6743/6743/87; Stevenson to Orde, 5 November 1935, PRO, FO 371/19373; Fuller to Achilles, 4 October 1937, NA, RG 59, Box 1475, 511.4A6A/333.

79 The PCOB contention appeared in a draft report circulated to OAC representatives. The OAC decided not to publish the minutes of the acrimonious debate. Fuller's report on twenty-first OAC meeting (18 May–6 June 1936), NA, RG 59, LF 55D607, Box 33; LNd C.278.M.168.1936.XI (1 July 1936), p. 20; League to FO, 26 November 1935, PRO, FO 371/19371; twenty-first OAC session, provisional minutes of private meeting, 29 May 1936, LNA, S.212–19, File 1.

80 OAC session minutes, 1935–39.

81 W. McAllister, "How Hungary Inadvertently Rescued Nazi Germany: International Drug Control and Opium as a Strategic Material," paper delivered at the National Policy History Conference, Bowling Green State University, June 1997; twenty-fourth OAC session minutes, LNd C.209.M.136.1939.XI. (8 July 1939), pp. 19–22; Fuller's report on the twenty-second OAC session, 30 August 1937, NA, RG 59, LF 55D607, Box 33.

82 Small memo, 18 December 1937, NA, RG 59, LF 55D607, Box 4, File: "Desomorphine."

83 Walker (1989), op. cit., ch. 6; McWilliams, op. cit., pp. 92–5; King, op. cit., ch. 8. Blanco's rebellion constituted a direct challenge to Anslinger's position. Anslinger and Sharman ceased all communication with Blanco and ignored his entreaties for reconciliation. See McAllister (1996), op. cit., pp. 211–12.

84 Delevingne to Fuller, 22 October 1935, and Fuller to Sharman, 31 October 1935, PAC, RG 29, Vol. 589, File 322–1–3; FO to Dominions Office, 10 August 1934, PRO, FO 371/18204; Lyall to Anslinger, 26 November 1937, AP, Box 3, File 3; Fuller's report on the 1939 OAC session, NA, RG 59, LF 55D607, Box 34, File: "twenty-fourth Session, OAC"; Moorhead to Chamberlain, 6 July 1934, BP, Box 10, File: "H. H. Moorhead."

In the deteriorating economic and political conditions of the later 1930s, a similar fragmentation of approaches and questioning of foundational assumptions occurred among those dealing with many social welfare issues. C. Miller, "Lobbying the League: Women's International Organizations and the League of Nations," PhD dissertation, St. Hilda's College, Oxford, 1992, pp. 167–9, 183–232.

85 All OAC sessions from 1934–39 included discussion of production control. For archival records see:
Great Britain. PRO, FO 371/21045 (April–May 1937); PRO, FO 371/21046 (May–September 1937); PRO, FO 371/22197 (April 1938); IOpC meetings, 23 February and 4 November 1938, HO 45/20414; CO to FO, 24 January 1939, and HO to FO, 4 May 1939, PRO, FO 371/23584.

Canada. PAC RG 25, Vol. 1758, File 1936-8-B, Part 2 (February–June 1937); Delgorge to Fuller, PAC, RG 29, Vol. 589, File 322-1-3, Part 2; Sharman to Ekstrand, 16 December 1938, and Skelton to Wrong, 23 December 1938, PAC RG 25, Vol. 1758, File 1936-8-B, Part 3; Sharman's report on the twenty-fourth OAC session, PAC RG 25, Vol. 1758, File 1936-8-B, Part 4; Rive to Sharman and External Affairs, 19 June 1939, PAC, RG 25, Vol. 1759, File 1936-8-B, Part 4.

United States. FBNA, ACC 170-71-A-3554, Box 7, File 0355, Folder #3 (October 1936–April 1937); Fuller's report on the twenty-second OAC session, 30 August 1937, NA, RG 59, LF 55D607, Box 33; Moorhead to Buell, 22 March 1937 and 12 May 1938, BP, Box 10, File: "H. H. Moorhead"; FBNA, ACC 170-71-A-3554, Box 7, File 0355, Folder #6 (December 1938); Fuller's report on the twenty-third OAC session 24 August 1938, NA, RG 59, LF 55D607, Box 34; Sharman to Anslinger, 5 January 1939, AP, Box 3, File 1; FPA executive Committee minutes, 9 March 1932–22 March 1939, FPAA, Micro 48, Reel 1.

League of Nations. twenty-first OAC session, provisional minutes of private meeting, 29 May 1936, LNA, S. 212–19 (working papers of Renborg and Steinig, 1931–46), File 1; Renborg memo, (?1936 or 1937?), LNA, C.1805 (DSB/Washington office records), File 2 (Raw Opium Conference); Renborg to Ekstrand, undated May 1938, 28 June 1938, undated July 1938 and 16 July 1938, all in LNA, S. 212–20 (working papers of Renborg and Steinig, 1931–46), File 7 (correspondence 1938–1944).

AOIB, nos 24–26 (1938–39).

86 W. McAllister, "Mrs. Outside/Mrs. Inside: The Contrasting Styles and Impact of Elizabeth Washburn Wright and Helen Howell Moorhead in International Drug Control Negotiations," paper delivered at the Society for Historians of American Foreign Relations Annual Meeting, June 1995.

87 Sharman's report on the twenty-third OAC session, 31 August 1938, PAC, RG 29, Vol. 589, File 322-1-3, Part 2, secret section, 6.

88 AOIB, no. 19, 31 October 1932, p. 2; Small to Eddy, 22 April 1936, SP, MS.C. 333, Box 2, File: "Eddy"; Bobst (President of Hoffmann-LaRoche, NJ) to Anslinger, 29 April 1936, SP, MS.C. 333, Box 2, File: "Ho-Hu"; Anslinger to Sharman, 1 April 1936, and Sharman's report on the twenty-third OAC session, 31 August 1938, PAC, RG 29, Vol. 589, File 322-1-3, Part 2; Sharman's report on the twenty-first OAC session, 10 August 1938, PAC, RG 25, Vol. 1758, File 1936-8-B, Part 2; PCOB Secretary's confidential progress report, 6 September 1937, LNA, R.5045, 12A/30666/1405; DSB Secretary's progress report, 6 October 1937, LNA, R.5108, 12B/31071/1674; Anslinger's report on the twenty-third OAC session, 15 June 1938, AP, Box 10, File 12; Fuller's report on the 1938 OAC session, 24 August 1938, NA, RG 59, LF 55D607, Box 34, File: "23rd Session, OAC"; decisions taken at the 13th DSB session (August–September 1938), LNA, R.5108, 12B/35822/1674; Erwin G. May to Anslinger, 16 January 1939, AP, Box 3, File 1; documents relating to the 1939 OAC session, NA, RG 59, LF 55D607, Box 34, File: "24th Session, OAC"; Sharman's report on the 24th OAC session, 25 July 1937, PAC, RG 25, Vol. 1759, File 1936-8-B, Part 4, 8–9 (secret); Secretary's progress report DSB 14th session, 20 October 1938, LNA, R.5108, 12B/35784/1674; series of reports by Renborg to Secretary-General's office, all dated

18 July 1939, LNA, S.212–20 (Working papers of Renborg and Steinig, 1931–46), File 2 (Steinig 38–40).

89 Reilly to Yencken, 20 December 1938, PRO, FO 371/22196; Charles to Randall, 26 January 1939, Felkin to Randall, 10 February and 30 May 1939, all in PRO, FO 371/23578; PCOB minutes, thirty-eighth session, second meeting, 14 April 1939, LNA, R.5047, 12A/38108/1405; Joseph Dittert, interview, Geneva, 21 April 1993.

90 J. Barros, *Betrayal from Within: Joseph Avenol, Secretary-General of the League of Nations, 1933–1940*, New Haven, Yale University Press, 1969, pp. 14–25, 186–8; E. Ranshofen-Wertheimer, *The International Secretariat: A Great Experiment in International Administration*, Washington, Carnegie Endowment for International Peace, 1945, p. 152–6; Dubin, op. cit., pp. 42–72.

91 McAllister, op. cit., pp. 216–17.

92 Executive Committee minutes, 26 April and 24 May 1939, FPAA, Micro 48, Reel 1; Renborg to Walters, 31 August 1939 and Felkin memo, undated (probably April 1940), LNA, S.561, File 1 (1939–40).

93 The Army–Navy Munitions Board defined *Strategic Materials* as "essential to the national defense for the supply of which in war dependence must be placed in whole, or in part, on sources outside the continental limits of the United States, and for which strict conservation and distribution measures will be necessary." *Critical Materials* were defined as "essential to the national defense, the procurement problems of which in war, while difficult, are less serious than those of strategic materials due to greater resources or to a lesser degree of essentiality, and for which strict conservation and distribution measures will probably be necessary." The composition of both lists fluctuated, usually between twelve and twenty-five items on each, as conditions and supplies changed. Opium migrated between the two categories depending on stocks and predictions about future need. Hemp, the best substitute for manila fiber, jute, sisal, and silk, usually remained on the Critical list. Memo, Army–Navy Munitions Board, Commodities Division, 3 April 1934, NA, RG 225, Entry 10, Box 1, File: "Strategic Materials – Requirements of the US"; Feis to Hull, 12 December 1935 and 5 February 1937, NA, RG 59, 811.24/1041, Special Board on Strategic Materials report, 18 August 1936, and "Strategic and Important Critical Materials," 5 October 1937, NA, RG 59, 811.24/1049; US Army and Navy Munitions Board, *The Strategic and Critical Materials*, hearings on H.R. 2969, 3320, 2556, 2643, 1987, 987, and 4373, House Committee on Military Affairs, Seventy–Sixth Congress, First Session, February–March 1939; US Military Academy, *Strategic and Critical Raw Materials*, West Point, Department of economics, government, and history, 1940 and 1944; Henderson to Bell, 13 November 1940, RG 179, Box 1802, file 544.31132; Henderson to Maxwell, 12 March 1941, RG 179, Box 1796, file 544.2113; J. Marshall, *To Have and Have Not: Southeast Asian Raw Materials and the Origins of the Pacific War*, Berkeley, University of California Press, 1995, chs 1–2; A. Eckes, *The United States and the Global Struggle for Minerals*, Austin, University of Texas Press, 1979, chs 2–4.

94 Hartung to Anslinger, 5 March 1943, NA, RG 59, LF 55D607, Box 4, File: "Coca."

95 Maywood's primary customer, the Coca-Cola company, utilized a decocanized coca extract entitled "merchandise no. 5" as a part of its flavoring syrup. In the late 1920s Maywood had conducted experimental manufacture in Peru to supply Coca-Cola bottling plants outside the United States. Maywood abandoned the experiment, but agreed to keep its buildings in repair in case the need should arise to commence cocaine manufacture. Documents dated 1933–1938 in NA, RG 59, LF 55D607, Box 4, File: "Coca-Cola extract"; Anslinger to Hoover, 29 January 1941, FBNA, ACC 170-74-5, Box 17, File: "Postwar narcotic problems, general" (1230).

96 None of the standard works dealing with the history of marijuana regulation in general and the 1937 Marihuana Tax Act in particular recognize the international dimension or critical materials aspect discussed here. See William B. McAllister, "Drug Control and Its Discontents: The Marihuana Tax Act of 1937 Revisited," paper delivered at American Society of Criminology Annual Meeting, November 1998.

Congress authorized the War Hemp Program in 1942. The War Production Board authorized cultivation of 300,000 acres for 1943. The Agriculture Department furnished seed and produced a promotional motion picture entitled *Hemp for Victory* (1942), the Commodity Credit Corporation bought the product, and the Defense Plant Corporation built dozens of mills to process hemp into cordage. In some areas farmers used German prisoners of war or displaced Japanese-Americans to harvest the crop (and paid the government for their services). War Hemp Program records, NA, RG 161, Entry 7 (1941–1946); J. Kelly, "'Hemp for Victory:' The Rise and Fall of the American Hemp Industry During World War II," MA thesis, University of Kentucky, 1992; R. Marsh, "The Illinois Hemp Project at Polo in World War II," *Journal of the Illinois State Historical Society*, 1967, vol. 60, no. 4, pp. 391–410; J. Hopkins, *A History of The Hemp Industry in Kentucky*, Lexington, University of Kentucky Press, 1951, pp. 210–15; J. Garland, "Hemp: A Minor American Fiber Crop," *Economic Geography*, 1946, vol. 22, pp. 126–32.

97 Anslinger's leverage was reduced because he needed pharmaceuticals' cooperation in acquiring other strategic items such as quinine. Interdepartmental conference memo, 11 August 1939, NA, RG 59, 811.24.

98 Brokmeyer Bulletin, 30 March 1939, AP, Box 10, File 8; Simon to Anslinger, 5 February 1940, AP, Box 2, File 2.

99 Sharman to Pensions and National Health Minister, 3 August 1938, and Skelton to Sharman, 25 August 1938, PAC, RG 25, Vol. 2622, File 8-AC-40; NA, RG 59, LF 55D607, Box 7, File: "Opium poppy cultivation in the United States" (December 1938–March 1939); Anslinger to Sharman, 22 December 1938, FBNA, ACC 170-71-A-3554, Box 7, File 0355, Folder #6; Sharman–Anslinger correspondence, 5 and 23 January 1939, and Anslinger to Thomas, 3 April 1939, AP, Box 3, File 1; *Courier Journal* (Louisville, Kentucky), 9 March 1940, AP, Box 2, File 10; opium stocks report, 24 April 1942, RG 179, Box 1694, file 533.252; McWilliams, op. cit., pp. 95–6.

100 Similar patterns developed in other areas of international interwar social work, and especially affected feminist issues. Miller, op. cit., pp. 94, 154, 166–8.

5 Preservation, perseverance, promise – 1939–46

1 Lester to Renborg, 29 July 1941, LNA, C.1803, no.2 (1941–46).
2 Judd to Moorhead, 16 June 1945, FBNA, ACC 170-74-12, Box 39, File 1230-13.
3 W. McAllister, *A Limited Enterprise: The History of International Efforts to Control Drugs in the Twentieth Century*, PhD dissertation, University of Virginia, 1996, pp. 226–9. For more on the Bruce Committee see M. Dubin, "Toward the Bruce Report: the economic and social programs of the League of Nations in the Avenol Era," in *The League of Nations in Retrospect*, Berlin and New York, Walter de Gruyter, 1983, pp. 42–72.
4 McAllister, op. cit., pp. 230–41.
5 A. Rovine, *The First Fifty Years: The Secretary General in World Politics, 1920–1970*, Leyden, A. W. Sijthoff, 1970, pp. 158–66; J. Barros, *Betrayal from Within: Joseph Avenol, Secretary-General of the League of Nations, 1933–1940*, New Haven, Yale University Press, 1969, pp. 210–14.
6 Rovine, op. cit., pp. 152–61; Barros, op. cit. pp. 214–258; NA, RG 59, 500.C/1016 (June–August 1940); Tittman to SD, 17 June 1940, NA, RG 59, 500.C 113/187.
7 Steinig had performed important work since joining the Opium Section in 1930. Although Renborg held the title of Secretary to the DSB, Steinig wrote the draft report, did much of the statistical work, maintained liaison with the PCOB, and travelled on sensitive missions to negotiate with governments. Steinig also dealt with most questions concerning implementation of the drug conventions. See "Note concerning the work of the Opium Section" in Renborg to Lester, 18 July 1939, LNA, S. 212–20, no. 2 (1938–40). For Steinig's escape see McAllister, op. cit., pp. 232–5.
8 For negotiations concerning the transfer see documents dated July–September 1940, LNA, S.561, no.1 (1939–40); NA, RG 59, 511.4A2A (July–September 1940); Fuller to Thompson, 28 June 1940, NA, RG 59, 500.C/1018; Hull to Tittman, 29 June 1940, LNA, S.561, no. 5, File: "Transfer to USA"; Sweetser to Felkin, 16 July 1940, and Sweetser to Adeylotte, 10 August 1940, SP, Box 18, File: "Princeton invitation"; Tittman to SD, 5 August 1940, NA, RG 59, 500.C/1034; Anslinger to Sharman, 10 November 1940, AP, Box 2, File 2. For FDR's approval see Long memo, 13 September 1940, NA, RG 59, 511.4A2A/1005.
9 For negotiations concerning the scope of drug control operations and personnel transfer, see LNA, S.561, no.1, File: "Transfer to USA, 1939–40" (September–December 1940); LNA, S.561, no.5, File: "Transfer to USA, 1940–42" (December 1940–March 1941); Lester to Hambro, LNA, C.1619, no.1 (Princeton Office Files); Felkin to Chatterjee, 2 December 1941, and Felkin to Lester, 6 December 1941, LNA, C.1632, no.2 (Princeton Office files, Opium, general, 1940–46); NA, RG 59, 511.4A2A (September–December 1940); Tittman to SD, 8 October and 12 December 1940, NA, RG 59, 500.C/1054&1055; FBNA, ACC 170–74–12, Box 39, File 1230-2, Special File 1939–48 (September–November 1940); FBNA, ACC 170-74-5, Box 17, File 1230 (General League of Nations), File:"1940–41" (October 1940); Swift to Moorhead, 23 October 1940, Anslinger memo, 4 November 1940, Anslinger to Sharman, 18 December 1940, Delevingne to Steinig, 15 December 1940, all in FBNA, ACC 170-74-5,

Box 17, File:"Post-war narcotics problems-general file (1230); PRO, FO 371/24749 (October–December 1940); Chatterjee to Makins, 8 January 1941, PRO, FO 371/28069.

10 H. May, *The Reminiscences of Herbert L. May*, OHRO, pp. 83–7; Joseph Dittert, interview, 21 April 1993; Louis Atzenwiler, interview, 30 April 1993.

11 Plaintive letters spurred Lester to alter his position. Alexander Loveday worried about the penury inflicted on League officials in pricey Washington. He noted that Felkin ". . . lives in a garret on his old clothes, sees nobody and does not entertain at all and spends his life in doing his work. I do not think he has any choice. . . . But I do not think it is good for the League." Loveday to Lester, 2 July 1941, LNA, C.1619, no.2. See also McAllister, op. cit., pp. 241–2.

12 McAllister, op. cit., pp. 241–4.

13 Quote: Felkin memo, 25 March 1941, NA, RG 59, 511.4A2A/1065. Felkin to Chatterjee, 2 January 1941, and Felkin to Lester, 6 January 1941, LNA, C.1632, no.2 (Opium Office, General, 1940–46); HO minutes, 9 January 1941 and 16 February 1943, PRO, HO 45/21792; PRO, FO 371/28069 (February–October 1941); Felkin to Chatterjee, 15 February 1941, and Felkin to Loveday, 1 April 1941, LNA, C.1631, no.6; AP, Box 2, File 21 (21 February–1 March 1941); Anslinger memo, 10 March 1941 and Sharman to Anslinger, 11 March 1941, FBNA, ACC 170-74-5, Box 17, File: "Post-war narcotics problems – General file" (1230); Sharman to Wrong, 13 May 1941, PAC, RG 25, Vol. 2692, File 8-B-40, Part 1; Lester to Jacklin, 12 October 1943, LNA, C.1803, no.2 (1941–46); PCOB minutes, November–December 1943, and April 1946, LNA, R.5048 12A/42294 and 43026/1405; Roberts minute, 4 April 1944, PRO, FO 371/39378; Steinig memo, 31 May 1944, LNA, C.1803, no.3 (1942–46); Norton to Chatterjee, 4 August 1944, PRO, FO 371/40509; PCOB to Lima, 9 October 1944, NA, RG 59, 511.4A2A/10-944; DSB confidential report, 10 November 1945, LNA, C.1803, no.5 (1941–45); May, op. cit., pp. 87–89; Dittert, interview, 21 April 1993.

14 Felkin to Lester, 13 April 1941 (quote) and 11 February 1942, LNA, C.1618, no. 2 (1941–45).

15 J. Edgar Hoover–Anslinger correspondence, 24 and 29 January 1941, Sharman to Anslinger, 11 March 1941, all in FBNA, ACC 170-74-5, Box 17, File:"Post-war narcotics problems – Geneva file" (1230); AP, Box 2, File 21 (26 February–4 March 1941); NA, RG 59, 511.4V (March–September 1941); Renborg to Lester, 27 December 1941, LNA, C.1803, no.2 (1941–46); W. Walker, (ed.), *Drugs in the Western Hemisphere: an Odyssey of Cultures in Conflict*, Wilmington, Scholarly Resources, 1996, pp. xx, 115–18; P. Gootenberg, "Reluctance or Resistance? The Export of Cocaine (Prohibitions) to Peru, 1900–1950," in P. Gootenberg (ed.), *Cocaine: Global Histories*, London, Routledge, 1999; J. Gagliano, *Coca Prohibition in Peru: The Historical Debates*, Tucson, University of Arizona Press, 1994, pp. 147–8; SP, Box 34, File:"Renborg, Bertil A." (June–July 1941); Anslinger to Sharman, 4 March 1941, AP, Box 2, File 21; PAC, RG 25, Vol. 2692, File 8-B-40, Part 1 (March–April 1941); PAC, RG 25, Vol. 2693, File 8-E-40 (January–March 1941); Sharman to Anslinger, 7 April 1941, FBNA, 170-74-5, Box 17, File: "Post-war narcotics problems – General file" (1230);

SP, Box 35, File:"Steinig, L." (May 1935); Renborg to Loveday, 13 December 1941, LNA, C.1632, no.1.

16   McAllister, op. cit., pp. 246–8.

17   Quote: Renborg to Lester, 26 April 1941, LNA, S.561, no.6. Aghnides to Sweetser, 15 May 1941, SP, Box 30, File: "Aghnides, Thanassis"; Loveday to Lester, 9 July 1941, LNA C.1619, no.2; PAC, RG25, Vol. 2692, File 8-B-40, Part 1 (March–April 1941); Felkin to Loveday, 23 September 1941, LNA, C.1620, no.5 (1941–42); Moorhead to Delevingne, 18 September 1942, FBNA, ACC 170-74-12, File 1230-2, Special File 1939-48. Some suspected Renborg of harboring German sympathies, or at least of a lack of discretion. Atzenwiler believed federal authorities opened Renborg's mail. Atzenwiler, interview, 30 April 1993; Dittert, interview, 21 April 1993; Rive to Robertson, 1 February 1941, PAC, RG 25, Vol. 2693, File 8–E–40. See also Barros, op. cit., p. 205.

18   The 1912 Hague agreement, the two 1925 Geneva treaties, the 1931 Geneva and Bangkok accords, and the 1936 anti-trafficking convention.

19   LNA, C.1620, no.5 (September 1941–February 1942); Sharman–Anslinger correspondence, 17 November and 3 December 1941, AP, Box 2, File 21; Sharman to Wrong, 22 November 1941, PAC, RG 25, Vol. 2692, File 8-B-40, Part 1; numerous documents dated December 1941–June 1942 in FBNA, ACC 170-74-5, Box 17, File 1230-A, Folder 1 (1942–43); Sharman to Anslinger, 8 December 1941, PAC, RG 29, Vol. 602, File 325-1-4.

20   NA, RG 59, LF 55D607, Box 34, File:"26th Session, OAC" (February 1942–April 1945); documents dated February–July 1942, FBNA, ACC 170-74-5, Box 17, File 1230-A, Folder #1 (1942–43); Renborg to Lester, 13 February and 11 June 1942, LNA, C.1620, no.5 (1941–42); Renborg to Lester, 30 June 1942, NA, RG 59, 511.4A6A/358; Renborg to Sharman, 29 July 1942, and Sharman to Anslinger, 1 August 1942, FBNA, 170-74-5, Box 17, File 1230–A, Folder #2 (August–December 1943); documents dated October–November 1942 in LNA, C.1620, no.7, (1942–44); Renborg to Vigier, 7 December 1942, LNA, R.5146, 12B/41129/8707; Reynolds to Williams, 21 January 1944, PRO, FO 371/39369; PAC, RG 25, Vol.2692, File 8-A-40 (March 1944); NA, RG 59, 500.C1197 (June 1943–April 1944).
  For increasingly acrimonious exchanges concerning Renborg, see Moorhead to Delevingne, 18 September 1942, FBNA, ACC 170-74-12, File 1230-2, Special File 1939-48; numerous communications dated May 1944–November 1945 in LNA, S.561, nos 2–4 (1944–45); Delevingne to Moorhead, 10 February 1944, FBNA, ACC 170-71-A-3554- box 7, file 0355, Folder 7; Lester to Hambro, 26 February 1945, LNA, S.554, no.4 (1945–46); Loveday memo, 16 March 1945, LNA, P.25, no.1 (miscellaneous correspondence); FBNA, ACC 170-74-12, Box 39, File 1230-13 (July–August 1945); Anslinger to Sharman, 24 July 1945, AP, Box 2, File 19; Renborg memo, 15 August 1945 and Renborg to Felkin, 3 April 1946, LNA, R.4934, 12/7288/7288; files concerning closing Washington offices dated 1945–46 in LNA R.5025 12/43113. Atzenwiler, interview, 30 April 1993; Dittert, interview, 3 May 1993; Loveday to Lester, 28 October 1942, LNA, C.1619, no.3; Loveday to Lester, 21 February and 26 June 1944, LNA, C.1619, no.5.

21   NA, RG 59, 841.114 N16 Merck and Company (1940–41); Anslinger to Sharman, 28 March 1940, PAC, RG 29, Vol. 589, File 322-1-3, Part 2; Morgenthau to Anslinger, 9 May 1940, AP, Box 3, File 23; Anslinger to

Gaston, 27 April 1940, AP, Box 2, File 21; Morlock memo, 3 June 1940, and Macatee to SD, 23 December 1940, NA, RG 59, 860H.114 Narcotics/ 254&287 FO 371/24749:F4073/4073/87 (August 1940–January 1941); Jonson to FO, 23 September 1940, PRO, FO 371/24748; Villiers minute, 1 October 1940, PRO, FO 371/24749; SD to Istanbul, 22 November 1940, NA, RG 59, 867.114 Narcotics/1199; Sharman to Skelton, 24 December 1940, and Sharman to Robertson, 1 March 1941, PAC, RG 25, Vol. 2693, File 8-E-40; Wrong–Sharman correspondence, 5 May and 22 November 1941, PAC, RG 25, Vol. 2692, File 8-B-40, Part 1; Gaston to Hull, 9 May 1941, NA, RG 59, LF 55D607, Box 7; Morlock memo, 23 December 1941, NA, RG 59, LF 55D607, Box 8; Morlock to Berle, 31 December 1941, and Morlock memo, 24 June 1942, NA RG 59, 511.4A1/2239&2257; Morlock memo, 26 March 1942, NA, RG 59, LF 55D607, Box 7, File: "Opium poppy cultivation in the United States"; Anslinger to Thompson, 21 July 1942, AP, Box 2, File 20; FBN memo, 2 September 1942, FBNA, ACC 170-74-12, Box 39, File 1230-8; Engert to SD, 19 December 1942, NA, RG 59, 511.4A6A/1770; Sharman to Anslinger, 3 November 1943, FBNA, 170-74-5, Box 17, File 1230-A, Folder #2 (August–December 1943); Howard to SD, 3 August 1945, RG 59, 102.196/8-345; Leche to FO, 2 July 1946, and Coles to Goodwin, 26 July 1946, PRO, FO 371/59608.

22 Federal officials studiously avoided endorsement of the 1925 Geneva convention, to which the United States was not a party.

23 See note 21 above and W. Walker, *Drug Control in the Americas*, Albuquerque, University of New Mexico Press, 1989, pp. 127–32; Walker (ed.), 1996, op cit., pp. xx, 115–18; P. Gootenberg, "Reluctance or Resistance? The Export of Cocaine (Prohibitions) to Peru, 1900–1950," in P. Gootenberg (ed.), op cit., D. Kinder and W. Walker, "Stable Force In a Storm: Harry J. Anslinger and United States Narcotic Foreign Policy, 1930–1962," *Journal of American History*, 1986, vol. 72, no. 4, pp. 920–1.

24 Established firms protested allowing new players to enter the field. The old-line companies claimed that they could meet the country's needs and still manufacture for export. Bomb damage to one factory and the prospect of increased foreign earnings, however, impelled the Home Office to approve the new applications. PRO, HO 45/21792:582,132/336 (December 1940–January 1941).

25 Minutes of meeting between Anslinger and pharmaceutical representatives, 26 March 1942, NA, RG 59, LF 55D607, Box 7, File:"Opium poppy cultivation in the United States." For 1942 opium control bill: NA, RG 59, LF 55D607, Box 10.

26 Richardson to SD, 23 November 1940, and Taylor to SD, 28 January 1941, NA, RG 59, 867.114 Narcotics/1200 and 1208; Renborg to Morlock, 18 August 1941, NA, RG 59, LF 55D607, Box 4, File: "Cocaine"; Everett to SD, 17 and 26 March 1941, NA, RG 59, 511.4A2A/1061 and 1064; Steinig to Anslinger, 16 April 1941, FBNA, 170-74-12, Box 39, File 1230-8. Blanco continued a variety of machinations until his death in August 1945. Morlock memo, 10 October 1945, NA, RG 59, LF 55D607, Box 2, File: "A.E. Blanco."

27 Everett–Felkin correspondence, 1 and 11 November 1939, LNA, R.5146, 12B/39251/8707; Anslinger to Fuller, 16 October 1940, and Tittman to SD,

22 October 1940, NA, RG 59, 511.4A2A/1020 and 1022; Felkin to May, 22 October 1940, LNA, S.561, no.1, File: "Transfer to USA."

28 J. McWilliams, *The Protectors: Harry J. Anslinger and the Federal Bureau of Narcotics, 1930–1962*, Newark, University of Delaware Press, 1990, pp. 152–75; A. Block and J. McWilliams, "On the Origins of American Counter-intelligence: Building a Clandestine Network," *Journal of Policy History*, 1989, vol. 1, no. 4, p. 353–72. For examples of domestic criticism during the war years that necessitated Anslinger's vigilance, R. Carroll, "The Weed with Roots in Rhetoric: Harry J. Anslinger, Marijuana, and the Making of American Drug Policy," PhD dissertation, University of Pittsburgh, 1991, ch. 2.

29 Even before Pearl Harbor, Anslinger had encouraged American physicians and pharmaceutical companies to practice conservation. Anslinger to Gaston, 27 April 1940, AP, Box 2, File 21; Morlock memo, 23 December 1941, NA, RG 59, LF 55D607, Box 8, file on drug import and export regulations; Morlock to Berle, 31 December 1941, and Morlock memo, 24 June 1942, NA, RG 59, 511.4A1/2239&2257 Anslinger to Gaston, 2 May 1942, and Anslinger to Thompson, 28 October 1943, AP, Box 2, File 20; Morlock to Berle, 12 August 1942, and Berle to Nelson, 22 August 1942, NA, RG 59, LF 55D607, Box 3, File: "Drugs-manufacture in the US." For executive order see Federal Register, 7 October 1942 and 28 May 1943. Anslinger insisted on treaty ratification before acceding to Afghanistan's desperate pleas for medicaments: NA, RG 59, 511.4A6A (1942–43), especially Engert to SD, 19 December 1942, 511.4A6A/1770.

30 Numerous documents in NA, RG 59, 867.114 Narcotics (January 1942–June 1945); FBNA, ACC 170-74-12, Box 10, File 0840-172, folders on Iranian opium and Indian opium (1942–44); FBNA, ACC 170-74-12, Box 9, File 0840-172, Folders 4B (1943) and 4C (1944); Anslinger to Gaston, 21 July 1942, AP, Box 2, File 20; Morlock memo, 2 October 1942, Hollis to Acheson, 2 October 1942, Hollis memo, 5 October 1942, all in NA, RG 59, LF 55D607, Box 14, File: "Act to control production and distribution of opium poppy and products" (H.R.7568); Morlock? memo, 20 January 1943, NA, RG 59, LF 55D607, Box 10, File: "Opium poppy cultivation in the US"; Johnson to SD, 1 June 1943, NA, RG 59, 800.114N16/665; Anslinger to Thornton, 22 July 1943, FBNA, ACC 170-71-A-3554, Box 18, File 0660 Great Britain, Folder 1 (1928–42); Sharman to Anslinger, 3 June 1944, FBNA, ACC 170-74-12, Box 39, File 1230-13; Morlock memo, 17 November 1944, NA, RG 59, 800.114 Narcotics/11-1744; Gaston to SD, 19 January 1945, NA, RG 59, 867.114 Narcotics/1-1945; Sharman to Anslinger, 12 May 1945, FBNA, 170-74-12, Box 19, File 1230-13; Kinder and Walker, op. cit., pp. 920–1; Walker (1989), op. cit., pp. 153–69; Walker (1996), op. cit., pp. 145–6.

31 Moorhead coined the term.

32 Numerous documents dated August–October 1942 in FBNA, ACC 170-74-5, Box 17, File 1230-A, Folder 1 (1942–43); Morlock to Anslinger, 11 September 1942, NA, RG 59, LF 55D607, Box 16, File: "Opium – suppression of opium smoking"; Anslinger to Thompson, 15 December 1942, AP, Box 2, File 20. Morlock memo, 1 September 1942, NA, RG 59, LF 55D607, Box 16, File: "Opium – suppression of opium smoking"; Executive Committee minutes, 16 December 1942, FPAA, Micro 48, Reel 1.

33 Anslinger to Renborg, 31 December 1942 (quote), Sharman to Anslinger, 4 January 1943, Renborg to Anslinger 18 January 1943, all in FBNA, ACC 170-74-5, Box 17, File 1230-A, Folder 1 (1942–43); Anslinger to Morlock, 9 January 1943, Morlock to Ward, 15 January 1943, Morlock memo, 16 March 1943, all in NA, RG 59, LF 55D607, Box 16, File: "Opium – suppression of opium smoking"; Renborg memo, 10 January 1943, LNA, C.1620, no.6 (1943–44).

34 Meetings held on 4 December 1942, 13 January 1943, and 17 March 1943. NA, RG 59, LF 55D607, Box 15, File: "Opium smoking, suppression of, minutes of Foreign Policy Association meetings"; McCoy to McCarthy, 19 January 1943, and Morlock memo, 16 March 1943, NA, RG 59, LF 55D607, Box 16, File: "Opium – suppression of opium smoking"; Renfrew to Anslinger, 25 January 1943, FBNA, ACC 170-75-17, Box 8, File 1690-10, FPA file; Executive Committee minutes, 26 May 1943, FPAA, Micro 48, Reel 1.

35 Morlock memo, 11 March 1943 (quote), and numerous communications in August 1943, all in NA, RG 59, LF 55D607, Box 16, File: "Opium – suppression of opium smoking"; numerous documents dated May–August 1943 in FBNA, ACC 170-74-5, Box 17, File 1230-A, Folder 1 (1942–43).

36 PRO, FO 371/34545 (February–October 1943); PRO, FO 371/34546 (October–November 1943); IOpC meetings, 7 September and 27 October 1943, PRO, HO 45/20414; Anslinger to Sharman, 24 July 1945, AP, Box 2, File 19; LNd C.77.M.76.1945.XI (25 July 1945).

37 Notes attached to Boetzelaer to SD, 29 September 1943, Sharman to Anslinger, 18 September 1943 and 3 November 1943, all in FBNA, ACC 170-74-5, Box 17, File 1230-A, Folder 2 (August–December 1943); Morlock memos of 18 and 20 September 1943, Renborg memo dated November 1943 and attached comment by Morlock, 28 February 1944, all in NA, RG 59, LF 55D607, Box 16, File: "Opium – suppression of opium smoking"; Sharman to Anslinger, 23 November 1943, FBNA, ACC 170-71-A-3554, Box 7, File 0355, Folder 7; Steinig to Delevingne, 1 December 1943, LNA, C.1803, no.10 (1943–45); AP, Box 2, File 19 (January 1944).

38 Moorhead and Steinig favored an "opium combine" that would limit production in exchange for guaranteeing producers minimum prices and a share of the licit market. That the notion of an "opium combine," or "international opium corporation," surfaced during this time is not surprising; international arrangements to stabilize commodity prices featured regularly in discussions about the postwar economic order. Moorhead noted that if profits from an international opium corporation could be shared with Iranian opium farmers, their standard of living and ability to purchase from the United States would increase. If, for example, more American automobiles were likely to be sold abroad, Congress would find it easier to approve a plan that smacked of monopoly. Morlock, Anslinger, and Sharman, however, feared such an arrangement would prove too cumbersome in practice. They favored direct pressure tactics. Nevertheless, producing governments expressed interest in a "joint sales agreement" and American negotiators continued to entertain the possibility. In addition to the two subsequent footnotes, see Executive Committee minutes, 28 October 1942, FPAA, Micro 48, Reel 1.

39 McAllister, op. cit., pp. 269–71.

40 FBNA, ACC 170-74-12, Box 39, File 1230-13 (June 1944–August 1945);
FBNA, ACC 170-74-5, Box 17, UNO Folder #2 (September–December
1945) and UNO Folder #3 (January–April 1946); NA, RG 59, LF
55D607, Box 7, File:"Herbert L. May (January–March 1945); McDairmid
to Kotschnig, 17 September 1945, and SD memo, 30 November 1945, NA,
RG 59, LF 55D607, Box 16, File: "PCOB"; Morlock memo, 18 September
1944, NA, RG 59, LF 55D607, Box 17, File: "Opium Section, League of
Nations"; Morlock memo, 18 January 1945, NA, RG 59, LF 55D607, box
34; Gaston to Morlock, 16 March 1945, NA, RG 59, 500.C1/3-1645;
Gaston to Morlock, 10 May 1945, NA, RG 59, 800.114 Narcotics/5-1045;
NA, RG 59, 511.4A2A (January–June 1945); NA, RG 59, 500.C1197
(September 1945–January 1946); NA, RG 59, 501.BD Narcotics (March–
April 1946); document SD/E/NAR/1, 31 August 1946, NA, RG 59, LF
82D211, Box 47; PAC, RG25, Vol. 2694, File 8-PW-40, Part 1 (June 1944–
November 1945); position paper USGA/Gen/13, (undated, 1946) WNRC,
RG 84, Box 169; LNA, C.1804, no.4 (December 1944–May 1945); Felkin
to Lester, 16 February 1945, and Renborg to Lester, 19 November 1945,
LNA, S.561, no.4 (1944–45); Felkin to Lester, 7 June 1945, LNA, S.561,
no.6; Steinig–Lester correspondence, June–July 1945, LNA, C.1803, no.2
(1941–46); numerous letters, February–October 1945, LNA, C.1803, no.10
(1943–45); Renborg to Reynolds, 6 February 1945, PRO, HO 45/23162;
IOpC meetings, 21 November 1945, 18 January 1946, 24 April 1946,
9 May 1946, all in PRO, HO 45/20414; AP, Box 2, File 19 (January–July
1945); May, op. cit., pp. 62–64, 91. For 1946 Protocol see S. Chatterjee,
Legal Aspects of International Drug Control, The Hague, Martinus Nijhoff,
1981, pp. 326–7.
41 McAllister, op. cit., pp. 271–6.
42 McAllister, op. cit., pp. 267–9. Anslinger, for example, located key members
of the German narcotics services and had them rehabilitated post haste.
Anslinger to Russell, 5 October 1945, FBNA, ACC 170-71-A-3554, Box 16,
File 0660 (Egypt).

6 Trouble in paradise – 1945–53

1 Governments and the UN organized their documentation concerning
drug-related issues in such a manner that many key sources deal with
numerous topics. Fully footnoting each subject covered in this chapter
would require repeated citations from the same sources. To avoid such a
morass, see the list of important records covering multiple issues below.
General documents of secondary importance are cited in W. McAllister,
"A Limited Enterprise: The History of International Efforts to Control
Drugs in the Twentieth Century," PhD dissertation, University of
Virginia, 1996, note 363. Documents highlighting one issue are cited in
the usual manner.
Canada. PAC, RG 29, Volumes 549–51, File 320-5-5, Parts 2 through 7
(1947–53). Grande to Holmes, 27 February 1951, and Hardy memo,
28 April 1953, PAC, 25, ACC 86-87/160, Vol. 2, File 8-R-2-40, part 1.
Great Britain. Narcotics-related IOC documents in the following volumes of
PRO, CAB 134: 379; 381; 387; 389; 390; 396; 397; 398; 408; 410; 411;

944; 945; 949; 950. PRO, FO 371/67642 (April–August 1947). IOC(48)111, 14 June 1948, PRO, FO 371/72915. *United Nations*. Annual PCOB reports, E/OB/1 through E/OB/9 (1946–53). Annual DSB reports, E/DSB/3 through E/DSB/10 (1946–53). For proceedings of CND Sessions, reports to ECOSOC, General Assembly actions, and other UN communications, see documents in E.CN.7 (1946–53). *United States*. From NA, RG 59: 340.1 AH (1950–53); 501.BD Narcotics (1946–49); LF 82D211, Box 45, File SD/E/CN.7 (1947–53). NA, RG 353, LF 122, Boxes 100–101 (1947–48). FBNA, ACC 170-74-5, Boxes 14–15, File 1230-1, folders on 1st through 9th UN sessions (1947–53). INTERVIEWS: Louis Atzenwiler, 30 April and 1 May 1993; Joseph Dittert, 21 April 1993. LETTER: Charles Vaille, 4 May 1994. For an overview of the postwar system, see K. Bruun, L. Pan, and I. Rexed, *The Gentlemen's Club*, Chicago, University of Chicago Press, 1975, Part II.

2 Grande to Holmes concerning Sharman's report on the fifth CND session, 27 February 1951, PAC, RG 25 (ACC 86-87/160), Vol. 2, File 8-R-2-40, Part 1.

3 For Moorhead's death see FPA Directors meeting, 23 March 1950, FPAA, Micro 48, Reel 1; Anslinger to May, 17 March 1950, and Rea to Anslinger, 6 May 1950, AP, Box 2, File 15; obituary in *New York Times*, 10 March 1953. For Wright's death see *New York Times*, 14 February 1952.

4 Felkin to Anslinger, 9 May 1946, FBNA, ACC 170-74-12, Box 39, File 1230-2, Folder 1; memo on relation of DSB to UN, 10 May 1946, LNA, R.5146, 12B/43890/8707.

5 Felkin memo on PCOB budget, 16 May 1946, UNA, DAG-16/2.1-1, G4.1/ 46 (PCOB and DSB); Aaronson memo, 14 November 1946, UNA, DAG-16/2.1-1, G4.2 (PCOB & DSB); Hall memos, 24 June 1949 and 15 August 1950, NA, RG 59, LF 55D249, Sandifer subject files, Box 7 (Advisory Committee on Administrative and Budgetary Questions, UN); Gautier to Lie, 22 December 1949, Chisholm to Lie, 3 August 1951, Price to Chisholm, 17 August 1951, all in UNA, RAG-2/196-1, 205/03; Lande to Huang and Bolton, 30 August 1951, UNDCPA, Inventory 81/1-1, Item 1, File SOA/ GA/208/6/01.

6 UNA, DAG-16/1.1.3, Box 9, File: "Narcotics Commission" (1946–48); Morlock memo, 29 January 1947, NA, RG 59, 501.BD Narcotics/1-2947; PAC, RG 29, Vol. 548, File 320-5-5 (February–April 1947); Sharman to Morlock, 7 May 1947, and Sharman to Anslinger, 11 September 1947, PAC, RG 29, File 320-5-5, Part 2; Sharman to Steinig, 20 April 1948, PAC, RG 29, File 320-5-5, Part 3; Fulton to Harney, 19 January 1952, FBNA, ACC 170–73–1, Box 6, File 0120–40, Vol. 1.

7 The title of the WHO medical committee changed several times. For simplicity I refer to it throughout as the Expert Committee. Bruun, Pan, and Rexed, op. cit., chs 4–5; S. Chatterjee, "The WHO Expert Committee on Drug Dependence," *International and Comparative Law Quarterly*, 1979, vol. 28, no. 1, pp. 27–51.

8 Anslinger–Sharman correspondence, 30 December 1947 and 2 January 1948, PAC, RG 29, Vol. 549, File 320-5-5, Part 2; Walsh to SD, 19 January 1948, and Holland to Walsh, 4 February 1948, NA, RG 59, 501.BD

Narcotics/1-1948&2-248 Sharman to Anslinger, 2 March 1948, PAC, RG 25, Vol. 2693, File 8-E-40; British UN Delegation to FO, 23 July 1948, PRO, FO 371/72911. For USSR pronouncements about the WHO taking responsibility for drug control see Swayzee to Kotschnig, 1 July 1948, NA, RG 59, 501.BD Narcotics/7-148; Anslinger to Sharman, 2 July 1948, PAC, RG 29, Vol. 549, File 320-5-5, Part 3; Sharman to Menzies, 14 July 1948, RG 25, Vol. 3356, File 8-PW-40, Part 3.

9 Numerous documents dated November 1951–January 1952 in UNA, RAG-2/82-10 (WHO).

10 PAC, RG 29, Vol. 551, File 320-5-5 (July 1953).

11 For lack of Soviet cooperation during the 1930s and 1940s, see HO minute, 9 August 1932, PRO, HO 45/21788; Chatterjee to FO, 5 January 1944, and FO minute, 4 May 1944, PRO, FO 371/39362; Steinig to May, 24 May 1945, LNA, C.1803, no. 9 (1944–46); Steinig to Lester, 28 May 1945, LNA, C.1803, no. 2 (1941–46). The initial postwar spat concerned Fascist Spain's participation in the control regime. McAllister, op. cit., pp. 288–90. See also R. Gregg, "The International Control System for Narcotic Drugs," in L. Simmons and A. Said (eds), *Drugs, Politics, and Diplomacy: the International Connection*, Beverly Hills and London, Sage, 1974, ch. 12.

12 Hiss memo, 28 September 1946, NA, RG 59, LF 55D323, Box 11; Morlock memo, 18 February 1947, NA, RG 59, 501.BD Narcotics/2-1847; American UN delegation document SD/E/OB/1 (?February 1947), NA, RG 59, LF 82D211, Box 47; American UN delegation documents SD/E/CN.7/1 and 9, 20 February 1947 and 3 May 1947, NA, RG 59, LF 82D211, Box 45; Anslinger to Sharman, 5 November 1947, PAC, RG 29, Vol. 549, File 320-5-5, Part 2; Steinig to Felkin, 15 December 1947, WHOA, 1st gen. (1946–50), 463-1-9; IOC(48)19, 20 January 1948, and IOC(48)30 (Revise), 11 February 1948, PRO, CAB 134/387; IOC(48)3rd meeting, 27 January 1948, PRO, CAB 134/386; IOC(48)30, 24 January 1948, PRO, FO 371/72907; British UN delegation to FO, 6 March 1948, PRO, FO 371/72908; Atzenwiler, interview, Geneva, 1 May 1993.

13 After several years of western hand-wringing concerning how to respond, the issue degenerated into a routine matter; Soviet protestations passed without comment or action.

14 For example, when a vacancy occurred on the PCOB in 1947, Steinig wanted to fill the position with a Russian. Doing so would satisfy the secretariat's natural inclination toward inclusiveness. American sentiment, however, precluded Anslinger from supporting such a move.

15 For example, Siragusa to Anslinger, 2 May 1960, FBNA, ACC 170-74-5, Box 16, File 1230-1, Folder: 15th UN Session, #2.

16 McAllister, op. cit., pp. 267–9; *The Reminiscences of Herbert L. May*, OHRO, 90; Dittert, interview, Geneva, 21 April 1993; W. Walker, *Drug Control in the Americas*, Albuquerque, University of New Mexico Press, 1989, ch. 8; NA, RG 59, 102.14 and 102.1402 (1945–49); NA, RG 59, 800.114 Narcotics (1945–49); Foley to Morlock, 5 January 1947, NA, RG 59, 893.114 Narcotics/1-1547; SD memo, 27 June 1947, NA, RG 353, LF 122, Box 98, meeting 11 of the Departmental Committee on International Social Policy; Sharman to Anslinger, 26 January 1948, PAC, RG 29, Vol 549,

File 320-5-5, Part 3; Sharman to Grande, 20 May 1952, PAC, RG 29, Vol. 550, File 320-5-5, Part 7.

17 Anslinger's men had engaged in cowboy diplomacy since the early 1930s and rivalries existed between the FBN and other Treasury agents (especially Customs) sent abroad to deal with drug trafficking. See, for example, Anslinger to Harper, 31 January 1934, NA, RG 56, Entry 193, Box 191, file: Treasury Department, Narcotic Bureau, 1933–40; Fuller to Edgar, 29 April 1940, NA, RG 59, 500.C 1197/403A; J. Jonnes, *Hepcats, Narcs, and Pipedreams: A History of America's Romance with Illegal Drugs*, New York, Scribner, 1996, pp. 106–9, 157–8; H. Friman, *Narcodiplomacy: Exporting the US War on Drugs*, Ithaca, NY, Cornell University Press, 1996, p. 56; D. Kinder, and W. Walker, "Stable Force In a Storm: Harry J. Anslinger and United States Narcotic Foreign Policy, 1930–1962," *Journal of American History*, 1986, vol. 72, no. 4, pp. 918–19; P. Gootenberg, "Reluctance or Resistance? The Export of Cocaine (Prohibitions) to Peru, 1900–1950," in P. Gootenberg, (ed.), *Cocaine: Global Histories*, London, Routledge, 1999.

18 Guliani to Anslinger, 16 May 1947, PAC, Vol. 549, File 320-5-5, Part 2; British UN delegation to FO, 24 September 1948, PRO, FO 371/72912; SD to Kotschnig, 3 June 1949, NA, RG 59, 501.BD Narcotics/6-349; British UN delegation to FO, 14 April 1950, PRO, FO 371/88824; Felkin to SD, 24 June 1950, NA, RG 59, 398.53/6-2450; Friman, op. cit., pp. 88–9.

19 W. Walker, *Opium and Foreign Policy: The Anglo-American Search for Order in Asia, 1912–1954*, Chapel Hill, University of North Carolina Press, 1991, pp. 164–8; Friman, op. cit., pp. 64–5; Penfield memo, 5 February 1947, NA, RG 59, 501.BD Narcotics/2–547; IOC(47)52, 21 February 1947, PRO, CAB 134/381; Departmental committee meeting on international Social Policy, 27 June 1947, NA, RG 353, LF 122, Box 98; FBNA, ACC 170-74-5, Box 14, File 1230-1, Folder: 2nd UN session (September 1947–January 1948).

20 Menzies to Hossick, 30 December 1947, PAC, RG 25, Vol. 2622, File 8-AC-40; comment paper SD/A/C.3/73 prepared for American delegation to UN General Assembly, 27 August 1948, WNRC, RG 84, 1945–49, Box 174; Anslinger article entitled "Synthetic Narcotic Drugs", undated (?1949), AP, Box 9, File 1; Hutson–Anslinger correspondence, 14 September and 3 October 1949, FBNA, ACC 170-71-A-3554, Box 18, File 0660 Great Britain, Folder 2 (1943–52); S. Chatterjee, *Legal Aspects of International Drug Control*, The Hague, Martinus Nijhoff, 1981, pp. 327–30; P. Bean, *The Social Control of Drugs*, New York, Halstead Press, 1974, p. 46; PRO, FO 371/72907 (beginning December 1947) and following volumes consecutively through FO 371/72912 (ending October 1948); IOC(48)172, 20 September 1948, CAB 134/391; Boyer to Acheson, 12 January 1950, NA, RG 59, 862.3971/1-1250.

21 McAllister, op. cit., pp. 299–301; W. Walker (ed.), *Drugs in the Western Hemisphere: an Odyssey of Cultures in Conflict*, Wilmington, Scholarly Resources, 1996, p. 131; J. Gagliano, *Coca Prohibition in Peru: The Historical Debates*, Tucson, University of Arizona Press, 1994, pp. 150–61.

22 NA, RG 59, 867.114 Narcotics (1947–48); Siragusa to Anslinger, 11 August 1950, and Kuniholm to SD, 3 October 1950, NA, RG 59, 102.14/8-750 & 10-350; NA, RG 59, 882.53 (1950–52).

23 Anslinger to Russell, 18 December 1945, FBNA, ACC 170–71–A–3554, Box 16, File 0660 (Egypt); Morlock memo, 18 January 1946, NA, RG 59, 511.4A2A/1–1846; Morlock memo, 22 January 1946, and Wilcox to Merrill, 11 November 1946, NA, RG 59, 891.114/1–2246, Greenfield to Anslinger, 5 April 1946, NA, RG 59, 845.114 Narcotics/4-546; PRO, FO 371/59608 (May–June 1946); Morlock memo, 18 June 1946, NA, RG 59, 114N16/6-1846; Anslinger to Morlock, 22 August 1946, NA, RG 59, 501.BD Narcotics/8-2246.

24 Quote: Landon to Butterworth, 23 April 1948, FBNA, ACC 170-74-5, Box 14, File 1230–1, Folder: 3rd UN Session, #2. Walker (1991), op. cit., pp. 162–4, 176–86; R. Cribb, "Opium and the Indonesian Revolution," *Modern Asian Studies*, 1988, vol. 22, no. 4, pp. 701–22; London Embassy to SD, 18 August 1945, NA, RG 59, 511.4A5/8-1845; IOpC meeting, 20 September 1945, PRO, HO 45/20414; Cummings memo, 11 April 1947, NA, RG 59, 845C.114 Narcotics/4-1747; Raynor memo, 30 April 1948, WNRC, RG 84, Subject Files, Box 85, File: "Narcotics 1946–49"; Executive Committee minutes, 28 October 1948, FPAA, Micro 48, Reel 1; Thornton to SD, 26 August 1948, PRO, FO 371/88825:US1811/79; Stone to SD, 28 November 1949, NA, RG 59, 800.114 Narcotics/11-2849; SD memo, 3 August 1951, NA, RG 59, 340.1 AH/8-351; A. McCoy, *The Politics of Heroin: CIA Complicity in the Global Drug Trade*, New York, Lawrence Hill, 1991, pp. 15–17, 109–15, 127–61.

25 Y. Zhou, "Nationalism, Identity, and State Building: The Anti-Drug Crusade in the People's Republic, 1949–1952," in T. Brook and B. Wakabayashi (eds), *Opium in East Asian History*, Berkeley, University of California Press, 2000; K. Meyer and T. Parssinen, *Webs of Smoke: Smugglers, Warlords, Spies, and the History of the International Drug Trade*, Lanham, Maryland, Rowman and Littlefield, 1998, ch. 10; Walker (1991), op. cit., pp. 168–75, 186–8; McCoy, op. cit., pp. 124–5; NA, RG 59, 893.114 Narcotics (1946–47). Note, however, that Chinese use of other substances, especially tobacco, rose – the polydrug phenomenon remained intact.

26 NA, RG 59, 891.114 (1945–49); NA, RG 59, 888.53 (1950–54); IOC(50)32, 4 February 1950, PRO, CAB 134/403; Haggerty to SD, 4 April 1951, NA, RG 59, 868.53/4-1451; H. Mowlana, "The Politics of Opium in Iran: A Social-Psychological Interface," in Simmons and Said, op. cit., pp. 161–7.

27 Quotes, respectively, from IOC(48)111, 14 June 1948, PRO, FO 371/72915; IOC(49)123, 20 June 1949, PRO, CAB 134/398; 1950–51 PCOB report, UNd E/OB/7, p. 9.

28 McAllister, op. cit., p. 307.

29 For objections to the proposed customs regulations by other branches of the federal government, see Jones to SD, 13 September 1951, NA, RG 59, 411.00234-N/9-1351.

30 Miller to Nichols, 21 June 1954, and Mellen to Wolf, 17 July 1958, NA, RG 59, 711.64/6-2154&7-858.

31 The 1912 Hague Convention, the 1925 Prepared Opium Agreement, the 1925 International Opium Convention, the 1931 Limitation Convention,

the 1931 Bangkok agreement, the 1936 Illicit Trafficking treaty, the 1946 Protocol transferring League authority to the UN, and the 1948 Synthetic Narcotics Protocol.

32 Anslinger initiated a series of preliminary steps to support his overall plans, including an abortive UN mission to South American coca states, launching a quasi-scientific UN-sponsored journal called the *Bulletin on Narcotics*, and embarking on a quixotic program to identify the geographic origins of opium through chemical analysis. See McAllister, op. cit., pp. 313–19. See also Gagliano, op. cit., pp. 154–60; Walker (1996), op. cit., p. xxi; Gootenberg, op. cit., in Gootenberg, op. cit.

33 ECOSOC resolutions 159 II D (VII), 3 August 1948 and 246 D (IX), 6 July 1949.

34 See, for example, H. May, *Narcotic Drugs and Atomic Energy: Analogy of Controls*, New York, American Association for the United Nations, 1946.

35 Morlock memo, 19 September 1949 and Thomas to Magnuson, 9 December 1949, NA, RG 59, 893.114 Narcotics/9-1949&12-1249 PRO, FO 371/88826 (November–December 1950).

36 Merrill to SD, 3 December 1949, NA, RG 59, 867.114 Narcotics/12-349.

37 Morlock memo, 19 May 1950, NA, RG 59, 102.14/5-1950; PRO, FO 371/88825 (June–July 1950); May, op. cit., p. 64.

38 position paper SD/E/CN.7/12, 1 August 1950, NA, RG 59, LF 82D211, Box 45; IOC(50)138, 8 August 1950, PRO, CAB 134/406; IOC(50)176, 15 September 1950, PRO, CAB 134/407; IOC(50)206, 3 November 1950, PRO, CAB 134/408; IOC(51)9, 30 January 1951, PRO, CAB 134/410.

39 Steinig to Anslinger, 14 February 1951, NA, RG 59, 811.53/2-1451; IOC(51)43, 3 April 1951, PRO, CAB 134/410; External Affairs memo, 14 April 1951, PAC, RG 25, Vol. 2, File 8-R-1-40, Part 1; position paper for thirteenth ECOSOC, 30 July 1951, PAC, RG 25, Box 3471, File 7-1-1951-1.

40 DND memo, June 1951, UNDCPA, Inventory 81/1, Item 60; SOA 208/7/01; Steinig to Greenfield, 18 August 1951, UNDCPA, Inventory 81/1, Item 59, SOA 208/4/01; IOC(51)170, 1 November 1951, PRO, CAB 134/413.

41 Renborg fluttered around the periphery until the early 1960s, unsuccessfully maneuvering to rejoin the elect. Whenever he smelled an opportunity he published an article either praising UN efforts or disparaging them, depending on how he thought the wind was blowing. McAllister, op. cit., pp. 276–7, 328, 354–6.

42 Anslinger to Hoo, 6 November 1951, and Anslinger to Penteado, 26 November 1951, AP, Box 2, File 14; Anslinger to May, 13 October 1952, NA, RG 59, LF 55D607, Box 7, File: Herbert L. May; Anslinger to Sharman, 28 August 1951, PAC, RG 29, Vol. 550, File 320-5-5, Part 7.

43 Myrdal to Kerno, 2 May 1950, UNA, RAG 2/323–9, File 323–4–01; UNDCPA, Inventory 81/1, SOA 204/2/01, Item 52 (June–October 1951); Lande to Huang and Bolton, 30 August 1951, UNDCPA, Inventory 81/1-1, Item 1, File SOA/GA/208/6/01; Lande to Steinig, 14 January 1952, UNDCPA, Inventory 81/1, SOA 205/04, Item 52; Sharman to Anslinger, 12 July 1951, PAC, RG 29, Vol 550, File 320-5-5, Part 6; Vaille to Anslinger, 23 November 1951, and Vaille to Sharman, 31 January 1952, PAC, RG 29, Vol. 550, File 320-5-5, Part 7; Anslinger to Kotschnig,

11 February 1953, FBNA, ACC 170-74-12, Box 38, File 1230-1, Folder 1; Vaille, letter, 4 May 1994.

44 PAC, RG 25, Vol. 2, File 8-PW-40, Part 4 (July–August 1950); McInnes memo, 22 August 1951, PAC, RG 25, Vol. 2, File 8-R-1-40, Part 2; PAC, RG 25, Vol. 2, File 8-R-2-40, Part 1 (April–June 1953); PAC, RG 25, ACC 86–87/159, Vol. 1, File 8-T-40, Part 1 (March 1953–January 1954).

45 For threats to the FBN's position in the late 1940s and early 1950s, see McAllister, op. cit., pp. 332–3; R. Carroll, "The Weed with Roots in Rhetoric: Harry J. Anslinger, Marijuana, and the Making of American Drug Policy," PhD dissertation, University of Pittsburgh, 1991, ch. 5, pp. 23–30.

46 Hulten to Anslinger, 5 August 1947, NA, RG 59, 501.BD Narcotics/8-547; DiLucia to Anslinger, 4 October 1947, AP, Box 2, File 19; Moorhead to Rogers, 23 November 1948, AP, Box 2, File 17; Morlock memo, 17 March 1949, NA, RG 59, LF 55D607, Box 17; Washington Embassy to Ottawa, 20 November 1951, PAC, RG 25, Vol. 1, File 8-B-40, Part 3; AP, Box 2, File 13 (November–December 1952); PS, Vol.14, No. 42, 29 November 1952, 8–9; Hickerson to Anslinger, 12 May 1953, NA, RG 59, 398.53-NA/5-1253; SD memo, 4 December 1953, FBNA, ACC 170-73-1, Box 6, File 0210-40 (Vol 1).

47 FBNA, ACC 170-74-5, Box 18, File: 1953 Opium Conference (October 1952–July 1953); IOC(52)52, including addenda 1 and 2, 15 May 1952, PRO, CAB 134/945; IOC(52)181, 8 December 1952, PRO, CAB 134/947; Huang to Yates, 12 November 1952, UNDCPA, Inventory 81/1, Item 60, File SOA 208/6/08; IOC(53)48, 21 April 1953, PRO, CAB 134/950; Canadian Delegation report, 18 June 1953, and Cameron to External Affairs, 14 August 1953, PAC, RG 25, Vol. 2, File 8-R-2-40, Part 2; US Delegation report, 29 July 1953, NA, RG 59, 398.53/7-2953; UK Delegation report, IOC(53)133, 6 August 1953, PRO, CAB 134/951; Sharman to Anslinger, 19 February 1954, FBNA, ACC 170-74-5, Box 15, File 1230-1, Folder: 10th UN session #1.

48 Those clauses nevertheless garnered the attention of disarmament negotiators, who scrutinized the inspection and enforcement provisions for their applicability to the arms–limitation question. Vaille, letter, 4 May 1994.

49 Bulgaria, Greece, India, Iran, Turkey, USSR, and Yugoslavia.

50 See for example Sharman to Anslinger, 19 February 1954, FBNA, ACC 170-74-5, Box 15, File 1230-1, Folder: 10th UN session #1.

7 The long march to the Single Convention – 1953–61

1 Important records covering multiple issues are listed below. See Chapter 6, note 1, for rationale. General documents of secondary importance are cited in W. McAllister, "A Limited Enterprise: The History of International Efforts to Control Drugs in the Twentieth Century," PhD dissertation, University of Virginia, 1996, note 417. Documents highlighting one issue are cited in the usual manner.

Canada. PAC, RG 29: Vol. 8, File 322-2-17, Part 4 (May 1954).

Great Britain. Narcotics-related IOC documents in the following volumes of PRO, CAB 134: 954; 956; 958; 964; 965; 966; 1268; 1269; 2062; 2063; 2064; 2066; 2067; 2068; 2073; 2074; 2078; 2084; 2085. PRO, FO 371/

129981 (March–May and August 1957); PRO, FO 371/137060 (April–July 1958).
United Nations. Annual PCOB reports, E/OB/9 through E/OB/17 (1953–61). Annual DSB reports, E/DSB/10 through E/DSB/19 (1953–62). For proceedings of CND Sessions, reports to ECOSOC, General Assembly actions, and other UN communications, see documents in E.CN.7 (1953–61). UNA, RAG 3/9–176, Files: SO 421/1, SO 421/11, SO 430, SO 440, SO 441, and SO 443 (1957–60).
United States. From NA, RG 59: 340.1AH (1953–54) and 340.19 (April 1955–July 1959). FBNA, ACC 170–74–12, Box 38, File 1230–1, Folder 2 (December 1956–January 1957); FBNA, ACC 170–74–5, Boxes 15–16, File 1230–1, Folders on 11th through 16th UN sessions (1953–61).
INTERVIEWS: Louis Atzenwiler, 30 April and 1 May 1993; Joseph Dittert, 21 April, 26 April, and 3 May 1993.
LETTERS: Louis Atzenwiler, 6 October 1993, 2 December 1993, 16 May 1994, 14 September 1994; Charles Vaille, 4 May 1994; Norma Walker, 6 May 1994; R. S. Tufnell, 9 August 1994; Janine Yates, 23 April 1994.

2 Steinig to Atzenwiler, 28 December 1951, UNA, RAG-2/82-10 (WHO).
3 Confidential PCOB report on the illicit traffic E/OB/W.252/Rev.1, 21 June 1954, attached to Greenfield to Anslinger, 24 August 1954, FBNA, ACC 170-74-12, Box 39, File 1230-2, Folder 1.
4 For Board attempts improve statistical reporting, continued sparring with the UN over administrative support, and issues surrounding the Board's independence, see McAllister, op. cit., note 421.
5 In addition to the public pronouncements of the Board and Body, see Sharman's private doubts: Sharman to Anslinger, 12 August 1954, FBNA, ACC 170-74-5, Box 15, File 1230-1, Folder: 10th UN session #1.
6 Schachter to Yates, 30 April 1956, UNA, DAG-3/3.1.4., Box 32 (Schachter).
7 For difficulties with PCOB nominees and the "personal union" issue see McAllister, op. cit., pp. 349–50 and note 424.
8 Yates to Trevelyan, 24 June 1958, UNDCPA, Inventory 80-1, Series G.XVIII, Item 31, File 4/3/1 (232969); Lande to Yates, 8 October 1959, and Lande to Schachter 23 November 1960, UNDCPA, Inventory 80-1, Series G.XVIII, Item 105, File 15/1/2 (26211); Atzenwiler, interviews, 30 April and 1 May 1993.
9 McAllister, op. cit., pp. 350–1.
10 Huang to Anslinger, 29 August 1955, AP, Box 2, File 11; FBNA, ACC 170-74-12, Box 38, File 1230-1, Folder #2 (March and August 1956); Anslinger–Huang correspondence, AP, Box 2, File 10 (February 1956–February 1957); Huang to Anslinger, 28 July 1958, AP, Box 2, File 11; Yates–Schachter correspondence, 8 and 17 September 1958, UNA, DAG-3/3.1.4, Box 32.
11 In addition to note 1, see Atzenwiler, interviews, 5 May 1993.
12 J. Jonnes, *Hepcats, Narcs, and Pipedreams: A History of America's Romance with Illegal Drugs*, New York, Scribner, 1996, ch. 10; R. Carroll, "The Weed with Roots in Rhetoric: Harry J. Anslinger, Marijuana, and the Making of American Drug Policy," PhD dissertation, University of Pittsburgh, 1991, ch. 4–7; J. McWilliams, "Through the Past Darkly: The Politics and Policies of America's Drug War," in W. Walker (ed.), *Drug Control*

Policy: Essays in Historical and Comparative Perspective, University Park, Pennsylvania, Penn State University Press, 1992, pp. 17–20; D. Kinder, "Bureaucratic Cold Warrior: Harry J. Anslinger and Illicit Narcotics Traffic," *Pacific Historical Review*, 1981, vol. 50, no. 2; A. Lindesmith, *The Addict and the Law*, Bloomington, Indiana University Press, 1965; R. King, *The Drug Hang-up: America's Fifty-Year Folly*, New York, Norton, 1972, chs 14–24; W. Eldridge, *Narcotics and the Law: A Critique of the American Experiment in Narcotic Drug Control*, Chicago, University of Chicago Press, 1962; Galliher, Keys, and Elsner, "Lindesmith v. Anslinger: An Early Government Victory in the Failed War on Drugs," *Journal of Criminal Law and Criminology*, 1998, vol. 88, no. 2, pp. 661–83.

13 McAllister, op. cit., pp. 357–9.

14 McAllister, op. cit., pp. 359–60; Galliher, Keys, and Elsner, op. cit.

15 PAC, RG 25 (ACC 86-87/336), Vol. 2, File 8-R-40, Part 6 (May 1958) and Part 7 (May–June 1958); Hossick to Green, 9 July 1958, PAC, RG 29, Vol. 225, File 320-5-9, Part 11.

16 Quote: IOC(58)46, 12 June 1958, PRO, CAB 134/2068.

17 McAllister, op. cit., pp. 362–3.

18 McAllister, op. cit., pp. 378–80. For other interpretations see A. McCoy, *The Politics of Heroin: CIA Complicity in the Global Drug Trade*, New York, Lawrence Hill, 1991, p. 17; J. McWilliams, "Covert Connections: the FBN, the OSS, and the CIA," *The Historian*, 1991, vol. 53, no. 4, pp. 659–78; Kinder, op. cit., pp. 182–9; D. Kinder, and W. Walker, "Stable Force In a Storm: Harry J. Anslinger and United States Narcotic Foreign Policy, 1930–1962," *Journal of American History*, 1986, vol. 72, no. 4, pp. 918–25; W. Walker, *Drugs in the Western Hemisphere: An Odyssey of Cultures in Conflict*, Wilmington, Scholarly Resources, 1996, p. 167.

19 P. Giffen, S. Endicott, and S. Lambert, *Panic and Indifference: The Politics of Canada's Drug Laws*, Ottawa, Canadian Centre on Substance Abuse, 1991, chs 12–13.

20 PAC, RG 25, ACC 86-87/160, Vol. 1, File 8-R-40, Part 1 (March–November 1953), Part 2 (April 1953), and Part 3 (March–May 1954).

21 Reid to Pearson, 15 March 1955 and Léger to Pearson, 22 March 1955, PAC, RG 25, Vol. 1, File 8-R-40, Part 4; PAC, RG 29, Vol. 224, File 320-5-9, Part 9 (March 1955–August 1956).

22 See note 1, especially US and UN citations and Vaille communications.

23 See note 1, especially British citations.

24 In addition to note 1, see NA, RG 59, 891.53 (1955–59).

25 During the 1950s, India's share of raw opium exports varied between 30 and 60 percent. During periods of crop failure in other producing countries (1959–60, for example) India's share rose as high as 80 percent.

26 NA, RG 59, 888.53 (1955–59); Anslinger to Vaille, 7 September 1955, FBNA, ACC 170-74-12, Box 38, File 1230-1, Folder 2; Vaille to Anslinger, 17 May 1956, FBNA, ACC 170-74-5, Box 15, File 1230-1, Folder: 11th UN session; Green to Gauntlett, 10 January 1958, PRO, FO 371/137058; Riddleberger to US officers in Near East and Middle East, 7 July 1959, NA, RG 59, 102.14/7-759.

27 It is likely that a connection existed between the CIA-backed putsch that placed the Shah in control and Iran's change of heart concerning opium. The FBN had close ties to the OSS/CIA, and FBN undercover agents may

have been operating in Iran at the time of Mossadeq's ouster. A private quid pro quo arrangement, in addition to control advocates' disapproval of previous Iranian behavior, would seem the most likely explanation for Teheran's abrupt reversal of policy.

28 McAllister, op. cit., pp. 372–4; Anslinger to Morlock, 28 April 1955, FBNA, ACC 170-74-5, Box 15, File 1230-1, Folder: 10th UN session, #2; NA, RG 59, 340.19 (1956); UNA, RAG 2/323–9, LEG 323/5/01 (January–April 1956); Vaille to Anslinger, 17 May 1956, FBNA, ACC 170-74-5, Box 15, File 1230–1, Folder: 11th UN session; Tabibi to Anslinger, 15 October 1956, and Kotschnig memo, 15 February 1957, FBNA, ACC 170–74–5, Box 16, File 1230-1, Folder: 12th UN Session; PRO, FO 371/129979 (January–February 1957); PAC, RG 25, ACC 86-87/336, Vol. 2, File 8-R-40, Part 5 (March–June 1957); PRO, FO 371/129981 (April–December 1957); PRO, FO 371/137059 (January 1958); PRO, FO 371/137060 (March–June 1958).

29 NA, RG 59, 882.53 (1955–59); Flues to Anslinger, 12 May 1958, FBNA, ACC 170-74-5, Box 16, File 1230-1, Folder: 14th UN Session; Anslinger to Yates, 25 November and 15 December 1958, FBNA, ACC 170-74-12, Box 38, File 1230-1, Folder 3.

30 FBNA, ACC 170-74-5, Box 15, File 1230-1, Folder: 10th UN session #2 (March 1955).

31 McAllister, op. cit., p. 375.

32 In addition to note 1, see McCoy, op. cit., pp. 17–18, 23, 93–113, 127–248; Kinder and Walker, op. cit., p. 923; Hoare to FO, 15 April 1957, PRO, FO 371/129981; HO to Gauntlett, 18 July 1957, PRO, FO 371/129980; Stephens to Gauntlett, 30 April 1958, PRO, FO 371/137060. During the first Indochina war, opium featured prominently in French and Vietminh strategic decision-making. The Dien Bien Phu campaign, in particular, was primarily a fight over controlling the region's opium revenue. D. Porch, *The French Secret Services: From the Dreyfus Affair to the Gulf War*, New York, Farrar, Strauss & Giroux, 1995, chs 13–14; McCoy, op. cit., p. 122.

33 J. Gagliano, *Coca Prohibition in Peru: The Historical Debates*, Tucson, University of Arizona Press, 1994, pp. 147–73; P. Gootenberg, "Reluctance or Resistance? The Export of Cocaine (Prohibitions) to Peru, 1900–1950," in P. Gootenberg (ed.), *Cocaine: Global Histories*, London, Routledge, 1999; Atzenwiler, interview, 30 April 1993; Sharman to Anslinger, 22 July and 12 August 1954, FBNA, ACC 170-74-5, Box 15, File 1230-1, Folder: 10th UN session #1; Rubottom to Flues, 24 June 1959, NA, RG 59, 102.14/6-2459. For concerns about recrudescence of coca trafficking: Yates–Anslinger correspondence, 7 and 15 December 1959, FBNA, ACC, 170-74-5, Box 16, File 1230-1, Folder: 15th UN session #1.

34 In addition to note 1, see McAllister, op. cit., pp. 380–5. See also C. Even-Zohar, "Drugs in Israel: A Study of Political Implications for Society and Foreign Policy," L. Simmons, and A. Said (eds), *Drugs, Politics, and Diplomacy: the International Connection*, Beverly Hills and London, Sage, 1974, ch. 8; A. Block and J. McWilliams, "On the Origins of American Counterintelligence: Building a Clandestine Network," *Journal of Policy History*, 1989, vol. 1, no. 4, p. 367.

35 In addition to note 1, see McAllister, op. cit., pp. 385–7; K. Bruun, L. Pan, and I. Rexed, *The Gentlemen's Club*, Chicago, University of Chicago Press, 1975, pp. 204–12; L. Simmons, and A. Said, "The Politics of Addiction," in Simmons and Said, op. cit., p. 9; Gagliano, op. cit., p. 160.

36 In addition to note 1, see C. Jackson, "Before the Drug Culture: Barbiturate/Amphetamine Abuse in American Society," *Clio Medica*, 1976, vol. 11, no. 1, pp. 47–58; L. Grinspoon and P. Hedblom, *The Speed Culture: Amphetamine Abuse in America*, Cambridge, Harvard University Press, 1975, pp. 11–26; M. Seevers, "Use, Misuse, and Abuse of Amphetamine-Type Drugs from the Medical Point of View," p. 10 and J. Rawlin, "Street Level Abusage of Amphetamines," pp. 51–7, in J. Russo (ed.), *Amphetamine Abuse*, Springfield, Thomas, 1968; N. Zinberg, *Drug, Set, and Setting: The Basis for Controlled Intoxicant Use*, New Haven, Yale University Press, 1984, p. 186; P. Bean, *The Social Control of Drugs*, New York, Halstead Press, 1974, p. 116; J. Burnham, *Bad Habits: Drinking, Smoking, Taking Drugs, Gambling, Sexual Misbehavior, and Swearing in American History*, New York, New York University Press, 1993, p. 124–5; F. Zimring, and G. Hawkins, *The Search for Rational Drug Control*, Cambridge, Cambridge University Press, 1992, p. 60; H. Friman, *Narcodiplomacy: Exporting the US War on Drugs*, Ithaca, NY, Cornell University Press, 1996, p. 95; M. Smith, *A Social History of the Minor Tranquilizers: The Quest for Small Comfort in the Age of Anxiety*, New York, Pharmaceutical Products Press, 1991. Anslinger had avoided domestic psychotropics control since first suggested in the 1930s. D. Musto, *The American Disease*, Oxford, Oxford University Press, 1987, pp. 222–3.

37 Curran to Hossick, 5 August 1954, PAC, RG 29, Vol. 8, File 322-2-17, Part 4; Rose to Dulles, 1 September 1954, NA, RG 59, 398.53/9-154; Boening to Anslinger, 8 November 1955, and Vaille to Anslinger, 20 June 1956, FBNA, ACC 170-74-12, Box 38, File 1230-1, Folder #2; Hoover to Ankara, 10 November 1955, NA, RG 59, 102.14/11-1055; FBNA, ACC 170-74-5, Box 15, File 1230-1, Folder: 13th UN session (May 1956); IOC(56)53, 27 June 1956, PRO, CAB 134/1269; Hoare to Gauntlett, 6 March 1957, PRO, FO 371/129982:UNS1816/5; McIlvane to SD, 23 June 1957, NA, RG 59, 340.19/6-2357; NA, RG 59, 340.51 (July 1957); SD to Athens, 25 November 1957, NA, RG 59, 340.51/11-2557; Holmes to Cameron, 26 November 1957, PAC, RG 25 (ACC 86-87/336), Vol. 2, File 8-R-40, Part 6.

38 No synthetic narcotic manufacturing industry existed in France, so Vaille did not have to worry about upsetting any domestic constituency.

39 Vaille was not a member of the PCOB. The incident caused a major flap among drug diplomats, not least because it dislodged Herbert May from the DSB. McAllister, op. cit., pp. 392–6.

40 In addition to note 1, for negotiations leading to the third draft: Bevans to Calderwood, 24 April 1957, NA, RG 59, 102.14/7-2457; Holmes to Cameron, 26 November 1957, PAC, RG 25 (ACC 86-87/336), Vol. 2, File 8-R-40, Part 6; memo to Yates, 28 February 1958, UNDCPA, Inventory 80-1, Series G. XVIII, Item 27, File 3/2/1 (23221); PAC, RG 29, Vol. 225, File 320–5–9, Part 11 (September–October 1958); Lande to Yates, 28 October 1958, UNDCPA, Inventory 80-1, Series G.XVIII, Item 6, File 2/1/3 (23607); Green to Hossick, 15 December 1958, PAC,

RG 29, Vol. 225, File 320-5-9, Part 12; UNDCPA, Inventory 80-1, Series G.XVIII, Item 103, File 14/2/2 (24230) (June 1959 and July–November 1960); Jay to Murray, 30 March 1960, PAC, RG 25, Vol. 2, File 8–E–40, Part 2; Pharmaceutical Manufacturers' Association comments on third draft, 1 December 1960, FBNA, ACC 170-74-12, Box 37, File 1230 (SC) #1.

41 For example, Tietjens to Foley, 26 September 1947, FBNA, ACC 170-71-A-3554, Box 8, File 0355, Folder 4 (1936 Convention); Swayze to Gross, 23 October 1947, NA, RG 59, LF 55D607, Box 27, File: 1936 Convention.

42 See W. McAllister, "Conflicts of Interest in the International Drug Control System," in Walker (1992), op. cit., pp. 143–66. The archival record reveals that this article is in certain respects inaccurate. The "groupings" discussed should be modified as noted here. The examination of the Single Convention's provisions, especially in comparison with the 1971 Psychotropic Convention, remains valid.

In addition to note 1:

For negotiation of the Single Convention see IOC(61)3, 11 January 1961, PRO, CAB 134/2082; UNA, DAG-1/1.2.2., Box 71, File: "Narcotic Drugs–Single Convention" (May 1959–September 1961); FBNA, ACC 170-74-12, Box 38, File 1230 (SC), Folder 3 (February–March 1961) and Folder 4 (April 1961); IOC(61)61, 9 May 1961, PRO, CAB 134/2084.

For Yates's assessment of the Single Convention see Yates to Narasimhan and Yates to Kotschnig, 5 May 1961, UNA, DAG-1/1.2.2, Box 71. See also United Nations, *Commentary on the Single Convention on Narcotic Drugs, 1961*; S. Chatterjee, *Legal Aspects of International Drug Control*, The Hague, Martinus Nijhoff, 1981, chs 7–10.

43 French officials ignored a growing Marseilles-based "French connection" as long as traffickers did not market their wares domestically. The FBN could not apply sufficient pressure on Paris without revealing the extent of its own failure to keep heroin out of the US.

44 Hayes to Anslinger, 5 June 1953, FBNA, ACC 170-74-5, Box 15, File 1230-1, Folder: 9th UN session; FBNA, ACC 170-74-12, File 1230 (SC) #1 (May 1957); Anslinger–Bevans correspondence, 28 April and 5 October 1959, NA, RG 59, 811.3971/4-2859 and 10-559; Hayes to Anslinger, 16 March 1960, AP, Box 2, File 7.

45 Single Convention, Article 17.

46 Atzenwiler, interview, 30 April 1993.

8 Crucible – 1961–73

1 Important records covering multiple issues are listed below. See Chapter 6, note 1, for rationale. General documents of secondary importance are cited in W. McAllister, "A Limited Enterprise: The History of International Efforts to Control Drugs in the Twentieth Century," PhD dissertation, University of Virginia, 1996, note 471. Documents highlighting one issue are cited in the usual manner.

Canada. PAC, RG 25, Vol. 2, File 8-R-40, Part 9 and FP (June 1963); PAC, RG 25, Vol. 53, File 45-9-1, Part 1 (August–December 1968); PAC, RG 25, Vol. 54, File 45-9-1, Part 4 (December 1971–April 1972) and Part 5 (May–August 1972); PAC, RG 25, Vol. 54, File 45-9-1-1, Part 1

(January–February 1964), Part 3 (1967-68), and Part 4 (January–May 1969); PAC, RG 25, Vol. 55, File 45-9-1-1, Part 8 (June 1971), Part 9 (July–September 1971), Part 10 (October–December 1971), Part 12 (April 1972), Part 13 (October–December 1972); PAC, RG 25, Vol. 55, File 45-9-1-6, Part 2 (January–March 1972).
Great Britain. IOC(62)38, 1 May 1962, PRO, CAB 134/2089; IOC(62)58, 20 June 1962, PRO, CAB 134/2090.
United Nations. Annual PCOB reports, E/OB/17 through E/OB/23 (1961–67). Annual INCB reports, E/INCB/1, 9, 13, 17 (1968–72). For proceedings of CND Sessions, reports to ECOSOC, General Assembly actions, and other UN communications, see documents in E.CN.7 (1961–72). From UNA: DAG-1/1.2.2, Box 72, File 8 (February 1963); DAG-1/1.2.2, Boxes 70-71, Narasimhan's correspondence and files on narcotics (1958–72); DAG-3/3.4.5, Box 19, File: Heenan Narcotics Correspondence (December 1967–October 1968). WHOA, 3rd Gen., A2/36/3 (March 1966). UNDCPA, Inventory 80-1, Series G.XVIII, Item 24, File 3/1/2(30596) (August 1967-March 1968).
United States. From FBNA: ACC 170-74-5, Boxes 16-17, File 1230-1, Folders on 17th–21st UN Sessions (1962–67); ACC 170-74-12, Box 39, File 1230-2, Folder 2 (June 1962–June 1965) and Folder 3 (May 1966–March 1967); ACC 170-74-12, Box 38, File 1230-1, Folder 4 (January 1965–August 1967); ACC 170-74-12, Box 38, File 1230, Book 9 (April 1966); ACC 170-74-12, Box 38, File: Misc PCOB (November 1967). From AP: Box 2, File 11 (June 1963); Box 2, File 3 (July–October 1963); Box 2, File 2 (January–February 1964); Box 2, File 1 (June 1968–May 1969); Box 11, File 25 (April 1968 and January 1969). From IP, Box: "Speeches 1969–73, UN CND Papers", File UN/CND (November 1970–February 1973).
INTERVIEWS: Joseph Dittert, 26 April 1993, 3 May 1993; John Ingersoll, 28 August 1994, 10 April 1995; Paulsen K. Bailey, 10 May 1993; Liselotte Waldheim-Natural, 20 May 1993; Ross Chapman, 10 February 1994; Lawrence Hoover, 23 April 1994; Neal Chayet, 12 and 14 December 1993; Robert Angarola, 2 December 1993.
LETTERS: Janine Yates, 23 April 1994; R. S. Tufnell, 9 August 1994; Charles Vaille, 4 May 1994;
OTHER COMMUNICATIONS: Vladimir Kuśević, cassette tape responses, February and July 1994; Letter from István Bayer including his paper entitled "Genesis and development of the international control of psychotropic substances" prepared for the US National Institute for Drug Abuse in 1989, chapter 2.
2 Curran to Cole, 11 April 1968, PAC, RG 25, Vol. 54, File 45-9-1-1, Part 3.
3 Daniel Patrick Moynihan to the Attorney General, 11 February 1969, IP, Box: BNDD International Historical Papers, etc, File: "Historical Documents."
4 Herbert L. Packer, quoted in P. Bean, *The Social Control of Drugs*, New York, Halstead Press, 1974, p. 91.
5 For a more detailed account, see McAllister, op. cit., pp. 410–18.
6 D. Kinder, "Shutting Out Evil: Nativism and Narcotics Control in the United States," in W. Walker (ed.), *Drug Control Policy: Essays in Historical and Comparative Perspective*, University Park, Pennsylvania, Penn State University Press, 1992, p. 120.

7 Anslinger to Ingersoll, 2 September 1969, IP, Box: BNDD Papers and Letters, File "personal correspondence."
8 For the upsurge in drug use and reactions thereto see: UNITED STATES: D. Musto, *The American Disease*, Oxford, Oxford University Press, 1987, ch. 10; H. Morgan, *Drugs in America: A Social History, 1800–1980*, Syracuse, NY, Syracuse University Press, 1981, ch. 8; J. McWilliams, *The Protectors: Harry J. Anslinger and the Federal Bureau of Narcotics, 1930–1962*, Newark, University of Delaware Press, 1990, ch. 8; J. Jonnes, *Hepcats, Narcs, and Pipedreams: A History of America's Romance with Illegal Drugs*, New York, Scribner, 1996, Part III; R. King, *The Drug Hang-up: America's Fifty-Year Folly*, New York, Norton, 1972; M. Smith, *A Social History of the Minor Tranquilizers*, New York, Pharmaceutical Products Press, 1991; R. Carroll, "The Weed with Roots in Rhetoric: Harry J. Anslinger, Marijuana, and the Making of American Drug Policy," PhD dissertation, University of Pittsburgh, 1991, conclusion; Chein, *et al.*, *The Road to H: Narcotics, Delinquency, and Social Policy*, New York, Basic Books, 1964; H. Becker, *Outsiders: Studies in the Sociology of Deviance*, New York, Free Press, 1997; V. Garrett, "Substance Abuse Treatment in Southern California: The History and Significance of the Antelope Valley Rehabilitation Centers," *Journal of Policy History*, 1996, vol. 8, no. 2, pp. 181–205; R. Mullen and N. Arbiter, "Against the Odds: Therapeutic Community Approaches to Underclass Drug Abuse," in P. Smith (ed.), *Drug Policy in the Americas*, Boulder, Westview Press, 1992, ch. 12; D. Courtwright, "Morality, Religion, and Drug Use," pp. 234–7, and A. Brandt, "Behavior, Disease, and Health in the Twentieth Century United States: The Moral Valence of Individual Risk," pp. 58–72, in A. Brandt and P. Rozin (eds), *Morality and Health*, New York, Routledge, 1997; P. Stares, *Global Habit: The Drug Problem in a Borderless World*, Washington, Brookings Institution, 1996, pp. 24–7; R. Bonnie and C. Whitebread, *The Marihuana Conviction: A History of Marihuana Prohibition in the United States*, Charlottesville, University of Virginia Press, 1974, ch. 12; E. Brecher, *Licit and Illicit Drugs*, Boston, Little, Brown, & Company, 1972, ch. 57; J. Burnham, *Bad Habits: Drinking, Smoking, Taking Drugs, Gambling, Sexual Misbehavior, and Swearing in American History*, New York, New York University Press, 1993, pp. 124–5; D. Healy, *The Antidepressant Era*, Cambridge, Mass., Harvard University Press, 1997; E. Epstein, *Agency of Fear: Opiates and Political Power in America*, New York, Putnam, 1977, but only in conjunction with P. Rachal, *Federal Narcotics Enforcement: Reorganization and Reform*, Boston, Auburn House, 1982, especially pp. 67–70, which refutes Epstein's thesis.
CANADA: P. Giffen, S. Endicott, and S. Lambert, *Panic and Indifference: The Politics of Canada's Drug Laws*, Ottawa, Canadian Centre on Substance Abuse, 1991, chs 11–16; DNHW memo, 28 March 1962, PAC, RG 25, Vol. 2, File 8-R-40, Parts 9 and FP.
BRITAIN: S. MacGregor (ed.), *Drugs and British Society: Response to a Social Problem in the Eighties*, London, Routledge, 1989, ch. 2; V. Berridge and B. Thom, "The Relationship between Research and Policy: Case Studies from the Postwar History of Drugs and Alcohol," *Contemporary Drug Problems*, 1994, vol. 21, pp. 599–629; P. Bean, *The Social Control of Drugs*, New York, Halstead Press, 1974, ch. 6; V. Berridge, "Aids, Drugs, and History,"

in Roy Porter and Mikulas Teich (eds), *Drugs and Narcotics in History*, Cambridge, Cambridge University Press, 1995, ch. 10. THE NETHERLANDS: M. de Kort and D. Korf, "The Development of Drug Trade and Drug Control in the Netherlands: A Historical Perspective," *Crime, Law, and Social Change*, 1992, vol. 17, pp. 123–44; M. de Kort, "The Dutch Cannabis Debate, 1968–1976," *Journal of Drug Issues*, 1994, vol. 24, no. 3, pp. 417–27; G. van de Wijngaart, *Competing Perspectives on Drug Use: The Dutch Experience*, Amsterdam, Swets & Zeitlinger, 1991; C. Kaplan, "The Uneasy Consensus: Prohibitionist and Experimentalist Expectancies behind the International Narcotics Control System," *Tijdschrift voor criminologie*, 1984, vol. 26, pp. 98–109; M. de Kort, "Doctors, Diplomats, and Businessmen: A History of Conflicting Interests in the Netherlands," in P. Gootenberg (ed.), *Cocaine: Global Histories*, London, Routledge, 1999; E. van Luijk, "A Lesson from history on the issue of drug legalisation: The case of the opiumregie in the Dutch East Indies, 1890-1940," June 1991, unpublished paper, Netherlands Institute for Advanced Study; E. van Luijk and J. van Ours, "How to control drugs: the lessons from the opiumregie in the Dutch East Indies, 1894–1940," 1993, unpublished paper, Vrije Universiteit, Amsterdam.
WESTERN EUROPE, including Scandinavia: H. Albrecht and A. Kalmthout, *Drug Policies in Western Europe*, Freiburg: Max-Planck-Institut für ausländisches und internationales Strafrecht, 1989, pp. 465–71; P. Stangeland (ed.), *Drugs and Drug Control*, Oxford, Oxford University Press/Norwegian University Press, 1987; A. Ehrenberg, (ed.), *Penser la Drogue, Penser les Drogues* (3 volumes), Paris, Editions Descartes, 1992; H. Friman, *Narcodiplomacy: Exporting the US War on Drugs*, Ithaca, NY, Cornell University Press, 1996, pp. 90–115; S. Scheerer, "The New Dutch and German Drug Laws: Social and Political Conditions for Criminalization and Decriminalization," *Law and Society Review*, 1978, vol. 14, no. 4, pp. 585–606; Scheerer, *Die Genese der Betäubungsmittelgesetze in der Bundesrepublik Deutschland und in den Niederlanden*, Göttingen, Schwartz, 1982; H. Bossong, C. Marzahn, and S. Scheerer (eds), *Sucht und Ordnung: Drogenpolitik für Helfer und Betroffene*, Frankfurt, Extrabuch, 1983; P. Reuter, M. Falco, and R. MacCoun, *Comparing Western European and North American Drug Policies*, Santa Monica, Rand Corporation, 1993.
AFRICA: B. Du Toit, *Cannabis in Africa*, Rotterdam, A. A. Balkema, 1980, chs 1–2.
AUSTRALIA: I. McAllister, R. Moore, and T. Makkai, *Drugs in Australian Society*, Melbourne, Longman Cheshire, 1991.
INDIA: M. Khan, *Drug Use Amongst College Youth*, Bombay: Somaiya Publications, 1985, ch. 1.
ISRAEL: C. Even-Zohar, "Drugs in Israel: A Study of Political Implications for Society and Foreign Policy," in L. Simmons, and A. Said (eds), *Drugs, Politics, and Diplomacy: the International Connection*, Beverly Hills and London, Sage, 1974, ch. 8.
JAPAN: Friman, op. cit., pp. 65–85; K. Meyer, "Fast Crabs and Cigarette Boats: A Speculative Essay," in Walker (1992) op. cit., pp. 83–4.
LATIN AMERICA: P. Gootenberg, "Reluctance or Resistance? The Export of Cocaine (Prohibitions) to Peru, 1900–1950," in P. Gootenberg (ed.), *Cocaine: Global Histories*, London, Routledge, 1999; J. Gagliano, *Coca*

Prohibition in Peru: The Historical Debates, Tucson, University of Arizona Press, 1994, pp. 162–3.
NEW ZEALAND: Secretary of Foreign Affairs, Wellington to New Zealand UN delegation, 3 May 1971, PAC, RG 25, Vol. 55, File 45-9-1-1, Part 8.
SOUTHEAST ASIA: A. McCoy, *The Politics of Heroin: CIA Complicity in the Global Drug Trade*, New York, Lawrence Hill, 1991, pp. 248–61.
USSR: J. Kramer, "Drug Abuse in the Soviet Union," *Problems of Communism*, 1988, vol. 37, no. 2, pp. 28–40.
YEMEN: S. Weir, *Qat in Yemen: Consumption and Social Change*, London, British Museum Publications, 1985, chs 3–4.
CUBA apparently experienced an increase in drug use and trafficking: Havana Embassy to External Affairs, 19 April 1967, PAC, RG 25, Vol. 53, File 45-9-1, Part 1.
For world overviews, see reports by governments on drug use in annual CND and PCOB/INCB publications and such WHO documents as J. Kramer, and D. Cameron, *A Manual on Drug Dependence*, Geneva, World Health Organization, 1975; P. Hughes, *et al.*, "Extent of Drug Abuse: An International Review with implications for Health Planners," *World Health Statistics Quarterly*, 1983, vol. 36, nos 3-4, pp. 394–497; WHO, *Youth and Drugs*, Geneva, WHO, 1973.

9 Combine Burnham's thesis, op. cit., especially ch. 5, about the vice-industrial complex, with P. Rozin, "Moralization," in Brandt and Rozin, op. cit., pp. 379–401, for a powerful assessment of the changes in attitudes toward drugs (and social conventions more generally) during the 1960s and 1970s.

10 V. Sharpe and A. Faden, *Medical Harm: Historical, Conceptual, and Ethical Dimensions of Iatrogenic Illness*, Cambridge, Cambridge University Press, 1998, Part I.

11 M. Silverman, and P. Lee. *Pills, Profits and Politics*, Berkeley, University of California Press, 1974; M. Silverman, *The Drugging of the Americas: How Multinational Drug Companies say one thing about their Products to Physicians in the United States and another to Physicians in Latin America*, Berkeley, University of California Press, 1976; M. Silverman, P. Lee, and M. Lydecker, *Prescriptions for Death*, Berkeley, University of California Press, 1982; K. Najmi, *Drugs Policy in Developing Countries*, London, Zed Books, 1992, ch. 1.

12 P. Haas, "Introduction: epistemic communities and international policy coordination," *International Organization*, 1992, vol. 46, no. 1, especially pp. 14–16, discusses in a generalized way the role that transnational expert groups (epistemic communities) can play during times of paradigmatic upset. E. Haas, *When Knowledge is Power: Three Models of Change in International Organizations*, Berkeley, University of California Press, 1990, elucidates the general phenomena of adaptation in international organizations, especially during periods of stress.

13 See notes 1 and 8 above, especially American references, and FBNA, ACC 170-73-1, Box 6, file 0120-40, Vol. 3 (1962); Curran to Nutting, 6 February 1962, PAC, RG 25, Vol. 2, File 8-R-40, Parts 9 and ff; AP, Box 2, File 5 (January–July 1962); AP, Box 2, File 4, (September 1962–February 1963); Anslinger statement to California Pharmaceutical Association, 7 March 1963, AP, Box 9, File 2.

14 See notes 1 and 8 above, especially Canadian references.

15 See notes 1 and 8 above, especially British references.
16 See notes 1 and 8 above, especially Dutch, Western European, and UN references.
17 McAllister, op. cit., pp. 427–30.
18 *Expansion of the CND*   *Expansion of the Board*
   1946 = 15 states   1928 (PCOB) = 8 Members
   1961 = 21   „   1968 (INCB) = 11   „
   1966 = 24   „   1977 (INCB) = 13   „
   1972 = 30   „
   1983 = 40   „
   1991 = 53   „

19 For examples of government maneuvering to gain (or avoid) a seat on the CND, Cusack to Anslinger, 4 January 1962 and Siragusa to Anslinger, 10 January 1962, FBNA, ACC 170-74-12, Box 38, File 1230-1, Folder 3; PRO, FO 371/166946 (February–March 1962 and December 1962–January 1963); Anslinger to Yates, 17 February 1962 and DND memo, 27 December 1962, UNDCPA, Inventory 80-1, Series G.XVIII, Item 27, File 3/2/5(28737); Cleveland to Hendrick, 2 April 1963, FBNA, ACC 170-74-5, Box 16, File 1230-1, Folder: 18th UN session; Bell to Anslinger, 17 June 1964, AP, Box 2, File 2.
20 McAllister, op. cit., pp. 430–4.
21 In addition to note 1, for negotiations preceding the 1971 Psychotropic Conference see: AP, Box 2, File 5 (May–June 1962); Lande to Yates, 18 May 1962, UNDCPA, Inventory 80-1, Series G.XVIII, Item 24, File 3/1/2(30596); Barbiturates position paper, 12 April 1963, FBNA, ACC 170-74-5, Box 16, File 1230-1, Folder: 18th UN session; FBNA, ACC 170-74-5, Box 17, File 1230-1, Folder: 20th UN session (May 1965); Lande to WHO, 25 November 1966, WHOA, 3rd Gen., A2/36/3; PAC, RG 25, Vol. 54, File 45-9-1-1, Part 1 (December 1965), Part 3 (December 1968), Part 4 (January–July 1969), Part 5 (January–December 1970) and Part 6 (September 1970); Isoré to Lande and Halbach, 10 March 1967, UNDCPA, Inventory 80-1, Series G.XVIII, Item 25, File 3/1/4(37991); WHOA, A2/112/2 (April 1967 and March–July 1969); Ansar Khan to Isoré, 7 June 1967, UNDCPA, Inventory 80-1, Series G.XVIII, Item 24, File 3/1/4(37991); Pharmaceutical Industries' Association (UK) statement, 13 February 1968, FBNA, ACC 170-74-12, Box 38, File 1230-1 (new substances); FBNA, ACC 170-74-12, Box 38, File 1230-1-A (July–September 1966 and June 1968); UNA, DAG-3/3.4.5, Box 19, Heenan narcotics correspondence (December 1966, February–September 1968, and October 1969); WHO to UN, 8 October 1969, WHOA, 3rd. Gen, A2/36/3; S. Chatterjee, "The WHO Expert Committee on Drug Dependence," *International and Comparative Law Quarterly*, 1979, vol. 28, no. 1, pp. 27–51. For pharmaceutical company tactics to defend products, see J. Graham, "Amphetamine Politics on Capitol Hill," *Trans-action*, 1972, vol. 9, no. 3, pp. 14–16, 18–22, 53; E. Valenstein, *Blaming the Brain: The Truth about Drugs and Mental Health*, New York, Free Press, 1998, especially ch. 8.
22 In addition to note 1, see W. B. McAllister, "Conflicts of Interest in the International Drug Control System," in Walker (1992), op. cit., pp. 143–66; "United Nations Conference for the adoption of a Protocol on Psycho-

tropic Substances, Official Records" (2 volumes), UNds E/Conf.58/7 and E/ Conf.58/7/Add.1; PAC, RG 25, Vol. 54, File 45-9-1-1, Part 7 (December 1970–February 1971); Chapman to Edelstein, 28 April 1971, PAC, RG 25, Vol. 54, File 45-9-1-1, Part 8; UNA, DAG-1/1.2.2, Box 71 (January 1971); PS, vol. 33, no. 2 (11 January 1971), pp. 22–3; PS, vol. 33, no. 12 (22 March 1971), p. 11; IP, Box "Speeches 1969–73, UN CND Papers," File: UN/CND (January–April 1971); IP, Box "BNDD International, Historical Papers," File: Senate Committee on Foreign Relations Fulbright), Psychotropic Substances (May 1971 and February 1972); S. Chatterjee, *Legal Aspects of International Drug Control*, The Hague, Martinus Nijhoff, 1981, ch. 12.

23 V. Kuśević, "Drug Abuse Control and International Treaties," *Journal of Drug Issues*, 1977, vol. 7, no. 1, pp. 38–40; Kuśević, cassette tape responses, February 1994.

24 For examples of strongarm tactics initiated by the US delegation, see McAllister, op. cit., p. 450.

25 The only derivatives included in the original treaty were the isomers of tetrahydrocannabinol (THC – the active ingredient in marijuana and other cannabis products.) This exception only reinforces the contention made here. See item 10 in Schedule 1.

26 Letter from István Bayer including his paper entitled "Genesis and development of the international control of psychotropic substances" prepared for the US National Institute for Drug Abuse in 1989, chapter 2.

27 Anslinger to SD, 27 November 1967, AP, Box 2, File 1; PAC, RG 25, Vol. 53, File 45-9-1, Part 2 (September 1970); LeClair to External Affairs, 9 September 1970, PAC, RG 25, Vol. 54, File 45-9-1-1, Part 6; PAC, RG 25, Vol. 55, File 45-9-1-1, Part 8 (May–June 1971), Part 9 (July 1971), Part 10 (December 1971–January 1972), and Part 11 (January–February 1972); PAC, RG 25, Vol. 54, File 45-9-1, Part 4 (December 1971); Raton to Wattles, 21 October 1971, and Stavropoulos to Winspeare-Guicciardi, 16 February 1972, UNA, Central Files, OLC 15 Narcotics, DAG-3/3.11.2., Box 2; K. Bruun, L. Pan, and I. Rexed, *The Gentlemen's Club*, Chicago, University of Chicago Press, 1975, pp. 243–59. See also J. McWilliams, "Through the Past Darkly: The Politics and Policies of America's Drug War," in Walker (1992) op. cit., pp. 20–4; W. Walker, *Drugs in the Western Hemisphere: An Odyssey of Cultures in Conflict*, Wilmington, Scholarly Resources, 1996, p. 167.

28 See note 27 and PAC, RG 25, Vol. 53, File 45-9-1, Part 2 (March and July 1970); Vernon to Edelstein, 10 August 1970, PAC, RG 25, Vol. 54, File 45-9-1-1, Part 6.

29 See note 27 and Anslinger to Stribavy, 28 October 1968, and Hoover to Anslinger, 16 April 1969, AP, Box 2, File 1; Kuśević to Narasimhan, 14 October 1968, UNA, DAG-1/1.2.2., Box 70; Canadian CND delegation to Ottawa, 23 January 1969 and Teheran Embassy to External Affairs, 15 April 1969, PAC, RG 25, Vol. 54, File 45-9-1-1, Part 4; Cusack to Anslinger, 30 October 1969, PAC, RG 25, Vol. 53, File 45-9-1, Part 1.

30 McCoy, op. cit., pp. 275–386.

31 In addition to note 1, see PAC, RG 25, Vol. 55, File 45-9-1-1, Part 12 (March–April 1972); Chapman to McKim, 1 May 1972, PAC, RG 29, Vol. 8, File 322-2-14; R. Gregg, "The International Control System for

Narcotic Drugs," in Simmons and Said, op. cit., pp. 294–5; Bruun, Pan, and Rexed, op. cit., pp. 259–68.
32 In addition to note 1, see ibid., pp. 212–21; UNA, DAG-1/1.2.2, Box 72, File 8 (January–April 1970); PAC, RG 25, Vol. 53, File 45-9-1, Part 2 (August–September 1970); PAC, RG 25, Vol. 54, File 45-9-1-1, Part 6 (September–October 1970); Cusack to Anslinger, 30 October 1970, PAC, RG 25, Vol. 53, File 45-9-1, Part 1; PAC, RG 25, Vol. 55, File 45-9-1-1, Part 9 (August–October 1971).
33 Kuśević to Ingersoll, 6 July 1972, UP, Box "Speeches 1969–73, UN CND papers," File: UN/CND.

9 Crosscurrents – 1972–2000

1 Lacking access to the archival sources necessary for a full historical analysis, this chapter offers an overview of the principal trends since 1972. For proceedings of CND Sessions, reports to ECOSOC, General Assembly actions, and other UN communications, see documents in E.CN.7 (1972–present). For annual INCB reports, see documents in E/INCB/17 (1972–present). The UNDCP website *http://www.undcp.org/index.html* also contains useful overviews and updates.
2 The discussion of "adaptation" through "turbulent nongrowth," applied to international organizations in E. Haas, *When Knowledge is Power: Three Models of Change in International Organizations*, Berkeley, University of California Press, 1990, especially ch. 6, contains some useful observations of more general applicability.
3 Key states ratifying prior to August 1976 included Bulgaria, Egypt, France, India, Mexico, Sweden, Thailand, and Yugoslavia. Those ratifying during 1977–78 included Pakistan, West Germany, Greece, and the USSR. Somewhat tardy were Hungary (1979), Peru and the United States (1980), Italy and Turkey (1981). Latecomers included the United Kingdom (1986), Canada (1988), Japan (1990), the Netherlands (1993), Belgium (1995), and Switzerland (1996). Austria and Iran had not ratified as of 31 December 1997.
4 Paul Bailey, Secretary of the DND, called the process an "amendment by resolution," referring to resolutions passed by the CND, ECOSOC, and UN General Assembly urging nations to comply with enhanced voluntary reporting standards. Paulsen K. Bailey, interview, 10 May 1993. Betty C. Gough, interview, 19 October 1993; Joseph Dittert, interviews, 26 April 1993, 3 May 1993; Liselotte Waldheim-Natural, interview, 20 May 1993; Robert Angarola, interview, 2 December 1993 and telephone interview, 14 December 1993; Herbert Schaepe, interview, 18 May 1993; A. Bahi, interview, 4 May 1994; PAC, RG 25, Vol. 55, File 45-9-1-1, Part 13 (November–December 1972); Lambo to Chrusciel, 28 June 1973 and Sartorious memos of 1 February and 20 April 1977, all in WHOA, 3rd Gen., A2/36/4; S. Chatterjee, "The WHO Expert Committee on Drug Dependence," *International and Comparative Law Quarterly*, 1979, vol. 28, no. 1, pp. 27–51.
5 W. Walker and B. Bagley (eds), *Drug Trafficking in the Americas*, New Brunswick, Transaction Publishers, 1994; W. Walker, *Drug Control in the Americas*, Albuquerque, University of New Mexico Press, 1989, pp. 189–223;

J. McWilliams, "Through the Past Darkly: The Politics and Policies of America's Drug War," in W. Walker (ed.), *Drug Control Policy: Essays in Historical and Comparative Perspective*, University Park, Pennsylvania, Penn State University Press, 1992, pp. 24–9.

6 Precursors to psychotropics – the US had long advocated control over narcotic precursors.

7 Mathea Falco, interview, 16 September 1993; Gough, interview, 19 October 1993; D. Courtwright, "Morality, Religion, and Drug Use," in A. Brandt and P. Rozin (eds), *Morality and Health*, New York, Routledge, 1997, pp. 234–42; F. Zimring and G. Hawkins, *The Search for Rational Drug Control*, Cambridge, Cambridge University Press, 1992, p. 159.

8 Bailey, interview, 10 May 1993; R. J. Samsom, letter, 23 August 1993; R. Gregg, "The International Control System for Narcotic Drugs," in L. Simmons, and A. Said (eds), *Drugs, Politics, and Diplomacy: the International Connection*, Beverly Hills and London, Sage, 1974, ch. 12; P. Smith (ed.), *Drug Policy in the Americas*, Boulder, Westview Press, 1992; F. Bresler, *Interpol*, London, Sinclair-Stevenson, 1992, chs 9 and 16; M. Anderson, *Policing the World: Interpol and the Politics of International Police Co-operation*, Oxford, Clarendon Press, 1989, chs 1–2, 5; J. Jonnes, *Hepcats, Narcs, and Pipedreams: A History of America's Romance with Illegal Drugs*, New York, Scribner, 1996, Part IV. See also for examples of US pressure on other governments: P. Stares, *Global Habit: The Drug Problem in a Borderless World*, Washington, Brookings Institution, 1996, pp. 27–37; IP, Box: Speeches, 1969–73, UN CND Papers, File: UN/CND (June and October–November 1972); Bonn Embassy to External Affairs, 21 April 1972, PAC, RG 25, Vol. 55, File 45-9-1-1, Part 12; Thibault to Ottawa, 1 August 1972, PAC, RG 25, Vol. 54, File 45-9-1, Part 5; External Affairs circular to various posts, 24 October 1972, PAC, RG 25, Vol. 55, File 45-9-1-1, Part 13.

9 United Nations Convention Against Illicit Traffic in Narcotic Drugs and Psychotropic Substances. Registered 11 November 1990, UN Treaty Series, No. 27627.

10 As of 31 December 1997 Austria, Indonesia, Iraq, Israel, Switzerland, and Thailand had not ratified.

11 Jean-Francois Gaulis (spokesman for the International Federation of Pharmaceutical Manufacturers' Associations), interview, 6 May 1993. Neil Chayet, interviews, 14 December 1994, and Chayet Papers, deposited with the author; Ingersoll's comments on Chayet's testimony, 4 February 1972, IP, Box: International Historical Papers, File "Senate Ctee. on Foreign Relations (Fulbright)." For an example of industry objections to increased "voluntary" reporting: brief written by Robert T. Angarola, attorney representing Hoffmann-La Roche and Roche Products, to DEA, 17 December 1993. Copy in possession of author. See also R. Hansen, "International Issues of Drug Regulation," *Zeitschrift für die gesamte Staatswissenschaft*, 1983, vol. 139, no. 3, pp. 568–77; M. de Kort, "The Dutch Cannabis Debate, 1968–1976," *Journal of Drug Issues*, 1994, vol. 24, no. 3, pp. 424–5; C. Kaplan, "The Uneasy Consensus: Prohibitionist and Experimentalist Expectancies behind the International Narcotics Control System," *Tijdschrift voor criminologie*, 1984, vol. 26, pp. 98–9; W. von Wartburg, *Drogenmissbrauch und Gesetzgeber*, Basel and Stuttgart, Birkhäuser, 1974; H. Bossong, C. Marzahn, and S. Scheerer (eds), *Sucht und Ordnung: Drogenpolitik für*

Helfer und Betroffene, Frankfurt, Extrabuch, 1983; V. Berridge (ed.), *Drugs Research and Policy in Britain*, Aldershot, Gower, 1990.
12 Smith, op. cit.; Stares, op. cit., pp. 37–46, 94; A. McCoy, *The Politics of Heroin: CIA Complicity in the Global Drug Trade*, New York, Lawrence Hill, 1991, chs 8–9. During the 1980s abuse apparently reappeared in mainland China. K. Meyer and T. Parssinen, *Webs of Smoke: Smugglers, Warlords, Spies, and the History of the International Drug Trade*, Lanham, Maryland, Rowman & Littlefield, 1998, pp. 274–5.
13 See Stares, op. cit., especially ch. 3, for comparison of "negative" and "positive" control measures; Chatterjee, op. cit.
14 *Declaration of the International Conference on Drug Abuse and Illicit Trafficking and Comprehensive Multidisciplinary Outline of Future Activities in Drug Abuse Control*, UNd ST/NAR/14.
15 For the CMO see UNd ST/NAR/14 (1988); for the Systemwide Action Plan see UNds E/1990/39 (including addenda) and A/RES/S-17/2. See also UNd A/RES/45/179 (21 December 1990); J. Donnelly, "The United Nations and The Global Drug Control Regime," in Smith, op. cit., ch. 19.
16 Bailey, interview, 10 May 1993; Waldheim-Natural, interview, 20 May 1993; Schaepe, interview, 18 May 1993; A. Bahi, interview, 4 May 1994. For administrative turf battles caused by the creation of UNFDAC see W. McAllister, "A Limited Enterprise: The History of International Efforts to Control Drugs in the Twentieth Century," PhD dissertation, University of Virginia, 1996, pp. 474–5.
17 Bailey, interview, 10 May 1993.
18 For developments in Japan and Germany representative of this phenomenon, see H. Friman, *Narcodiplomacy: Exporting the US War on Drugs*, Ithaca, NY, Cornell University Press, 1996, pp. 73–84, 106–11.

Conclusion

1 K. Meyer and T. Parssinen, *Webs of Smoke: Smugglers, Warlords, Spies, and the History of the International Drug Trade*, Lanham, Maryland, Rowman & Littlefield, 1998, pp. 279–80, note this phenomenon more generally.
2 This happened in the Netherlands as early as the 1920s. M. de Kort, "Doctors, Diplomats, and Businessmen: A History of Conflicting Interests in the Netherlands," in P. Gootenberg (ed.), *Cocaine: Global Histories*, London, Routledge, 1999.
3 Informal restrictions or local controls drove research and development agendas even in the later nineteenth century. J. Spillane, "Modern Drug, Modern Menace: The Legal Use and Distribution of Cocaine in the United States, 1880–1920," PhD Dissertation, Carnegie Mellon University, May 1994, ch. 4
4 For example, see the control–polydrug-use relationships discussed in Spillane, op. cit., especially pp. 2–3, 20–30, 228–42; F. Zimring and G. Hawkins, *The Search for Rational Drug Control*, Cambridge, Cambridge University Press, 1992, especially p. 60; J. Westermeyer, "The Pro-Heroin Effects of Anti-Opium Laws in Asia," *Archives of General Psychiatry*, 1976, vol. 33, pp. 1135–9.
5 Some theories of drug use emphasize that addiction proneness, personality type, and/or biomedical factors can impact the propensity to become depen-

dent. For a convenient summary see I. McAllister, R. Moore, and T. Makkai, *Drugs in Australian Society*, Melbourne, Longman Cheshire, 1991, ch. 1.

6 As early as 1928, shortly before the 1925 Opium Convention went into effect, the Dutch noted that a huge surge in coca orders largely emptied Amsterdam warehouses. de Kort, op. cit., in Gootenberg, op. cit.; S. Karch, *A Brief History of Cocaine*, Boca Raton, Florida, CRC Press, 1998, pp. 11–12. Key titles outlining this phenomena include Meyer and Parssinen, op. cit.; P. Stares, *Global Habit: The Drug Problem in a Borderless World*, Washington, Brookings Institution, 1996, especially ch. 4; A. McCoy, *The Politics of Heroin: CIA Complicity in the Global Drug Trade*, New York, Lawrence Hill, 1991; P. Scott and J. Marshall, *Cocaine Politics: Drugs, Armies, and the CIA in Central America*, Berkeley, University of California Press, 1998. See Bibliographic Essay in W. Walker (ed.), *Drug Control Policy: Essays in Historical and Comparative Perspective*, University Park, Pennsylvania, Penn State University Press, 1992, pp. 167–73, for other titles of varying usefulness. K. Meyer, "Fast Crabs and Cigarette Boats: A Speculative Essay," pp. 64–88 in Walker's edited volume offers insightful comments about continuities in drug smuggling. For an interesting though inadequately conceptualized argument, see Westermeyer, op. cit. See also A. Block and W. Chambliss, *Organizing Crime*, New York, Elsevier, 1981, despite its untenable marxist argument and poor documentation.

7 See the well-argued thesis in W. Walker, *Opium and Foreign Policy: The Anglo-American Search for Order in Asia, 1912–1954*, Chapel Hill, University of North Carolina Press, 1991.

8 See Walker's developing analysis of inter-American drug control efforts and resistance thereto that focuses on cultural and sub-cultural factors. W. Walker (ed.), *Drugs in the Western Hemisphere: An Odyssey of Cultures in Conflict*, Wilmington, Scholarly Resources, 1996, especially pp. xv–xxiv, 64, 167–8, 195–7, 229–30, 251–60; Walker, "International Collaboration in Historical Perspective," in P. Smith (ed.), *Drug Policy in the Americas*, Boulder, Westview Press, 1992, pp. 265–81; Walker, *Drug Control in the Americas*, Albuquerque, University of New Mexico Press, 1989. See also A. Hasenclever, P. Mayer, and V. Rittenberger, *Theories of International Regimes*, Cambridge, Cambridge University Press, 1997, especially ch. 5; G. Edwards and A. Arif (eds) *Drug Problems in the Socio Cultural Context: A Basis for Policies and Program Planning*, Geneva, World Health Organization, 1980; M. De Rios, *Hallucinogens: Cross-Cultural Perspectives*, Albuquerque, New Mexico University Press, 1984; C. Even-Zohar, "Drugs in Israel: A Study of Political Implications for Society and Foreign Policy," in Simmons and Said, op. cit., p. 186.

9 E. Nadelmann, *Cops Across Borders: The Internationalization of US Criminal Law Enforcement*, University Park, Penn State University Press, 1993. R. Gregg, "The International Control System for Narcotic Drugs," in L. Simmons and A. Said (eds), *Drugs, Politics, and Diplomacy: the International Connection*, Beverly Hills and London, Sage, 1974, p. 300, refers to western "cultural arrogance." Stares, op. cit., pp. 5–9, notes that the west is now exporting its addiction problem to the rest of the world. See also D. Rasmussen and B. Benson, *The Economic Anatomy of a Drug War: Criminal Justice in the Commons*, Lanham, Maryland, Rowman & Littlefield, 1994.

Bibliography

Manuscript sources

Official documents

Austria
Vienna
  UN Drug Control Program Archives

Canada
Ottawa
  Public Archives of Canada
    Record Group 25: Records of the Department of External Affairs
    Record Group 29: Records of the Department of National Health and
    Welfare

Great Britain
Kew
  Public Record Office
    Cabinet Records
      CAB 24: Cabinet Papers
      CAB 27: Cabinet Papers
      CAB 134: International Organizations Committee
    Foreign Office
      FO 371: General Correspondence, Political
    Home Office
      HO 45: Home Office files, Dangerous Drugs
London
  India Office Archives
    Economic and Overseas Department papers, 1924–46
      L/E/7
      L/E/8

Switzerland
Geneva
  League of Nations Archives
  World Health Organization Archives

United States
Bethesda, Maryland
  National Library of Medicine
    Lyndon F. Small Papers
New York
  United Nations Archives
Suitland, Maryland
  Washington National Records Center
    Record Group 84: Foreign Service Posts of the Department of State
    Record Group 170: Records of the Federal Bureau of Narcotics
Washington, DC
  Manuscript Division, Library of Congress
    Raymond Leslie Buell Papers
    Arthur Sweetser Papers
  National Archives
    Record Group 56: Department of Treasury General Records, Federal
      Bureau of Narcotics
    Record Group 59: General Records, Department of State
    Decimal Files
    Lot File 55D249: Durwood Sandifer subject files
    Lot File 55D323: Misc. records from predecessor units of the Bureau of
      International Organization
    Lot File 55D607: Subject File Relating to Control of Narcotics Traffic,
      1903–55
    Lot File 82D211: Position papers, Bureau of International Organization
      Affairs and its predecessors, 1945–74
    Record Group 84: US Mission to the United Nations
    Record Group 161: War Hemp Program, Commodity Credit Corporation
    Record Group 179: War Production Board
    Record Group 225: Army and Navy Munitions Board, War Department
    Record Group 353: Records of Interdepartmental and Intradepartmental
      Committees, Department of State
    Lot File 122: International Social Policy Committee

Private collections

United States
Asheville, North Carolina
  John Ingersoll Papers, in possession of Mr. Ingersoll

Charlottesville, Virginia
Neil Chayet Papers, in possession of author
Chevy Chase, Maryland
FDC Reports, Inc.
The Pink Sheet
Madison, Wisconsin
State Historical Society of Wisconsin
Minutes of the Foreign Policy Association Executive Committee meetings
New York
Butler Library, Columbia University
Oral History Research Office
The Reminiscences of Herbert L. May
Pentagon City, Virginia
DEA Library
Anti-Opium Information Bureau publications, other unpublished papers, theses, and government documents
University Park, Pennsylvania
Pattee Library, Pennsylvania State University
Harry J. Anslinger Papers

Published official documents

Great Britain
Foreign Office, *The Opium Trade, 1910–1941*, FO 415: Correspondence Respecting Opium, PRO. 6 vols, Wilmington, Scholarly Resources, 1974.
League of Nations documents
Category III: League Health Committee
Category IX: Arms Control and Disarmament
Category XI: Advisory Committee on the Traffic in Opium and Other Dangerous Drugs (Opium Advisory Committee)
United Nations
Commission on Narcotic Drugs records and reports (UN documents designated E/CN.7/. . .)
Drug Supervisory Body reports (UN documents designated E/DSB/. . .)
International Narcotics Control Board reports (UN documents designated E/INCB/. . .)
Permanent Central Narcotics Board reports (UN documents designated E/PCNB/. . .)
Permanent Central Opium Board reports (UN documents designated E/OB/. . .)
United Nations Conference for the Adoption of a Single Convention on Narcotic Drugs, New York, 24 January–25 March 1961, Official Records, New York, United Nations, 1964. (2 Volumes, UN documents E/CONF 34/24 and E/CONF 34/24/Add. 1)

Commentary on the Single Convention on Narcotic Drugs, 1961, New York, United Nations, 1973.

United Nations Conference for the Adoption of a Protocol on Psychotropic Substances, Official Records, New York, United Nations, 1973. (2 volumes, UN documents E/Conf.58/7 and E/Conf.58/7/Add.1)

Commentary on the Convention on Psychotropic Substances done at Vienna on 21 February 1971, New York, United Nations, 1976. (UN document E/CN.7/589)

Commentary on the Protocol Amending the Single Convention on Narcotic Drugs, 1961 done at Geneva on 25 March 1972, New York, United Nations, 1976. (UN document E/CN.7/588)

Bulletin on Narcotics, New York, United Nations.

United States

Congressional Record

US Army and Navy Munitions Board, *The Strategic and Critical Materials*, hearings on HR 2969, 3320, 2556, 2643, 1987, 987, and 4373, House Committee on Military Affairs, Seventy-Sixth Congress, First Session, February–March 1939.

US Department of Agriculture, *Hemp for Victory*, motion picture, 1942, director Raymond Evans, distributed on videocassette by The Institute for Hemp.

US Military Academy, *Strategic and Critical Raw Materials*, West Point, Department of economics, government, and history, 1940 and 1944.

Newspapers

The Times, London
New York Times
Wall Street Journal
Washington Post

Books

Abel, Ernest L., *Marihuana, The First Twelve Thousand Years*, New York, McGraw-Hill, 1982.

Albrecht, Hans-Jörg, and Anton van Kalmthout, *Drug Policies in Western Europe*, Freiburg, Max-Planck-Institut für ausländisches und internationales Strafrecht, 1989.

Anderson, Malcolm, *Policing the World: Interpol and the Politics of International Police Co-operation*, Oxford, Clarendon Press, 1989.

Austin, Gregory A., *Perspectives on the History of Psychoactive Substance Abuse*, Rockville, Maryland, National Institute on Drug Abuse (NIDA Research Issues Series no. 24), 1978.

Barros, James, *Betrayal from Within: Joseph Avenol, Secretary-General of the League of Nations, 1933–1940*, New Haven, Yale University Press, 1969.

Barrows, Susanna and Robin Room (eds), *Drinking: Behavior and Belief in Modern History*, Berkeley, University of California Press, 1991.

Bean, Philip, *The Social Control of Drugs*, New York, Halstead Press, 1974.

Becker, Howard S., *Outsiders: Studies in the Sociology of Deviance*, New York, Free Press, 1997.

Berridge, Virginia (ed.), *Drugs Research and Policy in Britain*, Aldershot, Gower, 1990.

Berridge, Virginia, and Griffith Edwards, *Opium and the People: Opiate Use in Nineteenth Century England*, London, Allen Lane/St. Martin's Press, 1981.

Binneveld, Hans and Rudolf Dekker (eds), *Curing and Insuring: Essays on Illness in past times: the Netherlands, Belgium, England, and Italy, 16th–20th centuries*, Hilversum, Verloren Publishers (Erasmus University Rotterdam), 1993.

Block, Alan A. and William J. Chambliss, *Organizing Crime*, New York, Elsevier, 1981.

Bonnie, Richard J. and Charles H. Whitebread II, *The Marihuana Conviction: A History of Marihuana Prohibition in the United States*, Charlottesville, University of Virginia Press, 1974.

Bossong, Horst, Christian Marzahn, and Sebastian Scheerer (eds), *Sucht und Ordnung: Drogenpolitik für Helfer und Betroffene*, Frankfurt, Extrabuch, 1983.

Brandt, Allan M. and Paul Rozin (eds), *Morality and Health*, New York, Routledge, 1997.

Brecher, Edward M., *Licit and Illicit Drugs*, Boston, Little, Brown, & Company, 1972.

Bresler, Fenton, *Interpol*, London, Sinclair-Stevenson, 1992.

Brook, Timothy and Bob Tadashi Wakabayashi (eds), *Opium in East Asian History*, Berkeley, University of California Press, 2000.

Bruun, Kettil, Lynn Pan, and Ingemar Rexed, *The Gentlemen's Club*, Chicago, University of Chicago Press, 1975.

Burnham, John C., *Bad Habits: Drinking, Smoking, Taking Drugs, Gambling, Sexual Misbehavior, and Swearing in American History*, New York, New York University Press, 1993.

Chatterjee, S. K., *Legal Aspects of International Drug Control*, The Hague, Martinus Nijhoff, 1981.

Chein, Isidor, Donald L. Gerard, Robert S. Lee, and Eva Rosenfeld, *The Road to H: Narcotics, Delinquency, and Social Policy*, New York, Basic Books, 1964.

Courtwright, David T., *Dark Paradise: Opiate Addiction in America before 1940*, Cambridge, Mass., Harvard University Press, 1982.

Crosby, Alfred W., *Germs, Seeds, and Animals: Studies in Ecological History*, Armonk, NY, M. E. Sharpe, 1994.

Curtin, Philip D., *Cross-Cultural Trade in World History*, Cambridge, Cambridge University Press, 1984.

De Rios, Marlene Dobkin, *Hallucinogens: Cross-Cultural Perspectives*, Albuquerque, New Mexico University Press, 1984.

Du Toit, Brian M., *Cannabis in Africa*, Rotterdam, A. A. Balkema, 1980.

Eckes, Alfred E., *The United States and the Global Struggle for Minerals*, Austin, University of Texas Press, 1979.

Edwards, Griffith and Awni Arif (eds), *Drug Problems in the Socio Cultural Context: A Basis for Policies and Program Planning*, Geneva, World Health Organization, 1980.

Ehrenberg, Alain (ed.), *Penser la Drogue, Penser les Drogues* (3 volumes), Paris, Editions Descartes, 1992.

Eisenlohr, Louise E. S., *International Narcotics Control*, London, Allen & Unwin, 1934.

Eldridge, William Butler, *Narcotics and the Law: A Critique of the American Experiment in Narcotic Drug Control*, Chicago, University of Chicago Press, 1962.

Epstein, Edward Jay, *Agency of Fear: Opiates and Political Power in America*, New York, Putnam, 1977.

Evans, Peter B., Dietrich Rueschemeyer, and Theda Skocpol (eds), *Bringing the State Back In*, Cambridge, Cambridge University Press, 1985.

Fay, Peter Ward, *The Opium War, 1840–42*, New York, Norton, 1976.

Forbes, Henry W., *The Strategy of Disarmament*, Washington, Public Affairs Press, 1962.

Foreign Policy Association, *International Control of the Traffic in Opium: Summary of the Opium Conferences Held at Geneva, November, 1924, to February 1925* (pamphlet no. 33, 1924–25 series), New York, Foreign Policy Association, 1925.

Friman, H. Richard, *Narcodiplomacy: Exporting the US War on Drugs*, Ithaca, NY, Cornell University Press, 1996.

Gagliano, Joseph A., *Coca Prohibition in Peru: The Historical Debates*, Tucson, University of Arizona Press, 1994.

Gastinel, Jean, *Le Trafic des stupéfiants*, Aix-en-Provence, 1927.

Gavit, John Palmer, *Opium*. New York, Brentano's, 1927.

Giffen, P. J., Shirley Endicott, and Sylvia Lambert, *Panic and Indifference: The Politics of Canada's Drug Laws*, Ottawa, Canadian Centre on Substance Abuse, 1991.

Goodman, Jordan, *Tobacco in History: The Cultures of Dependence*, London, Routledge, 1993.

Goodman, Jordan, Paul E. Lovejoy, and Andrew Sherratt, *Consuming Habits: Drugs in History and Anthropology*, London, Routledge, 1995.

Gootenberg, Paul (ed.), *Cocaine: Global Histories*, London, Routledge, 1999.

Gordon, Ernest, *The Anti-Alcohol Movement in Europe*, New York, Revell, 1913.

Grant, Rebecca and Kathleen Newland (eds), *Gender and International Relations*, Bloomington, Indiana University Press, 1991.

Greenberg, Michael, *British Trade and the Opening of China, 1800–1842*, Cambridge, Cambridge University Press, 1951.

Grinspoon, Lester, *Marihuana Reconsidered*, Cambridge, Mass., Harvard University Press, 1977.

Grinspoon, Lester and James B. Bakalar, *Marihuana, The Forbidden Medicine*, New Haven, Yale University Press, 1993.

Grinspoon, Lester and Peter Hedblom, *The Speed Culture: Amphetamine Abuse in America*, Cambridge, Mass., Harvard University Press, 1975.

Haas, Ernst B., *When Knowledge is Power: Three Models of Change in International Organizations*, Berkeley, University of California Press, 1990.

Harden, Victoria A., *Inventing the NIH: Federal Biomedical Research Policy, 1887–1937*, Baltimore, Johns Hopkins Press, 1986.

Harding, Geoffrey, *Opiate Addiction, Morality, and Medicine*, New York, St. Martin's, 1988.

Hasenclever, Andreas, Peter Mayer, and Volker Rittenberger, *Theories of International Regimes*, Cambridge, Cambridge University Press, 1997.

Headrick, Daniel R., *The Tentacles of Progress: Technology Transfer in the Age of Imperialism, 1850–1940*, Oxford, Oxford University Press, 1988.

Healy, David, *The Antidepressant Era*, Cambridge, Mass., Harvard University Press, 1997.

Himmelstein, Jerome L., *The Strange Career of Marihuana: Politics and Ideology of Drug Control in America*, Westport, Conn., Greenwood Press, 1983.

Hoijer, Olof, *Le Trafic de l'opium et d'autres stupéfiants*, Paris, Editions Spes, 1925.

Hopkins, James F., *A History of The Hemp Industry in Kentucky*, Lexington, University of Kentucky Press, 1951.

Jennings, John M., *The Opium Empire: Japanese Imperialism and Drug Trafficking in Asia, 1895–1945*, Westport, Conn., Praeger, 1997.

Jonnes, Jill, *Hepcats, Narcs, and Pipedreams: A History of America's Romance with Illegal Drugs*, New York, Scribner, 1996.

Karch, Steven B., *A Brief History of Cocaine*, Boca Raton, Florida, CRC Press, 1998.

Khan, M. Z., *Drug Use Amongst College Youth*, Bombay, Somaiya Publications, 1985.

King, Rufus, *The Drug Hang-up: America's Fifty-Year Folly*, New York, Norton, 1972.

Kohn, Marek, *Dope Girls: The Birth of the British Drug Underground*, London, Lawrence & Wishart, 1992.

Kramer, J. F. and D. C. Cameron, *A Manual on Drug Dependence*, Geneva, World Health Organization, 1975.

Krasner, Stephen D. (ed.), *International Regimes*, Ithaca, NY, Cornell University Press, 1983.

Kreutel, Margit, *Die Opiumsucht*, Stuttgart, Deutscher Apotheker Verlag, 1988.

Kuehl, Warren F., *Seeking World Order: The United States and International Organization to 1920*, Nashville, Vanderbilt University Press, 1969.

Kuehl, Warren F. (ed.), *Biographical Dictionary of Internationalists*, Westport, Conn., Greenwood Press, 1983.

Kuehl, Warren F., and Lynne K. Dunn, *Keeping the Covenant: American Internationalists and the League of Nations, 1920–1939*, Kent, Ohio, Kent State University Press, 1997.

LaMotte, Ellen, *The Opium Monopoly*, New York, Macmillan, 1920.

—— *The Ethics of Opium*, New York, The Century Company, 1924.

The League of Nations in Retrospect: Proceedings of the Symposium, Berlin and New York, Walter de Gruyter & Co., 1983.

Leffler, Melvyn P., *The Elusive Quest: America's Pursuit of European Stability and French Security, 1919–1933*, Chapel Hill, University of North Carolina Press, 1979.

Lewin, L. and W. Goldbaum (Kommentar), *Opiumgesetz (Gesetz zur Ausführung des internationalen Opiumabkommens vom 23. I. 1912), nebst internationalen Opiumabkommen und Ausführungsbestimmungen*, Berlin, Stilkes Rechtsbibliothek Nr. 75., 1928.

Liais, Michel, *La Question des stupéfiants manufacturés et l'oeuvre de la Société des nations*, Paris, Société anonyme du recueil sirey, 1928.

Lindesmith, Alfred R., *The Addict and the Law*, Bloomington, Indiana University Press, 1965.

Lodwick, Kathleen Lorraine, *Crusaders Against Opium: Protestant Missionaries in China, 1874–1917*, Lexington, University of Kentucky Press, 1996.

Lowes, Peter D., *The Genesis of International Narcotics Control*, Geneva, Librairie Droz, 1966.

Lubbock, Basil, *The Opium Clippers*, Glasgow, Brown, Son & Ferguson, 1933.

Lyons, F. S. L., *Internationalism in Europe, 1815–1914*, Leyden, A. W. Sijthoff, 1963.

McAllister, Ian, Rhonda Moore, and Toni Makkai, *Drugs in Australian Society*, Melbourne, Longman Cheshire, 1991.

McCoy, Alfred W., *The Politics of Heroin: CIA Complicity in the Global Drug Trade*, New York, Lawrence Hill, 1991.

MacGregor, Susanne (ed.), *Drugs and British Society: Responses to a Social Problem in the Eighties*, London, Routledge, 1989.

McWilliams, John C., *The Protectors: Harry J. Anslinger and the Federal Bureau of Narcotics, 1930–1962*, Newark, University of Delaware Press, 1990.

Marshall, Jonathan, *To Have and Have Not: Southeast Asian Raw Materials and the Origins of the Pacific War*, Berkeley, University of California Press, 1995.

May, Herbert L., *Narcotic Drugs and Atomic Energy: Analogy of Controls*, New York, American Association for the United Nations, 1946.

Meyer, Kathryn, and Terry M. Parssinen, *Webs of Smoke: Smugglers, Warlords, Spies, and the History of the International Drug Trade*, Lanham, Maryland, Rowman & Littlefield, 1998.

Milner, Helen V., *Interests, Institutions, and Information: Domestic Politics and International Relations*, Princeton, Princeton University Press, 1997.

Moorhead, Helen Howell, *International Administration of Narcotic Drugs, 1928–1934*, Geneva, 1935.

Morgan, H. Wayne, *Drugs in America: A Social History, 1800–1980*, Syracuse, NY, Syracuse University Press, 1981.

Morgan, Laura Puffer, *A Possible Technique of Armament Control*, Geneva, Geneva Studies (vol. 11, no. 7), 1940.

Musto, David, *The American Disease*, Oxford, Oxford University Press, 1987.

Nadelmann, Ethan A., *Cops Across Borders: The Internationalization of US Criminal Law Enforcement*, University Park, Penn State University Press, 1993.

Najmi, Kanji, *Drugs Policy in Developing Countries*, London, Zed Books, 1992.

Northcroft, D. M., *Women at Work in the League of Nations*, London, Page & Pratt, 1923.

Ostrower, Gary B., *Collective Insecurity: The United States and the League of Nations in the Early Thirties*, Lewisburg, Bucknell University Press, 1979.

—— *The League of Nations From 1919 to 1929*, Garden City Park, New York, Avery Publishing Group, 1996.

Owen, David Edward, *British Opium Policy in China and India*, New Haven, Yale University Press, 1934.

Parssinen, Terry M., *Secret Passions, Secret Remedies: Narcotic Drugs in British Society, 1820–1930*, Philadelphia, Institute for the Study of Human Issues, 1983.

Pila, J. Joseph, *Le Trafic des stupéfiants et la Société des nations*, Paris, 1926.

Polachek, James M., *The Inner Opium War*, Cambridge, Mass., Harvard University Press, 1992.

Porch, Douglas, *The French Secret Services: From the Dreyfus Affair to the Gulf War*, New York, Farrar, Straus & Giroux, 1995.

Porter, Roy and Mikulas Teich (eds), *Drugs and Narcotics in History*, Cambridge, Cambridge University Press, 1995.

Rachal, Patricia, *Federal Narcotics Enforcement: Reorganization and Reform*, Boston, Auburn House, 1982.

Ranshofen-Wertheimer, Egon F., *The International Secretariat: A Great Experiment in International Administration*, Washington, Carnegie Endowment for International Peace, 1945.

Rasmussen, David W. and Bruce L. Benson, *The Economic Anatomy of a Drug War: Criminal Justice in the Commons*, Lanham, Maryland, Rowman & Littlefield, 1994.

Reed, James, *The Missionary Mind and American East Asia Policy, 1911–1915*, Cambridge, Mass., Harvard University Press, 1983.

Reuter, Peter, Mathea Falco, and Robert MacCoun, *Comparing Western European and North American Drug Policies*, Santa Monica, Rand Corporation, 1993.

Risse-Kappen, Thomas (ed.), *Bringing transnational relations back in: non-state actors, domestic structures and international institutions*, Cambridge, Cambridge University Press, 1995.

Rovine, Arthur, *The First Fifty Years: The Secretary General in World Politics, 1920–1970*, Leyden, A. W. Sijthoff, 1970.

Rush, James R., *Opium to Java: Revenue Farming and Chinese Enterprise in Colonial Indonesia, 1860–1910*, Ithaca, NY, Cornell University Press, 1990.

Russo, J. Robert (ed.), *Amphetamine Abuse*, Springfield, Charles C. Thomas, 1968.

Scheerer, Sebastian, *Die Genese der Betäubungsmittelgesetze in der Bundesrepublik Deutschland und in den Niederlanden*, Göttingen, Schwartz, 1982.

Schuker, Stephen A., *The End of French Predominance in Europe*, Chapel Hill, University of North Carolina Press, 1976.

Scott, Peter Dale, and Jonathan Marshall, *Cocaine Politics: Drugs, Armies, and the CIA in Central America*, Berkeley, University of California Press, 1998.

Sharpe, Virginia A. and Alan I. Faden, *Medical Harm: Historical, Conceptual, and Ethical Dimensions of Iatrogenic Illness*, Cambridge, Cambridge University Press, 1998.

Silverman, Milton, *The Drugging of the Americas: How Multinational Drug Companies say one thing about their Products to Physicians in the United States and another to Physicians in Latin America*, Berkeley, University of California Press, 1976.

Silverman, Milton, and Philip R. Lee, *Pills, Profits and Politics*, Berkeley, University of California Press, 1974.

Silverman, Milton, Philip R. Lee, and Mia Lydecker, *Prescriptions for Death*, Berkeley, University of California Press, 1982.

Simmons, Luiz R. S. and Abdul A. Said (eds), *Drugs, Politics, and Diplomacy: the International Connection*, Beverly Hills and London, Sage, 1974.

Skran, Claudena M., *Refugees in Inter-War Europe: The Emergence of a Regime*, Oxford, Clarendon Press, 1995.

Smith, Mickey C., *A Social History of the Minor Tranquilizers: The Quest for Small Comfort in the Age of Anxiety*, New York, Pharmaceutical Products Press, 1991.

Smith, Peter H. (ed.), *Drug Policy in the Americas*, Boulder, Westview Press, 1992.

So, Alvin Y., *The South China Silk District: Local Historical Transformation and World-System Theory*, Albany, State University of New York Press, 1986.

Spence, Jonathan, *Chinese Roundabout: Essays in History and Culture*, New York, Norton, 1992.

Spinelli, Lawrence, *Dry Diplomacy: The United States, Great Britain and Prohibition*, Wilmington, Scholarly Resources, 1989.

Stangeland, Per (ed.), *Drugs and Drug Control*, Oxford, Oxford University Press/ Norwegian University Press, 1987.

Stares, Paul B., *Global Habit: The Drug Problem in a Borderless World*, Washington, Brookings Institution, 1996.

Stein, Stuart Derek, *International Diplomacy, State Administrators, and Narcotics Control*, Brookfield, Vermont, Gower, 1985.

Stelle, Charles Clarkson, *America and the China Opium Trade*, New York, Arno Press, 1981.

Swann, John P., *Academic Scientists and the Pharmaceutical Industry: Cooperative Research in Twentieth-Century America*, Baltimore, Johns Hopkins University Press, 1988.

Taylor, Arnold H., *American Diplomacy and the Narcotics Traffic*, Durham, NC, Duke University Press, 1969.

Terry, Charles, and Mildred Pellens, *The Opium Problem*, New York, Bureau of Social Hygiene, 1928.

Tesh, Sylvia Noble, *Hidden Arguments: Political Ideology and Disease Prevention Policy*, New Brunswick, Rutgers University Press, 1988.

Trocki, Carl A., *Opium and Empire: Chinese Society in Colonial Singapore, 1800–1910*, Ithaca, NY, Cornell University Press, 1990.

Valenstein, Elliot S., *Blaming the Brain: The Truth about Drugs and Mental Health*, New York, Free Press, 1998.

Veatch, Richard, *Canada and the League of Nations*, Toronto, University of Toronto Press, 1975.

Walker, William O. III., *Opium and Foreign Policy: The Anglo-American Search for Order in Asia, 1912–1954*, Chapel Hill, University of North Carolina Press, 1991.

—— *Drug Control in the Americas*, Albuquerque, University of New Mexico Press, 1989.

—— (ed.), *Drug Control Policy: Essays in Historical and Comparative Perspective*, University Park, Pennsylvania, Penn State University Press, 1992.

—— (ed.), *Drugs in the Western Hemisphere: An Odyssey of Cultures in Conflict*, Wilmington, Scholarly Resources, 1996.

Walker, William O. III, and Bruce Bagley (eds), *Drug Trafficking in the Americas*, New Brunswick, Transaction Publishers, 1994.

Walters, F. P., *A History of the League of Nations*, London, Oxford, 1952.

Walvin, James, *Fruits of Empire: Exotic Produce and British Taste, 1660–1800*, London, Macmillan, 1997.

von Wartburg, Walter P., *Drogenmissbrauch und Gesetzgeber*, Basel and Stuttgart, Birkhäuser, 1974.

Weindling, Paul (ed.), *International Health Organisations and Movements, 1918–1939*, Cambridge, Cambridge University Press, 1995.

Weir, Shelagh, *Qat in Yemen: Consumption and Social Change*, London, British Museum Publications, 1985.

van de Wijngaart, Govert Frank, *Competing Perspectives on Drug Use: The Dutch Experience*, Amsterdam, Swets & Zeitlinger, 1991.

Willoughby, Westel W., *Opium as an International Problem: The Geneva Conferences*, Baltimore, Johns Hopkins University Press, 1925.

Wong, J. Y., *Deadly Dreams: Opium, Imperialism, and the Arrow War (1856–1860) in China*, Cambridge, Cambridge University Press, 1998.

World Health Organization, *Youth and Drugs*, Geneva, WHO, 1973.

World Organization: A Balance Sheet of the First Great Experiment, Washington, American Council on Public Affairs, 1942.

Zabriskie, Alexander C., *Bishop Brent: Crusader for Christian Unity*, Philadelphia, Westminster Press, 1948.

Zimring, Franklin E. and Gordon Hawkins, *The Search for Rational Drug Control*, Cambridge, Cambridge University Press, 1992.

Zinberg, Norman E., *Drug, Set, and Setting: The Basis for Controlled Intoxicant Use*, New Haven, Yale University Press, 1984.

Articles

Acker, Caroline Jean, "Addiction and the Laboratory: The Work of the National Research Council's Committee on Drug Addiction, 1928–1939," *Isis*, 1995, vol. 86, pp. 167–93.

Adshead, S. A. M., "Opium in Szechwan, 1881–1911," *Journal of Southeast Asian History*, 1966, vol. 7, no. 2, pp. 93–9.

Berridge, Virginia, "Drugs and Social Policy: The Establishment of Drug Control in Britain, 1900–30," *British Journal of Addiction*, 1984, vol. 79, pp. 17–29.

Berridge, Virginia, "War Conditions and Narcotics Control: The Passing of Defence of the Realm Act Regulation 40B," *Journal of Social Policy*, 1978, vol. 7, no. 3, pp. 285–304.

Berridge, Virginia, and Betsy Thom, "The Relationship between Research and Policy: Case Studies from the Postwar History of Drugs and Alcohol," *Contemporary Drug Problems*, 1994, vol. 21, pp. 599–629.

Block, Alan A., "European Drug Traffick and Traffickers between the Wars: The Policy of Suppression and its Consequences," *Journal of Social History*, 1989, vol. 23, pp. 315–37.

Block, Alan A. and John C. McWilliams, "On the Origins of American Counterintelligence: Building a Clandestine Network," *Journal of Policy History*, 1989, vol. 1, no. 4, pp. 353–72.

Brown, J. B., "Politics of the Poppy: The Society for the Suppression of the Opium Trade, 1874–1916," *Journal of Contemporary History*, 1973, vol. 8, no. 3, pp. 97–111.

Buell, Raymond Leslie, "The International Opium Conferences with Relevant Documents," *World Peace Foundation Pamphlets*, 1925, vol. 7, nos 2–3, pp. 39–330.

Chatterjee, S. K., "The WHO Expert Committee on Drug Dependence," *International and Comparative Law Quarterly*, 1979, vol. 28, no. 1, pp. 27–51.

Conroy, Mary Schaeffer, "Abuse of Drugs Other than Alcohol and Tobacco in the Soviet Union," *Soviet Studies*, 1990, vol. 42, no. 3, pp. 447–80.

Cribb, Robert, "Opium and the Indonesian Revolution," *Modern Asian Studies*, 1988, vol. 22, no. 4, pp. 701–22.

Davis, Kathryn W., "The Soviet Union and the League of Nations, 1919–1933," *Geneva Special Studies*, 1934, vol. 5, no. 1, pp. 3–23.

Edwards, Griffith, "Drugs and Society: Opium and After," *Lancet*, 1980, pp. 351–4.

Galliher, John F., David P. Keys, and Michael Elsner, "Lindesmith v. Anslinger: An Early Government Victory in the Failed War on Drugs," *Journal of Criminal Law and Criminology*, 1998, vol. 88, no. 2, pp. 661–83.

Galliher, John F. and Allyn Walker, "The Puzzle of the Social Origins of the Marihuana Tax Act of 1937," *Social Problems*, 1977, vol. 24, no. 3, pp. 367–76.

Garland, John, "Hemp: A Minor American Fiber Crop," *Economic Geography*, 1946, vol. 22, pp. 126–32.

Garrett, Valery, "Substance Abuse Treatment in Southern California: The History and Significance of the Antelope Valley Rehabilitation Centers," *Journal of Policy History*, 1996, vol. 8, no. 2, pp. 181–205.

Graham, James M., "Amphetamine Politics on Capitol Hill," *Transaction*, 1972, vol. 9, no. 3, pp. 14–16, 18–22, 53.

Haas, Peter M. "Do regimes matter? Epistemic communities and Mediterranean pollution control," *International Organization*, 1989, vol. 43, no. 3, pp. 377–403.

——— (ed.), "Knowledge, Power, and International policy coordination," *International Organization*, 1992, vol. 46, no. 1.

Hansen, Bert, "America's First Medical Breakthrough: How Popular Excitement about a French Rabies Cure in 1885 Raised New Expectations for Medical Progress," *American Historical Review*, 1998, vol. 103, no. 2, pp. 373–418.

Hansen, Ronald W., "International Issues of Drug Regulation," *Zeitschrift für die gesamte Staatswissenschaft (Journal of Institutional and Theoretical Economics)*, 1983, vol. 139, no. 3, pp. 568–77.

Hughes, P. H., *et al.* "Extent of Drug Abuse: An International Review with implications for Health Planners," *World Health Statistics Quarterly*, 1983, vol. 36, nos 3–4, pp. 394–497.

Jackson, Charles O., "Before the Drug Culture: Barbiturate/Amphetamine Abuse in American Society," *Clio Medica*, 1976, vol. 11, no. 1, pp. 47–58.

Johnson, Bruce D., "Righteousness Before Revenue: The Forgotten Moral Crusade Against the Indo-Chinese Opium Trade," *Journal of Drug Issues*, 1975, vol. 5, pp. 304–26.

Kaplan, Charles D., "The Uneasy Consensus: Prohibitionist and Experimentalist Expectancies behind the International Narcotics Control System," *Tijdschrift voor criminologie*, 1984, vol. 26, pp. 98–109.

Kinder, Douglas Clark, "Bureaucratic Cold Warrior: Harry J. Anslinger and Illicit Narcotics Traffic," *Pacific Historical Review*, 1981, vol. 50, no. 2, pp. 169–91.

Kinder, Douglas Clark and William O. Walker III, "Stable Force In a Storm: Harry J. Anslinger and United States Narcotic Foreign Policy, 1930–1962," *Journal of American History*, 1986, vol. 72, no. 4, pp. 908–27.

de Kort, Marcel, "The Dutch Cannabis Debate, 1968–1976," *Journal of Drug Issues*, 1994, vol. 24, no. 3, pp. 417–27.

de Kort, Marcel and Dirk J. Korf, "The Development of Drug Trade and Drug Control in the Netherlands: A Historical Perspective," *Crime, Law, and Social Change*, 1992, vol. 17, pp. 123–44.

Kramer, John M., "Drug Abuse in the Soviet Union," *Problems of Communism*, 1988, vol. 37, no. 2, pp. 28–40.

Kuśević, Vladimir, "Drug Abuse Control and International Treaties," *Journal of Drug Issues*, 1977, no. 1, pp. 35–53.

McWilliams, John C., "Covert Connections: the FBN, the OSS, and the CIA," *The Historian*, 1991, vol. 53, no. 4, pp. 659–78.

Marsh, Robert, "The Illinois Hemp Project at Polo in World War II," *Journal of the Illinois State Historical Society*, 1967, vol. 60, no. 4, pp. 391–410.

Marshall, Jonathan, "Opium and the Politics of Gangsterism in Nationalist China, 1927–1945," *Bulletin of Concerned Asian Scholars*, 1976, July–September, pp. 19–48.

Maule, Robert B., "The Opium Question in the Federated Shan States, 1931–36: British Policy Discussions and Scandal," *Journal of Southeast Asian Studies*, 1992, vol. 23, no. 1, pp. 14–36.

Miners, N. J., "The Hong Kong Government Opium Monopoly, 1914–1941," *Journal of Imperial and Commonwealth History*, 1983, vol. 11, no. 3, pp. 275–99.

Nadelmann, Ethan A., "Global Prohibition Regimes: the Evolution of Norms in International Society," *International Organization*, 1990, vol. 44, no. 4, pp. 479–526.

Newman, R. K., "India and the Anglo-Chinese Opium Agreements, 1907–14," *Modern Asian Studies*, 1989, vol. 23, no. 3, pp. 525–60.

Papachristou, Judith, "American Women and Foreign Policy, 1898–1905," *Diplomatic History*, 1990, vol. 14, no. 4, pp. 493–509.

Pittman, Walter E., "Richmond P. Hobson and the International Limitation of Narcotics," *Alabama Historical Quarterly*, 1972, vol. 34, pp. 181–93.

Reasons, C., "The Politics of Drugs: An Inquiry in the Sociology of Social Problems," *Sociological Quarterly*, 1974, vol. 15, pp. 381–404.

Renborg, Bertil A., "The Grand Old Men of the League of Nations," *Bulletin on Narcotics*, 1964, vol. 16, no. 4, pp. 1–11.

Richards, J. F., "The Indian Empire and Peasant Production of Opium in the Nineteenth Century," *Modern Asian Studies*, 1981, vol. 15, no. 1, pp. 59–82.

Sandos, James A., "Northern Separatism During the Mexican Revolution: An Inquiry into the Role of Drug Trafficking, 1910–1920," *Americas*, 1984, vol. 41, no. 2, pp. 191–214.

Saper, Anthony, "The Making of Policy through Myth, Fantasy and Historical Accident: The Making of America's Narcotic Laws," *The British Journal of Addiction to Alcohol and other Drugs*, 1974, vol. 69, no. 2, pp. 183–94.

Scheerer, Sebastian, "The New Dutch and German Drug Laws: Social and Political Conditions for Criminalization and Decriminalization," *Law and Society Review*, 1978, vol. 14, no. 4, pp. 585–606.

Seyf, Ahmad, "Commercialization of Agriculture: Production and Trade of Opium in Persia, 1850–1906," *International Journal of Middle East Studies*, 1984, vol. 16, no. 2, pp. 233–50.

Skjelsbaek, Kjell, "The Growth of International Nongovernmental Organization in the Twentieth Century," *International Organization*, 1971, vol. 25, no. 3, pp. 420–42.

Taylor, Arnold H., "Opium, American–Chinese Relations, and the Open-Door Policy." *South Atlantic Quarterly*, 1970, vol. 69, pp. 79–95.

Traver, Harold, "Opium to Heroin: Restrictive Opium Legislation and the Rise of Heroin Consumption in Hong Kong," *Journal of Policy History*, 1992, vol. 4, no. 3, pp. 307–24.

Van Wettum, W. G. "Les Conférences de l'opium à Genève (3 novembre 1924–19 février 1925) et leurs résultats mis en regard de ceux de la conférence de la Haye (1912)," *Grotius*, 1926, pp. 63–78.

Walker, William O. III, "Drug Control and the Issue of Culture in American Foreign Relations," *Diplomatic History*, 1988, vol. 12, no. 4, pp. 365–82.

Westermeyer, Joseph, "The Pro-Heroin Effects of Anti-Opium Laws in Asia," *Archives of General Psychiatry*, 1976, vol. 33, pp. 1135–9.

—— "Social Events and Narcotic Addiction: The Influence of War and Law on Opium Use in Laos," *Addictive Behaviors: An International Journal*, 1978, vol. 3, no. 1, pp. 57–61.

Dissertations and other unpublished material

Acker, Caroline Jean. "Social Problems and Scientific Opportunities: The Case of Opiate Addiction in the US, 1920–1940," PhD dissertation, University of California at San Francisco, 1994.

—— "Partners in the Quest: The Search for a Nonaddicting Analgesic and the Development of an American Pharmaceutical Infrastructure in the 1930s," paper delivered at the American Historical Association Annual Meeting, January 1996.

Burkman, Thomas, "Opium in China and the League of Nations," paper delivered at the Conference on Opium in East Asian History, University of Toronto–York University Joint Centre for Asia Pacific Studies, May 1997.

Carroll, Rebecca, "The Weed with Roots in Rhetoric: Harry J. Anslinger, Marijuana, and the Making of American Drug Policy," PhD dissertation, University of Pittsburgh, 1991.

Dennis, Donald Phillips, "From Isolationism to Internationalism: 75 Years of the Foreign Policy Association, 1918–1993," unpublished manuscript, 1994.

Diebel, Terry L., "Struggle For Cooperation: The League of Nations Secretariat and Pro-League Internationalism in the United States, 1919–1924," UN Library, Geneva, unpublished thesis, 1970.

Kelly, John Andrew, "'Hemp for Victory:' The Rise and Fall of the American Hemp Industry During World War II," MA thesis, University of Kentucky, 1992.

Lin, Man-houng, "The Opium Market in China, 1820s–1906," paper delivered at the Conference on Opium in East Asian History, University of Toronto–York University Joint Centre for Asia Pacific Studies, May 1997.

van Luijk, Eric W., "A Lesson from history on the issue of drug legalisation: The case of the opiumregie in the Dutch East Indies, 1890–1940," June 1991, unpublished paper, Netherlands Institute for Advanced Study.

van Luijk, Eric W. and J. C. van Ours, "How to control drugs: The lessons from the opiumregie in the Dutch East Indies, 1894–1940," 1993, unpublished paper, Vrije Universiteit, Amsterdam.

McAllister, William B., "A Limited Enterprise: The History of International Efforts to Control Drugs in the Twentieth Century," PhD dissertation, University of Virginia, 1996.

—— "Parallel Tracks: Similarities Between the Questions of Arms and Drugs, 1919–1939," unpublished manuscript, 1996.

—— "Mrs. Outside/Mrs. Inside: The Contrasting Styles and Impact of Elizabeth Washburn Wright and Helen Howell Moorhead in International Drug Control Negotiations," paper delivered at the Society for Historians of American Foreign Relations Annual Meeting, June 1995.

—— "How Hungary Inadvertently Rescued Nazi Germany: International Drug Control and Opium as a Strategic Material," paper delivered at the National Policy History Conference, Bowling Green State University, June 1997.

—— "Drug Control and Its Discontents: The Marihuana Tax Act of 1937 Revisited," paper delivered at American Society of Criminology Annual Meeting, November 1998.

Miller, Carol Ann, "Lobbying the League: Women's International Organizations and the League of Nations," PhD dissertation, St. Hilda's College, Oxford, 1992.

Spillane, Joseph F., "Modern Drug, Modern Menace: The Legal Use and Distribution of Cocaine in the United States, 1880–1920," PhD dissertation, Carnegie Mellon University, May 1994.

Interviews, telephone interviews, and written communications with individuals

Angarola, Robert. Interview, Washington, 2 December 1993 and telephone interview, 14 December 1993.

Arif, Awni. Interview, Geneva, 7 May 1993.

Atzenwiler, Louis. Interviews, Geneva, 30 April and 1 May 1993; letters, 6 October 1993, 2 December 1993, 16 May 1994, 14 September 1994.

Baghdoyan, Sebouh. Discussions, Vienna, May 1993.

Bahi, Abdelaziz. Interview, Geneva, 4 May 1993.

Bailey, Paulsen K. Interview, Vienna, 10 May 1993.

Bayer, István. Letter, including paper entitled "Genesis and development of the international control of psychotropic substances" prepared for the US National Institute for Drug Abuse in 1989.

Chapman, Ross. Interview, Ottawa, 10 February 1994.

Chayet, Neil. Telephone interviews, 12 and 14 December 1993 and papers donated by Mr. Chayet to author.

Dittert, Joseph. Interviews, Geneva, 21 April, 26 April, and 3 May 1993.

Falco, Mathea. Interview, Washington, 16 September 1993.

Gaulis, Jean-Francois. Interview, Geneva, 6 May 1993.

Gough, Betty C. Interview, Washington, 19 October 1993.

Hoover, Lawrence. Interview, Harrisonburg, Virginia, 23 April 1994.

Ingersoll, John. Interviews with author, Charlottesville, Virginia, 28 August 1994, and Asheville, North Carolina, 10 April 1995.

Kusević, Vladimir. Responses to questions by cassette tape, February and July 1994.

Lecavalier, Jacques . Interview, Ottawa, 7 February 1994.

May, Everette. Letters, 31 May and 29 July 1994.

Samsom, R. J. Letter, 23 August 1993.

Schaepe, Herbert. Interview, Vienna, 18 May 1993.

Tufnell, R. S. Letter, 9 August 1994.

Vaille, Charles. Letter, 4 May 1994.

Waldheim-Natural, Liselotte. Interview, Vienna, 20 May 1993.
Walker, Norma. Letter, 6 May 1994.
Wattles, Gurdon. Letter, 20 April 1994.
Yates, Janine. Letter, 23 April 1994.

Index

single secretariat, *see* simplification
smuggling, *see* illicit trafficking
Spain, 139–40, 145
statistics 5–6, 47–9, 61, 71–2, 77,
111, 114, 128, 135–6, 141–2, 158,
163–6, 179, 181, 186–8, 206–9,
231, 241–4
Steinig, L. 138–44, 149, 153–4,
159–62, 173–9, 182–3, 189, 204,
249
stimulants 160, 201, 219, 227, 234,
252
stockpiles 71, 98, 106, 130–2, 144–6,
169, 181–2, 196, 208
strategic materials 130–2, 135–6,
144–9, 167–71, 251–3
"strict control" coalition 229, 231
supply control 3–5, 25–6, 37, 44,
49–50, 53, 56, 63–4, 77–9, 86,
101–2, 120, 125–7, 133, 144,
147–9, 154–7, 160–1, 165, 171,
178, 182–5, 200, 210–11, 218–21,
236, 239–40, 243–4, 246–50, 253;
alternatives to 5, 50, 77, 125–7,
133–5, 167–9, 210–11, 220, 224,
238, 244–5
Sweden 92, 141, 179, 228
Sweetser, A. 45, 74
Switzerland 126, 136–8, 195;
international drug policy 33–4, 57,
60–1, 66, 71–2, 80, 94, 110, 141,
206, 223, 232
synthetic drugs 126, 149, 152, 156–7,
164–5, 170–1, 176, 180–2, 198,
203–5, 209, 235–6

Taft, W. H. 28
taxes on drugs 10–11, 13, 22, 35
technical assistance 197, 200–3, 211,
221, 236–7, 242
technology, role in control and drug
development 3–4, 14–16, 38, 152,
156, 160, 164, 176, 180, 194,
246–53
Ten Year Agreement of 1907 24–7,
38, 44, 59, 69, 114, 251
Thailand 67, 167, 198
tobacco 9–11, 14, 247
trade, licit 1, 9–10, 136, 247–8;
regulation of 111–12, 126, 144,

167, 170, 173–4, 179–82, 186, 195,
198
treaties, conventions, protocols and
other international agreements;
1907 Indian–Chinese–British
agreement, *see* Ten Year
Agreement; 1912 International
Opium Convention 30–9, 46, 50,
61, 71, 74, 82, 100, 108, 117,
143–5, 239, 250; 1925 Agreement
concerning Manufacture of,
Internal Trade in and Use of
Prepared Opium (first Geneva
conference) 59–61, 67–9, 75, 105,
110; 1925 International Opium
Convention (second Geneva
conference) 59–65, 69–77, 80–7,
91, 96–100, 108, 117, 119–24, 133,
158, 161, 164, 187, 230, 248, 251;
1931 Convention, preliminary
conference 89–92; 1931
Convention for Limiting the
Manufacture and Regulating the
Distribution of Narcotic Drugs
1–4, 92–101, 105–11, 118–24,
132–3, 145, 158, 164, 181, 187,
226, 230, 248, 251; 1931
Agreement for the Control of
Opium Smoking in the Far East
(Bangkok Agreement) 106; 1936
Illicit Trafficking Convention
120–3, 205, 208, 243; 1946
Protocol signed at Lake Success
154; 1948 Synthetic Narcotics
Protocol 164–5, 172, 178; 1953
Protocol for Limiting and
Regulating the Cultivation of the
Poppy Plant, the Production of,
International and Wholesale
Trade in, and use of Opium 168,
176, 179–99, 202–10, 216–18, 249;
1961 Single Convention on
Narcotic Drugs 5, 143, 172–3, 175,
178, 183, 186, 189–90, 192–5,
202–11, 215–18, 222, 225, 227–9,
231, 234, 251; 1971 Convention on
Psychotropic Substances 224,
228–35, 238–42; 1972 Protocol
Amending the 1961 Single
Convention 235–6, 238; 1988